EXPLAINING WAR

EXPLAINING WAR

Selected Papers from the Correlates of War Project

J. DAVID SINGER
and Associates

Foreword by BRUCE M. RUSSETT

SAGE Publications   Beverly Hills   London

For information address:

SAGE Publications, Inc.
275 South Beverly Drive
Beverly Hills, California 90212

SAGE Publications Ltd
28 Banner Street
London EC1Y 8QE, England

Printed in the United States of America

Library of Congress Cataloging in Publication Data
Main entry under title:

Singer, Joel David, 1925-
    Explaining war.

    Bibliography: p.
    1. War. 2. World politics. 3. International relations. I. Title.
U21.2.S56   301.6'334   79-5452
ISBN 0-8039-1248-X
ISBN 0-8039-1249-8 pbk.

Contents

Foreword

BRUCE M. RUSSETT

"You know more than you think you do," begins Dr. Benjamin Spock reassuringly, in his world-famous *Baby and Child Care*. By contrast, I begin each of my courses in world politics with the challenge, "You know less than you think you do." In doing so I mean not to belittle my students' comprehension, but rather to emphasize that all of us—students, research scholars, and policy makers—know much less about world politics than we like to think we know. Most conventional wisdom turns out to be far less than wisdom. The base of rigorously articulated and tested theory on which we can construct our analyses, and on which decision makers can rely for action, is extremely tenuous.

But just because most decisions in the realm of world politics must now be taken with little more than intuition to guide them does not mean that we need or should rest contentedly in such a state. Scholars have long sought to systematize knowledge about why nations go to war; in the modern era the lifetime work of Quincy Wright, Lewis Frye Richardson, and a handful of others laid down some of the foundations for a science of peace and war. Those of us who currently labor at the task are much in their debt, ambitious to develop what they began. Of the several major research projects which, during the past two decades, have been devoted to this job, David Singer's Correlates of War (COW) project is one of the oldest, best-known and most productive. It is the one which most explicitly takes the work of Wright and Richardson—especially the former—for its model. Its contributions to the literature of our field include both an enormous base of painstakingly constructed data and a large body of monographic hypothesis-testing studies. In a newly emerging and evolving field, characterized by no established paradigm and by wide disagreement about philosophy of science, some of the work has become controversial. But there is no controversy about the central role that this project has played in defining the field of scientific international politics, and of establishing standards of scientific probity. It represents a corpus of work with which every serious scholar of the field must come to terms. Furthermore, the project has been especially notable for the highly responsible manner in which its data base has been made generally and promptly available to other scholars. Many students have cut their scientific wisdom teeth on analyses using the data base; any scholar wishing to challenge the project's method or theoretical application has the opportunity (and the duty) to rework its data base as s/he wishes.

Theoretically and methodologically the project has matured in response to wider developments in the discipline—and indeed has often stimulated those developments. There has been a progression, partly evidenced in the selections in this book, from data-making and relatively simple correlational analyses to more deductive theory-building and very complex statistical analysis and simulation. Characteristic of nearly all components of the project, however, has been an emphasis on theory and analysis at the macrolevel; that is, analyses focusing on characteristics of the international system, or of nation-states as actors. This emphasis on highly aggregated units of analysis is explicit and consistent through most of the work thus far emerging. I understand it as a conviction that the most important, persistent influences on the war-proneness of states are to be found at such a level. In this it is part of the grand sociological tradition shared, in very different ways and with different theoretical details, by such writers as Marx and Durkheim. It is, frankly, a conviction which I find for the most part congenial and compelling. The case for it is well argued by Nazli Choucri and Robert North (1974, p. 9) in their analysis of the forces leading to World War I:

> The dynamics of national growth and expansion, the conflict of national interests, patterns of growth in military expenditures, alliance-formation, and violence-behavior . . . were not the immediate cause of WWI. The processes set the stage, armed the players, and deployed the forces, but they did not join the antagonists in combat. They created the conditions of an armed camp within which the assassination of the Austrian archduke was sufficient to trigger an international crisis and a major war.

Even should the particular August 1914 crisis have been surmounted by wiser decision makers, the underlying international dynamics of national expansion were certain to create further crises. Ultimately one of those crises would have escalated out of control. Thus one should first come to understand the great forces that will regularly produce situations fraught with the threat of war, rather than zero in on the behavior of decision makers who, although they may be able to extricate themselves from one crisis, cannot expect to do so repeatedly in an environment where basic systemic forces are continually producing crises.

Such a judgment obviously will offend many analysts (and especially policy makers!). In the scholarly role of pursuing "pure science," one looks primarily for variables that will explain a substantial portion of the variance in given behavior. One is searching, in other words, for a "powerful" theory that will, when carefully articulated and tested, in crude statistical terms, produce a high R^2. As practitioner of "pure science" one is not so readily concerned with whether that variance can actually be controlled; that is, whether the explanatory variables are themselves readily "manipulable" by policy makers. The first step is understanding, and perhaps prediction. A "peace scientist" will of course care about finding practical means of promoting peace, but will not necessarily expect the immediate application demanded by a policy maker, nor need to serve the vested interests which constrain a policy maker's choice of policy goals and instruments.

The policy maker, quite the contrary, is primarily concerned with what s/he can manipulate. His or her eyes are much more likely to light up in reaction to an explanation that identifies something that can be controlled, than by one that identifies broad historic forces over which the policy maker has little control. Manipulability is of prime interest, prediction next, and "mere understanding" of little import. By this characterization, the policy maker is likely to be much more interested in anything that can explain how a crisis might possibly be resolved short of war than in knowing about forces that brought about the crisis, and over which s/he has little control. Or at least over which s/he is willing to have little control. The role of "pure scientist" macroanalyst may not be a popular one even if such a scientist's findings are accepted. Suppose one were to show that large, bureaucratically unwieldy states are more war-prone, or that great powers with system-wide hegemonic interests are more likely to be involved in world-endangering crises, or that the dynamics of capitalism or communism produce expansionist, aggressive, and war-prone behavior. Would a policy maker for such a government want to take the steps that would reduce the power of his/her state, or fundamentally change its socioeconomic system, even if the steps could be identified? I think this perspective makes a substantial contribution to understanding why macroanalysis is not so well regarded in some circles, and less well-regarded the closer one draws to the circle of the prince.

The work of the Correlates of War project nevertheless remains, as I stated above, one of a very few major social scientific projects that are critical to the development of any scholarly understanding of war that can perhaps be achieved during our era. Some of its assumptions and procedures can be challenged on philosophical, methodological, or theoretical grounds, but the project cannot be ignored. Furthermore, its basic assumptions ask us to define our own roles more clearly. Would we be holder of the *imperium*, or tribune of the people; adviser to the prince, or watchdog over the prince? I believe Singer and his associates would largely choose the latter role in these pairs.

Because many of the chapters in this book were initially published under my editorial auspices (principally in the *Journal of Conflict Resolution* beginning in 1973) I was asked to write this "blessing." And because I share many of the author's basic assumptions I find the request an appropriate and congenial one.

Introduction

J. DAVID SINGER

With the kind words of Bruce Russett's foreword fresh in mind, it behooves me to strike a fairly modest stance in this introduction. Thus, rather than devote it to a friendly backward glance at these selections from papers written by my colleagues and myself during the 1970s, let me address the larger body of research that seeks to help us explain— and ultimately eliminate—international war. Two general questions will be probed. First, how far have we come to date in our search for such an explanation, and second, what are the problems that remain in our way and what research strategies are implied for the near future? On both of these themes, the opening essay in the collection will serve as a convenient point of departure, despite the fact that it was originally prepared nearly a decade ago. Written to help commemorate the pioneering work of Quincy Wright, it (and the companion essay by Gochman) helps to set the stage for the eleven essays that follow by specifying certain criteria for evaluating our scientific progress and by then summarizing the extent to which our knowledge base, circa 1970, satisfied those criteria.

SOME SIGNS OF PROGRESS

Turning briefly to the progress-to-date question, it would be comforting to say that we have made a significant breakthrough in the explanation of interstate war during the 1970s. But we clearly have not, and after examining some indicators of how far we *have* come, I will suggest some possible explanations for the distressingly slow pace, along with some thoughts on how that pace might be accelerated. Most of the scientific work in Europe, Japan, and North America during the past decade is accurately mirrored in this collection, in both the encouraging and discouraging senses of the word. The encouraging side is that these essays, and the hundred or so others that have been published in our field in the 1970s, clearly move us ahead in the acquisition of correlational knowledge. Much of that work has led to the clarification of key concepts and the construction of reliable and apparently valid indicators of them, the generation of valuable data sets, and the illumination of several cross-temporal relationships.

We know a bit more now about the covariations among many of our putatively explanatory variables, and about their covariations with the incidence of international war. A fair amount of brush-clearing has occurred and a not insignificant number of myths about international conflict have been brought into question, if not persuasively demolished. Perhaps more important, recent research has shown that the traditional formulation of our questions has often been too primitive and that some of the hypotheses with which we work stand in need of drastic reformulation.

One of the more promising signs of this progress is the frequency with which some early findings of intercentury differences in the Correlates of War project have been confirmed by others within and without the project. Of course, some would see this as distressing rather than promising, because it tends to discredit our search for long-run empirical generalizations and law-like regularities. Leaving aside those who view the world in idiographic terms, and are thus relieved to know that the factors making for war in one epoch or region are different from those at work in other spatial-temporal settings, there are grounds for optimism in these results. First, they support our suspicion that diplomatic historians have been empirically justified in suggesting that the decade around 1900 was more than an artifact of the calendar and that the international system did indeed go through some critical transformations. Second, they strengthen confidence in our methods of observation and analysis by converging with a widely recognized historical fact.

Thirdly, and most germane here, these findings can have a salutary effect on our research strategies in two ways. One of these is to compel us to search systematically for those factors that most powerfully discriminate between the nineteenth- and twentieth-century settings. If, as some have speculated, the politicization of diplomacy has hindered the efficacy of the balance of power mechanism in regulating and coordinating major power behavior, we might try to develop various indicators of the diffusion of that politicization across time and across nations. Using one or more of them as control variables, we might then go on to ascertain the extent to which the parameter shifts or reversals then diminish or disappear. The same might be done with certain indicators of change in weapons technology or in diplomatic communication patterns.

The other and equally useful result of these findings is their ability to remind us that the world is indeed less than constant. Not only do the physical, structural, and cultural attributes of the system, its regions, and its actors change; the effects of these attributes and the way they impinge on one another also change. This is not to acquiesce in the antiscientific proposition that the system of 1975 is "totally different" from that of 1945 or 1885, and thus not comparable to those earlier periods, or in the assertion that since the relationship among variables is inconsistent, there is no use in searching for historical regularities. To the contrary, these inconstancies and alleged incomparabilities make the task more interesting, as well as more difficult. That is, they require us to not only construct models that are theoretically more sophisticated, but ones that also have our hypothesized parameter shifts explicitly built into them.

Another promising development in the 1970s has been the increase in the number of people, relatively as well as absolutely, whose research is in the historical experiment mode. While recognizing the reality of the problems discussed above, plus the more obvious ones of a small population of cases, the elusiveness of historical traces, and the inability to run our experiments over and even, the shift away from the laboratory, the experimental game, and the man-machine simulation is, in my view, an encouraging one. Because many peace researchers found "the light better" under the laboratory lamp post than down the dimly lit street of international history, the 1960s saw a great deal of research that was admittedly high on quality, but painfully low on relevance. Whether we had students role-playing as defense ministers or experimental subjects choosing among game theoretic options, these putative simulations of international politics could hardly be other than heuristic in their value. Similarly, the all-machine simulations of the past, heavy on mathematicization and dubious axioms, have increasingly given way to those that are more solidly data-based and whose axioms themselves are more in accord with political, economic, and psychological realities. We now see, partially in the wake of the *Limits to Growth* study, simulations that increasingly approximate representations of the historical referent world. In these, we can not only check out the extent to which a variety of postulated decision rules are consonant with given combinations of inputs and outputs, but we can also deal with the fact that each successive case in the historical process has some effect on the cases that follow.

SOME REMEDIABLE PROBLEMS

From the knowledge-generating perspective, these encouraging trends must be set alongside certain *dis*couraging ones. Perhaps most salient on the negative side of the ledger is our painfully slow growth in the sheer quantity of research that has been undertaken and completed. Although it is true that we have published about as much data-based research on the explanation of war in the 1970s as we did from the Peloponnesian Wars to 1970, we should not forget how pitifully small that quantity is. If *Beyond Conjecture* (Jones and Singer, 1972) has indeed identified virtually every such published study, those many millennia saw barely 160, almost all of which were in English. In our files for the volume that will cover the decade since, I find just about the same number of journal articles. On the other hand, this more recent output has been supplemented by nearly two dozen book-length investigations; equally important, a fair fraction of this work—perhaps 10 percent—has been conducted outside of North America.

A second discouraging fact is our failure to achieve any significant theoretical breakthrough. It is one thing to begin the slow aggregation of existential and correlational propositions regarding the incidence of war and the phenomena that covary with or precede it, but quite another to bring these findings together in such a way as to constitute a compelling explanation. As the cliché reminds us, correlation may be a necessary ingredient for the establishment of a so-called causal explanation, but it is far from sufficient. Although there is considerable room for diversity as to what constitutes a satisfactory explanation, I would contend that we need more than strong and statistically improbable covariation between our outcome variables and the predictor or explanatory variables in our models. Nor should goodness of fit between a statistical model and our observed historical realities be accepted as anything more than an indication that we *may* be on the right track. Thus, it is also dubious to assert that since a given statistical model postulates a given process, a close fit between data and model demonstrates that such a process actually obtained in the referent world.

To go a step further, some would contend that a well-articulated and mathematically elegant version of one's verbalized hunches does, if the goodness of fit is high, permit us to infer that it thus explains the empirical processes and outcomes that it is designed to represent.

Although I fully agree that the careful and explicit articulation of our models should receive the highest priority, and that rigorous and systematic empirical testing of those models should follow close behind, it is one thing to produce a clear and parsimonious description of the referent world, and quite another to claim that we have explained the observed outcomes. There are three important considerations here. First, we would do well to drop the mystical concept of causality from our epistemological repertoire. Too many different outcomes can arise out of basically similar events and conditions, and too many different sets of events and conditions can eventuate in basically similar outcomes; how might we decide which is the "causal" chain? Some would argue that the observed and inferred chain that most accords with our a priori and formal model is the causal one, but since we can usually articulate and test several such models with relative success, this would seem to be an inconclusive criterion.

This consideration leads to my second point: social causality is rarely if ever demonstrable in either the inductive or deductive sense. Such a demonstration would typically require proof that a given outcome only occurs under the specified conditions and events, and never occurs without them; it is difficult to imagine how we could satisfy these "necessary and sufficient" requirements. As a result, causality is likely to remain forever in the eye of the idiosyncratic beholder.

We can, however, escape most of these metaphysical pitfalls by shifting from the concept of causality to that of explanation. Although there still remains the problem of intersubjective agreement as to which model and which results provide the most compelling explanation, this approach recognizes the plurality of possible explanations, indicates how well we are doing in our search for the best explanation of a given set of outcomes, and permits us to build incrementally from existential and correlational knowledge to increasingly persuasive and parsimonious explanatory models. My third point, then, is that we approximate explanatory knowledge as the consensus among competent social scientists increases. But that consensus, we might hope, will rest on more than the superficial plausibility or cognitive comfort of the contending models. Rather, it should rest on the explicitness and clarity of the model, the rigor of the empirical tests, and the accuracy of the assumptions made or implied by the models. More specifically, these assumptions—though they must help to simplify the complexities of the individual and collective behavior that allegedly link our background conditions to our explained outcomes—must be congruent with existing knowledge of such behavioral regularities. Just as an operations research model that utterly *ignores* such psychological and behavioral links cannot be accepted as explanatory, neither can an econometric model (to take another example) whose assumptions are *at variance with* the findings of social and experimental psychologists.

Another problem and source of disappointment lies in the methodological sector. Despite appreciable progress on the index construction and data-making front, leading to the conversion of vague but important concepts into scientifically useful indicators, we have been painfully slow in developing better procedures for the analysis of the resulting data sets. Very simply, we have followed all too closely our electoral behavior colleagues in political science, who in turn seem to have emulated work in the econometrics field. This consequent reliance on one variation or another of the linear regression strategy has probably not hampered our search for correlational regularities, and that work is quite essential to the early stages of any new area of investigation. But as the "natural history" phase of our science increasingly blends with our drive for the specification and verification of explanatory models, the regression mode has its drawbacks.

First, it tends to put a premium on accounting for the variance (some still say "explaining" variance!) in our outcome variables by piling up the more plausible factors on the predictor side of the equation in order to maximize the multiple correlation coefficient. This usually leads to emphasis on the relative potency of the allegedly independent variables, rather than to a recognition that: (a) they are probably *not* independent of each other, but will show appreciable multicollinearity; and (b) their interactions with one another are more important in determining our outcomes than are their separate and "independent" effects.

A second consequence of this reliance on the regression mode has been the preoccupation with interval and ratio-scale data. The methods textbooks usually tell us that our data-analysis techniques should be geared to the quality of our data, usually meaning the fineness of the scales, rather than the accuracy of the observations. And it follows that if we have interval or ratio-quality data, we should use the most powerful data-analysis techniques in order that we not "throw away" useful information. This, in turn, leads us to ignore the value of data that has not yet been measured intervally and that does not lend itself to some obvious metric measurement. Thus, we are more likely to leave out of our models those variables whose operationalization and measurement looks difficult, rather than go ahead with a cruder, but perhaps equally accurate and more valid, indicator in ordinal or nominal form. More seriously, it leads us to ignore the analytic power of alternative data-analysis paradigms, ranging from the chi-square through discriminant analysis to prediction logic. In all of these, the outcome variable may be measured in nominal (war versus nonwar, for example) or ordinal form, expressing such important phenomena as the ranking of nations or the degree of centralization in an international organization. Nor must the predictor variables be measured in the same form as the outcome; any combination of scales is possible.

Moreover, by shifting from the regression mode to these various contingency table analyses, we are compelled to think in more explicitly theoretic/explanatory terms. That is, instead of asking which factors contribute how much to a given outcome, we now ask which outcomes do and do not occur under which conditions and combinations of conditions, or after which events and sequences of events. Although there are certain liabilities in this kind of dichotomous and trichotomous thinking, one of which is to denigrate subtlety and gradation of magnitudes, the advantages are quite substantial. Not only, as intimated above, are we more likely to attend to the interaction effects of two or more predictor/explanatory variables; we are also more likely to look for and discover the boundary lines between and among classes of cases. In addition, rather than use some sort of data transformation to "bring in" our outliers, as is often required by regression analysis, we not only stay closer to the distribution of outcomes as they actually occurred in the referent world, but also attend more explicitly to those deviant cases and try to explain—rather than ignore—them.

One final source of discouragement, it seems to me, is found on the knowledge-utilization side. Although our progress in the *generation* of knowledge has been painfully slow, that pace seems breathtaking in contrast to the rate at which political elites and the attentive public have taken an interest in the findings, concepts, and methods of recent research on conflict and war. Worse yet, when the more quantitative work *is* brought into the policy community, it is often of the "quick and dirty" variety, or so designed as to fit the preconceptions of the client practitioner. Most decision makers, journalists, and alert citizens are quite unaware of the difference between the impressionistic essay and the study that rests on reproducible evidence, perhaps assuming that quantitative analysis is quite all right when toting up military or industrial capabilities, but somehow irrelevant when it comes to describing the global systems' structure or the behavior of its nations.

As suggested above, this is partly due to the sparseness of our research findings to date, not to mention the fact that most of these findings are of little direct use to elites or counterelites. But it is also a function of poor education on our part. From the way in which we write up our research procedures and results, to the texts we use and the lectures we give in the classroom, through our failure to be as rigorous and scientific in public debate as we are in scholarly research, we have ourselves contributed to this dangerous state of affairs. If research into war and international conflict is not to be only an intellectual exercise, with no relevance to the central issue of our times, we will have to attend as closely to our educational roles as to our research responsibilities.

In sum, research on the explanation of international war in the 1970s presents a mixed and not altogether discouraging picture. As the essays in this volume and the larger corpus of work produced outside of our project demonstrate, there is discernible growth in both the quantity and quality of this research. From Asia to North America and from Western Europe to South America, we find a slowly increasing number of scientifically trained peace researchers. Especially encouraging is the shift away from a near-obsession with a priori and preoperational models of imperialism, so that the Marxian orientation now seems likely to get as serious attention as the more commonly analyzed realpolitik models. Just as the received wisdom of the bourgeois national interest orientation has gradually come in for systematic empirical examination, it now looks as if the ideological rhetoric of the radical left will be increasingly subjected to a sympathetic but rigorous and scientific examination.

A final issue in ur progress toward the understanding and diminution or elimination of war is that of the shared paradigm. Our critics are fond of pointing out how diverse and incompatible are the assumptions, models, methods, and findings in the international politics field, suggesting that we will make little progress until we move toward a common scientific paradigm. And often we are told to emulate such fields of investigation as electoral behavior or macroeconomics. In my judgment, there can be *too much* consensus in a field, especially when that field is characterized more by the science of discovery than the science of verification. There are to date few grounds for embracing any particular set of methods within the scientific mode and even fewer for accepting any of the contending theoretical orientations. We just do not know enough yet, and the current diversity is a healthy rather than a dangerous condition. I would even argue that commitment to a common paradigm in any macro-social science discipline today is a sign of atrophy and stagnation, rather than of scholarly advance. Our theoretical and methodological diversity is to me a sign of health, curiosity, and vigor, auguring well for the future of the field.

On the other hand, we may be going too far in this direction for the good of cumulative growth and subsequent theoretical convergence. First, we need greater consensus regarding the criteria by which we evaluate one another's research proposals, designs, and findings. Because we fear falling prey to a new orthodoxy, we tend to be overly tolerant on matters of research design, and often acquiesce in the lazy argument that scholars must be free to use the methods "appropriate" to their problem. The principle is sound, but in practice it means that we often accept utterly preoperational methods of observation, obviously biased sampling, and alarmingly loose analyses of "the data." This is carrying tolerance so far as to violate the meaning of science.

A second front on which greater consensus might help is that of typology and concept. There is little excuse for us to ignore one another's vocabularies and to produce yet another highly idiosyncratic addition to our polyglot collection of typologies and taxonomies; the burden of proof should rest squarely on the perpetrators of these dubious innovations. Similarly, despite some modest progress, we still tend to define and to measure our key terms in an unnecessarily diverse and confusing manner. As a result, our models often appear much less convergent than they really are, and our findings remain less comparable and integratable than they need to be. A new and dynamic science needs plenty of diversity, but until we insist on some minimal degree of methodological rigor and a modicum of semantic responsibility, the chances for cumulative growth toward a normal science will remain even lower than they already are.

CONCLUSION

To conclude, it is a pleasure to see these essays brought together in a single volume, where they might be of greater use to our peace research colleagues, to undergraduate and graduate students of international conflict, and perhaps even to those practitioners who are curious about the scientific approach to foreign policy. They not only illustrate the sorts of questions that we ask and the ways in which we have gone about trying to answer them; they also illuminate the strengths and weaknesses that have been discussed above. They thus offer an accurate insight into the activities of a research enterprise whose past performance may be a bit disappointing, but whose promise —in both intellectual and political terms—is extraordinary.

From *A Study of War* to Peace Research

SOME CRITERIA AND STRATEGIES

J. DAVID SINGER   *Chapter 1*

If Georges Clemenceau is noted for point-ing out that the *conduct* of war is too impor-tant to be left to the militarists, it is Quincy Wright who reminds us that the *analysis* of war is too important to be left to the intuition-ists. After years and volumes of literary specu-lation on the causes of international war, it was he who undertook the first systematic search for those empirical regularities which might shed some light on the origins of war among nations (Wright, 1942).[2] He was not, however, completely alone. At about the same time that his monumental project was getting underway at the University of Chicago, two other scholars were undertaking comparably systematic and ambitious studies of the prob-lem. One was the sociologist Pitirim Sorokin, whose work on war is reported in Volume III of his *Social and Cultural Dynamics* (1937) and the other was Lewis Richardson, the physicist whose output remained largely unread until the posthumous publication in 1960 of

Arms and Insecurity and *Statistics of Deadly Quarrels.*[3]

In the conversion of war from a subject of speculation and propaganda to one of scien-tific analysis, all three of these pioneers, as well as others, have played key roles. The purpose of this paper, however, is not so much to appraise the work of the past as to suggest an orientation toward that of the future. While the need remains for a systematic appraisal and codification of existing research, and the framework proposed here could indeed be used for it, space permits only a superficial backward glance.[4] The paper will concentrate, therefore, on a set of dimensions for describing, and criteria for evaluating,

---

[1] This is a condensed and reoriented version of a paper originally prepared for the Quincy Wright *Festschrift* (Lepawsky, Buehrig, and Lasswell, 1971). John Goormaghtigh, Karl Deutsch, Dieter Senghaas, and Allen Whiting contributed useful comments on earlier drafts.

[2] Nor did he stop with the completion of this opus. As a few of his papers cited in the references make clear, he continued to reappraise and reconsider the problem almost up to the day of his death.

[3] The reader's attention is called to the thorough, and extremely generous introduction to *Statistics of Deadly Quarrels,* by Wright and Carl Lienau, who jointly edited this portion of Richardson's work after his death in 1953. Characteristic, too, of Wright's thoroughness and generosity are the frequent allusions to, and inclusions of, Sorokin's work in *A Study of War.*

[4] I had originally intended to incorporate in this discussion a summary of all the known data-based findings relevant to each set of variables, but it turns out that this would extend the paper even further beyond the prescribed number of pages. I will, however, cite the most relevant of these studies, and many of them will be included in a forthcoming volume (Singer and Jones, 1971) in which some 130 or so data-based articles on international politics will be abstracted in considerable detail.

Originally published in the *Journal of Conflict Resolution,* Vol. 14, No. 4, December 1970.

social science knowledge on the causes of international war, and will conclude with some suggested strategies for picking up where Wright and his distinguished colleagues stopped. Let me emphasize at the outset that I see the pursuit of knowledge on the causes of war as a central concern of what has come to be called peace research, but by no means as the entire concern. Moreover, I have no doubts that research on war and its causes is no less legitimate, or appropriate, an object of scientific inquiry than, let us say, automobile "accidents," influenza epidemics, inventory control, or rocket launchings. This is not to ignore the problems of eventual applicability of our findings, or to deny the ignorance, taboos, and political constraints that may prevent or delay the acceptance and utilization of knowledge on the causes of war. But that is another set of problems, and while equally researchable, need not concern us here.[5] My hope, then, is to offer some ideas, based to a large extent on the Correlates of War project underway at the University of Michigan, which may contribute to the efficient acquisition and codification of knowledge on the causes of modern international war. To do so, I will look first at the qualitative dimensions along which such knowledge may be evaluated, and then go on to its more substantive aspects.

Two Criteria: Quality and Relevance

Whenever we seek, or claim, knowledge on the causes of war (or any other phenomena), there are two sets of criteria that need to be satisfied. The first concerns the scientific *quality* of the putative or anticipated knowledge, and the second concerns its explanatory *relevance*. Let us deal with the first briefly and then dwell upon the second at somewhat greater length.

---

[5]A relatively optimistic view is expressed in Singer (1970), while a sharply pessimistic one is in Rapoport (1970).

THE QUALITY OF OUR KNOWLEDGE

One possible way of evaluating the quality of social scientific knowledge is to reduce it into its component assertions or propositions, translate these (when necessary) into clear and operational language, and then ascertain where each such proposition or cluster of propositions falls along each of three dimensions.[6]

The first, *accuracy* dimension, reflects the degree of confidence which the relevant scientific community can have in the assertion at a given point in time; this confidence level is basically a function of the empirical or logical evidence in support of the proposition, but may vary appreciably both across time and among different scholars and schools of thought at any particular moment. The second dimension reflects the *generality* of the proposition, ranging from a single fact assertion (of any degree of accuracy) to an assertion embracing a great many phenomena of a given class. Third is the *explanatory* dimension: is the assertion essentially correlational or largely explanatory? With these three dimensions, we can construct some sort of epistemological profile of any proposition or set of propositions, and can classify and compare a given body of knowledge with another, or with itself over time. It should be emphasized, however, that all three dimensions are rough and merely ordinal in nature, and that there is no intention of treating them as interval or ratio scales, at least for the present.

For those of us concerned with understanding the causes of war, the objective is to move as rapidly as possible on all three dimensions.

---

[6]The position taken here is that we have something less than knowledge until it can be communicated in relatively operational form to most of the relevant intellectual community. A personal insight or vague intuition even if it can be "understood" by others may *lead* to knowledge, but does not yet constitute knowledge in the Western, scientific sense of the word.

What we seek are propositions in which the most competent, skeptical and rigorous scholars can have a high degree of confidence, although they may have originally been put forth on the basis of almost no empirical evidence at all. They will be propositions which are highly causal in form, although they may have been built from, and upon, a number of propositions which come close to being purely descriptive.[7] And they will be general rather than particular, although the generalizations must ultimately be based on the observation of many particular cases. From an immediate policy-oriented point of view, we may admittedly be more interested in understanding the possible causes of the *next* likely (and therefore, more specific) war, but my view is that the route to such understanding (and hopefully, prevention) is an indirect rather than a direct one, which must first run through an understanding of war in general. Until we can understand and explain a *class* of phenomena, we cannot explain a *single case* of that class, even though we may nevertheless do a fair job of predicting the outcome of that case and describing some of the conditions which surround it.[8]

Given these criteria, let me now try to appraise very briefly the quality of the past, present, and preferred future state of our knowledge on the causes of international war. As I see it, between the establishment of the international system (*circa* the Treaty of Utrecht in 1713, or the Treaties of Westphalia in 1648 if one prefers the earlier date) and the pre-World War II period, there was little important change in the quality of our knowledge regarding war and its causes. Admittedly the diplomatic and military historians of that epoch gradually added to our knowledge, giving us an increasing number of simple facts; these descriptive statements, while usually of high accuracy, seldom generalized beyond one or two cases, and when they sought to embrace a number of connected variables in the search for explanation, the confidence level almost invariably decreased.[9] In addition to a gradual increase in knowledge of the high confidence, but low generality and low explanatory, types, this period saw a remarkable degree of work in the form of speculative treatises on the causes of war. At a high level of generality, and seeking or claiming a considerable degree of explanatory power, these collections of assertions (based as they

---

Those social scientists who take too literally the example of the physical (or even the biological) sciences will be quick to urge that the inductive road (paved as it is with small and costly blocks of evidence) is hardly the most efficient route to knowledge and that propositions deduced from some larger theory are cheaper to come by and easier to defend. True enough, but where are the social science equivalents of the theories of gravity, thermodynamics, celestial mechanics, and so forth? By even the most modest criteria, we have precious little theory from which to deduce our propositions.

[7] A quotation from Wright (1957) is apposite here: "A case history, if composed without a theory [sic] indicating which of the factors surrounding a conflict are relevant and what is their relative importance, cannot be compared with other case histories, and cannot, therefore, contribute to valid and useful generalizations. On the other hand, a theory, if not applied to actual data, remains unconvincing . . ." (p. 265). And later in the same article: "Comparison would be facilitated if quantifications, even though crude, are made whenever possible" (p. 275). In a later article (1965) he very much follows his own advice.

[8] While disagreeing with those social scientists who hold that there is no such thing as an explanation when dealing with only a single case, I do concur that such explanations can seldom command much confidence. They may be plausible, but one can almost invariably come up with equally plausible, but incompatible, explanations. In choosing between competing explanations, we must either gather more and more detailed information on the single case, or place it into a *class* of cases for which a general explanation has already been developed. As a matter of scientific efficiency, the latter is much to be preferred.

were on very few high confidence factual assertions and very few cases) could hardly command much confidence today.[10] In the prescientific era, such conjectural "explanations" may have been widely accepted in some scholarly and political circles, but since the single fact assertions on which they often rested were not operationally defined and measured, and were therefore not comparable and cumulative, one may regard them today only as stimulating, albeit often original, sources of hypotheses.

The only exceptions I know which contradict the above evaluations are the scattered studies undertaken by a few nineteenth and early twentieth century economists. Because of their greater familiarity with quantitative data, operational measurement, probabilistic reasoning, and a propensity toward longitudinal and comparative analyses, several economists with an interest in the causes of war were able to add some modest knowledge of a fairly accurate, general, and explanatory sort. My impression, however, is that they were preoccupied primarily with business cycles, and only secondarily with the place of war in these cycles.[11]

But despite this assistance from the economists and economic historians, it was not until the late 1930s that an important qualitative change in our knowledge of war and its causes began to take place. Spearheaded primarily by Wright, Richardson, and Sorokin, we began for the first time to fill in some of that "knowledge space" characterized by relatively high confidence and generality and in the middle-to-high sector on the explanation axis. Following the lead of these pioneers—the first two of whom continued this work in the post-World War II period—the peace research movement of the late 1950s and the 1960s begun to generate inputs at many points along all three of our evaluative dimensions. We will return to this in the concluding section.

THE RELEVANCE OF OUR KNOWLEDGE

No matter how high the quality of our knowledge on the accuracy, generality, and explanatory dimensions, it may still be of no value in understanding or reducing the incidence of war. It must, in the final test, be relevant to the problem we seek to solve. A well-integrated body of true and general propositions may explain something *other than* how wars begin, escalate, or endure. But whereas many scientists might readily agree as to the *quality* of a given body of knowledge, the criteria for appraising its *relevance* are less obvious. Thus, rather than go on a private epistemological excursion into such criteria, let me turn to a consideration of those variables and models which for one researcher at least seem most relevant to the problem which so engaged Quincy Wright and those of us who follow in his footsteps.

The Search for Explanatory Variables

THE OUTCOME VARIABLE: MEASURING THE INCIDENCE OF WAR

In order to fit existing or anticipated knowledge into any explanatory framework and then evaluate the extent to which it correlates with, predicts, or accounts for the incidence of war, it is absolutely imperative that we first attend to that phenomenon whose occurrence we hope to explain. That is, if we hope to *explain* and account for the incidence of war, we must first discover: (a) what its incidence *has been*, and

---

[10] Some partial listings of this voluminous literature are to be found in Wright (1935), Bernard (1944), Bouthoul (1951) and Richardson (1960a).

[11] Among these are: Secerov (1919), Schumpeter (1939), and Frisch (1949). Only the first of these is devoted primarily to the search for an explanation of war. Another economist, Bloch (1903), sought to demonstrate how a variety of economic, demographic, and technological factors would soon put an end to war.

(b) what conditions and events *correlate with* the presence of, absence of, and magnitude of war. As obvious as this statement may be, only a fraction of those who seek to understand and explain the causes of war have ever bothered to generate such data or to utilize that of those who did. In addition to Wright himself, the only others who have tried to provide an operational description of the incidence of international war over any appreciable spatial and temporal domain are Sorokin (1937), Richardson (1960a), Urlanis (1960), and Singer and Small (1971). Let me summarize and compare several of these efforts.

First of all, Wright sought to identify for the period 1480–1940 "all hostilities involving members of the family of nations, whether international, civil, colonial, or imperial, which were recognized as states of war in the legal sense, or which involved over 50,000 troops." While his population of international wars is not complete, and his inclusion criteria are occasionally idiosyncratic, he produced (1942) the first definitive catalogue for the post-medieval epoch. And while Wright did not gather data on the casualties sustained in these wars, he did identify the major protagonists, the dates, and the general outcome for each of the 278 wars which fell into his net.

At about the same time, but apparently unbeknownst to one another, Sorokin and Richardson embarked on a similar enterprize. While Wright's listing covered about four centuries, Sorokin (1937, vol. 3) sought data on the incidence of war during the long period from the fifth century B.C. up to 1925. He was less interested in identifying the specific wars or their dates or protagonists than he was in estimating, for quarter-century periods and longer, the approximate number of wars, army sizes, numbers killed, and so forth. Given his theoretical purposes (1938), such figures were probably adequate, but for any detailed analysis of shorter-run fluctuations in a more restricted spatial and temporal setting, they are much too gross.

Covering a shorter time span than either Wright or Sorokin, but in considerably greater detail, Richardson (1960a) sought—not quite successfully—to identify all wars since 1820 in which more than 315 (the equivalent of his $\log_{10}$ magnitude of 2.5) fatalities were sustained. For each, whether civil or international, he attempted to identify not only the protagonists and dates, but most important, to make an accurate estimate of the battle-connected fatalities which eventuated from each such "deadly quarrel". Moreover—and at this point he became very pre-operational—he sought to specify the causes of each war on the basis of the military and diplomatic histories.[12]

Finally[13] there is the Singer and Small compilation which will soon appear under the title *The Wages of War, 1816–1965: A Statistical Handbook* (1971). Inspired by, and largely building upon the Wright and Richardson efforts, it represents the most comprehensive, operational and carefully compiled set of

---

[12] Several secondary analyses of Richardson's war estimate data have been published, seeking some chronological *pattern* in the ebb and flow of war, but not to *account for* that pattern in the explanatory sense; see Weiss (1963) and Denton (1966).

[13] Despite the prodigious work that obviously went into it, one cannot put the Urlanis (1960) compilation into the same class as the others. His coding rules are often unstated, seldom consistent from one table to another, and produce figures that are not compatible with one another; nor does he include and exclude wars according to any compelling and explicit criteria. Somewhat similar criticisms must be made of the recent report of the Institut Français de Polemologie (1968); it presents many figures over a long period of time, but gives not a single specific citation (a few authors are mentioned, but no sources) nor any coding or scaling rules.

There are, on the other hand, several careful and apparently accurate compilations which cover rather limited domains; among these are Harbottle (1904), Bodart (1916), and Dumas and Vedel-Peterson (1923). Finally, a devastating description of how a journalist's idle speculation on the incidence of war became accepted data in some of the "scholarly" literature is found in Haydon (1962).

data available for the time period. It makes no effort to get at the correlates or causes of the ninety-three wars which are reported, but rather seeks a full and detailed description of this outcome variable, measured in terms of the frequency, magnitude, severity, and intensity—plus trends and distributions of several types of international war. The data are organized initially by individual wars, but are then aggregated in order to show the distribution of different types of wars among different classes of nations for a variety of spatial and temporal domains. Our hope is that these materials will encourage the sort of rigorous and meticulous research which was hitherto not possible.

CLASSIFYING THE PREDICTOR VARIABLES

The number and variety of schemes for classifying and sorting out the possible causes of war is quite large, and the typology selected depends not only on a range of scientific considerations but upon many extra-scientific ones: nationality, age, sex, basic personality, education, prior research experiences, and not surprisingly, the fads and fashions of the moment as exemplified by those who employ us to teach, who finance our research, and who otherwise are in a position to pass judgment on our plans and our performance. In this section I will discuss what appears to be one of the more prevalent types of scheme, argue its inadequacies, and then move on to an alternative which seems to provide a satisfactory means of formulating substantive propositions, putting them to the empirical test, acquiring new knowledge, and codifying what we do know, think we know, and need to know.

The most widely used taxonomy is one which divides the alleged or potential explanatory variables into the standard disciplinary categories: political, economic, psychological, and sociological; some might include ideological factors under the political or the psycho-

logical categories, and technological factors under the sociological category. My objection to this sort of scheme is partly a function of its inherent inadequacies, and partly a response to the work of those who adhere to it.

Taking the latter grounds first, one is struck by the frequency with which many scholars move quickly from such an itemization to a concentration on just *one* of the categories, and proceed to "explain" the incidence of war almost exclusively in terms of that single cluster of variables. And, to nobody's surprise, the academics among us usually tend to select the variables of their own discipline. If such parochialism were to lead to the systematic collection of data for one or more variables in, for example, the economic or sociological sector, and then to the search for correlations between them and the onset of war, one could hardly complain. Such a procedure would enhance that critical mid-region of high confidence and high generality in our knowledge space. What it all too often leads to, however, is nothing but further speculation and conjecture. To the extent that single facts are brought to bear, they are neither representative nor operational, but a result of conscious or unconscious ransacking of the past in search of those few cases which tend to support the author's theoretical point of view.

My *a priori* objection is that no coherent model of an essentially explanatory nature can emerge from so restricted a set of independent and intervening variables. To put it simply and quite conventionally, if it is governments which decide on war and then manage its prosecution, no explanatory model which excludes political phenomena can be satisfactory. Even if we found that a certain cluster of economic or sociological or psychological variables were to correlate with, and account for a large percentage of the variance in, the frequency of, or magnitude of war in a given spatial-temporal domain, we would still be some distance from a satisfactory *explanation* of war. Just as I would argue that no explanation is scientifically adequate if it fails to account for the human perceptions and responses which link up the allegedly causal sequence, no explanation of war is adequate unless it specifies the decision process which links up the "objective conditions" with the military events themselves. There are, of course, many other formulations, and any one familiar with the "causes of war" literature will appreciate not only their diversity, but the ingenuity, learning, and dedication which they represent. However, rather than try to go over a great deal of old ground and summarize those formulations here, let me proceed to the delineation of a proposed alternative, in the context of a discussion on the substantive evaluation of our knowledge, possessed or anticipated.

In presenting this framework, it is well to keep in mind the demands that it should be able to satisfy. First it should be built around concepts that are as familiar as necessary, consistent only with the requirement that they reveal rather than conceal what our hunches and knowledge lead us to believe will be the most powerful explanatory variables. At this juncture, this is largely a matter of trained intuition. This brings us to the second requirement the ability of the scheme to embrace and codify, in a comparable and cumulative fashion, the most promising research which has so far been undertaken, as well as that which seems to lie ahead. Closely related is the need for it to be compatible with the concepts and findings of related disciplines. Third, it must permit the development of variables which are both valid and reliable, and, to satisfy the latter, the key constructs need to be as operational and quantifiable as possible, rather than vague and ephemeral. If a taxonomy is to contribute to the acquisition and codification of evidence which is not only theoretically promising, but methodologically cumulative and comparable, these are the

minimal criteria. Hopefully, the scheme which follows will turn out to satisfy these criteria.[14]

APPRAISING THE PREDICTOR VARIABLES

Since war is made, contemplated, and conducted by, and on behalf of, human beings organized into a variety of social entities, and is not made by relationships or roles or system properties (not to mention "social forces"), it makes perfect sense to build our taxonomy around those entities, however transitory and/or amorphous they may turn out to be. All sorts of social groups can and do wage war, but since our concern for the present is with international war, we can confine ourselves to the most relevant sub-national, national, and extra-national groups here, and neglect those of peripheral interest. These social groups range at the sub-national level from the family and primary work group up through all sorts of secondary associations to political parties, government agencies, legislatures, cabinets, and armies. When many such groups—at various levels of analysis and covering various functional sectors—are relatively unified and coordinated within a national territory, the resulting coalition may be called a nation. The nation or nation-state is the dominant unit of the contemporary international system, but for centuries before the emergence of that system, man was organized in many *other* types of social organizations. As other more effective groupings develop and attract the loyalty of their members, that pattern may be renewed, and it will be increasingly appropriate to refer to the *global*, rather than the *international* system. In any event, the nation is the major partici-

[14] One imaginative scheme, while less than operational, covers several levels of analysis, from the intra-psychic to the inter-national, and almost all sectors of human activity; see Deutsch and Senghaas (1969).

pant in modern international war, even though the probability of any such war, and its outcome, may well be more influenced by the various sub-national and extra-national groupings with which the nation shares the current world stage.

Every social unit may, in turn, be described in terms of three sets of attributes or properties: physical, structural, and cultural. Among the physical attributes are those of a geographic, technological and demographic nature. Among the structural attributes are the institutions and configurations normally associated with the labels: "political", "economic", and "sociological". And among the cultural (or better, psychocultural) attributes are the perceptions, preferences, and predictions of those individuals who comprise the entity (Singer 1968b).

Following the unfortunate tendency of the practitioners themselves, many scholars be they oriented toward the conjectural or the correlational have sought the causes of war in this very restricted set of variables. Certain nations in certain periods are labeled as aggressive or war-like (which may not be equivalent to war-prone) and their dominant structural, cultural, or physical attributes are assigned high explanatory status. Even though there has been little research leading to propositions of this sort in the high confidence, high generality, and correlational region of our knowledge space, these variables do not deserve to be jettisoned because of their propagandistic taint. While most of the inquiries into the effect of physical, structural, and cultural attributes on a nation's war-proneness suggest that they have little predictive or explanatory power (Cattell and Gorsuch, 1965; Rummel, 1968; Tanter, 1966; and Haas, 1968) a recent secondary analysis (Wilkenfield, 1968) points in the opposite direction; and Richardson (1960a) also seems to have uncovered some associations between the nations' attributes and their war-proneness.

In my view, bi-variate and multi-variate analyses using attribute variables should continue, on the assumption that, while helping to clear away the debris of political folklore, they will eventually fit into analyses which look at other classes of independent and intervening variables at the same time.

Another such class of variables is that of *relationships* between and among the nations and other entities in the system. These are of two types: *comparisons* and *connections*. The comparative type of relationship permits us to examine the similarities or differences between and among entities in order to see whether they help account for the war-proneness of particular pairs. Does it turn out that nations which are close together on such attributes as political ideology, or far apart on level of industrialization, are less war-prone than pairs whose attributes match in another fashion? The evidence here is also quite sparse, and the projects which have given greatest attention to this set of variables so far (Richardson, 1960a, and Rummel, 1963), show very mixed results. Shifting to the second type of relationship that of a connective nature we may profitably ask to what extent we can predict the frequency and magnitude of war for a given nation if we know something about its links and bonds to other nations, or to the war-proneness of a pair of nations on the basis of the interdependence and connections between them.

As with national attributes, the available evidence on relationships is both scanty and mixed. For the pre-World War II period, Wright developed some "distance" indicators that predicted well which pairs of nations would be at war against, and alongside of, one another (1942, App. XLIII). And Richardson found some association between the war-proneness of a pair and its linguistic and religious differences, but little association between economic inequality and such war-proneness; as to connective relationships, he found geographical contiguity to be an important predictor, prior military hostilities to be moderately important, and prior wartime alliances to have had little effect (1960a, Chaps. 5 and 6). Also relevant is the Singer and Small finding (1968) of a strong correlation between the number of alliance bonds a nation has and the amount of war it subsequently experiences. In sum, there seems to be a growing interest in relational variables as predictors to war (as well as to other phenomena), and my suspicion is that Wright was correct in urging us to attend to such comparisons and connections. Once more, though, the explanatory power of such variables will be considerably enhanced when they are combined with other sets of variables.

Let me shift back to attributes of social systems again, but at the international or global, rather than national, level of analysis. This sequence makes sense inasmuch as many of the international *system's attributes*, especially the structural ones, are based on the observation of *relationships among its members*. While there is a growing body of conjectural literature on the correlation between system properties and the incidence, or probability of war (Deutsch and Singer, 1964; Waltz, 1959), there is very little evidence on the strength and direction of this association; nor has there been much effort to develop operational measures of such variables.[15]

The problem is further confounded by the fact that some see war as a function of the system's inherent and *constant* properties, while others search for the association between *fluctuations* in such properties and

the fluctuation of war. Using the latter orientation, we found a very discernible *negative* correlation between alliance aggregation and subsequent war in the nineteenth century, and a stronger, but *positive* one, in the twentieth (Singer and Small, 1968); we also found practically no correlation between the amount of inter-governmental organization in the system and subsequent warfare (Singer and Wallace, 1970).[16] As to physical properties of the system, Rummel (1961) found some positive associations, as well as several negligible ones, between technological innovations and war. Regarding the perhaps most important system properties, psychocultural properties, there is almost no evidence on the extent to which shifts and fluctuations in the distribution of perceptions, perferences, and predictions may affect the frequency and magnitude of war. This set of variables, like the others already mentioned, has also received little empirical attention of a correlational nature, yet it is difficult to see much progress in understanding the causes of war until it, too, has been included in some systematic empirical investigations.[17]

So far, I have mentioned no behavioral variables and have focused solely on system or actor attributes (physical, structural, and cultural) and on relationships (comparative and connective) between and among actors. Some will contend that this represents an unfortunate emphasis and that the "real" causes of war will be found in the decisions of political

---

[15] Some data and measures of the attributes of the international system over the past century and a half are in Singer and Small (1966a, 1966b, 1968), and Wallace and Singer (1970). Also see the promising measures and data reported in Russett (1967), the pioneering effort of Deutsch *et al.* (1957), and the Princeton University project on "security communities."

[16] Also turned up in this inquiry was the strong correlation between the amount of war *ending* in any half-decade and the amount of new Inter-governmental Organization established in the following decade, suggesting that even though the historical effects of such organization on the incidence of war have not been impressive, public or private elites may believe otherwise.

[17] See, for some promising early efforts, such Stanford University studies as Holsti, North, and Brody (1968), and Zinnes (1968). For a systematic discussion of the problem, see Waltz (1959).

elites and the resulting actions of their nations. While fully concurring that an "ecological" theory of war would be incomplete at best, I would urge that serious attention to these attributes and relational variables is absolutely essential.[18] To look at behavioral events alone, or as parts of interaction sequences, is to court disaster unless they are examined along with —and in the context of— the physical, structural, and cultural setting within which they occur.

The problem is three-fold. First, as suggested earlier, governmental decisions and behavior represent the intervening variables between a set of ecological incentives and constraints (domestic and global) on the one hand, and war or no war as the outcome of conflict, on the other; they can only be understood in that sort of context. Second, until we can get at the discrepancies (if any) between the objective incentives and constraints and the way in which they are perceived, we will be far from understanding the behavior which leads toward or away from war. Third, until certain of the key ecological variables are identified and their own explanatory power ascertained, we will never know exactly how much control remained in the hands of the decision-makers and how much of the variance is accounted for by their behavior. One of the interesting differences between Wright and Richardson is that the former's work (1942, 1957, and 1965 particularly) seems to follow strongly from this point of view, while the bulk of the latter's theoretical efforts (1960b) focuses almost exclusively on behavioral and interactional phenomena. Some who have followed up Richardson's work on arms races have, happily, paid more attention to the

ecological setting within which such interaction sequences occur (Smoker, 1963).[19]

That there has been little operational data gathered on behavioral and interactional phenomena is not surprising; whether as outcome or as predictor variables, and whether related to war or anything else, it is extremely difficult to identify a population of behavioral events, draw a useful sample, and then classify or scale them. Despite that difficulty, however, a number of recent efforts suggest that the problems are far from insurmountable. First, there are the above-noted studies of the Stanford University project, focusing on the behavioral (as well as psychological) phenomena which characterized the period leading to World War I, the Cuban missile crisis, and other conflicts (Holsti, 1965; Holsti, North, and Brody, 1968; Zinnes, 1968; and North and Choucri, 1969). There are also the University of Southern California studies, examining the Berlin and Taiwan Straits crises of the post-World War II period (McClelland, 1968, and McClelland and Hoggard, 1969). Also advancing our capacity to describe and analyze inter-national conflict sequences in operational terms are Corson (1970), Azar (1970), and Burrowes (1969). More comprehensive, covering all pre-war conflicts in the system since the Congress of Vienna, but now only at the pre-test stage, is the typology and its rationale reported in Leng and Singer (1970).[20]

Appreciating the difficulty of coding and scaling the behavior and interaction of

---

This view is quite consistent with that which distinguishes between the remote and the immediate, the fundamental and the inciting, or the institutional and the behavioral causes of war as found in much of the speculative literature.

[19] Also in the behavioral sector is an oft-cited article (Abel, 1941) which purports to have "found" that tensions, misperceptions and other non-rational factors have seldom been important in the decision to go to war; rather, the study concludes that such decisions are taken cooly and well in advance of the onset of hostilities. However, there is not a shred of operational evidence reported, nor did a letter of inquiry to the author produce such evidence.

[20] For a thoughtful treatment of the ways in which complex diplomatic moves may be measured, see Moses *et al.* (1967).

national governments during conflicts, a number of peace researchers have shifted their attention to the "simulate" world. Such simulations take two basic forms: man–machine and all–machine (computer) simulation. While it is difficult to take the former type of study very seriously as a technique of discovery, these man–machine simulations have probably been valuable in the heuristic, suggestive, sense of the word.[21] More promising in its ultimate theoretical and policy payoffs, however, will be the computer simulation, in which we can more fully manipulate and examine the historical unfolding of the "real" world, as well as the world of the past (or of the future) as it *might* have unfolded. We will return to this research strategy in the conclusion.

To summarize this section, then, my view is that no one cluster of variables is likely to play a dramatic role as we gradually discover the causes of international war. It will almost certainly turn out that certain attributes do indeed make some nations more war-prone than others, but it will probably also turn out that these attributes are the ones which shift over time, making the stage of development or certain short-range perturbations more critical than such relatively fixed attributes as language or religion or ethnicity. I would, on the other hand, expect that these attributes—in order to exercise any consistent and powerful effect–have to interact with certain *relational* variables and with the attributes of the international system at the moment. A nation must, in a sense, be in the "right" setting if it is to get into war. Finally, there is little doubt that all of these ecological factors will have to be taken into account, and controlled for, if we are ever to understand the dynamic processes of behavior and interaction which are

so large a part of conflict. To talk about decision-making, political choice, strategy and the like in the absence of well-mapped environmental limits and opportunities is to exaggerate (or perhaps even *under*estimate) the autonomy and the power of those who act within such an environment.[22]

Conclusion

Let me try now to bring together the two sets of criteria which have been discussed separately, and on the basis of such a convergence see whether there is any one best research strategy for those of us seeking the causes of international war. If not, are there at least some fairly clear priorities that emerge? Now some will argue, in true academic tradition, that there is no one *best* way to do anything, that each of us should pursue his own line of inquiry, doing that which he does most competently and comfortably. And then, by some cosmological magic, all of these separate bits of knowledge will fall neatly into place, culminating in a single coherent theory.

While we need not set up a Manhattan Project or a PERT system (used to coordinate the discrete phases of the Polaris missile submarine project), it is naive to expect that the disparate frameworks, vocabularies, and empirical domains now represented in peace research will inevitably mesh and reinforce one another. At the same time, it would be presumptuous for any one scholar—and premature at this juncture—to spell out a single specific research program. Not only is the causes of war question merely *one* aspect of peace research, but the quality and the relevance of our knowledge on this one question are far from adequate as a basis for predicting the most efficient research path.

Having said this, however, let me propose

---

[21] The classical statement is in Guetzkow *et al.* (1963), and one of the more thorough experiments and reports is in Brody (1963); my reservations are in Singer (1965).

[22] The most systematic treatment of this problem remains Sprout and Sprout (1965).

and defend a general strategy which seems well-suited for the acquisition and codification of knowledge on the causes of international war. First, certain kinds of conjectural work could easily be dispensed with "for the duration." I refer to the sort of essay in which some single-cause "theory" is propounded, most often in terms of a biological, psychoanalytical, or economic variable. If one is persuaded that his propositions make sense, let him put the independent variable(s) in operational form, gather the necessary data, and see how the resulting time series correlate with the war data which are now available. If there is little or no established association, the enterprise will (if conducted competently) have nevertheless made some contribution to our knowledge. Even negative findings, while somewhat less valuable (since they are more probable and therefore convey less information), are very much worth turning up. I reject conjectural work on single cause ideas not only because I am convinced that no single variable will ever account for enough of the variance to justify yet another essay on the subject, but because just about every single cause conjecture has already been made. *If* a fairly thorough search of the literature reveals no prior discussion of the alleged causal factor, then a brief essay may well be merited, especially if it leads to an empirical investigation.

On the other hand, there is plenty of room for *multi*-variate conjecture, especially if the variables are stated in relatively operational form and if the relationships among them are explicitly spelled out in terms of an integrated model and hypothesized causal sequences. That is, despite the obvious paucity of evidence, and the apparent surfeit of speculation, there is still great need for pre-empirical, but scientific *thinking*, and the generation of hypotheses and models which could then be checked against evidence. But the payoffs in this speculative sector will almost certainly

come from scholars who are at home in scientific method and who know not only how to conduct rigorous research, but how to analyze a problem and the existing evidence in order to set up the really critical, rather than routine, experiments.[23] Furthermore, my prediction is that the really critical research designs will come from scholars who are relatively at home in several of the social science disciplines as was Wright (1955), and who think in general systems terms.

Having said all of this, however, there is little question in my mind that the greatest need is in the correlational sector. Our desperate requirement now is a data and findings base from which we may proceed to the systematic testing of a multiplicity of plausible explanations of war. Even as we wait and hope for the brilliant insight which may unlock the mystery, three points must be kept in mind. First, even if that brilliant conjecture is forthcoming, we will not recognize it, and should not believe it, until we have seen the evidence; and the more data we generate, the easier it will be to "check it out" when it comes along. Second, the more solid data at hand, and the more bi-variate and multi-variate analyses available, the more efficiently and persuasively we can look into and reject hunches or hypotheses that are inadequate. Conversely, in the absence of such data and the associated correlational analyses, the theoretical break-

---

[23] While experiments are generally associated with laboratory research in the physical or biological sciences, or in psychology and sociology, it should be noted that experiments may be conducted in two other settings as well. There is the "field experiment" in which the researcher waits for, or stimulates, the experimental condition in the natural setting, and the "historical experiment," in which he treats the unfolding of past events *as if* he did not know how they would turn out. An excellent discussion of the *critical* type of experiment, applicable to the field and historical, as well as to the laboratory setting, is Platt (1964).

through may be rejected because it is unconventional, implausible, or politically distasteful; just as bad, scientifically indefensible explanations may be embraced because they *are* plausible or acceptable, and because there is little evidence to refute them. Finally, the more data a creative social scientist has ready at hand, the more likely he is to come up with the critical insight; nothing is as suggestive of hypotheses as data and correlational matrices to a scholar who is not only thoughtful, but at home with statistical materials.

The view taken here is that the right combination of conjectural and correlational research could bring us close to a causal theory of war within a few years. Imaginative but disciplined conjecture can prevent us from embarking on a decade or more of mindless empiricism, and the gradual buildup of comparable and cumulative correlational findings can provide us with a growing knowledge base against which our conjectures may be tested. The idea, of course, is that we must move toward the construction and verification of multi-variate causal models just as quickly as our data and ideas permit.[24] These models, in turn, may be checked out in two ways. The first and most relevant is vis-a-vis the empirical realities of the international system as the tides of war ebbed and flowed.

But almost as important, as our models

improve and our data and correlational bases expand, is the resort to computer *simulations*, as suggested earlier. Our research has turned up 93 international wars during the past century and a half, most of which were preceded by conflicts and crises. From a humanitarian point of view, that may have been 93 wars too many, but from a scientific point of view it was too few. That is, not every combination of factors that *could* have occurred *did* indeed occur in actuality, and we therefore cannot be certain whether a particular combination of factors might have led to war, *had* that combination occurred. And conversely, for those combinations which did occur and were followed by war, we probably will not find enough historical cases in which all but one of the factors were the same and from which war did *not* ensue.

The virtue of a computer simulation is that it permits us to recreate such events and cases in a large variety of combinations, and if we know enough about the relations between and among certain variables in certain combinations, we can use that knowledge to simulate what would (or might) have happened had the combination been sufficiently different. In essence, a computer simulation is little more than an operational statement of one's theory, or alternative theories, in which different magnitudes of the separate variables are tried out in order to ascertain the effect, singly and in combination, of many differing magnitudes and rates of change in these variables. With it, we can discover, by means of sensitivity analysis of the model, at which thresholds these changes are likely to have critical effects. If the model itself is relevant, the variables are critical, and the data inputs are sound, such a simulation series can eventually add to our knowledge in a dramatic way.[25]

---

[24] In this connection, the incremental nature of empirical research must be emphasized. This means that the first scholar to examine the correlations between (let us say) international organization and war cannot be expected to look at every single type of organization in his opening study, but must restrict himself to a well-defined subset thereof. He or others may then follow up the original work by either including certain additional organizations or using a more refined breakdown of those which had originally been lumped together. In this way, we gradually improve the validity of our measures while moving toward increasingly sophisticated sets of models, and toward findings which are high on the accuracy, generality, and explanatory axes.

---

[25] In my judgment, we have barely begun to realize these possibilities, but promising starts are in

In sum, then, the view here is that international war is a problem as inherently researchable as most others we have faced, and that as our research improves in quantity, quality, and relevance, we can acquire and codify sufficient knowledge to be able to explain its presence, absence, or magnitude under a variety of conditions. Whether such knowledge will be applicable to conflicts and crises of the future, it is too early to tell, but in principle, it should be. And whether such knowledge will be put to use is, of course, another question entirely and one which also merits some modest research attention in the interim. If we can continue to carry on where Wright and his fellow pioneers left off, we may yet build the most valuable applied science that man has ever known.

J. David Singer (Ph.D. New York University, 1956) is Professor of Political Science at the University of Michigan and has also been associated with Vassar College, The Naval War College, and the Universities of Oslo and Geneva. Among his books are Financing International Organization *(1961);* Deterrence, Arms Control, and Disarmament *(1962);* Human Behavior and International Politics *(1965);* Quantitative International Politics *(1968);* The Wages of War, 1816-1965 *(1972); and* The Study of International Politics *(1976).*

Milstein and Mitchell (1969), and Bremer (1970); two useful sets of discussions are Bobrow and Schwartz (1968), and Coplin (1968), and a rigorous critique is in Alker and Bruner (1969). Representative of the more ambitious computer simulations in economics and urban studies, respectively, are Orcutt (1961) and Forrester (1970).

Studies of International Violence

FIVE EASY PIECES?

CHARLES S. GOCHMAN   *Chapter* 2

The study of international violence—and war, in particular—is a
time-honored profession. Among its practitioners have been philosophers
and historians, economists and mathematicians, sociologists, psychologists,
anthropologists, and political scientists. Not surprisingly, this wide
representation of disciplines has produced an equally diverse array of
explanations as to why international violence occurs, or does not occur.
These explanations range from the metaphysical belief in fate to the

AUTHOR'S NOTE: I would like to acknowledge the helpful comments of Stuart
A. Bremer and Thomas R. Cusack and the financial assistance of the University
Consortium for World Order Studies.

Originally published in the *Journal of Conflict Resolution,* Vol. 20, No. 3, September
1976.

realpolitik preoccupation with the struggle for power, from the unicausal to the multivariate, from the idiographic to the nomothetic. Although to date there does not appear to be a satisfactory explanation of the causes of international violence nor an adequate understanding of its consequences, there does seem to be a trend toward constructing multivariate models that are applicable to a large number of conflict events. The arguments and analyses presented in the five books that we shall review in this essay are all consonant with this trend. Four of the books fall squarely into the genre of literature called quantitative peace research, the fifth (Blainey, 1973) is better classified as an historical survey. In all five works we find a belief in the existence of historical regularity, a reliance on longitudinal data, and a preference for systematic examination of the evidence. But while the books under review highlight a multitude of ways in which quantitative research techniques are applicable to questions of war and peace, and while they offer some very interesting suggestions for modeling the international conflict process, they also serve as a reminder that we need to be cautious about the ways in which we use statistical and mathematical tools in our research and the manner in which we interpret the results of our analyses.

LITERATURE ON INTERNATIONAL VIOLENCE

In writing this essay my purposes are really threefold: first, to review some recently published literature on international violence; second, to identify some theoretical strands that these, at first sight, disparate works have in common; and third, to suggest how these strands might be woven into a conceptual framework to guide our search for the causes of international violence. I therefore begin with an examination of the central themes, empirical domains, and major findings and conclusions presented by the author(s) of each of the five volumes under review.

BLAINEY ON WAR

Geoffrey Blainey, professor of economic history at the University of Melbourne, has written a most readable treatise on *The Causes of War* (1973). His book is purportedly based upon a survey of all international wars fought during the period 1700-1971 A.D. I use the term "purportedly" because Blainey offers us neither an explicit definition of war nor a comprehensive compilation of these phenomena. This is a matter of no small moment. In the first place, the question "How do we recognize a war when we see it?" is not a trivial query; a great deal of discussion has evolved over whether particular battle-death thresholds or legalistic criteria should be elements of a definition of war (Wright, 1965; Singer and Small, 1972; Duvall, 1976). To further compound this difficulty by omitting a complete listing of the wars surveyed can only increase the reader's uncertainty about the reliability of the author's conclusions. For the inferences one draws from any analysis are dependent upon the population of cases that is selected for investigation; altering the cases may well alter the analytic results.

Be that as it may, Blainey's book is provocative and rich in ideas. Half of the pages are dedicated to exposing weaknesses in a number of commonly-held explanations of war and peace. And in this enterprise Blainey is at his best, judiciously marshaling historical counter-examples. Among the targets of his well-orchestrated onslaught are the notions that powerful statesmen, moderate peace treaties, humane ideas, closer commercial or cultural contacts, economic prosperity, or civil strife promote prolonged periods of peace among nation-states.

Once he has applied his scythe to this yielding field of popular belief, Blainey turns his hand to sowing his own interpretation of why states fight. His thesis is an interesting, if familiar, one. Simply put, "war is a dispute about the measurement of power" (p. 114). Wars are most likely to occur when decision makers in rival states disagree about the relative power capabilities of their respective countries. Wars usually end when they reach agreement on this issue. In this sense, war serves the function of accurately measuring the relative power of states.

What is particularly appealing about Blainey's argument is its simplicity and its symmetry. He contends that wars are never accidental, that they "can only occur when two nations decide that they can gain more by fighting than by negotiating" (p. 159). This is most likely to occur when decision makers overestimate, and thereby become overconfident about, their state's bargaining strength. To the extent that neither side can muster a decisive power advantage, and so long as the intervention of additional states appears to the combatants to be improbable or incapable of tipping the power scales, wars are likely to be prolonged. But once a decisive power difference is established, hostilities will most probably cease. For, as Blainey says, "the conflicting aims of rival nations are always conflicts of power" (p. 150), and the decisions to resolve these issues by warlike methods, to prolong hostilities, and to sue for peace are largely determined by assessments of relative strength.

While I find the argument appealing, Blainey's method for supporting his thesis is less than adequate. By and large—and despite statements to the contrary—Blainey is content to bolster his contentions by relying upon selected historical examples. Whereas this "pick the case that supports my argument" procedure is an efficient means for highlighting weaknesses in some contending explanations of war and peace and for illustrating the plausibility of one's own thesis, it is no substitute for a systematic examination of a relationship. The association between disagreements over relative power, on the one hand, and the occurrence, duration, and termination of war, on the other, cannot be established by Blainey's selective use of historical examples. In this light, it is interesting to note that Blainey repeatedly chides peace researchers for failing to recognize that the factors that "cause peace" (i.e., end wars) are simply the opposite of those that produce war. Yet he fails to examine the obverse of his principal hypotheses; he does not ask, for example, whether some wars are *not* preceded by disagreements over relative power or whether some disagreements over power do *not* erupt into wars. If he had asked such questions, he might well have been forced to undertake a more systematic investigation. Such questions compel the investigator to think in terms of percentages and statistical associations. If Blainey had so structured his inquiry, *The Causes of War* would be more than a well-written book that poses intriguing questions; it might well have made a major contribution to the scientific study of war and peace.

FERRIS ON POWER CAPABILITIES

Wayne Ferris, a political scientist, has also investigated the relationship between the relative capabilities of states and their involvement in international conflicts. His approach to the issue is, however, quite different from that of Blainey. We find in Ferris' *The Power Capabilities of Nation-States* (1973) very little historical narrative. Rather, we are confronted with a rigorous, well-documented, and, seemingly, highly-reproducible quantitative analysis. Ferris' stated purposes in his book are to construct an index of national power capabilities, and then systematically to relate this index to national involvements in conflicts, especially wars, during the period 1850-1965 A.D.

Ferris' theoretical argument has many similarities to Blainey's. He recognizes that there are a large number of factors that account for violent international conflicts, but he asserts that armed conflict can be viewed as being caused by primarily two factors: (1) the importance each party to a dispute attaches to a conflicting interest and (2) the probability that one party to the dispute can secure its interests by resorting to military force. In his data analysis, the first factor remains largely an unmeasured variable; the second is operationalized in terms of the power each party can bring to bear upon the other. Ferris reasons that the greater the likelihood that *one* party to the conflict can secure its interests by resorting to military force, the greater is the probability of war. This contention appears to be opposite to that which Blainey would argue. Ferris is positing that the likelihood of war is great when the disparity in power capabilities between opposing parties is *large*. Blainey, on the other hand, contends that war is most probable when *both* parties to the conflict are overconfident about their ability to secure their interests through the use of force and, presumably, this is most likely to occur when the power disparity between the opposing parties is *small*. [Editor's note: On this debate, see the articles by Garnham and Weede, *Journal of Conflict Resolution*, September 1976, which support the latter hypothesis.] But despite this admittedly important divergence, one cannot help but notice the basic similarities in their theoretical arguments. Both Ferris and Blainey hypothesize that the expectations of decision makers concerning the likelihood of obtaining national objectives by means of military force are based primarily upon an evaluation of relative power capabilities. Both also contend that these expectations can be distorted. Ferris posits that changes in the relative capabilities of states may introduce a destabilizing element into the decision-making calculus; Blainey lists a number of factors that can lead decision makers to overestimate their bargaining strength and, thereby, become overconfident about the likely outcome of armed conflict. Both Ferris and Blainey agree that, if a war erupts, the greater the power disparity between the adversaries, the shorter the war is likely to be. And finally, both concur that the more powerful adversary in a war is most likely to be victorious.

If their theses are similar, their approaches to data analysis are not. Ferris explicitly defines and operationalizes all the concepts in his hypotheses, he is careful to identify his data sources and list the cases to be examined, and he is rigorous and systematic in his data manipulation and analysis. This is not to say that his procedures are without fault. A number of his operationalizations appear arbitrary, for example, he defines "most wars" as 85% of wars and "a high level of power capabilities" as a two-to-one power advantage. No reasons are offered for these decisions. He relies upon statistics, such as product moment correlations, that are appropriate for ascertaining the association between *continuous* linear variables, when, in fact, the outcome variable in most of his analyses is *dichotomous.* He uses factor loadings from a nine-variable principal components analysis to weight the elements of a power index when he should have selected loadings from an eight-variable analysis. But, on the whole, Ferris' procedures are lucid, and even resourceful. One example of this is his carefully-reasoned, if complex, power capabilities index. Ferris defines "power capabilities" as those factors that enable one nation-state to threaten sanctions—in particular, the use of military force—against another state. He sees these factors residing in a nation's armed force strength, technological development, and economic and administrative capacity. In order to combine indicators of these factors into a single index of power, he employs a factor analytic technique (principal components analysis) to determine the extent to which the indicators tap a single dimension that might be called "power capabilities." The weight of each indicator in the power index is then deemed to be proportionate to the percentage of variance each indicator has in common with the "power capabilities" dimension. Another example of Ferris' resourcefulness arises when he is forced to develop a list of "nonconflict" cases. This is necessary in order to determine whether the power disparity between states involved in conflicts is dissimilar to that between states *not* involved in conflicts. To develop such a list, Ferris randomly selects for each state one year between 1850 and 1965 in which it was a member of the international system, and then randomly pairs this state in that year with one of its contiguous neighbors (since most international conflicts involve neighboring states). He thereby obtains a "randomly-generated" list of nonconflict dyads.

Ferris' analytic findings raise doubts about some of Blainey's conclusions, in particular, the one that associates (or, more accurately, can be inferred to associate) equality in relative power capabilities with involvement in war. Examining international conflicts listed by Wright (1965), Holsti (1966), and Singer and Small (1972), Ferris discovers that the greater the power disparities between states and the greater the change in such disparities, the higher the probability that these states will become involved in intense conflicts (i.e., ones that involve the threat or use of military force or are sufficiently serious to be brought before the League of Nations or the United Nations). However, at this point, even Ferris' own principal hypothesis falters. He finds that, given the existence of intense conflicts, neither power disparities between the antagonists nor changes in such disparities alter the likelihood that these conflicts will escalate into serious military hostilities (in which 317 or more combatants are killed). Additionally, and contrary to hypotheses of both authors, Ferris discovers that power capabilities disparity is *not* associated with either the duration of wars or the battle losses suffered by the combatants. But, he does find that two thirds of all wars fought between 1850 and 1965 are won by the more powerful adversary.

What is fascinating about Ferris' findings is that power disparity and changes in that disparity appear to have a different impact on the *initiation* of conflicts than on the *escalation* of these conflicts into more serious hostilities, and a different impact on the *duration and devastation* of combat than on the *probability of victory*. In short, his findings suggest—as, indeed, do some of my own (Gochman, 1975)—that variables have different effects at different points in the conflict process, and that variables that account for the onset of the process may well be different from those that account for its size or outcome.

NAROLL ET AL. ON DETERRENCE

The notion that the relative power capabilities of states are associated with their involvement in wars appears, yet again, in Raoul Naroll, Vern Bullough, and Frada Naroll's *Military Deterrence in History* (1974). The volume is a markedly enlarged version of an article of similar title that appeared originally in Pruitt and Snyder's *Theory and Research on the Causes of War* (1969). Naroll et al.'s approach in their book lies somewhere between that of Blainey and Ferris. As in Blainey, we are presented an historical survey, this time in the format of 20 case studies. But, as in Ferris, quantitative techniques are employed to investigate the authors' hypotheses.

Naroll et al.'s principal hypothesis is that "states assuming a defensive stance with strong military preparations and favorable diplomatic, geographic, political, and cultural circumstances . . . tend to avoid war" (p. 5). The thrust of their argument, i.e., that military strength promotes peace and security, is directly opposed to Ferris' contention that strength promotes war.

To test their supposition, Naroll et al. identify nine intellectually influential higher civilizations that have existed during the past 5,000 years, these being the Egyptian, Mesopotamian, Hebrew, Greco-Roman, Chinese, Hindu, Western, Islamic. and Russian civilizations. They then randomly select to study the decade 76-85 and, from all centuries for which historical records of the civilizations exist, they arbitrarily choose 17 cases for analysis. Five cases are drawn from each of the Greco-Roman, Chinese, and Western civilizations, and one each from the Islamic and Russian. To these 17 are added three decades from the Swiss Confederation, so as to increase the number of nonmonarchical cases. In all, the 20 decades selected span more than 2,000 years from 225 B.C. to 1785 A.D. The 20 cases, however, are in no way a random or stratified sample of the population of intellectually influential higher civilizations. And, therefore, it is impossible to ascertain whether findings from an analysis of these cases are in any way valid for the population of cases. The authors fully recognize this, having offered us a 100-page methodological introduction to research design and statistical inference. But their response to the dilemma is to tell us "to do as they say, and not as they do" (paraphrase, p. 27).

For each of the 20 spatial-temporal domains that are selected, Naroll et al. identify the state that is most active in international conflict (the Conspicuous State) and its primary diplomatic or military opponent (the Conspicuous Rival). Then, for these 20 "conspicuous dyads," the authors examine the intercorrelations among 29 predictor variables (having to do with military, geographic, diplomatic, cultural, and administrative factors) and three outcome variables: frequency of war (more accurately, months of war per decade), territorial growth, and territorial instability. The manner in which many of these variables are operationalized raises questions of reliability and validity. Much of the data coding, which is apparently done by the authors themselves, is impressionistic. And while "soft data" are to be preferred over no data, this reader would be very interested in the extent of inter-coder reliability, i.e., the extent to which different people independently coding the same material would produce the same results. Naroll et al. do not investigate this question; we are simply told that "this is only a pilot study and its theoretical results are inconclusive" (p. xlvii). But the results may be even less than inconclusive, since a number of data transformations may threaten the validity of the authors' conclusions. Naroll et al. transform all of the outcome variables so as to produce "pseudo-normal distributions." These transformations do not seem to be based upon theoretical considerations, but are rather the product of a trial-and-error process in which a computer is used to generate a wide range of alternative transformations, from which the authors select those that produced the most nearly Gaussian distribution. Naroll et al. tell us that such transformations insure that "statistically significant results from statistical tests based on the assumption of normality of distribution must chiefly reflect actual relationships of the data" (p.39). This explanation is a bit confusing, since the assumption to which Naroll et al. refer does not stipulate that the *sample* should be normally distributed, but that the underlying *population* of scores from which the sample is drawn should be so distributed (Hays, 1963). The authors, therefore, needlessly subject their data to complex and questionable transformations involving arcsines, arctangents, and square roots of logarithms. The theoretical interpretation of these transformed variables is not clear to me. An even more fundamental issue, however, is simply whether tests of statistical significance (for the purpose of drawing inferences about a population) are not beside the point, since the cases to be analyzed do not constitute a random or stratified sample of a population.

If we can overlook these methodological problems, the results of Naroll et al.'s analyses would seem to be consistent with Ferris' findings. By and large, Naroll et al. discover that neither military, geographic, diplomatic, cultural, nor administrative variables are strongly associated with the amount of war experienced by the "conspicuous dyad" during the period examined. Indeed, the only sizable correlations are among the predictor variables, where the authors find (not surprisingly) that several cultural variables are highly interrelated and (more surprisingly) that the locations of capital cities are associated with the absence of natural barriers and the presence of cultural and economic exchange. Thus, the location of capital cities would appear to be determined more by considerations of ease of communication and commerce than by desires for military safety. Although this is an interesting observation, it can hardly be said to be central to the deterrence question. The major conclusion to be drawn from the Naroll et al. study is that, in preindustrial times, neither military strength nor interstate ties were associated with the amount of war that erupted between the Conspicuous State and its major rival.

Inexplicably, the authors of *Military Deterrence in History* reach a different conclusion. After telling the reader that "for the Conspicuous State, at least, the search for peace and security through armed force is in vain," they conclude that *"those who live by the sword may indeed expect to perish by the sword"* (p. 343, my italics). No such conclusion can possibly be drawn from the findings of this study! Naroll et al. themselves clearly state at many points in the book that they find *no* strong relationship between any of their military variables and the outcome variables. Thus, while *Military Deterrence in History* is an interesting study and one that reflects a great deal of arduous and detailed historical investigation, the reader should be alert to the fact that it is replete with methodological difficulties.

MIDLARSKY ON WAR

Having examined three volumes that all focus on relative power capabilities as the principal factor accounting for national war involvement, we now turn to one that does not. This fourth book, Manus Midlarsky's *On War* (1975), is by far the most methodologically sophisticated, not to mention eclectic, volume under review. It is largely a collection of previously presented papers, which the author attempts to tie together using the rubric "environmental uncertainty reduction." Basically, this refers to the purported propensity of national decision makers to eliminate ambiguity in the international environment. Midlarsky argues that the use of force in international politics is an attempt to achieve certainty in situations in which normal political relations have failed.

Midlarsky's thesis is that decision makers are confronted by uncertainty whenever there exist a number of possible events, each having an approximately equal probability of occurring. Faced with such a situation, decision makers attempt to reduce this uncertainty by acting in such a manner as to increase the probability of particular events occurring, while decreasing the probability of others. If they have the power capabilities to alter these probabilities, yet are for other reasons constrained from doing so, there is a high likelihood that they will initiate violent acts—even resort to war—to achieve their ends.

Given this formulation, Midlarsky is interested in examining constraints on decision-making latitude. Some of these constraints he sees as voluntary, i.e., national leaders at times enter into international agreements that either limit the domain of their authority or commit them to take certain actions if specific conditions arise. Other constraints are more or less fixed, i.e., decision makers are often confronted by geographic or other environmental factors that are, by and large, not susceptible to their control. Midlarsky investigates both types of constraints. Using the concept of entropy (borrowed from physics and information science), he explores the extent to which membership in military alliances, the length of time spent in alliances, the number of borders a state has, the degree of multipolarity in the interstate system, the equi-distribution of military alliances across states, and the uncertainty (entropy) engendered by each of these factors are associated with the number of wars in which states become involved. He finds that for what he calls the central powers (Austria-Hungary, Germany, France, Russia, Turkey, Spain, Italy, Great Britain, the United States, and Japan) during 1815-1945 A.D. the associations are quite sizable, especially between the uncertainty measures and the number of wars.

It is exceedingly difficult to evaluate the significance of these findings. Much of the theoretical argument is highly abstract, and Midlarsky's mathematical presentation of the uncertainty (entropy) measure is not well-integrated with the substantive issue. For example, in physics, entropy is used as a measure of disorder and is associated with the *probability* that a particular molecular arrangement will occur in a closed thermodynamic system; in information science, entropy is a measure of information content and is associated with the *probability* that a given message will alter a recipient's subjective evaluation of the likelihood of an event occurring. For the purposes of political science, Midlarsky wishes to employ entropy as a measure of decision-making uncertainty. But rather than operationalize the concept in terms of the *probability* of an event occurring, as appears to be necessitated by the mathematical formulation of entropy, he utilizes such quantities as the *number* of borders that a state has and the *proportion* of total system alliances to which a state belongs. It is not clear to me what assumptions must be made if one is to substitute such quantities for probabilities, or whether or not these assumptions would be theoretically defensible. As a result, I am not sure how the entropy measure, as operationalized by Midlarsky, relates to the concept of decision-making uncertainty.

Another difficulty that I see in Midlarsky's work is his use of what might be called a "time exposure" research design. Rather than conduct time series analysis, he computes for each state in his spatial domain a mean or total score on every variable for the 1815-1945 period. He then calculates what, in effect, are cross-sectional correlations. For example, when investigating the association between alliance membership and national war involvement, Midlarsky correlates for each state its *total* number of alliance memberships over the 130-year period with its *total* number of war involvements during the same period. The fact that the summary scores for each state represent a 130-year period does not alter the cross-sectional nature of the design. It is important to note that the same correlation could be obtained if alliance membership (or alliance-induced uncertainty) increased the likelihood of war involvement or if precisely the opposite relationship existed, i.e., war involvement increased the likelihood of alliance membership (or alliance-induced uncertainty).

Indeed, the variables being correlated could produce the same statistical association without even being temporally proximate, e.g., *all* of a state's war involvements might have occurred *before* it ever joined an alliance (or at times when alliance-induced uncertainy was low). One result of this is that it is possible to obtain a positive cross-sectional correlation between two variables when the correlation over time between these variables may be negative, or vice versa. For example, suppose that there are three states which, over 130-years, have respectively a total of 10, 20, and 30 alliance memberships. If these three states were involved in a total of 10, 20, and 30 wars over the same period of time, then there would be a perfect positive "time exposure" correlation between alliance membership and war involvement. But if during the 130-year period it was the case that each of these three states became members of increasingly more alliances while at the same time they became involved in fewer wars, then the longitudinal (or "time series") correlation between alliance membership and war involvement would be negative. Thus, caution is warranted when interpreting the extent to which Midlarsky's correlational findings support his hypotheses.

Even Midlarsky's endeavor to demonstrate by means of causal inference the plausibility of his thesis raises questions. He wishes to show that his hypothesized causal sequence ALLIANCES $(X_1) \rightarrow$ UNCERTAINTY (X_2) $\rightarrow$ WAR (X_3) is better supported by the data than is the alternative sequence UNCERTAINTY $(X_2) \rightarrow$ ALLIANCES $(X_1) \rightarrow$ WAR (X_3). If the hypothesized sequence represents the true causal relationships, then the partial correlation between ALLIANCES (X_1) and WAR (X_3), controlling for UNCERTAINTY (X_2), should be zero, i.e., $r_{13 \cdot 2} = 0$ or equivalently $r_{13} = r_{12} r_{23}$ (Blalock, 1964). Similarly, if the alternative sequence represents the true causal relationships, then it should be the case that $r_{23 \cdot 1} = 0$ or equivalently $r_{23} = r_{12} r_{13}$. After testing the relative merits of the two sequences, Midlarsky concludes that his hypothesized causal sequence is better supported by the data. The primary question raised by this procedure for untangling causal relationships is whether or not the alternative sequence is even testable, since the concept of "alliance-induced uncertainty" is operationalized in such a way that it does not seem possible for there to be "uncertainty" without (i.e., prior to) "alliances." If, indeed, we are to allow "uncertainty" to exist prior to "alliances," then Midlarsky's hypothesized causal sequence can be confronted by a second plausible alternative sequence that he does not examine, namely, WAR $(X_3) \rightarrow$ UNCERTAINTY $(X_2) \rightarrow$ ALLIANCES (X_1). This second alternative sequence could not be tested against the hypothesized sequence using Midlarsky's correlational technique, because the prediction equation ($r_{13 \cdot 2} = 0$ or, equivalently, $r_{13} = r_{12} \, r_{23}$) would be precisely the same for both sequences.

Finally, and this is a point that I only mention in passing, I am somewhat curious about why Midlarsky analyzes the particular data sets that he does. More precisely, why does he rely upon old versions of data sets (for diplomatic importance, military alliances, interstate system membership, and interstate wars) when revised and extended versions of these data sets have been published (Small and Singer, 1969, 1973; Singer and Small, 1972)?

Thus far, I have only reviewed what amounts to one-half of Midlarsky's ambitious book. The first half of *On War* is a fairly cohesive, if somewhat abstract and highly complex, investigation of the concept of environmental uncertainty. The second half of the book, however, is comprised of chapters that can be only weakly, if at all, tied to the central theme. I will not, therefore, offer a detailed summary of this material; a cursory overview will have to suffice.

In the latter half of *On War,* the author looks at the association between status inconsistency and war, the diffusion of military coups from one naton-state to another, and the degree to which domestic factors are related to a state's involvement in international war. Midlarsky sees status inconsistency (i.e., the condition in which a nation-state is attributed less importance by the other members of the interstate system than might be expected on the basis of its capabilities) as an indicator of decision makers' inability to use their nation's capabilities to acquire system benefits. That this condition should be associated with environmental uncertainty, and thereby to war, is not obvious to me. I should think that a more convincing thesis would simply be that decision makers in status inconsistent states feel that their states are receiving less than their fair share of system benefits and, therefore, these decision makers may be predisposed toward demonstrating their dissatisfaction by means of armed force. Whatever the appropriate rationale, Midlarsky's investigation of 33 primarily European and Latin American states for the period 1870-1945 A.D. shows that status inconsistency is strongly and positively correlated with the number, magnitude, and duration of international wars. However, because of the way in which the data are aggregated (each state's total number of war involvements is correlated with its *mean* status inconsistency score for the 75-year period), it is, as discussed previously, impossible to determine whether status inconsistency leads to war, war to status inconsistency, or, indeed, if they are temporally proximate. Thus, it is not possible to evaluate the significance of these findings.

Midlarsky's examination of the spatial diffusion of military coups and the effects of domestic factors on international wars is even less obviously associated with the theme of environmental uncertainty than is the investigation of status inconsistency, yet his findings are nevertheless extremely interesting. He discovers that he can better account for Latin American coups between 1935 and 1949 A.D. with a diffusion model that posits that military coups in one country are the result of coups in other Latin American countries than with a model that attempts to account for the coups simply in terms of domestic factors such as modernization. And he finds in an examination of 18 preindustrial societies (Eisenstadt, 1963) that the magnitude and duration of war are better accounted for by domestic factors than is the occurrence of war. As a result of this latter finding, Midlarsky suggests a rather intriguing idea, namely, that the factors that account for the *onset* of war may be found largely in the international environment, whereas the factors that account for the *magnitude and duration* of war may best be sought in the domestic characteristics of the participants.

In its totality, *On War* is a very difficult book to read. It is complex, often mired in tortuous prose, and definitely not for the "quantitatively uninitiated." Many of the statistical associations reported in the book are of impressive magnitude, but a good number of the inferences drawn from these correlations are open to serious theoretical and methodological questions. Yet, despite all of its deficiencies, the book does present a host of fascinating ideas in a very imaginative fashion, and a great many of these ideas merit continued exploration.

CHOUCRI ON POPULATION DYNAMICS

The final book to be reviewed is Nazli Choucri's *Population Dynamics and International Violence* (1974). In it we are introduced to yet a third explanation of why nation-states become involved in international conflict. Choucri's thesis, and one that dates back to her work with Robert North at Stanford University, concerns a trilogy of factors: population, resources, and technology. The argument, in simplified form, is as follows. Human beings require certain resouces in order to survive, and they rely on technology (i.e., knowledge and skills) to convert these resources into usable products. Technology itself creates its own resource demands. The three factors (population, technology, and resources) interact with one another such that "an increase in the number of people and/or an increase in the level of knowledge and skills will create increased demands unless available resources increase commensurately" (North and Lagerstrom, 1971: 3). When demand is high, there is a tendency for decision makers to try to expand their state's control over resources external to the state. At times, such activities result in conflictual and violent interaction with other nation-states.

In the volume under review, Choucri examines only one of the factors in the trilogy, that being population. She looks at four aspects of population: size, composition, distribution, and changes in the preceding three aspects. Her intention is to discover what association these four aspects have to (1) the power relationships and (2) the propensities for violence between and among states in the interstate system.

The first part of the book is comprised of a propositional inventory linking the various aspects of population to conflict and violence. An individual chapter is devoted to each of the four aspects and the literature review, while disjointed, is extensive. In summarizing her propositional inventory and literature review, Choucri laments that political scientists have paid too little attention to the demographic influences on political behavior. She posits that population variables are always relevant in conflict situations because they help to define the limits of possible behavior. But the effects of population are generally indirect, usually operating within the confines permitted by technological capabilities and resource constraints.

The second part of the book is an empirical examination of the propositions set forth in the preceding section of the book. Choucri's strategy is to investigate 45 cases in which conflict and violence have occurred and then, by tracing back through the antecedent conditions, to identify the relative importance of population variables. The 45 cases are post-1945 third world conflicts, almost all of which are drawn from the CASCON (Computer Aided System for the Analysis of Local Conflicts) data files at Massachusetts Institute of Technology (Leiss, Bloomfield et al., 1967). A few cases, e.g., the Arab-Israeli war of October 1973, not in the CASCON files are included because of their importance or ready data availability.

For each case, coders judgmentally assessed the role of population variables in the conflict, the proximity of population variables to the outbreak of the conflict, and the impact of these variables upon subsequent developments. They did this by first answering a series of questions such as: "Does absolute population level, in terms of the sheer weight of numbers, contribute to a group's violent behavior?" (p. 95).

Next, the coders judged whether population factors acted as "parameters" that provided the context for the conflict, "multipliers" that exacerbated an existing conflict, or "variables" that changed during the course of the conflict or changed the nature of the conflict. Finally, the impact of each population factor on the conflict was coded on a six-point scale: no appreciable influence, background significance, minor irritant, major irritant, centrally important, and sole determinant.

Two methodological issues merit mention. The first, concerning the external validity of the study, is rather obvious. Since Choucri's data are derived entirely from post-1945 third world conflicts, inferences drawn from her investigation may have very limited applicability. That is to say, her findings may be valid only for the post-1945 third world. The second issue is more subtle. There is not really any data "analysis" in *Population Dynamics and International Violence.* Choucri simply reports the proportion of conflicts in which, according to her coders, population factors play a role. In the research by Ferris, Naroll et al., and Midlarsky, the investigators derived independent measures of the predictor variables and the outcome phenomena, and then attempted to determine whether there existed a statistical relationship between the two sets of measures. Choucri does not do this, rather she asks her coders to make this judgment and, then, reports the *coder's* subjective evaluations. These coders have to make some very difficult assessments, for example, they have to judge whether or not a population factor was the "sole determinant" of a conflict or whether the effect of a factor was that of a "multiplier" as opposed to a "parameter" or "variable." And they have to do this for relationships that Choucri herself describes as "complex, interactive, and mutually reinforcing" (p. 99). Thus, it becomes very important to know who the coders are and how high is the level of inter-coder reliability. Unfortunately, we are told neither of these; indeed, it is not clear whether there are multiple, or merely single, coders for each conflict case examined. I personally have some reservations concerning the degree of reliability that one can expect when coders must make subjective evaluations about very complex relationships. And I would be very interested in knowing whether Choucri employed experts, familiar with the cases under investigation, or "naive" coders to make these judgments. These are not idle concerns, for they relate directly to the reliability of Choucri's findings. Without knowing the answers to these issues, it is not possible to evaluate the significance of her results.

Leaving aside for the moment these matters of reliability and validity, let us turn to Choucri's findings. She reports that, in her coders' judgment, population factors played a role in 38 of the 45 local conflicts examined and, in 25 of these cases, demographic factors were of major, central, or sole importance. In assessing the impact of the various aspects of population, Choucri contends that prior emphasis on the *total size* of a population has been misplaced; what is "far more important is the size of the effective population, which contributes actively to overall national productivity and which can in fact be mobilized in any military confrontation" (p. 200). She further notes that population *composition* often sets the stage for violent conflict; segmental cleavages being endemically destabilizing, especially when reinforced along several dimensions. And interestingly, she reports that the *distribution* of population in relation to space (population density) appears to be much less important in the development of a conflict than the distribution in terms of available resources (population pressure), and that objective population pressure proves to be more critical than do perceptions of pressure. Finally, she states that "differential rates of population *change* [between states] are often a critical consideration in a conflict situation" (p. 202), shaping attitudes toward acceptable casualty losses and relative power, as well as exacerbating existing tensions.

What we are to make of these findings is difficult to say. As a scientific investigation, *Population Dynamics and International Violence* may have serious deficiencies, particularly in the area of data reliability. If, however, we view Choucri's investigation as merely a "reconnaissance" study, then it has a number of strengths, not least of which are a fine literature review and a multitude of ideas for subsequent research.

CONCEPTUALIZING THE CONFLICT PROCESS

Having now reviewed central themes and research findings presented in five recently published studies on international violence, it is legitimate to ask what, if anything, do they suggest that we need to do when we attempt to model the international conflict process? I think that they suggest three things. First, we need to specify what it is that motivates decision makers to use military force. Second, we need to identify those factors that might alter the probability that this motivation or propensity to use force will actually be manifested. And third, we need to recognize that the factors that produce conflicts may not be the same as those that account for the escalation, duration, or outcome of the conflicts. Let us look at each of these in turn.

THE PROPENSITY TO USE FORCE

In the five books, we find the authors alluding to three different rationales for why national decision makers might be motivated to use military force against other nation-states. It is interesting to note, in this regard, that all of the rationales are based upon unitary, (more or less) rational actor models. That is, there is no mention of bureaucratic or organizational politics (Allison, 1971); rather, political machinations within the state are black-boxed and the foreign policy elite are viewed as a single actor or as a group acting in concert.

One rationale for what motivates decision makers to use military force can be culled from Blainey's book (and is also consistent with Ferris' propositions). In the traditional literature, this rationale is usually referred to as the *realist* position. Defined most narrowly, the realist argument is based upon the principle that decision makers are continually attempting to increase the power capabilities of their states and to expand the territory over which they exercise control. As one well-known realist notes, statesmen "think and act in terms of interest defined as power" (Morgenthau, 1960: 5). The logic of the realist argument suggests that states become involved in international conflict as a result of decision makers' attempts to expand the domain of their control or because their state's reputation for power makes it a target for decision makers in other expansionist states.

A second rationale, different from the narrow interpretation of realism, is offered by Midlarsky. His argument is based upon the propensity of decision makers to reduce environmental *uncertainty*. According to this argument, decision makers are always confronted by a welter of possible alternative events; each might have a greatly different effect upon the decision makers' country. The essence of international politics, therefore, is the attempt to limit these possible alternatives, particularly in such a way as to increase the probability of favorable events occurring. For the most part, the manipulation of events (i.e., reduction of uncertainty) is carried out by nonviolent means. On occasion, however, prior international agreements or basically nonmalleable environmental factors make this impossible. Under such conditions, it is argued, decision makers have an increased propensity to use military force to achieve their ends.

A third rationale, that might be labeled a resource *necessity* explanation, underlies Choucri's study (although, in the particular book that we reviewed, she focuses on only one aspect of this wider rationale). The basic argument is that the continuing process of economic development necessitates that a state possess certain raw materials. If these resources are not available at home or cannot be purchased abroad at reasonable prices, then decision makers are forced to find alternative means for obtaining them. Under such pressure, decision makers may well resort to the threat or use of force. Even when raw materials can be obtained abroad, the argument continues, decision makers may be motivated to use force against third parties that are perceived to encroach upon, or threaten access to, these essential resources.

These are only three of many plausible explanations for why decision makers might be motivated to use military force. We can certainly think of others. For example, in reviewing Midlarsky's discussion of status inconsistency, I suggested the possible applicability of a *fair share* rationale. It might be argued, for instance, that each nation-state is entitled to particular benefits from the other members of the interstate system in accordance with some recognized norm. Perhaps the norm is that the more powerful a state, the greater the deference, decision latitude, or economic benefits it should receive. So long as states receive their fair share, no problems arise; when, however, decision makers perceive that their state is receiving less than its fair share of system benefits, they become predisposed toward demonstrating their dissatisfaction in the most salient manner possible in international politics, i.e., by a show of military force.

What is important to note about all of these rationales is that they are not explanations of why states become involved in *war,* defined as large-scale military violence between the armed forces of opposing political units. Rather they are attempts to account for why decision makers may be motivated to use military force or, more precisely, to initiate *unilateral military action.* If we can accept this distinction between the initial use of force by one state and the escalation of the conflict to reciprocated military actions, we can begin to understand such seemingly incompatible statements as "war can only begin and can only continue with the consent of at least two nations" (Blainey, 1973: 159) and "it does not take two nations to make a war but only one" (Naroll et al., 1974: 330). This distinction between unilateral and reciprocated action is often overlooked by those of us engaged in peace research. Almost all quantitative studies of international conflict, in which lengthy spans of time have been examined, have focused on war as the outcome variable. But, often, the rationales that underlie these analyses specify why statesmen may be motivated to *initiate* military action, not the conditions under which such action will be reciprocated or will escalate to more violent levels of hostilities.

CONSTRAINTS ON THE USE OF FORCE

This raises a second issue. A *predisposition* to use military force—whether it be motivated by the propensity to expand power, reduce uncertainty, acquire resources, or obtain a fair share of system benefits—is not the same as the *manifestation* of force. In only one of the books under review (Naroll et al., 1974) do the authors explicitly examine factors that might deter the use of force; indeed, they do this to the exclusion of any mention of what might have originally motivated decision makers to use force. But, in several of the other studies, the authors at least implicitly include in their discussions factors that might alter the probability that military force will be employed. Blainey, for example, suggests several variables that might make decision makers overconfident about their state's bargaining strength, among these are the belief that third parties will not aid an opponent nor take advantage of one's own preoccupation with a war, the existence of unity at home or domestic discord among the enemy, and forgetfulness about the realities and suffering of war. We would not want to say that such factors, themselves, motivate decision makers to use military force. Certainly, decision makers do not decide to initiate military action *because* they no longer remember the devastation caused by prior wars. Rather, *if* decision makers are already predisposed to use force (perhaps because they are trying to reduce environmental uncertainty or acquire needed resources, et cetera), *then* such factors as the international alliance structure, the existence of civil disorders, and the presence or absence of war-weariness among the populace may alter the probability that force will be manifested. Thus, I am suggesting that we can conceptualize the initiation of military action in terms of two sets of variables, one set that might be seen as the motivating impetus to conflict and a second set that can be comprised of mediating factors that alter the probability that force will actually be used.

CONFLICT AS A STAGE PROCESS

The factors that account for the initiation of a unilateral military act, however, may not be the same as those that account for whether such action will be reciprocated, or those that account for the magnitude, duration, or outcome of reciprocated action. Midlarsky, for instance, suggests that the factors that lead to the onset of violence may be found largely in the international environment, whereas those that account for the magnitude and duration of the violence may best be sought amongst the domestic characteristics of the participants. Ferris finds that the power disparity between antagonists and changes in that disparity appear to have a different impact on the initiation of conflicts than on the escalation, and a different impact on the duration and devastation of combat than on the outcome. In my own research (Gochman, 1975), I have observed that the effects of geographic contiguity and system polarity are different at different stages in the conflict process. And, in yet another study (Bremer, 1979), it has been found that while the most powerful states are most likely to initiate or become involved in interstate war, these wars are not, on the average, longer or bloodier than other interstate wars. Given this tentative evidence, I would speculate that the motivation for initiating military action has little to do with whether or not that action is reciprocated or the level to which the resulting hostilities will escalate. Rather, I would hypothesize that factors more immediate to the conflict, such as the alliance associations or the relative capabilities of the antagonists, would have the greatest impact on the escalation, duration, and outcome of violence.

If there is some validity to this agument, then it may be quite useful to think of the conflict process as a series of stages, each of which needs to be modeled. The conflict process could be divided in any number of ways, but a simple three-stage model would perhaps offer a good starting point. In the first stage, we would try to account for the initiation of unilateral military acts; in the second, we would predict whether or not the initial acts would be reciprocated in kind; and in the third, we would investigate the magnitude, duration, and outcome of military hostilities. Within this simple framework, we could compare the predictive power of a number of contending explanations of what motivates decision makers to use military force, e.g., the realist, uncertainty, necessity, and fair share rationales. If we can construct models of these contending explanations so that they differ on only a small number of dimensions—let us say, only with respect to the initial motivating factor, but not in terms of any of the mediating variables—we will begin to approximate that point in the development of a science when "critical tests" can be made (Platt, 1964). It is at that point, that what we refer to as "peace research" will have earned the title "peace science."

Charles S. Gochman (Ph.D. University of Michigan, 1975) is Assistant Professor of Political Science at the University of Pittsburgh. His fields of specialization include world politics and quantitative research methods, and his current research focuses on the causes and consequences of international conflict. He is now at work on a handbook of all major power serious disputes, 1816-1978.

Conflict in the International System, 1816-1977

HISTORICAL TRENDS AND POLICY FUTURES

MELVIN SMALL
J. DAVID SINGER
Chapter 3

This study examines the incidence of international violence in an attempt to identify historical cycles and trends in war and conflict. Drawing on an extensive collection of data on military confrontations and international and civil wars from 1816 to 1977, and using indicators of frequency, magnitude, and severity of these conflicts, no evidence of a long-term secular trend is found. Both international and civil wars were found to rise and fall together, with neither being a substitute for the other in any given historical period. Finding the post-1965 period lowest on five of eight normalized indicators of frequency, magnitude, and severity for all types of conflicts, it is noted that this decline is a brief one and that most of the factors that interrupted earlier declines still obtain. The failure to move toward disarmament, for example, leaves the international system fundamentally as war-prone as it has been since the Congress of Vienna.

An American sea captain who plied the oceans in the 1780s reported that his newly independent country was seen "in the same light by foreign nations as a well-behaved negro is in a gentleman's family" (Elliot, 1891:34). Far off the beaten track geographically speaking, the pariah republic was also far removed from the complicated diplomatic and martial games played in the

AUTHORS' NOTE: We are indebted to Richard Stoll, Michael Champion, Thomas Cusack, and Thomas Kselman for their contributions to the data and the analysis on which the chapter rests, and for their assistance in the presentation and interpretation of the results.

Originally published in C. W. Kegley, Jr. and P. J. McGowan (eds.) Sage Yearbook on Foreign Policy Studies, *Challenges to America,* 1979.

capitals of the Old World. One hundred years later, the United States was still on the fringes of the major power system; reciprocal interests were marginal, and her navy was inferior even to that of Chile. In his first inaugural address in 1885, Grover Cleveland recommended the "scrupulous avoidance of any departure from that foreign policy commended by the history, the traditions, and the prosperity of our Republic. It is the policy of independence . . . the policy of neutrality, rejecting any share in foreign broils and ambitions upon other continents . . . peace, commerce, and honest friendship with all nations; entangling alliances with none" (Richardson, 1904:301).

Obviously, as the United States enters her third century as an independent actor in the international system, the scenario has changed appreciably. Today, and for the foreseeable future, she is at the very center of that system. Her political, economic, and cultural activities affect the outcome of a war in the Horn of Africa, the price of wheat in India, and the wearing apparel of teenagers in Hungary. In addition, the system is no longer dominated by a handful of Christian Majesties who spoke the same language, figuratively as well as literally. Prominent players in the game now include not only newly independent states, but liberation and terrorist groups, intergovernmental and nongovernmental international organizations, producers' consortia, and multi-national corporations. All of these actors, ranging from the superpowers like the U.S. and the U.S.S.R. to the International Office of Epizootics, participate in a highly interdependent network using sophisticated technology and weaponry that would have seemed like science fiction not only to Grover Cleveland but to Franklin Roosevelt as well.

Today's system seems so complex, the pace of activity so rapid, and the stakes so high that the first American secretary of state, Thomas Jefferson, probably exercised more control over his nation's role in the international firmament than did Henry Kissinger, with all of the advanced communications (and weapons systems) available to him. Indeed, today's diplomats may well envy that small coterie who were able to keep the nation on an even keel through most of its history without "going to the brink" or "losing" a country.

But how different *is* the international system today compared to that of 50, 100, 200 years ago? While the system is clearly larger, the technology more advanced, and the boundaries more permeable, is it indeed more complex, more interdependent, or more dangerous? Are we, as many suggest, living in an age of conflict, a century of total war, an era of violent peace (Chambers, Harris, and Bayley, 1950; Aron, 1954; Mydans and Mydans, 1968)? Is the world more conflictful than it has been; is it becoming a more dangerous place for its citizens to inhabit?

Asked by statesmen, scholars, and journalists, such sweeping questions are answered with a multiplicity of conflicting projections, often based on the conventional wisdom of the day, buttressed by an anecdote or two from history. Thus, for some, the immediate future will be unlike any other period because of the disappearance of fossil fuels; or it will see a rebirth of the balance of power system of the 1870s; or it will experience global revolution as in 1848; or nuclear Armageddon will leave a few survivors back in the Stone Age. Such projections, while sometimes insightful and imaginative, are frequently based upon the most marginal evidence and an all-too-selective recall of diplomatic history.

We propose to examine trends in war and conflict in a systematic fashion, as we seek to describe where we have been and to suggest where we may be headed. Over the past decade or so, the Correlates of War Project has collected a wealth of data on international and domestic conflict ranging back to 1816. The presentation of some of these data here should enable us to chart more precisely the trends and cycles in the incidence of international violence. We undertake this task not merely out of historical curiosity, but because a more precise description of the past is a useful first step toward intelligent extrapolations about future levels of conflict in the global community. Such a description also provides a useful basis for analyzing American foreign policy in the 1980s.

There are, of course, many bases upon which to rest our forecasts of international events and conditions. Leaving aside such dubious methods as chicken entrail or tea leaf reading, we see five basic strategies. One is what might be called the "seat of the pants scenario," popularized by such futurologists as Kahn and Wiener (1967) and deJouvenal (1967), but well known in one guise or another in the foreign ministries of the world. At bottom, this is little more than combining a bit of imagination with a large dose of the contemporary folklore, and such a forecasting strategy rests on an all too flimsy foundation. The error rate of decision makers using this "method" is manifest in a long list of battle fatalities over the centuries, as well as in many disasters of a less dramatic sort.

Slightly more systematic is the Delphi method (Helmer, 1973), which has a number of specialists respond to a forecasting questionnaire, whose results are then pooled and returned to the respondents. In light of these tabulations, the respondents are asked to revise or confirm their original forecasts to see whether two or more iterations can lead to a clear consensus. In our view, this is merely a paper and pencil version of what occurs in foreign ministries every day, and while it does tell us something about the suggestibility of the specialists (Asch, 1952), it is perhaps even more dangerous than the less formalized version because it implies some of the aura of scientific method.

Then there are forecasts resting on either man-machine or all machine simulations, and while they *could* be effective, their success depends largely on the quality of the "theory" that informs the simulation. But given the state of codified knowledge (that is, theory) in our field, it would be a mistake to place much confidence in either form of simulation at this stage. Another type of analogy to the international system of tomorrow (and simulation is one) is that reflecting our understanding of apparently similar social systems, such as business firms, economic markets, universities, or social psychological experiments. Finally, and also resting on analogy, is the forecast based on history.

This will be our strategy here, despite the dangers inherent in it. As Harold Nicolson (1961:ii) reminded a British Foreign Office planning for the post-World War II period, "events are not affected by analogies; they are determined by combinations of circumstances. And since," he added, "circumstances vary from generation to generation, it is illusive to suppose that any pattern of history—however similar it may at first appear—is likely to repeat itself exactly in the kaleidoscope of time." We are not, in other words, oblivious to the discontinuities in world history, nor are we indifferent to the frequency with which repetitive patterns begin to appear, only to be shattered by some unexpected or rare event. But we also suspect that today's practitioners and observers—like observers in every generation—exaggerate the changes that are currently under way, even as they urge the incomparability of the several epochs that have gone before.

Further, we suspect that despite a major increase in popular participation as well as dramatic technological innovations, the game of nations has changed but little since Machiavelli codified the ancient rules of diplomatic conduct more than 450 years ago. The state system ushered in after Westphalia, or at least after the Congress of Vienna, is still with us today. The national (or multinational) state remains the dominant actor in the system, despite its limited ability to meet the basic needs of its citizens, and despite the recurrent focus on varieties of subnational and extranational entities that seem to challenge the dominant role of the state. Moreover, the substance of foreign policy decision rules has remained relatively constant across time, as well as across states whose structural and cultural characteristics appear to be quite different. Thus, even though many priorities as well as strategies continually shift, the *basic* goals and decision rules of foreign policy elites continue to revolve around national survival, autonomy, and power.

At bottom, of course, the relationship of our times to those that preceded it is an empirical question that analyses such as ours ultimately address. As noted above, each generation tends to think of itself as new or revolutionary.

However, at least to date, each appears to be not only affected by and intimately linked to previous ones, but also remarkably similar to those that went before. There is, of course, always the chance that we *have* come to a major watershed in world history, and that the events of recent decades *are* so unique as to constitute the sort of systemic transformation that occurs only once or twice a millenium. Perhaps; yet it might well be that the allegedly historically unique period in our lives is over. In a recent historical overview, Wilson (1977) argues that the 1920s offer important guidance for the future. In her view, the most recent past—the Depression, World War II, and the Cold War—were aberrations followed now by a period of "normalcy" comparable to that of the Harding-Coolidge-Hoover years. Similarly, Rosecrance et al. (1974) see a close parallel between the contemporary period and a prior one, but for them the referent is that of the 1870s.

Whether or not contemporary decision makers find Wilson's parallel compelling, most do think they can learn from the past. Unfortunately, their historic memories are often too selective, if not blatantly self-serving, to produce accurate or particularly credible forecasts. For only one of many examples, May (1973) reminds us how a misreading of history led American policy makers in the 1960s to perceive another Munich in Vietnam, and each of us has a favorite horror story about how a highly selective and distorted recall of the past has contributed to one foreign policy disaster or another.

THE HISTORICAL TREND DATA

Because history will continue to be studied for guidance to the future, it behooves us to examine it carefully and systematically. To do so, certain procedures must be followed from the beginning, so that even if our interpretations and inferences are erroneous, our historical data base will at least be accurate. Crucial to such accuracy is a set of categories that are logically exhaustive and mutually exclusive, resting on a set of classification rules that are unambiguous and reliable. In other words, one must devise a set of operational coding rules so that all possible cases of a particular type are first identified, after which each is assigned to the appropriate sub-category.

In the sections that follow, we have done exactly that. We have taken three basic types of political conflict—international wars, military confrontations short of war, and civil wars—and developed explicit and operational criteria by which all possible or "candidate" cases are examined. Those conflicts that satisfy the criteria for each type are assigned accordingly, and those that do not are left aside for the moment, to be reexamined at a later date. After we summarize the results of these procedures for all three types of conflict, we will turn to an interpretation of the data and an examination of the implications for foreign policy in the decades ahead.

International Wars

To describe historical trends in international war since 1816, we must first define what we mean by international war. To qualify for this designation, a sustained military conflict had to array at least one sovereign member of the interstate system against another member, or an independent nonmember, or a colony, and result in at least 1,000 battle deaths to the system member participant(s). Excluded here are internal wars involving only one political entity, as well as those scores of internation skirmishes and exchanges of fire that resulted in very few battle deaths. From 1816 through 1977, we found 103 such wars, of which 57 involved system members on both sides (interstate wars) and 46 involved a system member in combat with either a colony or another polity that did not qualify for system membership (extra-systemic wars).[1] A more complete explanation of our coding rules and research procedures relating to wars and system membership is found in *The Wages of War* (Singer and Small, 1972).

To make more meaningful comparisons over our long time span, we will subdivide it into seven distinct periods, conforming closely to the periodization used by most diplomatic historians. For the most part, their termini are found in years following major upheavals or substantial rearrangements in the international system. Thus, we look first at the years from the Congress of Vienna through 1849, the so-called Concert Period, largely shattered by the widespread revolutions that racked the continent in 1848-1849. We then demarcate a period from 1850 to 1870, in which the international system is in a state of flux as the Italian and German states are forged with blood and iron. The third period, 1871-1890, is the Age of Bismarck, marked particularly by the Iron Chancellor's successful isolation of his enemy, France. During the fourth period, from 1891 through 1914, an alliance system develops that results in the severe bipolarization of the European system and ends in the First World War, while the years following (1919-1939) comprise the conventional interwar period.

The identification of possible break points within the past 32 years (1946-1977) is of course somewhat more difficult, given our lack of historical perspective; later generations might well view it in a manner entirely different from the way we do today. Emphasizing the tentativeness of this decision, we examine first the years from 1946 through 1965, a period that experienced the worst of the Cold War and which is bounded by the breakup of the Grand Alliance at one end and the Americanization of the war in Vietnam at the other. Finally, our seventh period covers the most recent 12 years

(1966-1977), in which the international system seems to be in considerable flux.

We have not divided our temporal domain in this manner in order to test the validity of historians' periodizations—although that might be a useful exercise. Rather, for the purposes of this chapter, we accept the reasonableness of these break points, most of which seem to have been internalized by contemporary policy makers as well as scholars. Table 1, which shows the frequency of international wars, is similar in format to the tables that follow, with the first column indicating the number of years spanned by each of the historic periods. Five of the seven periods are of relatively equal length, but the first (1816-1849) is the longest and the last (1966-1977) is the briefest. The fact that not all periods are of the same length could make comparisons awkward, but the problem disappears when we "normalize" and present our calculations in terms of annual averages, or wars per year. The second column shows the average number of nations in the system during the period, a figure that ranges from 29 to 135. Then, in columns 3 through 5, we present the number of wars begun during each period, the average number of wars begun per year, and the number of wars begun per year, per system member. Thus, the figures in columns 4 and 5 control for both the differing size of the system and the differing lengths of the periods. Our final two columns deal with *national* war involvements or the *number of nations* that participate in wars, and thus do not necessarily reflect the same phenomena reported in columns 3 through 5. It is entirely possible to experience two different sorts

TABLE 1. FREQUENCY OF INTERNATIONAL WARS, 1816–1977

	1	2	3	4	5	6	7
Period	No. of Years	Avg. System Size	No. of Wars Begun	No. of Wars Begun Per Year	No. of Wars Begun Per Year Per Nation	No. of War Involve- Ments Per Nation	No. of War Involve- ments Per Nation Per Year
1816–49	34	29	21	.62	.021	1.00	.034
1850–70	21	39	19	.90	.023	2.43	.062
1871–90	20	34	12	.60	.017	.85	.025
1891– 1914	24	42	17	.71	.016	2.00	.047
1919–39	21	64	11	.52	.008	2.33	.037
1946–65	20	95	11	.55	.006	1.87	.025
1966–77	12	135	9	.75	.006	1.67	.012

of violent eras, one with a great many dyadic wars of perhaps brief durations, and another with a few, but very large or long, multilateral wars. Thus, in columns 6 and 7 are national war involvements per year and national war involvements per year per system member, respectively.

Because we will return to all six of the tables later in the chapter, this section will be used only for a brief introduction to each. Looking at Table 1, the first impression is that of a fairly steady decline in the frequency of international wars, going from 21 in the first period down to 9 in the final one. But when (in column 4) we average the figures to account for the differing lengths of these seven periods, the annual frequencies that emerge are clearly not indicative of any historical trend. Rather, we get the impression of a fluctuating pattern, perhaps suggesting a mild periodicity. When, however, we normalize for the number of nations in the system as well as the duration of the period, the downward trend reappears in column 5. And shifting to the annual frequency of national war involvements (as distinct from *systemic* war occurrences) in columns 6 and 7, we again find a discernible downward trend, but more fluctuating than that in column 5.

Of course, the *frequency* of international wars may not be the most valid indicator of historical patterns. More revealing may be the *amount* of war, measured in nation months (our indicator of magnitude) and in battle-connected deaths (or severity); from some points of view, the number of discrete wars is considerably less meaningful than their duration, the number of nations involved, and the fatalities that resulted. Thus, in Table 2, we find further evidence of a fluctuating pattern and again perhaps a very crude periodicity. That is, the periods that experience the most intense martial activity are generally followed by periods of somewhat less activity. When we normalize for the length of the period and size of the system (column 4), the pattern remains the same. Shifting to the severity (battle deaths) indicator in columns 5 and 6, we again see the rising levels from 1816 up through World War II, and then a dramatic decline. Notice also the temporary drop along all four of the magnitude and severity indicators during the period from 1870 to 1890. It should be emphasized that Tables 1 and 2 reflect the frequency, magnitude, and severity of wars *begun* in each period, rather than the amounts of war actually *underway*. Thus, the high magnitude and severity scores for the war in Vietnam (which began as a civil war, became an internationalized civil war in 1961, and then escalated to a full interstate war in 1965) show up only in the 1946-1965 period, when that bloody disaster began. No other period is affected by this coding rule, but it should be kept in mind.

TABLE 2. MAGNITUDE AND SEVERITY OF INTERNATIONAL WARS, 1816-1977

	1	2	3	4	5	6
Period	No. of Years	Avg. System Size	Nation Months of War Begun Per Nation	Nation Months of War Begun Per Year Per Nation	Battle Deaths Per Year From Wars Begun	Battle Deaths Per Year Per Nation From Wars Begun
1816–49	34	29	12.37	.47	9,997	359.3
1850–70	21	39	30.45	.80	37,076	998.7
1871–90	20	34	19.59	.59	18,280	564.0
1891–1914	24	42	37.82	.88	374,200	8525.8
1919–39	21	64	62.30	.98	789,400	12145.0
1946–65	20	95	67.20	.71	150,000	1579.0
1966–77	12	135	12.85	.09	9,551	70.1

Military Confrontations

Turning to a second indicator of martial activity, we now examine the incidence of military confrontations *short of war*. Here we are interested in all cases in which a system member threatens, displays, or actually uses military force while engaged in a serious dispute with another member of the system. Such actions range from verbal threats, mobilizations, and deployments, through seizures, border crossings, and bombardments.

Needless to say, the task of generating this particular data set is a formidable one. While research on *all* nation members of the system continues, we have completed our survey of the serious disputes only of the major powers.[2] These include not just confrontations between the majors themselves, but also those that minor powers were unlucky enough to engage in against majors. While this data set, then, is not quite comparable to those embracing the entire system, all of our investigations to date have shown that majors are involved in the bulk of the system's diplomatic and martial activities. Moreover, their interactions seem to set the tone for other nations' interactions during the various historic periods. Thus, we are fairly certain that major power disputes constitute a significant portion of all confrontations and that their patterns reflect those that obtain throughout the system.

The dispute data arrayed in Table 3 are a bit more difficult to interpret than those shown in the first two tables. More important than the number of confrontations that occurred in any period is the number that escalated into full scale war. Obviously, the most desirable international environment would

TABLE 3. FREQUENCY OF MILITARY CONFRONTATIONS INVOLVING AT LEAST ONE MAJOR POWER, 1816–1977

Period	1 No. of Years	2 Avg. System Size	3 Avg. No. Major Powers	4 No. of Confrontations	5 Avg. No. of Confrontations Per Year	6 No. of Confrontations Per Year Per Major	7 No. of Major Power Wars	8 Percent of Confrontations Ending In War	9 No. of Major vs Major Confrontations	10 No. of Major vs Major Wars	11 No. of Confrontations Per Year Per Nation
1816–49	34	29	5	29	.85	.17	6	21	8	0	.03
1850–70	21	39	5.5	34	1.60	.29	9	23	10	4	.04
1871–90	20	34	6	23	1.15	.19	2	6	4	0	.03
1891–1914	24	42	7.5	25	2.29	.14	7	17	17	2	.05
1919–39	21	64	6.5	51	2.43	.37	7	10	17	2	.04
1946–65	20	95	4.5	48	2.40	.53	4	8	16	1	.02
1966–77	12	135	5	24	2.00	.40	0	0	4	0	.01

be one with few confrontations and few wars. In the absence of such a prospect, however, we might prefer an environment in which confrontations continue to occur—or even increase—but in which few result in war, and our indicators are designed to pick up this distinction.

In column 3, we show the average number of major powers in the system during each period, a figure that ranges from 4.5 to 7.5, and columns 4, 5, and 6 report the number of military confrontations that occurred in each period, the average number per year, and the average number per year per major power. In column 7 is the number of major power wars, a figure that includes both major-major and major-minor wars; and this is followed (column 8) with the all-important indicator, the percentage of confrontations that escalated to war. Columns 9 and 10 are restricted to those confrontations and wars that involved major powers on both sides. The last column gives the number of confrontations per system member, reflecting the number of possible countries in the entire system with which a major power has the opportunity to join in highly disputatious behavior.

Reexamining this table, and especially column 5, we see that there have been more confrontations per year in the 20th century than in the 19th, with the Metternichian age appearing to be as crisis-free as the Austrian leader planned it to be. And this pattern holds even when we normalize for fluctuations in the number of major powers, as shown in column 6. While we are fairly confident in our data-gathering procedures, skeptics might ask whether this increase in the 20th century might not be a reporting error. After all, while a Soviet rocket rattle leaves traces in the media that cannot be ignored, perhaps our intrepid diplomatic historians have not picked up every comparable rumble emanating from Czar Nicholas I in the 1830s.

The data in columns 7 and 8 are more promising, however, and show that the probability of major power confrontations escalating into full scale war is generally lower in the 20th century than in the 19th. Indeed, since 1946, although we have averaged better than two major power confrontations per year, only four have led to war (Korea, Suez, Hungary, and Vietnam) and only one of those four involved a major on each side (Korea). And when we normalize for total system membership (column 11), our most recent period again appears to be the most pacific.

Civil Wars

If international war is not occurring more frequently or with more intensity than in the past, then perhaps the impression that we live in an age of conflict is because of the intranational wars that seem to abound in our time. Scarcely a day goes by without a news report of a bombing in Northern Ireland, a kidnapping in Argentina, or a raid in Angola. Many of these actions have international implications, since they may lead to informal political and economic involvement by other members of the system or, as in the case of war in Vietnam, full scale military intervention. Is it the incidence of civil unrest and war, then, that makes our time appear to be especially conflictful?

To answer this question, we have identified all of the civil wars experienced by system members since 1816 that resulted in at least 1,000 battle deaths per year. After a lengthy search through literally thousands of national histories, we found exactly 100 wars that met our coding criteria requirements. The severity threshold served, of course, to eliminate hundreds of coups and putsches from our purview, not to mention scores of riots, disturbances, and so forth.[3]

In Table 4, we again break down our 161-year span into several historic periods. Columns 3 and 4 offer the number of civil wars in each period, and the normalized civil wars per year, respectively. In column 5, we control for system size with civil wars per system member, and then normalize still further (column 6) with civil wars per member per year. Finally, in column 7, we show the percent of civil wars that were internationalized through the entry of an outside party on one or both sides.

Again, as with the international wars, there is no clear trend or periodicity in the civil war data, but the two types of war do seem to be related temporally to one another. Thus, we find, as earlier, the periods from 1816 to 1849 and from 1871 to 1890 to be more pacific than the 1850-1870 period separating them. And even more than with international wars, most of the

TABLE 4.   FREQUENCY OF CIVIL WARS, 1816–1977

	1	2	3	4	5	6	7
Period	No. of Years	Avg. System Size	No. of Civil Wars Begun	No. of Civil Wars Begun Per Year	No. of Civil Wars Begun Per Nation	No. of Civil Wars Begun Per Year Per Nation	Percent of Civil Wars Internationalized
1816–49	34	29	12	.35	.41	.012	25
1850–70	21	39	15	.71	.38	.018	7
1871–90	20	34	6	.30	.18	.009	0
1891–1914	24	42	17	.71	.40	.017	18
1919–39	21	64	11	.52	.17	.008	18
1946–65	20	95	26	1.3	.27	.014	27
1966–77	12	135	11	.91	.08	.007	36

indicators show periods of intense civil war activity generally succeeded by periods of somewhat less activity. As might be expected, the years from 1946 through 1965 witnessed the rapid decolonization of European empires and the subsequent struggle for power within the new states, leading to many civil wars. When we control for system size (column 5), however, these years appear less warlike than the period before World War I or the span from 1816 to 1870. And while the past 12 years rank second on the number of civil wars per year, controlling for system size makes this period easily the lowest in terms of the frequency of civil wars. Finally, column 7 suggests a different story: third party intervention has been rather constant, with the low point (no interventions) during the Bismarckian period, but with the post-World War II figures even higher than that following the Napoleonic Wars.

In Table 5, we shift from the frequencies of civil war to its magnitude and severity, as we did for international war in Table 2. In columns 3 and 4 are nation months of civil war begun per year and per year per system member, and in columns 5 and 6 are battle deaths per year and battle deaths per year per system member. In general, the severity and magnitude data do not change our impressions of the amount of civil war activity in the various periods. The one glaring exception is in battle deaths during the most recent period; although the years from 1966 through 1977 rank second lowest on nation months per year per system member (column 4), they rank third highest on battle deaths per year per system member. Even more ominous is the ranking of all civil wars by severity in battle deaths (not shown here); 13 of the first 15 most severe civil wars were fought in the 20th century, eight of

TABLE 5.   MAGNITUDE AND SEVERITY OF CIVIL WARS, 1816–1977

	1	*2*	*3*	*4*	*5*	*6*
Period	*No. of Years*	*Avg. System Size*	*Nation Months of War Per Year*	*Nation Months of War Per Year Per Nation*	*Battle Deaths Per Year*	*Battle Deaths Per Year Per Nation*
1816–49	34	29	14.7	.51	2,828	97.5
1850–70	21	39	26.6	.70	135,650	3,478.2
1871–90	20	34	3.6	.10	2,200	64.7
1891–1914	24	42	11.2	.27	15,498	392.6
1919–34	21	64	14.7	.23	46,100	720.3
1946–65	20	95	55.1	.58	107,920	1,136.0
1966–77	12	135	29.5	.14	133,250	987.0

those 13 were fought since 1946, and three of those occurred since 1965 (Nigeria, Bangladesh, and Cambodia).

Our data also reveal that European states, especially in the 20th century, have not experienced as many major civil wars as nations in the Western Hemisphere and other parts of the developing world. Indeed, since 1917, only Russia, Hungary, Spain, and Greece suffered major civil wars; and since 1945, no civil war that resulted in more than 1,000 deaths per year has occurred in the Old World, unless one were to shift the 1956 war in Hungary from the international to the civil war category.

SUMMARIZING THE HISTORICAL DATA

Before we turn to the delicate matter of future levels of conflict, it is important that we try to make sense of the patterns that have obtained in the past. In the process, we might also lay to rest some of the more widely accepted notions about conflict and violence in the current international system. Turning first to these notions, we find three that enjoy wide popular support.

The most general suggests that there has been a steady upward climb in the amount of violent conflict during the past century and a half, with today's world more conflictful, violent, and dangerous than at any time since the Napoleonic or even the Thirty Years' Wars. Certainly the World Wars were more destructive than any that preceded them, and they were not only close together in time, but were followed all too quickly by the Korean and Vietnamese Wars, neither of which could be thought of as an antiseptic war of skirmish and maneuver. Nor can we overlook the incredible rise in the destructiveness and range of offensive weapons, or the dramatic increase in militant and organized dissatisfaction in every region of the world and in nations of all types at all levels of economic and political development. Another possible contribution to this general belief is that of the media; a greater percentage of political events, in more graphic form, is more widely disseminated in less time than ever before.

But let us look at the data and see whether there is "less there than meets the eye." Are we indeed operating under some serious misperceptions, or conversely, is humanity moving steadily along a road whose end looks like Armageddon? In Table 6, we assemble a number of the indicators that were first presented separately, and use them to rank the seven periods along eight distinct dimensions of conflict and then along a ninth composite rank dimension.

As we examine these figures, it is important to remember the ways in which they are normalized, and thus the "null model" against which our

TABLE 6. THE INDICATORS COMPARED BY RANK AND SCORE WITHIN EACH PERIOD, 1816–1977

Period	1 International Wars Begun Per Year Per Nation	2 Nation Months From International Wars Begun Per Year Per Nation	3 Battle Deaths From International Wars Begun Per Year	4 Civil Wars Begun Per Year Per Nation	5 Nation Months From Civil Wars Begun Per Year Per Nation	6 Battle Deaths From Civil Wars Begun Per Year Per Nation	7 Confrontations Per Year	8 Percent of Confrontations Ending in War	9 Standardized Scores
1816–49	2 .021	6 .47	6 359	1 .41	3 .51	6 98	7 .85	2 21	+.04
1850–70	1 .023	3 .80	4 999	3 .38	1 .70	1 3748	5 1.60	1 23	+.84
1871–90	3 .017	5 .59	5 564	5 .18	7 .10	7 65	6 1.15	6 6	−.51
1891–1914	4 .016	2 .88	2 8526	2 .40	4 .27	5 393	3 2.29	3 17	+.45
1919–39	5 .008	1 .98	1 12145	6 .17	5 .23	4 720	1 2.43	4 10	+.13
1946–65	7 .006	4 .71	3 1579	4 .27	2 .58	2 1136	2 2.40	5 8	−.10
1966–77	6 .006	7 .09	7 70	7 .08	6 .14	3 987	4 2.00	7 0	−.85

observations are conducted. If, for example, we assume that the "normal" amount of conflict or violence in the international system depends on the number of people on the face of the earth, or the number of nations, or the total number of subnational and extranational as well as national actors, we would normalize accordingly. Or, if, as some might suggest, our expected levels of conflict should reflect the number of possible *pairs* of protagonists, the denominator in our normalization formula would be even larger. The range of plausible null models is all too large, and we have selected the more conventional and obvious normalizing unit: the number of nations in the category under scrutiny. Parenthetically, if one chooses to generalize and compare on the basis of the non-normalized scores found in Tables 1 through 5, that, too, rests on an implied null model: that system size, population growth, or number of possible pairs, etc. should have *no effect* on the incidence of violence and conflict.

Turning, then, to Table 6, we find that the bad news has been rather exaggerated. On six of the eight normalized indicators, the latest period ranks lowest (seventh) or next to lowest (sixth) of all the periods since the Congress of Vienna. And on the standardized composite score, this most recent period is clearly the lowest in wars and confrontations with the greatest negative value; even the preceding post-World War II period is far from the most conflictful. Further, no matter how one looks at these normalized indicators, there is virtually no evidence of a secular trend—up or down—in any of the columns.

On the other hand, calculating our coefficient of concordance (Kendall's W = .31) suggests that the periods do have a degree of commonality. That is, those that are low on one dimension tend to be low on the others (such as 1816-1849, 1871-1890, and 1966-1977) and those that are high are generally high (such as 1850-1870).

This pattern leads us, in turn, to consider a second but different general belief that seems equally unfounded; that while international confrontations and wars have declined since World War II, civil wars have been on the rise. But columns 4, 5, and 6 in Table 6 clearly belie that impression. Not only do neither of the post-1945 periods match the 1850-1870 period in the frequency and magnitude of civil violence, but the most recent period ranks lowest or second lowest on two of these three indicators when we normalize for system size (and, of course, length of the period).

An important corollary of this finding is that the "substitutability hypothesis" is far from supported. That is, some have urged that when the nations are involved in civil wars, there will be a decline in international wars, and vice versa. The evidence points, rather, in the opposite direction, with the above-noted tendency for some periods to witness high amounts of *both* civil and international war and others to see relatively low levels of both. Apparently, then, international and civil wars rise and fall together, but whether these fluctuations are experienced by the same or different nations has not yet been determined. Nor are we prepared to say here whether the same conditions account for both.

A final generalization is similar to the previous one, and appears to be equally unfounded. It suggests that the recent past has seen a decline in only one form of international war—that between sovereign states—in parallel with a rise in imperial or colonial wars. That is, the conventional interstate war so typical of 19th century Europe has allegedly been replaced by the war of national liberation, in which a western industrial state is pitted against a third world nation whose people are either resisting the imposition of foreign control or are in the process of throwing off a previously imposed imperial yoke. This proposition stands only if some inconsistent and/or unconventional coding criteria are invoked. For example, Kende (1971 and 1977) identifies 97 wars in the period 1944-1969, but he invokes no criteria for inclusion that rest upon either a minimal number of casualties, the political status of the combatants, or the degree of combat reciprocity. These are indeed examples of armed violence, but many cannot be classified as war in the conventional meaning of the term, especially since some of the cases qualify only because of the intervention—often unopposed—of foreign forces in the domestic conflicts of third world nations. Such cases may be reprehensible, but that does not make them wars. Very similar problems arise with the classifications developed by Wallensteen (1973) in his excellent study of the 1920-1968 period, and by Bouthoul and Carrére (1976a) in their more sweeping inquiry into the challenge of war.[4]

In sum, we found no long range secular trend, and any cyclical pattern—in the precise sense of the word—is more apparent than real.[5] All three types of conflict rise and fall together, and the only clear trend involves that which may have begun with Hiroshima and Nagasaki and continues up to the present day. This latter point will, of course, be central to our discussion in the next section, where we offer some possible explanations and some very tentative forecasts.

These, then, are the patterns revealed by our systematic examination of the incidence of wars and confrontations since 1816. While these data are not only interesting in their own right, and will also play a crucial role in testing a number of theoretical models of the correlates and causes of war, our interest here is more pragmatic and immediate. But before we shift to the more interpretive and speculative mode, it is important to summarize in one place the limitations of the evidence adduced in this chapter.

While these analyses rest on a highly operational and carefully generated data base, covering the entire globe and a very long time period, they are nevertheless quite limited. The statistical tools used for this exercise were fairly primitive. More sophisticated ones might turn up patterns that have so far remained unnoticed. And our interperiod break points, while consistent with those most often used by diplomatic historians, could be deceptive. It is, for example, possible that by shifting the boundaries between conceptual, spatial, or temporal categories, we can markedly affect the number of cases falling into each, and thus, the possibility of an "unintended gerrymander" could be affecting our temporal distributions. Then there is the fact that all of our data are aggregated at the international system level, thus concealing some potentially interesting patterns at the regional and national levels of aggregation.

Finally, there is the most sensitive issue of all: the extent to which our coding rules themselves affect the results. For example, does the 1,000 battle death threshold exclude a large number of international or civil wars, and would a threshold of 500 or 750 lead to the inclusion of many more cases? On the basis of our investigations to date, the answer is negative, but one would want to examine all candidate cases as well as those that fell into the mini-war and military confrontation categories to be sure. Similarly, as we noted in discussing the data sets generated by Kende (1977) and Wallensteen (1973), one's theoretical orientation can indeed affect the content of one's classification criteria. No matter how meticulous their articulation and application, the substantive reasoning behind the coding rules can markedly shape the data sets that emerge. Hence the importance of explicit coding criteria and careful application; and we trust both have been attended to here.

INTERPRETATIONS AND CONTINGENT FORECASTS

With these methodological caveats made clear, we may more prudently turn to the kinds of forecasts permitted by the data base and the elementary analyses to which it was exposed. Bearing in mind the points made in our introduction, what forecasts, if any, are permitted by these empirical findings? First of all, there are no discernible long-range trends, and therefore little temptation to propose a simple extrapolation into the future. Are there, however, any shorter-range trends to which we might turn for guidance?

Here the evidence is relatively clear, because there is a steady if modest decline since the World War II epoch on many dimensions. Returning to Tables 1 and 2, we find fairly credible downward trends in the annual frequencies of war involvements per nation as well as nation months of war begun and battle deaths from war begun, whether we control for system size or not. Similarly, for military confrontations that involve one or more major powers (Table 3), there is a post-World War II decline in their annual frequency, as well as in those confrontations involving a major on each side. Moreover, there is the dramatic decline in the frequency with which they escalate to war, with only 8% doing so after World War II, and none since 1965.

Shifting from *inter*national violence to that found at the *intra*national level, there is also a general downward trend, but of much shorter duration. That is, the annual frequency of civil wars (Table 4) rose sharply (and not surprisingly) in the two decades following World War II, but has declined markedly in the decade since then; however, the number of civil wars that became internationalized via large-scale foreign intervention has risen. The data in Table 5 show the same pattern, with annual nation months of civil war begun, plus battle deaths from those wars, both rising after World War II and then declining over the past 12 years.

Thus, to the extent these trends of the past three decades offer grounds for prediction, we might expect that the decades ahead will show a gradual decline in the frequency and destructiveness of war. But, aside from the dangers of simple extrapolation, there is the other problem alluded to earlier: the rather rough, but visible, periodicity in these data over the entire 160-odd years. It will be recalled that on many of the indicators, the relative peacefulness of the Concert period gave way to the extreme violence of the 1850s and 1860s, followed by a general decline in martial activities in the 1870s and 1880s. Then we experienced general increases in those activities through World War I, a decline during the inter-war years, and increases again after World War II. Finally, we have the relative decline that we have already described.

In summary, we can examine the long range century-and-a-half trend and find little pattern, examine the short range trend of the past few decades and predict a continuing general decline, or examine the crude periodicity and predict an upsurge in international and civil war as the current decline "bottoms out." The point should be manifest: in war and many other social phenomena, there are indeed temporal regularities, but few of them are inexorable. As Lewis Richardson (1960) reminds us, the statistical regularities in international combat rest on the human failures of the past, and their continuation into the future rests on the assumption that people *still* will not "stop to think." Thus, any forecasts we make in this sector should be *contingent* and conditional forecasts (Singer, 1973), rather than unconditional ones.

Does it follow from this that all of our systematic research into the past is of little value for policy purposes? To the contrary, the sort of data generated and reported here can turn out to be quite valuable in the policy context, but not as the basis for any mechanical projection of trends or cycles into the future. Rather, their main value will be in the formulation and testing of alternative explanations for the incidence of global violence, which, of course, was the original purpose.[6] Thus, as our theoretical models are tested against these outcome data, and gradually become accurate enough to account for the fluctuations and distributions across time and space, we will increasingly be able to build contingent forecasts on explanatory models. And, of all the bases from which to make forecasts, the explanatory model that has been tested against both the constancies and the dynamics of history is the most reliable.

Having argued against inexorability, and suggested that the thoughtful application of scientific knowledge can help shape our future, let us at the same time recognize that certain historical processes are *not* particularly vulnerable to conscious human intervention. If, for example, the structure and culture of today's international system are appreciably dependent on decisions and accidents that occurred decades or centuries ago, some finite degree of variance in system change will be beyond our control now. But just as it is useful to know how much of our future we *can* shape, it is also useful to know how much of it lies beyond our control. While systematic (and, we hope, cumulative) research goes on, we must, of course, act on the basis of what we know now, and one of the things we know with some confidence is that a certain momentum inheres in some of the processes now unfolding in the global system. Let us, therefore, close with a brief and rather speculative discussion of such possibilities in the context of certain trends that seem to be quite vigorous today. Needless to say, we will go well beyond our data here, and many of our forecasts should be examined alongside those papers in this volume that consider similar dimensions in considerably greater depth.

One of the trends that seems particularly germane to prospects for conflict in the next decade or so is that of weapons technology. In the major power stratum, the nuclear-missile combination gives so dramatic an advantage to the offense vis-a-vis the defense that almost all concerned consider strategic war an act of madness, engaged in only by accident or in desperation. Because the exotic defenses against either the warhead or the delivery vehicle—such as laser beams or magnetic force fields—seem unlikely to modify the offense-defense ratios in appreciable ways, the downward trend in major versus major war should continue. As our Table 3 data show, the major powers do continue to go to the brink, but less and less against one another, and so far they have always managed to halt the escalation process short of war. The fact that the 20 major versus major confrontations since V-J Day have gone to neither conventional nor nuclear war (except for China's "volunteers" who intervened in Korea as General MacArthur approached the Yalu) strongly suggests that the nuclear deterrent, as clumsy and fragile as it is, seems to exercise an inhibiting effect.

Another war-inhibiting trend that seems likely to continue is that of increased interdependence, which is operating in two sectors. One is implied in the above discussion, with the major powers becoming involved in a large fraction of minor versus minor confrontations, taking on a patron-client role, and thence exercising a restraining role through the granting and withholding of military and economic assistance. Since the missile crisis of 1962, the annual frequency of minor versus minor wars has increased slightly (Table 1), but given the increased number of actors, the normalized frequency has actually declined. More important, as Table 2 indicates, there has been a rather dramatic drop in the absolute *amount* of war as reflected in nation months and battle deaths. The second sector in which interdependence seems to be inhibiting international war is that of resources and trade. The evidence is less clear here, but because most conventional wars occur between neighbors, and because proximity is usually correlated with economic interdependence (and will probably be more so in the decades ahead), this inhibitory effect may well continue for some time.

A third factor at work is that of nation-building, and while this *can* be a source of conflict—over territory, seaports, resources, and prestige, for example—the inhibitory mechanisms are far from negligible. It is, for example, one thing for third world elites to engage in "wars" of words and maneuvers, and quite another to enter into sustained military combat with a neighbor's forces; since 1816, for the major powers at least, only about 10% of military confrontations ended in wars. With the steadily rising expectations and demands for material improvement, their citizens may enjoy the drama of parades, air shows, and some judicious sabre-rattling, but there seems to be increasing resistance to heavy military spending and to foreign military adventure. The significant exception appears to be Cuba, but as something of a client state for the U.S.S.R., much of the bill is footed by Moscow. And while the Cuban economy may be headed for trouble, the convergence between expectation and performance is—for the moment—sufficient for domestic stability. More typical would be Egypt, whose elites and public show every sign of turning away from military adventure and toward domestic development.

Closely related to this trend in the third world is the decline in ideology, by which we mean the tendency to take literally the political scriptures of the various founding fathers. One consequence of this is the tendency to view foreign conflicts in more pragmatic and less Manichean terms, thus reducing the frequency with which confrontations should escalate to war. Of course, this trend began even sooner in the first and second worlds, even though it may not have been widely noticed. Just as Soviet or Czechoslovakian factory workers have been cynical about their required courses in Marxism-Leninism for several decades, citizens in the West have gradually lost their appetite for a holy war against "Godless, Communist atheism," thanks in part to their costly war involvements in Algeria, Korea, Suez, and Indochina. A particularly compelling reflection of this trend at several strata and in many sectors of the global system is the recently consummated trade pact between China and Japan. Despite the long history of conflict, exploitation, and war—as well as ideological opposition—economic realities and diplomatic pragmatism seem to have taken precedence.

Having examined these data sets, and the relatively reassuring inferences they permit, let us return to our earlier point regarding the distinction between noncontingent and contingent forecasts. Most of the above inferences are, of course, noncontingent; they essentially assume that not much will happen to interfere with a continuing decline in the frequency of warfare. But, to reiterate, it would be quite irresponsible to rest our forecasts on simple extrapolation, and even more irresponsible to suggest that a nation's foreign and military policies be based on such extrapolations.

That is, even while there seem to be several trends that promise a decreasing likelihood of war, there are certain countertrends whose portent is much less reassuring. Most dramatic of these is, of course, that of military spending. Global expenditures for preparedness stood at about 107 billion U.S. dollars (1974 prices) in 1960, at about 201 billion in 1970, and by 1975, the figure was approximately 324 billion (Sivard, 1977). Even allowing for the dramatic growth in the world's population, the per capita military expenditure rose from 35 to 55 to 81 dollars over those three time points.

An attentive observer of the U.S. foreign policy scene over the past three decades would certainly note a rather bizarre pattern. That is, the dominant line on arms control and arms reduction has essentially been that articulated by such respected analysts as Morgenthau (1948) and Kennan (1957). Starkly stated, these shrewd theoreticians held that armaments are (a) merely the manifestation of political tension; (b) that this tension is a result of unresolved "political" differences; and (c) that such tension will decline as political differences are successfully negotiated. By extension, they suggested further that (a) these political differences can be negotiated prior to any meaningful arms reductions; (b) tensions can therefore be reduced prior to arms reduction; (c) arms reductions cannot be successfully negotiated until tensions are markedly reduced; and (d) once tensions *are* reduced, arms reduction will easily follow. The events of the past three decades show that these arguments were essentially incorrect. That is, we have seen some political settlement and some tension reduction in East-West relations; this is clearly the meaning of détente. But the final and most critical assumption in this scenario has been clearly refuted. There have, admittedly, been some arms *control* agreements, but arms *reduction*—as some of us predicted long ago (Singer, 1958) and have often reiterated since (Singer, 1962 and 1970)—just could not be expected.

Why should this be? The explanation is simple, except to those who are naive enough to believe that nations acquire and add to weapons stockpiles solely in response to external threats. While that external threat is essential to the initial moves and can help keep the momentum in the later stages of an armament race, the arm-for-defense-only model is woefully incomplete. The allocation of resources to preparedness, beyond certain minimal levels, is escalatory in its effects at home as well as abroad. First of all, each increment in military expenditure enhances the credibility of those in the *opposing nation* who claim that an external threat exists, and this enhances the likelihood of increased expenditures in that nation. Second, each such increment carries with it a modest—but devastatingly cumulative—redistribution of economic power *within* the nation, thus weakening the forces of restraint and prudence. In the end, those who advocate and benefit from bloated defense budgets become the "realists," and those who oppose this kind of "realism" are classified as soft and irresponsible, if not lacking in political virility and patriotism.

The extent to which this has occurred in the U.S. and the U.S.S.R., with the burden of proof shifted from the hawks to the doves, is not readily measured, but a content analysis of foreign policy debates or newspaper editorials or discussions on defense budgets would almost certainly reflect such a shift during these past three decades. Another reflection of this overall trend might be the size and budget of governmental and private organizations engaged in research, planning, or negotiations on arms reduction or disarmament; in the U.S. and the U.S.S.R. this has hardly been a "growth industry" when compared to the military establishment. Other indicators come to mind, but for now we will leave this as a matter of judgment.

Thus, it seems evident that the peace forces in the world are not exactly having their way, and that "preparedness" programs serve not only to misallocate resources within nations, but also to generate tensions between nations. Further, they absorb energies and funds that might help break the log-jam of economic development in the third world. Perhaps most dangerous of all, in the longer run, is the extent to which they inhibit efforts to develop, articulate, or experiment with policies that might lead to certain essential modifications in the global environment.

All of this leads, in turn, to consideration of a menacing *non*trend: the lack of real movement toward the disarmament of the world's nations and a concomitant growth in the political efficacy of supranational institutions. Despite the occasional international agreement on arms control—usually intended to make the system less prone to accidental war—little has happened to reverse the trends in vertical and lateral proliferation of nuclear and conventional weapon systems. And for the reasons outlined earlier, as well as the destabilizing effects of much of the new weapons technology, this leaves us with a system that is fundamentally as war-prone as it has been since the Congress of Vienna. Whether it is with conventional or nuclear weapons (assuming the difference is not obliterated by the deployment of enhanced radiation warheads or their miniaturization), whether it involves major powers or minors, and whether the theater is central Europe or Africa, war remains all too likely.

For the United States, the options are several, and may be crudely classified as passive, provocative, or adaptive. The first, or passive, option is that which has been followed for most of the post-World War II era by the U.S. and more erratically by the U.S.S.R. It consists essentially of accepting the strategic and other characteristics of the international environment, paying lip service to the need for system transformation, maintaining a military arsenal that is too large for strategic deterrence and too small for a credible first strike threat, and generally responding to external opportunities and threats in accord with the current distribution of power and interests at home. Remaining with this option seems an effective way of preserving the century-and-a-half-long tradition of from five to nine international wars every decade (Table 1) until the final one in the series.

The second, or provocative, option is that which has been advocated by an important domestic coalition that has not been strong enough to have its way nor weak enough to be ignored. With a few breaks at home (such as continuing economic dislocation, renewed racial/religious conflict) or abroad (such as increased Soviet bellicosity, major U.S. setbacks in the Third World), this coalition could move into a dominant role. With that might well come an even more rapid arms buildup, more vigorous military intervention, a more intense ideological assault on the enemies of the moment, and a general propensity to exploit the contemporary international environment. Given the physical impossibility of regaining the strategic and industrial preponderance enjoyed by the U.S. in the late 1940s, this strategy could readily produce a sharp upward trend in both the frequency and the severity of international war in the years ahead.

The third basic option would reflect an awareness of the international system's fundamental flaws and set about modifying the environment in a vigorous but incremental fashion. Recognizing the extent to which major power policies can worsen or improve—as well as perpetuate—the system's structure and culture, the U.S. could take a variety of initiatives in several sectors. Most pressing would be, in our judgment, the military-security sector, with economic and cultural initiatives playing a supporting role.

To shift from the passive to the adaptive option, while foreclosing the provocative option, will require (as Holsti and Rosenau point out in this volume) a conscious political decision on the part of America's elites. But there is little evidence of even the mildest tendencies in that direction. Our diplomatic, economic, and military policies remain as conventional and opportunistic as they have been since the Spanish-American War. Despite occasional initiatives, the central tendency has been to follow in the footsteps of those other major powers whose ascendancy and decline we have witnessed with fatal regularity.

In sum, the legitimacy and the expectancy of war remains all too firmly embedded in the structure and culture of the system and its nations, despite the modestly encouraging economic, technological, and psychological trends that we have noted here. Unless and until war and the preparation for war—psychic as well as material—are consciously rejected, all of these countervailing tendencies remain vulnerable to quick reversal. Most of the more visible auguries were equally promising in June of 1914, only weeks before the guns of August shattered the fragile structure of peace. For American foreign policy then, building a new political and security order will be the crucial test, but the omens are far from encouraging.

NOTES

1. We deal here with only 100 of the 103 international wars. Because we do not examine the years from 1915 through 1918 and from 1940 through 1945, three qualifying wars are omitted from the analyses: the extra-systemic wars between Russia and her nationalities beginning in 1917; between France and her colony in Vietnam in 1945; and between Holland and her colony in Indonesia in the same year. Conversely, we include the following wars that were continuing as of December 31, 1977: the two seccessionist wars against Ethiopia; the Cambodian (Kampuchea)-Vietnamese border war; and the Moroccan-Mauritanian war against the Polisario Front in the Sahara.

2. The major powers and their years of tenure are: England (1816-present); France (1816-1940 and 1945-present); Germany/Prussia (1816-1918 and 1925-1945); Austria-Hungary (1816-1918); Italy (1860-1943); Russia (1816-1917 and 1922-present); China (1950-present); Japan (1895-1945); and the United States (1899-present).

3. Because we do not consider here the period during which the Two World Wars were being fought, the following qualifying civil wars are omitted from the analyses: Russia, 1918-1921, and Greece, 1944-1949. Further, we do include two civil wars that were continuing as of December 31, 1977: those in the Philippines and Angola. It is also worth noting that there were civil wars in some of the nations that did not qualify early as sovereign system members, and hence our 19th century figures are accordingly lower than some might expect.

4. Other compilations that should be compared are Woods and Baltzly, 1915; Wood, 1968; and Bloomfield and Leiss, 1969.

5. If we define periodicity in terms of peaks and valleys of approximate magnitude, occurring at more or less equal intervals, we find no evidence for such a claim. Even using spectral analysis methods, which are explicitly designed to *find*, no less confirm, any clear cyclical patterns, we turned up nothing of significance.

6. This theoretical and empirical work continues apace; much of it has already been reported in the scholarly literature, and many of those articles will be assembled in several anthologies scheduled to appear in 1978 and 1979.

Melvin Small (Ph.D. University of Michigan, 1965) is Professor and Chairman of the Department of History at Wayne State University and has been a visiting lecturer at the University of Aarhus and Windsor University. He has authored Public Opinion and Historians *(1970), coauthored* The Wage of War *(1972), and published many articles dealing with diplomatic history and international politics.*

J. David Singer (Ph.D. New York University, 1956) is Professor of Political Science at the University of Michigan and has also been associated with Vassar College, The Naval War College, and the Universities of Oslo and Geneva. Among his books are Financing International Organization *(1961):* Deterrence, Arms Control, and Disarmament *(1962):* Human Behavior and International Politics *(1965):* Quantitative International Politics *(1968):* The Wages of War, 1816-1965 *(1972): and* The Study of International Politics *(1976).*

Alliance Polarization, Cross-Cutting, and International War, 1815-1964

A MEASUREMENT PROCEDURE AND SOME PRELIMINARY EVIDENCE

MICHAEL D. WALLACE   *Chapter 4*

Various authors have posited the relationship between alliance polarization and violent conflict in the global system as positive, negative, and curvilinear. Unfortunately, these hypotheses have not received a thorough test, as previous empirical studies of alliance polarization have tended to neglect (1) the configurational properties of alliance groupings, and (2) the nonmilitary dimensions of alignment. This paper attempts to construct measures of polarization and cross-cutting which take these properties into account. Configurations of alignment patterns are generated by subjecting data on military alliances, diplomatic representation, and intergovernmental organizations to Guttmann-Lingoes Smallest Space Analysis. Several mathematical procedures are developed to measure polarization and cross-cutting within and between these clusters.

Using these new indices, the relationships between and among polarization, cross-cutting, and international war are examined. It was found that both independent variables had only a weak linear relationship to war. However, polynomial regression uncovered a strong curvilinear relationship between military alliance polarization and war; periods in which polarization was extremely low or extremely high were far more likely to be followed by increased war, while a moderate level of polarization apparently reduced the likelihood of violent conflict.

Diplomats and scholars have long assumed a connection between the division of the world's nations into mutually exclusive alliance blocs and the outbreak of war, but there has never been a firm consensus as to how precisely the two are related (Rosecrance, 1966). Recently a major debate has developed in the international relations literature over the relationship between the polarization of the international system and the frequency

AUTHOR'S NOTE: An earlier version of this paper was presented to the annual meetings of the American Political Science Association, Washington, D.C., September 5-9, 1972.

Originally published in the *Journal of Conflict Resolution,* Vol. 17, No. 4, December 1973.

and magnitude of violent international conflict. From one perspective, a strongly bipolar international system such as that existing during the 1950s and early 1960s provides a good deal of stability (Waltz, 1967). The ubiquity of confrontation and crisis prevents aggressive expansion while providing for incremental change without war, and the existence of only two significant powers makes for greater certainty in international dealings.

A more common view, however, holds that highly polarized systems are dangerously unstable and war prone; far better are multipolar systems (for example, that existing between the Napoleonic Wars and World War I) characterized by relatively loose alignments (Deutsch and Singer, 1964; Singer, 1963). Loosely polarized systems provide more interaction opportunities and thus generate competing loyalties which may serve to prevent violent conflict (Coser, 1956: 76-77); by contrast, in "tight bipolar" systems all cleavage is ranged along one axis and hence takes on the character of a zero-sum game. Furthermore, the existence of many power centers means that aggressive actions on the part of anyone are relatively less threatening to the system as a whole.

A third hypothesis has it that the optimal level of polarization is somewhere between tight bipolarity and a loose multipolar system (Rosecrance, 1966). According to this view, a certain degree of polarization provides for the automatic equilibration of the international balance, and serves to dampen conflicts in the remainder of the system. At the same time, the system should be sufficiently multipolar to diffuse some antagonism away from the bipolar axis, and to limit the scope and costs of such crises as do occur.

Thus, the relationship between alliance polarization and war in the international system has variously been asserted to be negative, positive, and curvilinear. Unfortunately, there is insufficient empirical evidence to allow us to evaluate these three contradictory hypotheses with any degree of confidence. There have been only two systematic, data-based studies which touch upon the relationship between system polarization and international war—those by Singer and Small (1968) and Haas (1970)—and these appear to yield partially contradictory findings. Singer and Small found that polarization in the twentieth century international system (as measured by the amount of alliance aggregation) showed a strong positive association with the magnitude and severity of war, but that in the nineteenth century the association was negative. This would seem to suggest that in earlier times alliance polarization had a stabilizing effect on the system, but that in the changed circumstances of the contemporary era it has tended to increase the probability of violent conflict. Haas, on the other hand, found that for 21 historical systems in Europe, Asia, and Hawaii, system polarization as measured by the number of independent power centers exhibited a consistent negative association with the incidence, magnitude, and severity of war.

Quite apart from their findings, it is questionable whether the design of either study permits us to draw any firm conclusions about the relationship between alliance polarization and war. Although system polarization is normally linked conceptually with the number of independent power centers in the system and the tightness with which nations are bound to them (Deutsch and Singer, 1964), the Singer and Small study focuses only on the number of alliance bonds in the system as a whole. While the Haas study does develop an intuitive measure of the number of poles in the system, it employs only a binary measure of the tightness of alignment patterns. Moreover, neither study focuses to any significant degree on the *configuration* of alignment patterns; such factors as the relative distances between and among the various poles and the number of nations clustered outside the major military camps will not necessarily affect their indices.

In addition, both studies concern themselves only with the military aspects of alignment and do not consider the multitude of other pacts, accords, treaties, and commitments which may alternately overlap or cut across military alliance configurations. Many scholars would argue that insofar as these nonmilitary bonds parallel the defense links in the system, they serve to increase the likelihood of war by reinforcing alliance solidarity and exacerbating the cleavage among alliance groupings. Similarly, to the extent that these bonds cut across the structure of military commitments, they tend to reduce the probability of violent conflict by generating competing loyalties linking nations in different or opposing military camps (Coser, 1956; Rae and Taylor, 1970; Deutsch and Singer, 1964).

This paper will propose several indices of alliance polarization which will (1) focus on the neglected configurational properties of the systemwide network of military alignments, and (2) take into account the multidimensional character of alignment patterns by examining two types of nonmilitary bonds. It will then undertake to examine the statistical relationship between these different indices of polarization and crosscutting, and the magnitude and severity of international war.

The Raw Data

As with most research undertaken in connection with the Correlates of War Project, the temporal domain of this study is the 150-year period from 1815 to 1964. The spatial domain comprises all independent nation-members of the international system as specified by Singer and Small (1966a) and Russett et al. (1968). Data on the dependent variable consist of information on the number of nation-months of war, and the battle deaths accruing from wars begun in the system each year.[1] This basic information will be aggregated in several different ways. First, indices of the amount of interstate war (in which both sides in the conflict are nation-states), as well as indicators measuring the amount of international war (including colonial and imperial conflicts) will be used. Second, the data will be aggregated both annually, and for each five-year period beginning in 1815.

The first step in the construction of indices for the independent variable—the generation of raw data on international alignments—also traverses familiar ground. Three sets of data from the Correlates of War Project will be used. The first is the data on membership in formal military alliances collected by Singer and Small (1969, 1966b). Three classes of alliances are included: defense pacts, committing each signatory to intervene with military force on behalf of the others; neutrality pacts, committing each nation to refrain from intervention against any other signatory; and ententes, providing for consultation upon the outbreak of hostilities. The second data set comprises information on another sort of international commitment: membership in international governmental organizations (Wallace and Singer, 1970). Included here are all organizations established by international treaty and possessing a permanent secretariat, and since these are very few in number during the early nineteenth century, this data set is included only from 1865 to 1964. The final set of data identifies those pairs of nations which have formal diplomatic relations; included is any bilateral exchange of representatives at the chargé d'affaires level or above. The alliance data have been compiled annually; the international organization and diplomatic representation data are compiled at five-year intervals.

1. Following Singer and Small, a war is defined as an armed conflict engaging the armed forces of at least one state-member of the international system for a duration of at least two weeks in which at least 1,000 battle-related fatalities were suffered. For greater detail and the rationale behind these operational procedures, see Singer and Small (1972).

Data Transformation—the Dyadic Scores

If the raw data are to shed light on the configuration of alignment patterns, they must undergo several transformations. The first step is to permute the data so as to yield as much information as possible on the relationship between each pair of nations in the system. This is most easily done by coding it in the form of an n·n proximity matrix, where n represents the number of nations in the system at a given point in time, and the value of cell (i, j) represents the strength of closeness of the bond between nations i and j. There are several possible ways in which this might be done, and since the procedure followed at this stage will have a crucial bearing on the subsequent analyses, it is worthwhile to examine briefly the main alternatives.

The intergovernmental organization (IGO) data set presents us with little difficulty in this respect, reflecting as it does not one nor two but a large and heterogeneous number of internation bonds. Following Russett (1967), the proximity of a pair of nations may be measured using these data as the number of intergovernmental organizations to which both belong, normalized by the total number of organizations in the system (strictly speaking, this normalization is not necessary to the analysis per se, and is done only in order to permit comparability between analyses where the number of organizations varies).

By contrast, the alliance and diplomatic data sets offer no such easy solution. In each case, the raw data almost always represent only a single bond between each nation-pair (or at most two or three in the case of a pair in more than one alliance together). Thus, the simple solution used in the IGO case would yield a matrix with cell entries of 0 or 1, according to whether or not each nation-pair possessed a formal military or diplomatic tie. Such a matrix would have two drawbacks. First, it does not meet the crucial requirement that the cell entries accurately reflect the relative strength of the bonds between and among the nation-pairs, since all aligned pairs are not bonded with the same tightness, nor are all unaligned pairs equally distant. Second, even if this procedure were acceptable in principle, it would create problems when the data matrix was analyzed. As we shall see, the preferred analytic technique cannot handle such dyadic matrices, and the only usable alternative has many drawbacks.

A second possible approach would be to rank or scale the three types of formal alliances and the three types of diplomatic links which make up the raw data. While this procedure would produce more diversified cell entries, it proved impossible even to rank order either set of categories satisfactorily, let alone give them numerical values. For example, one might suppose that defense pacts should be rated above neutrality pacts and ententes, since they imply a much greater degree of formal commitment. Yet this would lead to the classification of such crucial links as those between the Axis powers from 1936 to 1939, or between Britain and France from 1904 to 1914, as less important than such hollow pacts as the Albanian-Italian alliance of 1927-1939. Given that any ordering based upon formal treaty provisions alone creates such anomalies, ranking the direct bonds cannot produce valid results without a great deal more information concerning the pacts themselves. An ordering of the types of diplomatic bonds is easier to justify but unfortunately the number of bonds in the lower two categories (minister resident and chargé d'affaires) undergoes such a sharp relative decline in the twentieth century that the usefulness of this classification is largely obviated.

Given these difficulties in formulating explicit coding rules to rank categories of military alliances, one might expect that a third alternative procedure—the use of an expert panel to rank the importance of the alliances themselves—would be unlikely to produce satisfactory results. And so indeed it proved. Attempting to rank alliance bonds in this fashion, the author quickly discovered that expert consensus simply did not exist; the dimensions of evaluation employed and the relevant information adduced varied widely among respondents, reducing reliability to unacceptable levels. Thus, while a complete or even partial ordering of formal military alliances based upon their relative importance represents a worthwhile goal for further research, it is clearly not something that can be generated from existing data.

Thus, the approach finally adopted proceeds quite differently. The initial assumption is that the tightness of the bond between two nations is a function not only of the direct bond between the pair, but also of the number of other nations with which they are mutually linked. For example, the fact that the United States and Great Britain have alliance and diplomatic ties with many of the same nations is deemed to indicate a closer bond than exists between nations whose only links in common are with each other. Applying this principle to the alliance data we may compute the matrix entries by counting the number of common alliance bonds possessed by each nation-pair (including of course any bond between the nations of the pair themselves) and normalizing by the number of nations in the system. In similar fashion, the diplomatic matrix entries are derived by counting the number of common diplomatic links possessed by a given pair, and dividing by the total number of nations. In either case, this yields a coefficient whose theoretical range is between one and zero and which represents the closeness of the pairwise bond between nations.

It goes without saying that this procedure is not unexceptional. To begin with, some would argue that this coefficient is more a measure of similarity between national alignment and diplomatic patterns than an index of the actual link between nations (Russett, 1967: 99-100). In defense it may be argued that the procedure used here differs from virtually all similarity measures in that it takes into account only those nations with which the pair are *jointly* bonded, and ignores those with which only one or neither member is linked.[2] A second objection might be that this coefficient in effect equates direct and all indirect links, whereas in fact we know that (1) direct bonds are more important than indirect ones, and (2) some indirect bonds—for example, those through a major power—may be more important than others. The point is well taken, but given that there exists no systematic procedure to weight the various links, it seems better to rely on the (admittedly unproven) assumption that the strength of an alliance bond is proportional to the simple *number* of indirect links, rather than to adopt some intuitive weighting procedure which might drastically reduce index reliability.

Data Reduction—the Configurations

Using the above procedures on the entire data set yields 150 derived data matrices corresponding to the annual alliance data from 1815 to 1964, thirty corresponding (approximately) to the quinquennial diplomatic data for the same period, and twenty taken every half-decade from 1865 to 1965 representing the IGO data. The next step is to analyze these 200 matrices so as to make visible the configurations of alignment patterns. Given that most of the matrices are quite large, this requires the

2. For example, the common 0-1 similarity coefficient phi is computed as

$$\phi_{ij} = \frac{\text{(number of cases where i and j are both 1)} + \text{(number of cases where they are both 0)} - \text{(number of cases where they disagree)}}{\text{total n}}.$$

By contrast, our coefficient alpha is

$$\alpha_{ij} = \frac{\text{number of cases where i and j are both 1}}{\text{total n}}.$$

use of some data reduction procedure. The most common analytical technique employed on problems of this type is factor analysis (Russett, 1967; Cattell, 1965b). But despite its widespread use, there are two reasons why it would be inappropriate to employ it here. First, factor analysis requires that the measures of dyadic alignment be in the form of a ratio scale, so that one may say, for example, that a score of twelve is precisely twice as large as a score of six. While the data to be used are in ratio scale form, it may be unwise to presume upon this too much. Since no procedure will be used to weight these formal ties according to their importance, one can hardly insist that twelve bonds represent twice as much alignment as six; it would be preferable to make the less ambitious claim that the twelve bonds merely constitute the greater degree of alignment.

However, the strong assumptions required by the factor analysis model are not limited to the input data, and herein lies the second problem. At several stages in its complex sequence of operations, a priori decisions must be made as to how the algorithm shall proceed. While often masquerading as "merely technical" matters, they have crucial theoretical implications. In deciding whether or not to normalize the factor matrix prior to rotation, one decides in effect whether or not a nation's affiliation with several groupings shall be deemed to attenuate its membership in each (Russett, 1967: 101-102); in choosing the number of factors to be extracted and rotated, one chooses the lower threshold below which a bond is considered "trivial" or "noise" (Cattell, 1965a: 211). The need to make such crucial theoretical decisions at the very outset weighs heavily against the procedure, given the still underdeveloped state of our knowledge.

Thus a different technique will be used here: the method of Smallest Space Analysis (SSA) developed by Guttmann and Lingoes (Guttmann, 1968; Lingoes, 1966; 1965). The chief distinctive feature of SSA vis-à-vis factor analysis is the less stringent demands it makes of the input data. It requires only that the data represent a monotone invariant (ordinal) scale, and not a true metric (ratio or interval) scale.[3] This difference goes a long way toward eliminating the methodological difficulties of factor analysis. For one thing, since this algorithm is only responsive to the rank orderings among the input coefficients and not their actual numeric values, it is

3. Actually there are two additional constraints that must be placed on the coefficients; they must be reflexive ($\alpha_{ij} = \alpha_{ji}$) and nonnegative ($\alpha_{ij} \geqslant 0$, $\alpha_{ii} = 0$). For this reason, Guttmann refers to the coefficients as defining a "semimetric" (Guttmann, 1968: 475).

much less sensitive to the imperfections in the method used to generate a coefficient of alliance bonding. Moreover, we are relieved of the burden of those complex analytic decisions which arise from the strong metric assumed in factor analysis; no new theoretical assumptions are required in order to generate a solution.[4]

SSA has other advantages besides overcoming these traditional bugbears. For one thing, since the algorithm operates without the restriction of a metric, the resulting solution is generally far less complex. Of particular importance is the fact that the dimensionality of the output configuration (the number of dimensions or factors) is usually much lower with SSA than with factor analysis; in fact, SSA always produces the minimum possible dimensionality with the constraints of a permissible "fit" (Guttmann, 1968: 501).[5] A second and somewhat related advantage is the ease with which the SSA output configuration may be represented spatially. Although the input matrix need not fulfill the requirements of a Euclidean space, the output configuration is transformed to do so by applying Guttmann's principle of rank-images (1968: 479-481); the distances between points in the output configuration will then fulfill all metric requirements while simultaneously preserving the original rank-order among the points to a very close tolerance. Since a good fit to most data can be obtained in very few dimensions, this allows us to represent the underlying relationships in the matrix as real distances in two- or three-dimensional space, greatly facilitating interpretation. The output will in fact constitute a multidimensional map of the international system whose features are the alignment patterns of nations.

Despite these advantages, there will inevitably be those who are leery of the SSA algorithm because of its newness and unfamiliarity. Yet, as noted above, the comparative sense of confidence engendered by the older technique is almost wholly spurious. In using it we are literally forced to make trouble for ourselves. We must make a series of difficult and complex analytic and theoretic decisions at the beginning of the analysis;

4. In principle, the user does have a choice to make with those matrices which violate the monotonicity condition, i.e., those containing ties. In practice, however, the assumption of "semi-strong" monotonicity (which allows the algorithm to break ties wherever possible) produces the most parsimonious solutions (Guttmann, 1968: 477).

5. Of course, the user must decide what tradeoff is to be made between dimensionality and fit. With the data matrices used here however, there was no need for hesitation. In virtually every case, two dimensions gave a good or at least satisfactory fit, and only minor improvements could be obtained with higher dimensionalities.

these return to haunt us by increasing the mathematical difficulties involved in arriving at a solution, and (far more seriously) by generating worrisome problems of interpretation at the end of the process. Thus, SSA should not be considered a still more esoteric substitute for factor analysis, but a welcome surcease from complexity and difficulty.

But the proof of the pudding is in the eating; what hath SSA wrought? It is obviously impossible to present results for all 200 matrices in this paper, so four configurations have been selected as examples. Figures 1 and 2 illustrate two alliance configurations a decade apart; 1953 and 1963. Figure 3 shows the two-dimensional diplomatic configuration for 1920, and Figure 4 the 1930 IGO configuration.

For the 1953 alliance matrix it is possible to obtain an excellent fit (Guttmann-Lingoes Coefficient of Alienation = .033) in only two

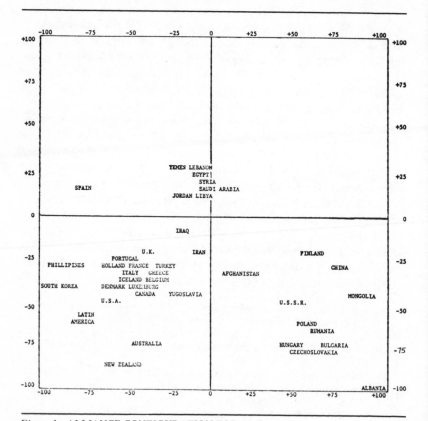

Figure 1: ALLIANCE CONFIGURATION FOR 1953

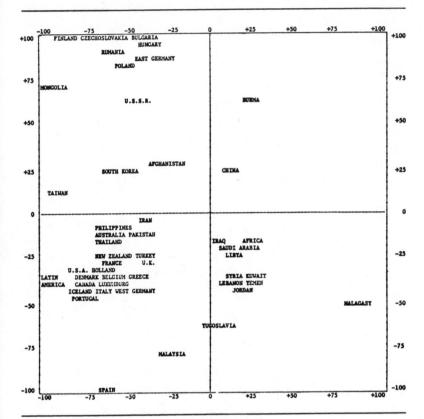

Figure 2: ALLIANCE CONFIGURATION FOR 1963

dimensions. A quick glance at the configuration confirms our intuitive understanding of the alignment patterns at the height of the Cold War. The system is dominated by the two superpowers, each ringed by its allies. There is no other major axis of alignment; indeed, if the solution is forced into a single dimension, the CA only increases to .063, indicating how closely the bipolar model fits this period. The only substantial group of "neutrals" is the Arab bloc, clustered off to one side somewhat closer to the Western than the Soviet camp.

The results for 1963 provide an interesting contrast with the bipolar pattern of a decade earlier. The two-dimensional fit is still excellent (CA = .038) but the mediocre fit in one dimension (CA = .110) indicates that the bipolar axis no longer dominates the system so completely. The two

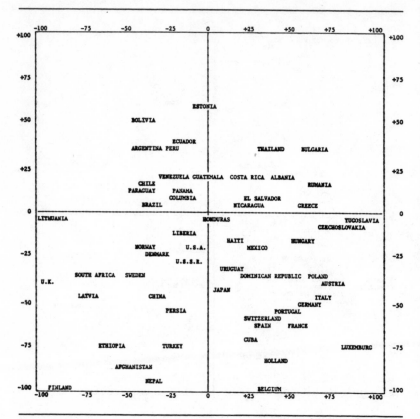

Figure 3: DIPLOMATIC CONFIGURATION FOR 1920

superpower blocs are still distinct, but they are now supplemented by a coterie of Afro-Asian nations lying some distance away from the East-West axis, constituting if you will a "Southern" cluster. This accords well with our intuitive understanding of the impact of the emerging Afro-Asian bloc after 1960.

A still more striking contrast is evident if we turn to the 1920 diplomatic configuration. Tight clusters and poles of any kind are virtually absent, giving way to several rather ill-defined and overlapping regions whose membership may be accounted for chiefly by geographical propinquity. Moreover, the two-dimensional fit is not as good (CA = .260). Taken together, these two results suggest a very complex and somewhat chaotic pattern of internation links, a finding certainly in conformity with

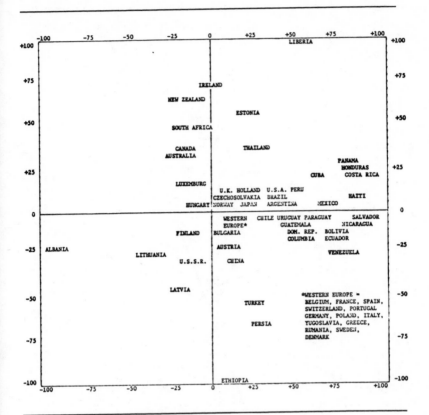

Figure 4: IGO CONFIGURATION FOR 1930

the standard historical description of the international system immediately after World War I.

The configuration produced by the 1930 IGO data stands somewhere midway between the simple structure and tight clusters of the Cold War alliance configurations and the diaphanous complexity of post-World-War-I diplomatic patterns. The system is dominated by two large, tight clusters, the one comprising the European states and Japan, the other the major American states. Unlike the alliance configurations, these groupings are quite close together; the IGO configuration is unipolar rather than bipolar, with the peripheral states of the system scattered loosely around a single, massive core. But despite this apparently simple structure, the two-dimensional fit is not exact (CA = .180), suggesting as in the previous example an underlying complexity not present in the alliance configurations.

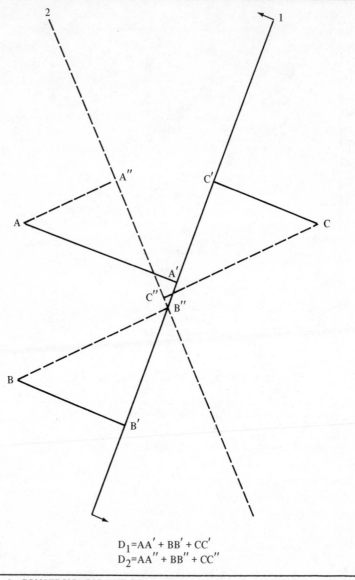

$$D_1 = AA' + BB' + CC'$$
$$D_2 = AA'' + BB'' + CC''$$

Figure 5: CONSTRUCTING THE POLARIZATION INDEX: A THREE-NATION
ILLUSTRATION

From these four examples, it seems clear that SSA does in fact succeed in producing readily interpretable configurations which possess relatively high face validity. Consequently, this method of analysis was used on all 200 derived data matrices. In all cases, the two-dimensional solution was used; while this sometimes results in a loss of detail, such standardization facilitates comparison and is mandatory for the last stage in the construction of indices of polarization and cross-cutting.

Constructing the Polarization Index

As we saw above, some notion of the degree of alliance polarization can be obtained merely by inspection of the SSA output. However, what is needed for the analysis which follows is a mathematical index reflecting precisely the degree of polarization which each configuration represents. Since the relative positions of the nations have been represented geometrically, it is now possible to construct such an index by giving geometric meaning to the concept of polarization. Clearly, where the system is highly polarized, the great majority of nations will be clustered in as few as two tightly knit groups at a considerable distance from one another. On the other hand, where polarization is low, the nations will form many loose clusters, distributed in random fashion throughout the space.

After considerable experimentation, a procedure was devised which allows us to express this visual difference in index form. To begin with, an axis was drawn in an arbitrary direction through the geometric center of the configuration. The second step was to calculate the perpendicular distances from each nation-point in the configuration to this axis, as shown in Figure 5. Third, these distances were summed, and the sum

$$D_1 = \sum_{i=1}^{n} d_{il}$$

corresponding to the initial axis position, was recorded. The fourth step was to rotate this axis about the center through $180°$, recomputing the sum of distances from the nation-points to the axis at intervals of $1°$. This yields a series of observations $D_1, D_2, \ldots, D_{180}$.

If we represent these points sequentially on a graph, a relationship between the resulting plot and the degree of polarization in the SSA configuration is immediately apparent. This can best be shown with reference to the two extreme cases illustrated in Figure 6. In the "perfectly" polarized case (where the configuration consists of two points, each representing a cluster of one-half the nations), rotating the axis will produce wide variation in the value of D. Where the axis passes directly through the two point clusters, D will approach zero; where it is perpendicular to a line drawn between them, it will reach a high maximum. It can be shown, in fact, that plotting the series D_1, D_2, . . ., D_{180} will yield a sine wave in this case. On the other hand, in the case of "minimum" polarization (where the nations are randomly scattered

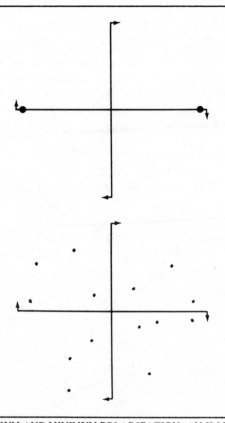

Figure 6: MAXIMUM AND MINIMUM POLARIZATION: AN ILLUSTRATION

throughout the space), D will scarcely vary at all as the axis is rotated; in the limiting case, plotting $D_1, D_2, \ldots, D_{180}$ yields a straight line.

This relationship between variation in D and the properties of the SSA configurations suggests a very simple algebraic representation for alliance polarization. If the value of D varies widely in the highly polarized configurations, but is nearly constant when there is little polarization, we can define an index of polarization

$$P = \frac{\sigma D}{\bar{D}} \, .$$

Computing this index for each year, we obtain 150 observations.

Refining the Index—The Weighted Values

In computing polarization as described above, each nation was assumed to make an equal contribution to the final score. This represents a distortion of our intuitive notion of polarization in that we normally consider the relative alignments of the larger and more powerful nations to affect system outcomes far more than alignments of smaller states. Moreover, the SSA output demonstrates that the most powerful nations are not always associated with the numerically largest clusters of nations. Thus, the measurement procedure as outlined thus far may tend to underestimate the importance of small poles containing strong nations, while overestimating the influence of weak, populous ones. To compensate for such distortion, it was decided to weight the impact of each nation by some factor reflecting its military capability. The resulting index would then respond to the *relative strength,* as well as the number and tightness of alliance clusters in the system. For this purpose, an additional set of data was adduced: information concerning the number of military effectives possessed by each nation at five-year intervals beginning in 1815 (for the coding rules used to collect these data, see Wallace, 1973).

These data were incorporated into the index by utilizing the physical concept of "moment," or the product of mass times distance from the axis. In computing the sum of the distances of nations from the axis, each distance was multiplied by a weight proportional to the size of the corresponding nation's military effectives. Thus for each position of the axis we obtained the sum of the moments about the axis

$$M = \sum_{i=1}^{n} (d_i \cdot w_i),$$

and as before, $M_1, M_2, \ldots, M_{180}$ were computed, yielding a weighted polarization score

$$P_w = \frac{\sigma M}{\overline{M}} .$$

Since the data on military effectives were only available at five-year intervals, only thirty quinquennial values of the weighted index could be computed.

Constructing Indices of Cross-cutting

In the comparative politics and voting study literature an individual is said to be "cross-pressured" if he or she belongs to several formal or informal groups whose political norms pull in different and often contradictory directions (Lipset, 1960). When there are a large number of such individuals, the political system as a whole is said to be "cross-cut"; this concept is usually defined as the proportion of pairs of individuals who share common loyalties or affiliations on some important systemic cleavages but are in different groupings on others (Rae and Taylor, 1970: 92). In operational terms, the amount of cross-cutting is usually computed either between a single pair of dimensions of affiliation (for example, religion versus race) or, where there are more than two salient cleavages, between each pair of dimensions considered separately. Because of the multitude of different formal links and organizational affiliations to be considered here, such pairwise computations would be far too lengthy and unwieldy. So a simplified procedure will be employed: instead of measuring cross-pressures with reference to pairs of specific links or affiliations, they will be considered a function of the differences among national patterns of allegiance and affiliation on each of the three *classes* of internation links examined in this study. In other words, for our purposes a cross-pressured nation is one whose formal military alignments bond it tightly to a different group of nations than those closely affiliated with it via diplomatic ties or common membership in IGOs.

Thus, when we speak of cross-cutting here it will be in a somewhat limited sense; we have in mind the degree to which the diplomatic and IGO bonds among nations generate patterns of formal allegiance different from those imposed by military alliance ties. Expressed in terms of the SSA configurations, cross-cutting will be said to occur when the geometric structures representing the patterns of diplomatic and IGO links among the nations in the system for a given year are not congruent with the corresponding structure representing the patterns of military alignment. To measure the precise degree of congruence between any pair of configurations, canonical regression analysis is employed. The set of Euclidean coordinates corresponding to each nation's position in a given SSA alliance configuration are regressed against the set of national coordinates derived from the diplomatic and IGO configurations for the same year. A high canonical R^2 between two sets of national coordinates implies a substantial degree of congruence and thus relatively little cross-cutting; conversely, a low canonical R^2 implies little congruence between the two configurations and consequently substantial cross-cutting. Continuing this procedure for all observations, we obtain (1) thirty quinquennial index values of the degree of cross-cutting between patterns of military alignment and those based on formal diplomatic ties, and (2) twenty index values of cross-cutting between military alignments and linkages based on shared IGO memberships. Note that since (a) these are negative indices of cross-cutting (i.e., the greater the index value, the less cross-cutting), and (b) we have posited a negative relationship between cross-cutting and war, the predicted direction of the correlation and regression coefficients will be positive.

Bivariate Relationships Among the Indices

What are the relationships among these measures of alliance polarization, cross-cutting, and the amount of war begun in the international system? Table 1 displays the product-moment correlations between the two indices of the first independent variable—alliance polarization— and the magnitude and severity of war begun in the subsequent annual (or quinquennial) period.[6] It is obvious that the correlations based on the

6. The perceptive reader may ask if the different measurement intervals used by the two indices may not account for many of the differences observed between them. In every case, the values for the unweighted index were reanalyzed on a quinquennial basis for comparison, and no significant differences were uncovered.

TABLE 1

BIVARIATE CORRELATIONS ALLIANCE POLARIZATION AND WAR BEGUN IN THE SYSTEM

Period/ War Index	Nation-months: Interstate War	Battle Deaths: Interstate War	Nation-months: International War	Battle Deaths: International War
Unweighted				
1815-1964	.13	.12	.15	.12
1815-1944	.14	.12	.16	.12
1815-1919	.15	.15	.18	.15
1850-1964	.17	.15	.21	.15
Weighted				
1815-1964	−.30	−.41	−.21	−.41
1815-1944	−.34	−.41	−.25	−.41
1815-1919	−.15	−.28	.00	−.27
1850-1964	−.35	−.46	−.26	−.45

unweighted index are negligible; whether we examine the 150-year period as a whole, or look at segments of this era, and regardless of the index of war used, no important relationship is observed. Looking at the weighted polarization scores, we see some improvement; there appears to be a noticeable negative relationship between this index and war. However, only three of the sixteen correlations are significant at the .05 level or better, and the percentage of variance explained never rises above twenty. Consequently, on the basis of these findings we can hardly claim this index shows a marked improvement on those used in other studies.

When we turn to Table 2 and examine the relationship between cross-cutting and war begun, disappointment is compounded by puzzlement. As with polarization the correlations are rather low: using the index

TABLE 2

BIVARIATE CORRELATIONS BETWEEN CROSS-CUTTING AND WAR BEGUN IN THE SYSTEM

Period/ War Index	Nation-months: Interstate War	Battle Deaths: Interstate War	Nation-months: International War	Battle Deaths: International War
Alliance-Diplomatic				
1815-1964	−.31	−.39	−.27	−.39
1815-1944	−.36	−.39	−.32	−.39
1815-1919	−.06	−.10	−.02	−.10
1850-1964	−.38	−.43	−.33	−.44
Alliance-IGO				
1865-1964	−.21	−.17	−.16	−.16

measuring alliance-diplomatic cross-cutting, only six of sixteen have less than a .05 probability of occurring by chance, and none of the correlations based on the alliance-IGO index are significant at this level. The results for the earliest (1815-1919) period are particularly poor, as the correlations for that time span are virtually zero. More important, the direction of relationship is opposite from that predicted; as they stand, these findings suggest that the greater the amount of cross-cutting between different types of internation bonds in the system, the greater the amount of lethal conflict that is likely to arise.

Must we conclude, then, that there is indeed no strong relationship between our independent variables and war, and that such as does exist runs counter to the dominant theoretical expectations? Or is it merely that there are flaws somewhere in the complex measurement processes outlined above? Before accepting either of these unpalatable explanations, it would be well to examine empirically other ways of accounting for the observed findings. Two of these suggest themselves immediately.

Multivariate Analysis

The first avenue to be explored is suggested by the strong conceptual links between polarization and cross-cutting. On the one hand, it is not too difficult to surmise a negative empirical relationship between the two variables (Deutsch and Singer, 1964); if the system's alliance structure is strongly polarized, it is more than likely that the opportunities for the construction of cross-cutting ties will be lessened, whereas if alliance polarization is low, such opportunities may well be increased. Thus, the observed positive relationship between cross-cutting and war may be a mere artifact of a strong negative relationship between polarization and these two variables. On the other hand, it is just as easy to hypothesize a strong interaction effect between our two independent variables. It may be that no amount of polarization will have much impact on the amount of war as long as there is sufficient cross-cutting or vice versa. If this were the case, the bivariate relationships between independent and dependent variables would yield misleadingly low results; only by examining the *combined* effect of polarization and cross-cutting would their true importance be apparent.

To test these possibilities, the weighted polarization index was entered into a multiple regression equation with the alliance-diplomatic index of

TABLE 3
WEIGHTED ALLIANCE POLARIZATION AND ALLIANCE-DIPLOMATIC
CROSS-CUTTING VERSUS WAR BEGUN IN THE SYSTEM

Period/ War Index	Nation-months: Beta-Weights for:			Battle Deaths: Beta-Weights for:		
	Polari-zation	Cross-Cut	R^2	Polari-zation	Cross-Cut	R^2
Interstate War						
1815-1964	−.22	−.24	.14	−.33	−.30	.24
1815-1944	−.26	−.28	.19	−.33	−.31	.25
1815-1919	−.14	−.01	.02	−.26	−.00	.08
1850-1964	−.26	−.30	.20	−.37	−.34	.30
International War						
1815-1964	−.14	−.22	.09	−.32	−.30	.24
1815-1944	−.17	−.26	.13	−.33	−.31	.25
1815-1919	.01	−.03	.00	−.26	−.01	.07
1850-1964	−.17	−.27	.14	−.37	−.34	.30

cross-cutting.[7] The regression beta-weights and R^2 values so produced are displayed in Table 3.

The results give little evidence of spurious relationships and virtually none at all of interaction effects. In almost every case, the beta-weights for both independent variables have the same sign as and are only very slightly lower than the zero-order correlations. Only in two rather minor ways do the multivariate findings give us additional information. First, they highlight the differences among time periods and war indices; the joint impact of polarization and cross-cutting appears to be greater on the magnitude than on the severity of war, and far greater in the twentieth and later part of the nineteenth centuries than in the pre-Versailles era. Second, these findings enable us to account for a considerably higher percentage of the variance in the amount of war, as much as 30% in some cases. Nevertheless, they merely compound the main puzzles of the bivariate findings—the low magnitude and unexpected direction of the relationships. To shed light on these, further refinement of the analysis will be necessary.

7. From here on in, only the weighted polarization index and the alliance-diplomatic cross-cutting index are used. These measures yield results which are in the same direction but of greater magnitude than those omitted.

Curvilinear Relationships

As mentioned at the outset, one school of thought holds that the relationship between polarization and conflict is curvilinear, and if this is true, then the strictly linear equations generated thus far will significantly underestimate the magnitude of the relationship. The next avenue to explore, then, is a possible curvilinear relationship, and this may be done by polynomial regression. Higher powers of the weighted polarization index were entered into the equations generated above by a stepwise regression procedure. Table 4 displays the beta-weights for those powers which were statistically significant when entered into the equation, along with the percentage of variance in the amount of war they jointly explain. A number of important results emerge.

First, the curvilinear fit in all cases represents a major improvement; for the 150-year period as a whole, the R^2 ranges as high as a striking .77, and in fact falls below .58 only for the pre-Versailles period. Proportional improvements over the linear fit occur in all of the shorter time periods as well, with the R^2 reaching .78 on two occasions. Thus, Rosecrance (1966) would appear to be correct about the curvilinear nature of the relationship.

Second, the signs of the betas seem to conform roughly with Rosecrance's hypothesis about the shape of the curve as well. In almost all cases, the form of the equation is

$$Y = a - b_1 x + b_2 x^2 - b_3 x^3 + b_4 x^4 + e$$

where $b_1 \geqslant b_2 \geqslant b_3 \geqslant b_4$. This suggests that war is more probable both at very low and at very high levels of polarization, while the chances of war are minimized by a moderately polarized alliance configuration. Thus, the finding of a negative linear relationship turns out to have been rather misleading. A negative slope does indeed characterize the relationship at lower levels of polarization, but once a critical threshold has been passed, polarization exerts very strong positive effects; as predicted by Deutsch and Singer (1964), a very highly polarized system is exceptionally war prone.

Third, polarization clearly plays a much more critical role in the later part of the post-Vienna era than in its earliest days. This variable consistently explains three to five times as much variance from 1850 to 1964 as from 1815 to 1919. This finding accords reasonably well with our intuitive expectations; most would agree that the international system in

TABLE 4
WEIGHTED POLARIZATION INDEX VERSUS WAR BEGUN IN THE SYSTEM

Period/ War Index	Power of Polarization	Nation-months: Interstate War		Battle Deaths: Interstate War		Nation-months: International War		Battle Deaths: International War	
		beta	R^2	beta	R^2	beta	R^2	beta	R^2
1815-1964	x	-.61	.61	-.78	.77	-.59	.58	-.78	.77
	x^2	.51		.70		.48		.70	
	x^3	-.41		-.63		-.38		-.63	
	x^4	.34		.57		.31		.57	
1815-1944	x	-.68	.70	-.78	.78	-.67	.70	-.78	.78
	x^2	.58		.69		.56		.70	
	x^3	-.48		-.62		-.47		-.62	
	x^4	.41		.56		.40		.56	
1815-1919	x	-.38	.15	-.34	.16	-.44	.20	-.35	.16
	x^2	.36		.30		.44		.31	
1850-1964	x	-.61	.60	-.77	.77	-.59	.58	-.77	.77
	x^2	.50		.69		.47		.69	
	x^3	-.39		-.61		-.36		-.61	
	x^4	.31		.54		.29		.54	

the twentieth century exhibits far less stability than in the nineteenth on a whole variety of dimensions (Singer et al., 1972) and is thus far more vulnerable to disturbing influences such as a high degree of alliance polarization.

The striking success of polynomial regression applied to the polarization-war relationship suggests that it might clarify the connection between cross-cutting and war as well. A plausible theoretical argument suggesting a curvilinear relationship can be adduced here, as well: it might be that heavily cross-cut international systems generate confusion and uncertainty in the minds of national decision makers about the identity of their respective allies and adversaries. Conceivably, such confusion could lead to less predictable (and consequently more lethal) crisis and conflict behavior. At the same time, systems with little or no criss-cross would lack the stabilizing influence of the countervailing links discussed earlier, and therefore the ideal state of affairs would be a moderate amount of cross-cutting. Turning to Table 5, we see this speculative argument partially confirmed. Apparently, a greater amount of war is associated both with very low and very high levels of cross-cutting, and relatively less war with moderate criss-cross. However, the relationship is by no means as powerful and unambiguous as with polarization; no significant curvilinear relationship exists for the 1815-1919 period, and even for the later periods the R^2 values never exceed a low .26. Furthermore, the indices of cross-cutting do not make a significant contribution to the polarization equation, regardless of the power to which they are raised; their high correlation with the polynomial terms of polarization merely generates a pathological degree of multicollinearity when they are included. Thus, while polynomial regression clarifies the puzzling direction of the linear relationship, it offers no evidence that cross-cutting is an important explanatory variable distinct from polarization.

Some Caveats

Before discussing the implications of these findings, it would be wise to stress their tentative nature. Despite the impressive magnitude of many of the R^2 coefficients, the pitfalls are many and deep. Five of these are worthy of particular note.

To begin with, the raw data used in this study reflect only the more formal and institutional linkages among nations. This author would argue along with others (Singer and Small, 1966b) that the pattern of formal relationships usually reflects, and is often virtually congruent with, the structure of informal links; but nevertheless it would be difficult to make

TABLE 5
POWERS OF THE ALLIANCE-DIPLOMATIC CROSS-CUTTING INDEX VERSUS WAR BEGUN IN THE SYSTEM

Period/ War Index	Power of Polarization	Nation-months: Interstate War		Battle Deaths: Interstate War		Nation-months: International War		Battle Deaths: International War	
		beta	R^2	beta	R^2	beta	R^2	beta	R^2
1815-1964	x	-.29	.15	-.41	.26	-.25	.11	-.41	.26
	x^2	.24		.36		.21		.36	
1815-1944	x	-.35	.21	-.41	.26	-.31	.16	-.41	.26
	x^2	.30		.36		.26		.36	
1850-1964	x	-.23	.17	-.37	.26	-.19	.13	-.37	.26
	x^2	.17		.30		.14		.30	

any definitive claims for the findings reported here unless they can be replicated using a broader data base.

Second, the complexity of the process used to measure the independent variables suggests that considerable caution be used in interpreting the results. At the crucial stages in this process—the calculation of a dyadic proximity coefficient, the derivation of a geometric configuration from the matrix, and the measurement of polarization and cross-cutting from the configurations—risky theoretical assumptions have been made. Only if and when these results are reproduced using alternative operational procedures rooted in different measurement hypotheses can they be considered more than tentative. Until that time, great caution should be employed in interpreting the findings.

Third, it is important to recall that the findings reported here apply only to relationships at the level of the system as a whole; one cannot, for example, make inferences from a nation's location in the alliance configuration to the magnitude of its war experience. To make such statements, studies must be undertaken which adduce data on national alliance position and war participation.

Fourth, as with all empirical studies employing only a few independent variables, the findings may be an artifact of the influence of some exogenous variable. As a consequence, these results only suggest—but do not prove—the existence of a strong causal relationship between alliance polarization and war, or the lack of such a relationship between war and the existence of cross-cutting internation bonds. Only further tests which incorporate alliance polarization into a more sophisticated multivariate model can give a definitive answer on this score (Wallace, 1972b).

Finally, this study does not touch upon the origins of alliance polarizations and cross-cutting; until we understand why configurations of formal bonds form and dissolve as they do, we have not discovered a true cause of war, but only one intermediate process leading to it. Once again, what is needed is a multivariate model incorporating the causal sequence of variables whose action eventuates in war.

Interpreting the Results

While important, these caveats should not be allowed to inhibit us from examining the theoretical and practical implications of the findings. This author has argued at length (Wallace, 1973; 1972a) that the paucity of hard evidence about the behavior of the international system, combined with the urgent need for policy-relevant research, gives new meaning to the traditional canons of scientific caution as they apply to our field. It is still important, of course, that tentative results be labelled as such and that we do not claim more than has been demonstrated. But we must exercise equal caution to ensure that no piece of information goes unnoticed. Given the strength, consistency, and direction of the present findings, there is every reason to believe that careful interpretation will produce much of value.

To begin with, the findings clearly vindicate those who have asserted the continuing importance of alliance patterns as an explanatory variable in the international system. Not only have these patterns been closely linked to interstate war over the century and a half from Vienna to Vietnam, but it would appear that their impact has actually been growing steadily. This influence is all the more significant in that it seems to be direct and immediate; unlike certain other factors which are apparently linked to war (Wallace, 1971), there was no need to introduce a long time-lag in order to maximize the statistical effect. In short, it would seem that alliance patterns represent a crucial avenue for exploration in the search for the causes of war.

But if the role of alliances is important, it is also complex. Even this exploratory paper clearly demonstrates that simple indices, bivariate statistics, and linear regression are completely inadequate to deal with the relationships between our independent variables and war. On the one hand, this would indicate that much more research must be done; given the complications unearthed in this one paper, it is likely that a great deal more remains to be discovered. Yet this routine request for further investigation must be tempered with a plea for sophistication. Only carefully designed mathematical procedures, based on sound theoretical reasoning, are likely to prevail in this area.

These findings have two important practical implications. The first concerns the dismantling of tight Cold War alliance groupings which has proceeded apace for almost a decade. If the results are to be believed, it is this change which has been most closely associated with the more temperate relations now existing between superpowers. Yet the decline of the polarization index from its post-World-War-II high in 1954 to its present (1970) value has scarcely been precipitous; it remains at a level which would lead us to "predict" a great deal of violent conflict in the next half decade. Thus, the evidence would suggest that additional "depolarization" would markedly reduce the likelihood of war. For the great powers, this implies that they should strive for accommodation, not on the basis of exclusive control over (and thus, tight alignment bonds with) particular areas of the globe, but rather by permitting and encouraging military guarantees which cross bloc lines. For smaller powers, it suggests that world peace can be better served by maintaining alignment flexibility than by becoming exclusively bound to one alliance grouping. Of course, given the curvilinear nature of the relationship between alliance polarization and war, this process ought not to be allowed to proceed to extremes or the likelihood of war will again rise; perhaps future research can determine the optimal configuration. Nevertheless, it is clear that the ideal level of internation alignment would be much more closely approximated by dismantling or redirecting many existing military pacts.

The second policy implication has to do with the prolonged and patient attempts made by many smaller and middle-rank nations to build diplomatic and organizational bridges across bloc cleavages. The findings presented above suggest that such attempts are, by themselves, unlikely to succeed; such cross-cutting links apparently do not appreciably reduce the likelihood of war unless the military ties themselves are dismantled or rearranged.

Taken together, then, these findings seem to contradict those who argue for the present web of regional and global military security treaties as the best method of maintaining world peace. It would appear, on the contrary, that not only is the present alliance structure likely to increase the probability of violent conflict in the system, but that its war-producing effects are scarcely mitigated by other, more pacific internation links. This is particularly significant in that the structure of Cold War military alliances has come to be accepted as a virtually unalterable fact of life even amongst those who advocate major changes in the foreign and military policies of the superpowers. If the results reported here are correct, we cannot afford such resignation; ways and means of dismantling this structure must be found. Hopefully, the growing spirit of change which pervades the foreign policy process in many countries of both blocs can be harnessed to provide the intellectual and political resources for this vital task.

Michael D. Wallace (Ph.D. University of Michigan, 1970) is Associate Professor of Political Science at the University of British Columbia, and has held several visiting appointments at the University of Michigan. He is the author of War and Rank Among Nations *(1973), and coeditor of* To Augur Well *(1979), and has written many articles on arms races and the causes of war.*

Systemic Polarization and the Occurrence and Duration of War

BRUCE BUENO de MESQUITA   *Chapter 5*

The literature concerned with the relationship between polarity and war generally focuses on decision maker responses to uncertainty. That literature assumes, implicitly, that foreign-policy decision makers are generally risk-acceptant or risk-avoidant under uncertainty. I suggest several alternative formulations, based on the assumptions that (a) uncertainty is promoted by change in the structure of the international system, rather than by the actual structure itself; and (b) risk-taking orientations are normally distributed among decision makers. Using data on the occurrence and duration of war during the past century and a half, and defining polarity as consisting of three attributes—the number of poles, and their tightness and discreteness—I find no support for the hypotheses found in the literature. Considerable support, however, emerges for the hypotheses derived from the assumptions proposed here. Most significantly, the occurrence and duration of wars during the twentieth century are found to be closely linked to increases in systemic tightness.

In searching for conditions that alter the likelihood of war, one might begin by focusing on (a) decision-making; (b) national attributes; (c) relations among nations; or on (d) structural attributes of the international system. It is likely that factors at each of these levels of analysis affect the likelihood of war. But, in making a first attempt to identify conditions necessary for war, I believe it will be most fruitful to begin with the structure of the international system, not because system-level factors offer the best explanation of war—they probably do not—but because, as background factors, system-level attributes play a crucial role in establishing the constraints imposed on decision makers.

AUTHOR'S NOTE: I would like to thank Michael Altfeld, Charles Gochman, Chung Hsiou Huang, Bruce Jacobs, Peter Lemieux, Walter Petersen, and J. David Singer for helpful comments on earlier versions of this manuscript. This paper was originally prepared for delivery at the 1974 meeting of the International Studies Association.

Originally published in the *Journal of Conflict Resolution,* Vol. 22, No. 2, June 1978.

The literature linking systemic attributes to war is, with few exceptions, both contradictory and largely speculative, rather than empirical. One area in which a fair amount of theoretical and empirical research has been carried out, however, concerns the relationship between systemic polarity and the likelihood of war. It is to that topic that this study is addressed.

THEORIES ON POLARITY
AND THE PROBABILITY OF WAR

Two aspects of polarity that are widely believed to affect the probability, and possibly the duration, of war are (a) the number of poles, blocs, or clusters of nations in the system; and (b) the bonds linking nations to one another, both within and across poles. Studies concerned with the number of poles focus on the bipolarity or multipolarity of the international system, while studies concerned with the bonds among nations focus on the tightness or looseness and discreteness or interactiveness of the system's poles.

The literature concerning each of these attributes is filled with contradictory hypotheses that often stem, in turn, from alternative assumptions about decision-making in the international arena. Yet, there is also a core of important assumptions that are largely accepted by theorists concerned with polarity and war. Rather than replicate the various arguments made in the literature—often without sufficient care to make assumptions explicit—I will provide a set of hypotheses derived from explicit assumptions that lead to the major empirical implications found in the literature on polarity. In addition, by varying some of the assumptions I will suggest alternative hypotheses about the relationship between systemic polarity and both the occurrence and duration of war.

Several assumptions, whether explicit or implicit, appear to be held in common by researchers concerned with polarity and war. First it is generally agreed that when nations join military alliances, or in some other way link their foreign policies to those of other nations, they restrict their decision-making options. For instance, members of an alliance may restrict their options by committing themselves to the active defense of their allies; or to remaining neutral during a particular conflict; or to consulting with their allies before deciding on a course of action. While, of course, nations do not always honor their formalized commitments, they do so often enough that most such commitments are taken seriously by decision makers. This assumption of reduced autonomy is essential to the pursuit of any investigation of polarity since the significance of a bloc of nations rests in the presumed unity of action by its members, at least in the face of some specified contingency. In fact, the assumption of unified action is essential for defining the number of autonomous actors in the international system as being equal to the number of blocs in that system.

Second, it is generally agreed that the level of decision maker uncertainty about the consequences of particular actions in the international arena increases as the number of autonomous actors—or poles—increases (Waltz, 1964; Deutsch and Singer, 1964). The reasoning underlying this assumption is, in fact, quite straightforward. As the number of autonomous actors increases, the potential sources of important information also increases, probably at a faster rate than the expansion in decision maker ability to analyze and interpret that information. Consequently, in any given short period of time decision makers know the content of a smaller percentage of the information circulating in the system than they would have known if there were fewer sources of information; hence, the increase in their uncertainty.

TWO VIEWS OF THE RELATIONSHIP BETWEEN THE NUMBER OF POLES AND WAR

Given the assumption that multipolar systems contain more uncertainty than bipolar systems, what implications are we to draw about the expected likelihood of war occurring somewhere in the international system? It is in response to this question that one finds sharp differences among students of polarity and war. Waltz (1964), for instance, concludes that uncertainty increases the probability that some decision maker will misjudge the intentions of some potential foe, or will miscalculate the consequences of his own nation's decisions. For Waltz, then, high levels of uncertainty—such as are assumed to be prevalent when the system is multipolar—increase the likelihood of war, while the low level of uncertainty accompanying bipolarity decreases the probability of war. But why should uncertainty encourage miscalculated behavior that is likely to produce a war? It should not unless one makes the additional assumption that decision makers are willing to take the risk of departing from their current pattern of actions, and undertake decisions with unknown or very uncertain consequences. That is, one must assume that decision makers under uncertainty are risk-acceptant in order to provide a logical basis for concluding that uncertainty increases the likelihood of war.

The proposition that bipolarity tends to be more conducive to peace than does multipolarity seems quite plausible. Yet, Deutsch and Singer (1964) explicitly reject this hypothesis in formulating their own, alternative argument. They agree that multipolar structures produce more uncertainty than do bipolar structures, but they conclude that increased levels of uncertainty reduce the probability of war. This conclusion may be reached by supposing that uncertainty encourages decision makers to behave cautiously, avoiding decisions that represent significant departures from the "tried and true" path they have followed in the past. If their previous decisions did not place them on a collision course with another nation, then it is very unlikely that their cautious behavior will place them on such a course. Consequently, the likelihood of war is very low. Of course, in order to make the supposition that uncertainty encourages caution it is necessary to assume that decision-making under uncertainty is largely risk-avoidant. Thus, Deutsch and Singer's hypothesis contradicts Waltz's hypothesis because they implicitly assume an opposite risk-taking propensity on the part of foreign policy decision makers.

ALTERNATIVE VIEWS OF THE NUMBER OF POLES AND THE LIKELIHOOD OF WAR

Both the argument that bipolarity tends to lead to peace and the argument that multipolarity tends to lead to peace seem plausible. Yet they obviously can not both be true. They can, however, both be false. If either of the critical assumptions of these two models—that is, (a) multipolarity increases uncertainty and (b) there is a uniform risk-taking orientation under uncertainty among foreign policy decision makers—is inconsistent with reality, then there is no reason to expect empirical support for the hypotheses deduced from these assumptions.

I contend that the uncertainty assumption is inconsistent with reality. Change, for instance, may be an important element contributing to uncertainty that is overlooked by the static view of polarity subscribed to in the literature. A more dynamic, change-oriented view of uncertainty produces very different empirical implications.

Let us assume that uncertainty results from an inability to anticipate the likely consequences of one's actions and that decison makers are capable of learning to discern patterns of action and reaction from their own and others' behavior. Then, so long as the system's structure does not change significantly, learned patterns from prior behavior will aid decision makers to anticipate the likely consequences of similar behaviors under similar circumstances. That is, if the system's structure—be it bipolar or multipolar—does not change, there will be little uncertainty. Conversely, if the system undergoes substantial changes, then decision makers probably experience considerable uncertainty. An important empirical implication of this dynamic uncertainty assumption is that neither bipolarity   nor multipolarity, with the attendant focus on the static structure of the system, satisfies an uncertainty condition that is related to the probability of war. Hence, if decision maker uncertainty primarily responds to shifts in the system's structure, rather than to the actual structure itself, then there should be no association between the number of poles in the system and the likelihood of war. On the other hand, if uncertainty is produced by change, and if the assumption of homogeneous risk-taking predispositions is maintained, then large changes in the number of poles in the system will either increase or decrease the probability of war, depending on whether one subscribes to a risk-acceptant or risk-avoidant view of decision-making.

Research on risk-taking suggests that the assumption that risk-taking orientations under uncertainty are homogeneous is almost certainly false (Pollatsek and Tversky, 1970; Fiorina, 1975; Bueno de Mesquita, 1975b). Therefore, I reject that assumption, preferring instead to assume that risk-taking is normally distributed, with the mode located at or near the risk-neutral position at any given time. Under this assumption, most decision makers would generally behave in a risk-neutral way, while some would be risk-acceptant and others risk-avoidant. Risk-neutral decision makers would be neither more cautious, nor more reckless under uncertainty than under other conditions. Hence, they would be neither more nor less likely to wage war as a result of an increase in the system's level of uncertainty. Risk-avoidant decision makers, as we have seen, would be more cautious, while risk-acceptant decision makers would be more prone to miscalculations, misperceptions, and possibly reckless actions under conditions of uncertainty. Given the assumption that risk-taking is normally distributed, and the empirical observation that serious international disputes likely to erupt into war are fairly uncommon, we may infer the following empirical expectation. The number of states that are both involved in serious disputes and have risk-acceptant foreign policy decision makers is small. Similarly, the number of states that are both involved in serious international disputes and have risk-avoidant decision makers is small. Because of this, the level of systemic uncertainty, by itself, neither increases nor decreases the likelihood of war. Consequently, neither the number of blocs, nor the magnitude of change in the number of blocs in the system is expected to be associated with the likelihood of war.

One final alternative view of uncertainty should be considered. The notion that uncertainty is closely linked to changes in the system's structure may be correct, but it may not be the case that the linkage depends solely on the magnitude of such changes. Instead, I assume that some changes increase uncertainty, while other changes decrease uncertainty. In the context of the present discussion, one would want to know whether an increase or decrease in the number of blocs of nations systematically affects the level of uncertainty experienced by decision makers. One might argue that as the number of blocs increases, while the total number of aligned states remains the same, the objectives of each bloc become more clearly defined. If this is so, then the increased specificity of objectives in each bloc is likely to reduce uncertainty about the expected behavior of the bloc members under certain contingencies. In this sense, an increase in the number of blocs reduces uncertainty. On the other hand, while the specificity of objectives may increase with an increase in the number of blocs, decision maker awareness of the objectives of each bloc may decrease. In this sense, an increase in the number of blocs increases uncertainty. In light of the observation that uncertainty might rise or fall for some decision makers as the number of blocs increases (or decreases), it seems unlikely that the direction of change in the number of blocs is consistently linked to uncertainty or to the likelihood of war. Consequently, we should not expect a relationship between the direction and magnitude of change in the number of blocs and the likelihood of war in the international system.

SUMMARY OF HYPOTHESES CONCERNED WITH
THE NUMBER OF POLES

(1) Bipolar systems are more likely to experience war than multipolar systems (Deutsch and Singer, 1964).

(2) Bipolar systems are less likely to experience war than multipolar systems (Waltz, 1964).

(3) The number of poles in the system is unrelated to the probability of war in the international system.

(4) The magnitude of change in the number of poles is unrelated to the probability of war in the international system.

(5) The magnitude and direction of change in the number of poles is unrelated to the probability of war in the international system.

INTRA- AND INTERBLOC RELATIONS AND WAR

Closely associated with the polarity of the international system is the degree to which nations within the same bloc share similar foreign policy objectives and the degree to which nations in different blocs have dissimilar foreign policy objectives. When nations in different blocs share some common objectives, one might assume that they will develop commitments between them that help draw their respective blocs closer together, thereby reducing uncertainty about each other's goals and objectives. This is, in very simplified terms, the argument underlying detente. From the perspective of detente, the reduction in uncertainty is expected to reduce the probability of war in the system. As we saw in the case of polarity, the opposite conclusion follows if one assumes that decision-making under uncertainty is generally risk-acceptant. And, following my assumption, if risk-taking under uncertainty is normally distributed, then there should be no relationship between the level of interaction—or discreteness—between blocs and the likelihood of war.

As with polarity, the magnitude of change in the discreteness of bloc boundaries may result in an increase in uncertainty, but such an increase can not be linked to the likelihood of war without assuming a homogeneous risk-taking orientation among decision makers. Given that such homogeneity is very unlikely, I hypothesize that discreteness—or detente, if you like—is unrelated to the probability of war in the system.

Finally, as with polarity, the direction of change in the discreteness of the system's blocs is probably not systematically related to changes in the level of systemic uncertainty. As blocs become more discrete, there is, by definition, a decrease in overlapping interests between blocs. This might readily be viewed as contributing to an increase in the amount of uncertainty in the system. However, as blocs become less discrete—as results when the number of overlapping interests between members of different blocs increases—it becomes increasingly difficult for decision makers to discern the boundaries separating one bloc from another. This may lead to uncertainty about the priority of commitments for members of interlinked blocs, thus contributing to an increase in decision maker uncertainty. We expect, therefore, that the direction of change in the discreteness of blocs, like the magnitude of that change, is unrelated to the likelihood of war.

As with the number of poles and the degree of interbloc interactions, there are several hypotheses that relate the level of intrabloc commitments—or tightness—to the probability of war. The most commonly held position may be characterized as follows. When all the members of a bloc are substantially committed to each other, it is difficult for any one member to venture on an independent foreign policy course that involves commitments to nations outside the bloc. From this assumption follows the observation that the more tight-knit the commitments within a bloc, the lower the probability that friendly inter-bloc relations will develop. Hence, the more tightknit the system's blocs are, the less likely that hostile sentiments between blocs will be mitigated by friendly interactions between individual members of different blocs. Consequently, the higher the level of tightness of commitments within blocs, the higher the probability of war (Kaplan, 1957).

The conclusion that tightness increases the likelihood of war is closely related, though not explicitly, to the uncertainty—risk-taking relationship discussed above. Tight blocs contain relatively unambiguous commitments between their members and, consequently, alleviate uncertainty about contingent behavior. Loose blocs, conversely, possess a high level of uncertainty. If risk-taking under uncertainty is uniformly distributed, then tightness may, as Kaplan suggests, increase the likelihood of war, or it may produce cautious behavior that decreases the probability of war. But, if as I assume, risk-taking is normally distributed, with the mode at or near the risk-neutral position, tightness should be unrelated to the probability of war. Similarly, changes in systemic tightness, when the direction of those changes is ignored, are likely to be unrelated to the probability of war. Tightness differs from the number of poles and from discreteness, however, when the magnitude *and* direction of change is considered.

TIGHTNESS, WAR, AND
EXPECTED UTILITY CALCULATIONS

As the tightness of poles increases, the nature of commitments among bloc partners becomes clearer so that, in the limit, one can be virtually certain of the support of allies fully committed to one another. As the system becomes looser, reflecting a decline in the nature of commitments between members of the same bloc, one becomes increasingly certain that one's "allies" will *not* be supportive in the face of some specified contingency. What implications does this difference between increasing and decreasing systemic tightness have for the likelihood of war?

In order to respond to the question just posed, additional assumptions about decision-making must be made explicit. First, I assume decision makers calculate their expected utility from such options as initiating wars. This assumption simply states that decision makers do not initiate wars without calculating the expected benefits and costs of such wars. Second, I assume that decision makers are utility maximizers, by which I mean that they do not initiate wars unless the expected benefits of the war exceed the expected costs of the war and of not initiating the war. This is, of course, the familiar rationality assumption found in social choice theory (Riker and Ordeshook, 1972). Finally, I assume that risk-taking is normally distributed and generally centered around risk-neutrality.

Let us posit some nation i whose decision makers are contemplating a war against some other nation j, with i's estimate of its expected net gain from such a war being P_{ij}. Because of the rationality assumption, i will not wage a war unless the expected net benefit from such a war is greater than or equal to some minimally required payoff, which I designate M_i. That is, if $P_{ij} < M_i$ war will not be waged. The problem is, of course that P_{ij} is not a known quantity. Therefore, the decision to wage war depends, in part, on what the relevant decision makers believe P_{ij} equals, or rather on whether they believe it is greater than or equal to M_i. Consequently, the relevant factor for consideration by decison makers is $p(P_{ij} \geq M_i)$—i.e., the probability that $P_{ij} \geq M_i$. It should be clear that, because of the assumption of normally distributed risk-taking propensities, as $p(P_{ij} \geq M_i) \rightarrow 0$, fewer and fewer decision makers would be willing to accept the risk that the true value of P_{ij} is less than M_i, and therefore, the probability of a decision maker finding his nation engaged in a serious dispute capable of escalating into a war, and having a sufficiently risk-acceptant outlook to consider war as a viable option also approaches zero.

Now, as commitments within the poles of the system become looser, fewer nations in alliances can count on their allies support, and consequently the only resources available to them for a war effort are their own resources. As the set of available resources declines, all other things being equal, $p(P_{ij} \geqslant M_i)$ also declines. Thus, when the tightness of the system is declining, indicating a reduction in commitments among allies, the a priori probability of a war beginning declines rapidly, with only risk-acceptant decision makers still being in a position to rationally contemplate war as a strategy.

As the system's tightness increases, then for decision makers in some nations, the increased clarity of commitments by their allies means an increase in their confidence that their allies resources are available to them in the event of a war. For others, the increase in tightness results from the withdrawal of weakly committed members of their pole, leaving the average level of commitment within the pole higher than it had been before. Thus, increasing tightness may be produced by the upgrading of commitments among allies, by the addition of new, but highly committed allies, or by the withdrawal of marginally committed allies. In the latter instance, the loss of a marginal ally means some loss of support, albeit probably marginally counted on support to begin with. Such a loss of support must, naturally, leave the estimate of P_{ij} reduced. Conversely, increased tightness produced by the upgrading of already existent ties, or by the addition of new, highly committed allies, increases the estimated value of P_{ij}. Thus, it is possible for $p(P_{ij} \geqslant M_i)$ to increase, decrease, or remain the same when the system's tightness increases. As the probability increases, the acceptable level of risk is surpassed for more and more decision makers, thereby increasing the likelihood of war. In this sense, increasing tightness is radically different from decreasing tightness, in that at least *some of the time* increasing tightness increases the likelihood of war, while decreasing tightness can only mean a decrease in the likelihood of war. Yet, it should be borne in mind that an increase in tightness does not mean that war is inevitable. After all, an increase in tightness may, as noted, lead to a decline in the probability that the war would yield adequate benefits. Furthermore, regardless of the level of tightness, it may be that decision makers estimate that $P_{ij} < M_i$, in which case they would not wage war.

In other words, increases in commitments within the system sometimes lead to war and sometimes do not, while decreases in commitments are expected almost always to produce a very low probability of war (or high probability of peace). In correlational terms this means that a modest positive relationship is expected between increases in systemic tightness and the probability of war.

SUMMARY OF HYPOTHESES LINKING COMMITMENTS TO WAR

(6) A system with a discrete bloc structure is more likely to experience war than one with many interbloc interactions (detente).

(7) The discreteness of the system's blocs is unrelated to the likelihood of war.

(8) Changes in the level of discreteness of the system's blocs is unrelated to the likelihood of war.

(9) Increases or decreases in the level of discreteness of the system's blocs is unrelated to the probability of war.

(10) The tighter commitments within blocs, the higher the probability of war (Kaplan, 1957).

(11) The tightness of blocs is unrelated to the likelihood of war.

(12) Changes in the level of tightness are unrelated to the likelihood of war.

(13) As the system becomes tighter, the probability of war increases.

THEORIES ON POLARITY AND
THE DURATION OF WAR

Many factors influence the duration of war, with systemic factors possibly being important background variables. It is unlikely that the duration of any war is causally linked to such systemic attributes as the number of poles, tightness, or discreteness. On the other hand, if we continue to assume that decision makers are utility calculators, then those systemic variables that affect confidence in utility estimates may be important indicators of the likely duration of contemplated wars. After all, the expected duration of a war significantly influences one's expected costs.

Rather than proceed with a very lengthy, step-by-step presentation of all the factors not expected to be related to the duration of war, let me say briefly that those variables that do not bear a relationship to the likelihood of war—with all that that implies about the information those variables provide for rational decision makers—are not expected to be related to the duration of war. Change in systemic tightness, on the other hand, is expected to bear a close relationship to the duration of ensuing wars. In particular, as decision makers perceive an increase in the likelihood of their nation becoming involved in a war, they undoubtedly attempt to secure access to resources that will increase their chances of emerging victorious. As commitments within the system become clearer, it becomes easier for decision makers to identify the actions they must take to increase their capabilities in the event of war. They may, for instance, mobilize domestic resources for the nation's defense. Additionally, they may seek assurances from their allies that support will be forthcoming in the event of war. Such assurances mean a larger pool of resources are available to a state expecting to be involved in a war. Of course, as a state's pool of resources increases, its ability to sustain its participation in a war also increases.

Since the war initiator was assumed to be an expected utility calculator and a utility maximizer, we should expect that most war initiators have greater capabilities than do their intended targets. Indeed, this has generally been the case at least since the Congress of Vienna (Singer and Small, 1972). An interesting consequence of the initiator's resource advantage at the outset of a war is that few nations can expect a significant payoff from fighting alongside the initiator. After all, their added resources generally cannot significantly alter the expected outcome of the war, giving the initiator little incentive to share the war's benefits with them (Starr, 1972). Without a share of the benefits, third states have little reason to aid the initiator. The initiator's target, on the other hand, often needs the assistance of third states to alter the war's expected outcome in its favor. In order to attract such support, the initiator's target is likely to offer to share any of its benefits from a victory with those states that aid it. Thus, a war initiator's target is likely to take advantage of increases in the clarity of commitments within the system to identify potential supporters for its cause. Such efforts on its part are likely to diminish the difference in capabilities between initiators and their targets when increases in the structural clarity of the system permit the target to identify and attract potential supporters. Of course, as the resource gap closes, one may expect the duration of the ensuing war to increase.

SUMMARY OF WAR-DURATION HYPOTHESES

(14) Neither the number of poles, nor changes in that number, are related to the duration of wars.

(15) Neither discreteness, nor changes in discreteness, are related to the duration of wars.

(16) While tightness is not related to the duration of war, increases in systemic tightness are associated with increases in the duration of ensuing wars.

MEASUREMENT OF THE VARIABLES

OUTCOME VARIABLES

The probability of war is, in principle, a continuous variable, but is treated as a dichotomous variable in this study. Each year between 1816 and 1965—the temporal domain here—in which one or more wars began is coded as having an occurrence of war equal to one, while years in which no war began are coded as zero.

Two types of war occurrence are included in the analyses. The first, referred to as *interstate war* consists of all interstate wars as defined by the Correlates of War project (Singer and Small, 1972). The second, referred to as *major power war,* is coded one for each year during which an interstate war began involving at least one major power, with major power status defined as by Singer and Small (1972). All other years score zero on major power war occurrence.

Keeping the distinction between interstate and major power wars, I employ a separate measure for the duration of each type. For the investigation of the hypotheses related to war duration the unit of analysis is the individual war, with the number of months the war lasted being the measure of its duration. When more than one war began in a single year, and there was no overlap in the wars' participants, each war's duration is counted separately. When one or more nations were combatants in two or more wars that began in the same year, I count each of those wars as one combined war. That is, I avoid double counting so that if, for example, one month is part of the duration of two wars in the set of wars with overlapping participants, then the month contributes only one month to the duration of the combined wars. Thus, while the Russo-Hungarian war and the Sinai War of 1956 are counted separately, the Russo-Finnish, Russo-Japanese, and World War II, each of which began in 1939 and each of which involved the Soviet Union, are counted as if they were all part of one war, with a duration of 75.1 months. All the wars, along with the duration of each, are listed in Singer and Small (1972).

PREDICTOR VARIABLES

The measurement of tightness (hereafter T), discreteness (hereafter D), and poles (hereafter IO) is described at length in Bueno de Mesquita (1975a). Suffice it to say here that these variables are calculated in terms of the similarity in the distribution of alliance commitments for each pair of nations each year. A correlation coefficient—tau b—defines the tightness of each pair of nations, while typal analysis—which produces results similar to factor analysis—is used to identify the bloc membership of each nation, and hence the number of poles in the system.[1] The mean of all within-bloc tau b scores defines systemic tightness, while the mean of all between-bloc tau b's defines the discreteness of the system's blocs. The number of poles is transformed, in accordance with the argument of Deutsch and Singer (1964), to reflect the number of interaction opportunities between blocs. This is done by calculating the number of possible pairs of blocs each year (i.e., if there are N blocs in a given year, then there are $(N^2 - N)/2$ pairs).

T and D effectively range between 0.00 and 1.00.[2] Both indicators are used without a time lag (T_{to} and D_{to}) and with a one-year lag, so that T_{t-1} and D_{t-1} are observed one year prior to the outcome variable. IO is also observed both with and without a lag.

In addition to measuring the tightness, discreteness, and interaction opportunities among poles in the system, the hypotheses require measures of the magnitude and direction of change in each of these indicators. The directional change in T, D, and IO is observed across each five-year period (with each period ending one year before the observation of the

1. Typal analysis yields results that maximize the within-cluster similarity of nations' alliance commitments, while maximizing the between-cluster dissimilarity in alliance commitments. Two other studies that used typal analysis with international relations data are Smoker (1968) and Newcombe et al. (n.d.). A study that demonstrates the substantial similarity between factor analysis and typal analysis is Lankford (1974).

2. Discreteness varies between zero and one for bipolar systems. Multipolar settings necessarily involve some degree of similarity in the bonding network of nations in different clusters. This is so because ideally no nation in one cluster will share any alliance with a member of another cluster. Consequently, members of clusters A and B share the fact of their nonalignment with members of clusters C, D, . . . , N. It should also be recognized that discreteness, being a measure of interbloc bonding, is undefined for years in which the system contained only one pole.

outcome variables). These variables are called ΔT, ΔD, and ΔIO, respectively. These same variables squared (to remove the direction of change) reflect the magnitude of change in the structure of the international system. All the indicators of both the magnitude and direction of change are lagged one year behind the outcome variables in order to assess their utility as early warning indicators of war, as well as to assess their role in influencing the occurrence and duration of war.

RESULTS

Because of the frequent finding that system-level attributes are differently related to war in the nineteenth and twentieth centuries (Singer and Small, 1968, 1972; Singer et al., 1972), the analyses are computed separately for each century. Before testing the hypotheses, the intercorrelations among the independent variables are examined to insure that each variable measures a different aspect of polarity. Tables 1a and 1b contain these intercorrelations. The patterns of intercorrelations in the two centuries are fairly similar, with the autocorrelations being by far the strongest relationships in the tables. None of the other intercorrelations are large enough to suggest a lack of independence among the predictor variables.

NUMBER OF POLES AND THE OCCURRENCE OF WAR

We turn now to the hypotheses concerning the relationship between the number of poles (or interaction opportunities) and the occurrence of war. These hypotheses are tested using estimated correlation coefficients derived from probit analysis (McKelvey and Zavoina, 1971; Zechman, 1974; Aldrich and Cnudde, 1975). The results are reported in Table 2.

The hypotheses derived from the assumption that bipolar systems contain less uncertainty than multipolar systems (Waltz, 1964; Deutsch and Singer, 1964) fail to find support in the evidence. Those hypotheses based on the assumption that changes in the number of poles is of more importance than the actual number itself prove to have no support in the evidence. As expected, the magnitude (but not direction) of change in interaction opportunities is not significantly correlated with the occurrence of war.

The direction of change in interaction opportunities is uncorrelated with the occurrence of all types of war except twentieth century inter-

TABLE 1A
Intercorrelations Among the Predictor Variables for the Nineteenth Century

	T_{t-1}	ΔT	$\Delta TSQR$	D_{t0}	D_{t-1}	ΔD	$\Delta DSQR$	IO_{t0}	IO_{t-1}	ΔIO	$\Delta IOSQR$
T_{t0}	.81[a]	.47[b]	−.28[b]	.39[c]	.39[d]	.02[e]	.18[e]	.28[g]	.22[a]	.03[b]	.18
T_{t-1}		.57[b]	−.30[b]	.35[c]	.38[d]	−.15[e]	.26[e]	.15[a]	.29[a]	.10[b]	.07
ΔT			−.16[b]	.08[c]	.02[d]	−.07[e]	.10[e]	.23[b]	.31[b]	.39[b]	.07
$\Delta TSQR$				.30[c]	.11[d]	.04[e]	−.30[e]	.07[b]	.61[b]	.16[b]	−.05
D_{t0}					.83[h]	.44[f]	−.23[f]	−.42[c]	−.30[c]	−.27[c]	−.01
D_{t-1}						.53[e]	−.30[e]	−.31[e]	−.41[e]	−.35[e]	−.16
ΔD							−.51[e]	.04[e]	.02[e]	−.50[e]	.53
$\Delta DSQR$								−.01[e]	−.05[e]	.05[e]	−.08
IO_{t0}									.73[a]	.43[b]	.59
IO_{t-1}										.66[b]	.61
ΔIO											.16

Ns equal (a) 83 (b) 78 (c) 55 (d) 54 (e) 34 (f) 29 (g) 84 (h) 46

NOTE: The discreteness variables are undefined for periods in which the nations in the system clustered into one pole. This is why the Ns are greatly reduced for all correlations involving discreteness (especially for data drawn from the nineteenth century). Additional observations are lost, of course, because of time lags or spreads in the variables. Both of these factors affect the number of reported observations throughout the analyses in this study.

TABLE 1B
Intercorrelations Among the Predictor Variables for the Twentieth Century

	T_{t-1}	ΔT	$\Delta TSQR$	D_{to}	D_{t-1}	ΔD	$\Delta DSQR$	IO_{to}	IO_{t-1}	ΔIO	$\Delta IOSQR$
T_{to}	.87	.41	.05	.07	-.05	.12	-.03	.59	.59	.27	.43
T_{t-1}		.50	.00	.08	.09	.24	-.12	.55	.59	.25	.45
ΔT			.48	.11	-.00	.36	-.13	.20	.29	.36	.19
$\Delta TSQR$				.02	-.11	.21	.07	.06	.15	.27	.17
D_{to}					.77	.02	.13	-.59	-.49	-.33	-.19
D_{t-1}						.09	.12	-.56	-.59	-.48	-.21
ΔD							-.79	.04	.04	-.18	.07
$\Delta DSQR$								-.08	-.07	.13	.03
IO_{to}									.91	.59	.59
IO_{t-1}										.72	.71
ΔIO											.37

NOTE: N = 66.

TABLE 2

Correlations Between the Number of Poles (IO)
and the Occurrence of War in the International System

	Interstate War	*Major Power War*	*N*
Occurrence of Nineteenth Century War			
IO_{t0}	−.10	−.16	84
IO_{t-1}	−.08	−.08	83
Δ IOSQR	−.04	−.25	78
Δ IO	−.11	−.12	78
Occurrence of Twentieth Century War			
IO_{t0}	.04	.10	66
IO_{t-1}	.04	.06	66
Δ IOSQR	.09	−.02	66
Δ IO	.33[a]	.24	66

NOTE: All coefficients are estimated correlation coefficients derived from probit analysis.
a. $p < .05$.

state wars. Here the result implies that the greater the increase in the number of poles, the higher the probability of war. This result suggests that the clarification of commitments achieved as a consequence of the increased specificity of bloc objectives—which presumably accompanies an increase in the number of poles—outweighs the increase in the quantity of information decision makers must evaluate as the number of poles increases, thereby facilitating the utility estimates necessary before choosing a strategy that might lead to war.

DISCRETENESS AND THE OCCURRENCE OF WAR

Because of the close conceptual link between the discreteness of the system's poles and the extent to which detente prevails among blocs, the results of this portion of the analysis should be revealing in terms of current foreign policy. As suggested by my assumptions of dynamic uncertainty and normally distributed risk-taking orientations, none of the indicators of discreteness are significantly correlated with the occurrence of war. Thus, bridging the gap between blocs by building alliances across them does not now, nor did it in the nineteenth century, affect the likelihood of war in the international system. The results are reported in Table 3.

TABLE 3

Correlations Between Discreteness (D)

and the Occurrence of War in the International System

	Interstate War	*Major Power War*	*N*
Occurrence of Nineteenth Century War			
D_{t0}	.15	.27	55
D_{t-1}	.00	.06	54
$\triangle$ DSQR	.15	−.01	34
$\triangle$ D	−.18	.05	34
Occurrence of Twentieth Century War			
D_{t0}	−.08	−.16	66
D_{t-1}	−.04	−.12	66
$\triangle$ DSQR	−.01	−.01	66
$\triangle$ D	−.06	.05	66

NOTE: All coefficients are estimated correlation coefficients derived from probit analysis. Discreteness is conceptually and mathematically undefined for those years (all of which occur in the nineteenth century) in which there was only one pole, and hence no opportunity for interbloc alliances.

TIGHTNESS AND THE OCCURRENCE OF WAR

Despite the persuasive arguments presented by Kaplan (1957), the tightness of the system's blocs bears no association with the occurrence of war. Indeed, in the nineteenth century, none of the measured aspects of tightness are significantly associated with the occurrence of war. In the twentieth century, however, as anticipated by the assumptions of utility-maximizing behavior and normally distributed risk-taking, increases in the tightness of the system increase the likelihood of both interstate and major power war. In fact, as expected, *war almost never occurs during periods of declining tightness.* Eighty-nine percent of the twentieth-century periods of declining tightness preceded years in which no war began, while 84% of the wars in the twentieth century began in years following a five-year rise in systemic tightness. Even in the nineteenth century more than three-fourths of the periods of declining tightness preceded years in which no war started, while 63% of the years in which wars began were preceded by rising systemic tight- ness. Furthermore, no war involving more than one nation on each side has occurred following a decline in systemic tightness at any time throughout the century and a half under investigation. Nearly 80% of all

TABLE 4
Correlations Between Systemic Tightness (T)
and the Occurrence of War

	Interstate War	Major Power War	N
Occurrence of Nineteenth Century War			
T_{t0}	.16	.15	84
T_{t-1}	.21	.22	83
Δ TSQR	.15	.02	78
Δ T	.11	.09	78
Occurrence of Twentieth Century War			
T_{t0}	.03	.14	66
T_{t-1}	.05	.14	66
Δ TSQR	.04	.20	66
Δ T	.29[a]	.47[b]	66

NOTE: All coefficients are estimated correlation coefficients derived from probit analysis.
a. $p < .05$
b. $p < .01$

wars involving more than one participant on either side occurred during periods of rising tightness. The correlation analysis for the relationship between the various indicators of systemic tightness and the occurrence of war are found in Table 4.

The impact of increasing systemic tightness—the best predictor of the occurrence of twentieth century war—may be greater than implied by the results. The analysis reported thus far assumes that all 66 years of the twentieth century that were examined experienced no contextual changes that might have altered the importance of systemic tightness. Yet, it is commonly assumed by decision makers, scholars, and laymen that the twentieth century includes three quite distinct periods. These periods are assumed to span the pre-World War I years, the interwar period, and the post-World War II nuclear age. The latter period is often thought to be so different from the prenuclear age that some even claim that patterns of behavior predating nuclear weapons are irrelevant for studies of contemporary world politics. To test the correctness of the assertion that there are three contextually distinct periods in the twentieth century, a dummy probit analysis of the following form was undertaken:

TABLE 5

Probit Analysis of the Clarity of Commitments, Historical Periods,
and the Occurrence of War, 1900-1965

	Interstate War		*Major Power War*
Constant	−.91		−1.46
D_1	.69	$(.42)^a$	.05 (.69)
D_2	.15	(.46)	.41 (.58)
$\triangle T$	2.06	$(1.20)^b$	3.34 $(1.51)^b$
$(\triangle T)(D_1)$	.19	(2.97)	5.29 (5.50)
$(\triangle T)(D_2)$	1.90	(6.62)	−2.69 (7.51)
Multiple R	.41		.59
Chi Square	6.44		9.67
Number of Cases	66		66
Significance	.20		.10
Durbin-Watson	2.16^c		2.36^c

NOTE: Numbers in parentheses are standard errors for the coefficients.
a. $p < .10$
b. $p < .05$
c. No significant serial correlation.

$$Y = a + b_1 D_1 + b_2 D_2 + b_3 \triangle T + b_4 (\triangle T)(D_1) + b_5 (\triangle T)(D_2)$$

where D_1 = a dummy variable coded one for the years 1900 through 1914, and zero for 1915 through 1965.

D_2 = a dummy variable coded zero for 1900 through 1945, and one for 1946 through 1965.

This general equation is interpreted as follows:

$a + b_1 D_1 + b_3 \triangle T + b_4 (\triangle T)(D_1)$ provides the maximum likelihood estimate of the probability that war would occur during the pre-World War 1 period.

$a + b_3 \triangle T$ provides the maximum likelihood estimate of the probability that war would occur during the interwar period.

$a + b_2 D_2 + b_3 \triangle T + b_5 (\triangle T)(D_2)$ provides the maximum likelihood estimate that war would occur during the years from 1946 to 1965.
The results of the probit analysis are found in Table 5.

Several interesting results emerge from Table 5. First, the post-World War II years are not significantly different from the interwar years, either in terms of the impact of changes in systemic tightness on the occurrence of war, or in terms of the many unspecified factors reflected by the intercepts. The suggestion that nuclear weapons have changed the world so much that generalizations from the prenuclear period are irrelevant appears to be dubious, at least with regard to the relationship between increased tightness and the occurrence of war.

Second, the pre-World War I period appears also to have been very similar to the other two periods, at least with respect to the relationship between changes in systemic tightness and the occurrence of war. Similarly, neither intercept for the pre-World War I period is significantly different from the intercept for the interwar years, although the pre-War intercept for Interstate War approaches statistical significance.

HYPOTHESES CONCERNING THE DURATION OF WAR

We turn now to an evaluation of the hypotheses concerning the relationship between systemic polarity and the duration of ensuing wars. These hypotheses are evaluated in terms of the familiar Pearson product-moment correlation.

Among those variables that reflect the static uncertainty assumption, only the number of interaction opportunities (with a one-year lag) is significantly correlated with any indicator of duration. Thus, with the exception of this one variable, which is correlated with the duration of major power wars in the nineteenth century, neither major nor general war duration in the nineteenth or twentieth century can be anticipated from the level of tightness, discreteness, or interaction opportunities in the international system. The undirectional magnitude of change in systemic tightness and in interaction opportunities is significantly associated with the duration of twentieth-century wars (only major power wars in the case of ΔIOSQR). One might infer from these results that uncertainty in the twentieth century encourages nations to prepare for war and hence to be capable of sustaining their participation. Such a conclusion, however, is premature. An examination of the direction in which these variables were changing prior to the onset of war reveals that long wars always followed periods of increasing tightness and increasing interaction opportunities, while short wars followed periods of unchanged or declining tightness and interaction opportunities. In fact, there was only one war in the twentieth century that

TABLE 6
Correlations Between Systemic Polarity and the Duration of War

	19th Century				20th Century			
	Inter-state	*N*	*Major Power*	*N*	*Inter-state*	*N*	*Major Power*	*N*
IO_{t0}	−.05	26	.14	15	.08	21	.20	11
IO_{t-1}	.00	26	.49[a]	15	.02	21	.16	11
Δ IOSQR	−.13	26	.28	15	.08	21	.56[a]	11
Δ IO	.22	26	.63[a]	15	.16	21	.52[a]	11
D_{t0}	.09	18	.17	9	−.17	21	.11	11
D_{t-1}	−.16	18	−.00	10	−.08	21	.11	11
Δ DSQR	−.06	13	.03	7	−.01	21	.23	11
Δ D	−.39[c]	13	−.07	7	.50[a]	21	.59[a]	11
T_{t0}	.25	26	.13	15	.08	21	.27	11
T_{t-1}	.27	26	.24	15	.09	21	.24	11
Δ TSQR	.22	26	.17	15	.76[b]	21	.69[b]	11
Δ T	.26[c]	26	.26	15	.69[b]	21	.90[b]	11

NOTE: All coefficients are Pearson product-moment correlation coefficients.
a. $p < .05$
b. $p < .01$
c. $p < .10$

followed a decline in interaction opportunities and only a handful that followed periods of declining systemic tightness.

The results for the direction and magnitude of change reveal some expected and some unanticipated patterns. Increases in systemic tightness, as anticipated, are significantly associated with the duration of war in the twentieth century, and approach significance in the nineteenth century. Surprisingly, increases in discreteness and in interaction opportunities are also significantly associated with some types of war duration in either the nineteenth or twentieth centuries. The consistency with which indicators of the direction of change are correlated with the duration of war suggests that they may each reduce the level of uncertainty in some fashion. In particular, it appears that as blocs become tighter, more discrete, and more specific in their objectives, at least during the twentieth century, decision makers become increasingly able to calculate their needs in the event of war and to find the means to satisfy those needs, thereby increasing the length of time they are capable of waging war. The results concerned with the duration of war may be found in Table 6.

TABLE 7
Regression Analysis of the Clarity of Commitments,
Historic Periods, and the Duration of War, 1900-1965

	Interstate War		Major Power War	
Constant	23.6		−11.6	
D_1	−13.6[a]	(9.3)	18.4[a]	(10.8)
D_2	−20.5[b]	(10.2)	17.9[a]	(9.1)
ΔT	72.3[c]	(27.7)	170.7[c]	(24.8)
$(\Delta T)(D_1)$	19.8	(58.3)	17.7	(55.6)
$(\Delta T)(D_2)$	133.8	(143.3)	158.4[a]	(85.3)
Multiple R	.77		.98	
Number of Cases	21		11	
F	4.34		21.12	
Significance	.05		.01	
Durbin-Watson	3.09[d]		3.05[d]	

NOTE: Numbers in parentheses are standard errors for the coefficients.
a. $p < .10$
b. $p < .05$
c. $p < .01$
d. No significant serial correlation.

As was the case with the occurrence of twentieth-century war, ΔT proved to be the best predictor of the duration of wars in the current century. I turn, therefore, to a dummy variable regression analysis of ΔT, making use, once again, of the three time periods specified earlier. Table 7, which contains the regression analysis, reveals a pattern somewhat similar to that reported for the occurrence of war. Only one post-World War II slope approaches being significantly different from the interwar slope, while none of the pre-World War I slopes are significantly different from the interwar period. Thus, the effect of ΔT on the duration of war has remained essentially unchanged during the first two-thirds of the twentieth century. What slight change there has been in the post-World War II period is in the direction of having small increases in tightness be followed by war durations that previously would have followed larger increases in tightness.

The intercepts reveal some interesting changes during the three periods. Wars in general were significantly shorter in the pre-World

War I and the post-World War II periods than they were during the interwar years (with the intercepts based on interstate war duration, for example, being 10, 23.6, and 3.1, respectively). The intercepts for major power wars, on the other hand, have generally increased, although not very significantly, in the post-World War II period. In the nuclear age virtually any decrease in ΔT implies a zero war duration—meaning either instantaneous defeat for one side or virtually no possibility of war during periods of declining tightness—while the interwar system required a .32 reduction in tightness to achieve the same level of security against war.

CONCLUSIONS

With the data analysis now complete, we may reflect on the potential significance of the findings. In doing so, I begin with their theoretical import, then their empirical significance, and finally examine their potential policy relevance.

Two common—though not always explicit—assumptions found in most studies of polarity are that uncertainty affects the likelihood of war and that the nature of the affect depends on whether decision makers are generally risk-acceptant or risk-avoidant. Implicit in this debate is the notion that risk-taking is uniformly distributed among foreign policy decision makers. This study also suggests that decision makers learn from past experience, so that such static variables as the number of poles, or their tightness, is unrelated to the probability of war. Second, I suggest that risk-taking orientations are an inherent—though not explicit—part of all research linking uncertainty to war. And, more importantly, that risk-taking predispositions are normally distributed among foreign policy decision makers, so that some are risk-acceptant, some risk-avoidant, and most are assumed to be generally risk-neutral. These assumptions led to very different implications about the expected relationship between aspects of systemic polarity and the occurrence and duration of war.

The evidence indicates that theories linking static aspects of polarity to war are generally false, while suggesting that the direction of change in systemic tightness, and to a lesser extent interaction opportunities, is very closely related to the occurrence and duration of war, especially in the twentieth century. The overall pattern that seems to emerge is that the occurrence and duration of nineteenth-century wars cannot be accounted for by focusing on the military alliance commitments among nations, while the occurrence and duration of twentieth-century wars can be accounted for to a fair degree by shifts toward greater clarity in alliance commitments among nations.

The consistently strong relationship between the direction of change in systemic tightness and the outcome variables for the twentieth century, coupled with the inconsistent relationship between the direction of change in discreteness and the same outcome variables, may have important policy implications. Because discreteness is closely linked conceptually to detente, the evidence here raises questions about the value of detente as a strategy for increasing the likelihood of world peace. Thus, while the evidence suggests that reduced discreteness may lead to shortened wars, it does not indicate that reduced discreteness decreases the probability of war. Decreases in systemic tightness, on the other hand, signal both a reduction in the occurrence and the duration of wars in the twentieth century. What is more, changes in tightness may be a useful early warning indicator of the likelihood of war. As noted earlier, 84% of the wars in the twentieth century began in years that followed periods of rising systemic tightness.

These results, which are predicated on assumptions about rationality and risk-taking, highlight the importance of assessing the impact of utility calculations and risk-taking predispositions on war choices, while calling attention to the inadequacy of generalizations derived from the assumption that uncertainty has a uniform effect on decision makers.

Bruce Bueno de Mesquita (Ph.D. University of Michigan, 1971) is Associate Professor of Political Science at the University of Rochester. Engaged in research on a rational-choice theory of war decisions, he has authored Personality, Risk, and Coalitions *(1975) and coauthored* India's Political System *(1976).*

From Bosnia to Sarajevo

A COMPARATIVE DISCUSSION
OF INTERSTATE CRISES

ALAN NED SABROSKY   *Chapter* **6**

This paper undertakes a comparative case study of the relationship between the onset of interstate crises and the incidence of war. Findings obtained from several different studies are integrated and extended into an analysis of changes in the major-power subsystem between the Bosnian Crisis of 1908-1909 (which was resolved without war) and the Sarajevo Crisis of 1914 (which escalated into the First World War). The outcomes of these crises are examined in the context of the changing pattern of major-power alliances, the distribution and the shift in distribution of major-power capabilities, and the pre-1914 arms race. The author finds a transformation in the major-power subsystem between 1905-1910 which significantly altered the existing European balance of power in favor of the Triple Entente. During the Sarajevo Crisis, the behavior of the decision makers on both sides reflected that transformation. The implications of these findings for conflict theory are summarized.

One of the more compelling questions raised in the study of international conflict involves the relationship between the onset of crises and the incidence of war. That is, why do some crises end in war, while others do not? Social scientists of all methodological persuasions have approached this problem from a variety of theoretical and empirical perspectives. The present paper proposes to bring together several aspects of these studies and to develop them further. In it, findings on several structural and behavioral variables will be integrated into a comparative discussion of the outcomes of the two major crises preceding the First

AUTHOR'S NOTE: Thanks are in order to J. David Singer, Karl W. Deutsch, Catherine M. Kelleher, Stuart A. Bremer, and Bruce Bueno de Mesquita for their helpful comments. Final responsibility, of course, is mine.

Originally published in the *Journal of Conflict Resolution*, Vol. 9, No. 1, March 1975.

World War: Bosnia (1908-1909) and Sarajevo (1914). Specifically, I will examine the behavior of the opposing decision makers in these crises in the context of (a) the pre-1914 alliance system, (b) the capabilities of the major powers in the contending alliances, and (c) the arms race underway in that period.

The concept of comparing one crisis that ended in war with another one that did *not* has been used before (e.g., Holsti, 1972; Paige, 1972). Unlike most such studies, however, both of the crises being examined in this paper involved the same set of states.[1] In addition, both crises originated in a particularly bitter conflict of interest between the same two states—Austria-Hungary and Serbia—in the same region. While the Bosnian Crisis was resolved without war, the Sarajevo Crisis escalated into the first of this century's world wars. By examining the systemic changes which took place between these two crises, we may improve our understanding of why that occurred, as well as developing some additional insights into international conflict in general.

THE TWO CRISES: GENERAL DISCUSSION[2]

Both the Bosnian Crisis of 1908-1909 and the Sarajevo Crisis of 1914 have been subjects of considerable interest for students of the origins of the First World War (e.g., Albertini, 1967; Fay, 1928; Gooch, 1928; Lafore, 1971; Remak, 1967). Briefly, the Bosnian Crisis developed from an abortive understanding concluded between the Russian and Austro-Hungarian foreign ministers at Buchlau in September 1908. According to that unwritten agreement, Austria-Hungary was to formally annex two nominally Ottoman provinces—Bosnia and Herzegovina—which had been administered by the Habsburgs since 1878. For its part, Russia would receive Austro-Hungarian support in its claims for access to the Mediterranean Sea through the Dardanelles. The exact terms of this arrangement are far from clear. In any event, Austria-Hungary announced the annexation in October 1908, before Russia had been able to gain the acquiescence of the other major powers to the opening of the Dardanelles to Russian warships. The crisis gradually escalated during the winter of

1. These states were England, France, Russia, Germany, Austria-Hungary, and Italy. Serbia, a nonmajor power, was also a participant in both crises.

2. For a comprehensive discussion of the Bosnian and Sarajevo crises, see Albertini (1967); Fay (1928); Lafore (1971); Reventlow (1916); Schmitt (1916); and Taylor (1954). A summary of the literature and an analysis of the implications of the Bosnian Crisis are in Sabrosky (1970).

1908-1909, with Serbia threatening war to prevent the "absorption" of territories over which it had claims, and Russia supporting Serbia. In March 1909, Germany presented what amounted to an ultimatum to Russia, telling it either to accept the annexation or to face the prospect of war against both Austria-Hungary *and* Germany. Under these circumstances, and unsupported by its allies, Russia withdrew its objections. Lacking Russian assistance, Serbia soon did likewise.

The Sarajevo Crisis occurred five years later, following the assassination of the heir to the Habsburg empire and his wife by a young Serbian nationalist. The incident, which occurred in the capital of Bosnia, involved a group of conspirators acting with the prior knowledge and material assistance of elements of the Serbian government and its General Staff. At first, it appeared that the crisis would abate. By late July, however, tension had mounted following an Austrian ultimatum to Serbia. As in 1908-1909, Germany stood by its ally. Unlike the earlier period, however, France supported Russia; the latter, in its turn, agreed to aid Serbia in the event of an Austrian attack. A complicated series of partial and full mobilizations, declarations of war, and movements across national frontiers in late July and early August finally involved five of the six European major powers in a general conflict. Japan, the only Asian major power in the system, declared war against Germany and Austria-Hungary a few weeks later. Italy followed suit in 1915, as did the United States in 1917.

GENERAL ANALYSIS

The empirical domain selected for analysis is the major-power subsystem during the period 1900-1914. This subsystem consisted of six European states—England, France, Russia, Germany, Austria-Hungary, and Italy—plus the United States and Japan. In 1900 there were really only two "core" alliances in existence. One was that between France and Russia, the other a "Dual Alliance" of Germany and Austria-Hungary (commonly referred to as the "Central Powers").[3] Italy was also allied to

3. Russia and Austria-Hungary were also allied in a Class III (Entente) pact from 1897-1908. Since it provided a link (however tenuous) between the two core alliances, its termination in the early stages of the Bosnian Crisis further underscores the deteriorating position of the Central Powers. This consideration notwithstanding, it was decided to exclude this Austro-Russian "gentlemen's agreement" (as it was known at the time) from the analysis. This was done because the Austro-Russian understanding was, as Taylor (1954: 370) aptly put it, "purely negative." That is, it was not an alliance which implied either active cooperation or an aggregation of capabilities, but rather a determination not to disturb the status quo in the Near East

the Central Powers in the Triple Alliance, although her adherence to that pact was uncertain even at the turn of the century. England, Japan, and the United States were still outside of the formal alliance network at that time, although they conducted normal diplomatic relations with all the major powers involved in the two coalitions. Nonmajor states are excluded from this study, although several subsequently became involved in the war and at least one of them (Serbia) was a key factor in its outbreak in 1914. This exclusion obtains because the actions of the nonmajor states appear to have been contingent on those of the major powers. That is, Serbia (and most comparable states) acted in what Wilkinson (1969: 5-12) called a "second-party" role, rather than in a "first-party" role which approximates major-power status.

THE SYSTEM OF ALLIANCES, 1900-1914

A central characteristic of the pre-1914 major-power subsystem was the existence of an extensive alliance network. This "system of alliances" eventually involved all of the major powers except the United States. There is a consensus among diplomatic historians to the effect that, without these alliances, the initial Austro-Serbian war probably would have remained limited to those two states. That is, the existence of these alliances facilitated the expansion of the original bilateral conflict (although the strength of that influence is uncertain). These intuitive judgments are partially supported by a recent study (Singer and Small, 1968) which suggests that there is a fairly strong, positive correlation between alliance aggregation, bipolarity, and the incidence of war in the twentieth century.

In discussing the pre-1914 alliance system, it is insufficient to consider only the final composition of the contending coalitions as they appeared in 1914. One must also look at the development of those coalitions before that time. Several changes in the membership of those coalitions, if they still maintained some type of balance, need not be destabilizing. A relatively smaller number of changes which upset that balance in favor of one of the coalitions, however, could have the opposite effect. We would expect both of these conditions to be reflected in the behavior of the decision makers on both sides. The impact of any changes, of course, would increase as the disparities in size and relative strength between the

---

at that time. However, if the reader prefers to include this alliance, that may be done without detracting from the thrust of the arguments in this paper. In fact (as I indicated above), it actually strengthens them somewhat.

opposing coalitions became more pronounced (Zinnes, 1967: 271; Kaplan, 1957: 23).

In one study of alliances (Small and Singer, 1969), the authors compiled a list of interstate alliances which fell into one of three classes. These were (I) defense pacts, (II) neutrality or nonaggression pacts, and (III) ententes. The Class I (defense) pacts were theoretically the strongest, followed by the neutrality/nonaggression pacts and ententes in that order. However, the authors noted (1969: 263) that twentieth-century "ententes" were often of greater significance than other classes of alliance. (This was particularly evident when an entente included England.) Between 1900 and 1914, eight major-power alliances (all of them bilateral) were concluded. One of these, an entente between Japan and the United States, lasted less than a year and is not considered in the discussion. None of the other seven alliances, however, included either Germany or Austria-Hungary. Italy, on the other hand, formed alliances with both France and Russia during this period. The former pact essentially neutralized Italy in the event of a Franco-German war; the latter alliance had the same effect with regard to any future Austro-Russian conflict. That is, after the conclusion of these two alliances, Italy's commitment to the Central Powers was little more than a diplomatic formality which lacked any substantive foundation. The alliances concluded in this period are summarized in Table 1. A graphic representation of the effect of these new alliances on the existing major-power subsystem appears in Figure 1.

By 1910 the situation had changed markedly from that which had existed in 1900. The Franco-Russian core alliance had been transformed into a considerably more impressive coalition of four major powers. Those major powers which had either formed new alliances or reinforced existing commitments (France, England, Russia, and Japan) would ultimately declare war against the Central Powers within a month of one another in 1914. Yet Italian equivocation between the two major pacts did not mean, however, that it was viewed as part of the Entente coalition. Italy was, at best, considered a neutral factor in any future war among the major powers. This general state of disequilibrium remained unchanged at the time of the Sarajevo Crisis in 1914. That is, it was not that the "balance of power" between a Triple Alliance and a Triple Entente failed to keep the peace in 1914. It was simply that the balance no longer existed at that time. Instead, a Dual Alliance of Germany and Austria-Hungary was opposed by a coalition of at least four (and with Italy, five) other major powers.

TABLE 1
MAJOR-POWER ALLIANCES, 1900-1914

	Members of Alliance	Date of Inception	Date of Termination	Class of Alliance
(1)	France	12/1900	1902	III
	Italy	(7/1902)[a]	1915	II
(2)	England	1/1902	1912	I
	Japan			
(3)	England	4/1904	1914	III
	France			
(4)	Japan	6/1907	1914	III
	France			
(5)	Japan	7/1907	1914	III
	Russia			
(6)	England	8/1907	1914	III
	Russia			
(7)	Italy	10/1909	1915	III
	Russia			

SOURCE: Singer and Small (1969).
a. The original Franco-Italian *entente* of 1900 was renegotiated and superceded by a stronger alliance in 1902. See the discussion in Taylor (1954: 406-408 ff).

CAPABILITIES OF THE MAJOR POWERS, 1900-1913

These alterations in the composition of the opposing coalitions were accompanied by a corresponding change in the relative capabilities of the two blocs. Precisely what constitutes national "capabilities" or "power," of course, is far from certain. Several different indicators of power and its relationship to the incidence of war have been suggested (e.g., German, 1960; Singer, Bremer and Stuckey, 1972; Alcock and Newcombe, 1970; Organski, 1968; Hermann and Hermann, 1967). The most comprehensive measure of power currently available is that developed on the Correlates of War Project at the University of Michigan (Singer, Bremer and Stuckey, 1972). Six separate indicators (total population, urban population, energy consumption, iron/steel production, military expenditures, and military personnel) are subsumed into a single gross indicator of national capabilities. This indicator is presented in the form of a certain "percentage share" of the total capabilities available to all of the major powers in the subsystem at a given time. These Major Power Capabilities Shares (MPCS) are then computed for the major powers in the interstate

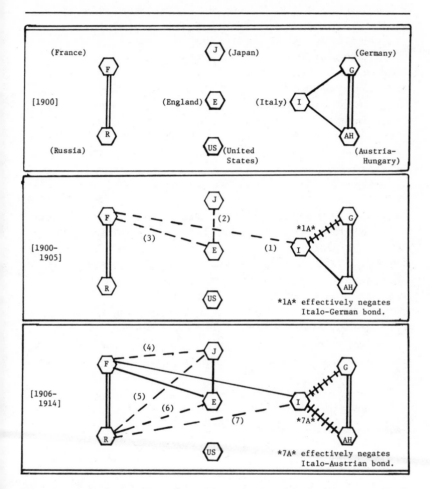

NOTE: Numbers on lines indicating new alliance bonds refer to alliances in Table 1.

===   "Core" alliances (Austro-German, Franco-Russian).

——   Other alliance bonds.

---   New alliance commitments undertaken during subject period (e.g., 1900-1905).

+++   Alliance bond negated by new (and conflicting) alliance commitment.

Figure 1: MAJOR-POWER ALLIANCES, 1900-1914

system at five-year intervals. These are presented for the period 1900-1913 in Table 2.

Throughout this period, the rank-order positions of five major powers remained constant. The United States, although nonaligned, stayed in first place; France, Austria-Hungary, Italy, and Japan continued to occupy the fifth through eighth places, respectively. However, there was a significant change in the rank-ordering of England, Germany, and Russia over this period. Germany and Russia each advanced one rank, to second and third place, respectively. England fell from second to fourth place. That is, England was not only passed by her most salient rival—Germany—but also by her newly acquired ally, Russia.

If only the *individual* major powers are considered, with or without the United States and Japan at the two extremes of the scale, this would suggest that Germany had first approached and then overtaken England in the contest for European leadership. That this culminated in a major war conforms to Organski's discussion of the consequences of such a "power transition" (1968: ch. 14). However, we are concerned with the aggregation of capabilities by opposing *coalitions*—one of the major objectives of alliance formation (Liska, 1968: ch. 1). We must therefore examine the changes in the relative distribution of power between the opposing coalitions which occurred from 1900 to 1914.

Precisely when a particular major power should be added to, or deleted from, a given coalition is often less than clear. There is, of course, no

TABLE 2
PERCENTAGE SHARE DISTRIBUTION OF MAJOR-POWER CAPABILITIES
(1900-1913)

| STATE | *Percentage Share of Major-Power Capabilities* | | | |
	1900	*1905*	*1910*	*1913*
France	10.1	9.8	9.6	10.4
Russia	16.1	16.5	16.5	16.7
England	20.6	16.5	15.0	14.1
Germany	16.7	16.9	17.2	18.2
Austria-Hungary	6.1	6.2	6.4	6.1
Italy	4.9	5.0	4.9	5.0
Japan	3.8	4.3	4.5	4.4
United States	21.6	24.9	25.9	25.0

SOURCE: Compiled from (FILE=LIST), "Percentage Share Distribution of Major-Power Capabilities" available at the Correlates of War Project, University of Michigan.

difficulty with regard to the Franco-Russian and Austro-German coalitions. For better or worse, they remained basically constant throughout the period in question. In addition, since the United States remained outside of the European system of alliances, its Major Power Capabilities Shares are not added to either of the opposing coalitions.

For the other major powers, the following rules were used. A major power was not added to a coalition until it was fully bonded to all existing members of that coalition. Likewise, a major power was not deleted from a coalition until it had concluded contradictory alliances which explicitly or implicitly negated the existing bonds to all of its original partners. That is, although England concluded an entente with France in 1904, it is not included in the Entente coalition (as it came to be known) until after it had signed a similar pact with Russia in 1907. Similarly, although Italy was partially neutralized by its alliances with France in 1900 and 1902, it is not deleted from the Central Powers coalition until after it had made similar arrangements with Russia in 1909.

Even with these coding rules, Japan presents something of a problem. It was fully bonded with England, France, and Russia by 1907. Its participation in these pacts certainly influenced the maritime balance of power to the detriment of the German position. Moreover, as we noted earlier, Japan promptly joined its three European major-power allies in declaring war against Germany and Austria-Hungary in 1914. Still, the First World War was essentially a European conflict, and the crises which finally resulted in that conflict were basically European-centered affairs. Therefore, in order not to bias unnecessarily the ratio of capabilities possessed by the contending European coalitions, I have not included Japan's capabilities shares with those of England, France, and Russia.[4] The resulting aggregations of the distribution and change in distribution of major-power capabilities shares from 1900 to 1914 are presented in Table 3. A graphic representation of those changes in the context of the transformed alliance systems appears in Figure 2.[5]

These findings are in sharp contrast to those obtained from a simple consideration of the individual major powers in the system. That is, the

4. Adding Japan's capabilities shares (MPCS) to those of the Anglo-Franco-Russian Entente does not alter significantly the ratio of power between the opposing coalitions. It does, however, reduce somewhat the "nonaligned" MPCS in the system, as Figure 2 indicates.

5. The strength of these formal alliance bonds, of course, would be increased by other factors, such as the existence of cultural or economic ties or by prolonged periods of amicable relations between the alliance partners.

TABLE 3
PERCENTAGE SHARE DISTRIBUTION OF MAJOR-POWER CAPABILITIES
(aggregated by coalitions)

| Year | Percentage Share of Capabilities | | Ratio of |
	[A] "Entente" Coalition	[B] "Alliance" Coalition	"Alliance" (B) / "Entente" (A) =
1900	France Russia = 26.2	Germany Austria = 27.7 Italy	1.06
1905	France Russia = 26.3	Germany Austria = 28.1 Italy	1.07
1910	France Russia = 41.1 England	Germany Austria = 23.6	0.57
1913	France Russia = 41.2 England	Germany Austria = 24.3	0.59

NOTE: Data have not been normalized to account for those major powers which are not included in the opposing coalitions on the above dates. Consequently, the aggregated percentage shares of major-power capabilities do not sum to 100.0%. In addition, the term "Alliance" in this table has been used to designate the coalition based on Germany and Austria-Hungary.
SOURCE: Compiled from (FILE=LIST), "Percentage Share Distribution of Major-Power Capabilities" available at the Correlates of War Project, University of Michigan.

period 1905-1910 marked a transition from a major-power subsystem characterized by two coalitions possessing approximately equal power, to a system marked by a significant imbalance between those coalitions. As the composition of those coalitions shifted, the share of major-power capabilities available to each had also shifted to a great extent. When one realizes that Japan (and possibly Italy as well, although this is less certain) could also be added to the roll of Entente members by 1910, the disparity between the two coalitions becomes even more striking.

ARMS RACES, 1908-1914

It can, of course, be argued that such gross capabilities shares do not accurately reflect the "real" power of a state. That is, it is not so much the possession (or lack) of a large population or a high level of energy

MAJOR-POWER ALLIANCE CONFIGURATION, 1900

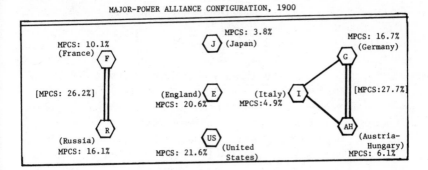

MAJOR-POWER ALLIANCE CONFIGURATION, 1914

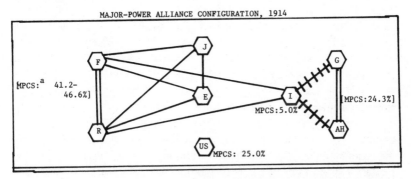

NOTE: MPCS = "Major-Power Capabilities Shares." Numbers in brackets [ ] are the *aggregated* MPCS in the "Entente" and "Alliance" (Central Powers) coalitions.
a. Lower value does not include Japan's MPCS; the higher value does. Some would include Japan in the Entente coalition, while others (as has been discussed in the body of this paper) would not. The reader may take either option—both support the analysis in the text. In addition, neither value for the Entente in 1914 includes Italy's MPCS, nor are the latter included in the Alliance MPCS for that year.

Figure 2: CHANGES IN THE DISTRIBUTION OF MAJOR-POWER CAPABILITIES SHARES, 1900-1914

consumption which is a valid indicator of real, rather than potential power, but only those capabilities reflected in "military" variables. This argument was essentially used by Richardson (1960a), among others, in his discussion of various arms races. Richardson used military expenditures alone as an indicator of the military competition between states. This indicator of "war preparedness" is not only the least complex of the possible indicators of an arms race. It also possesses a certain face validity in that, ceteris paribus, a state which spends twice as much as another on the same range of military goods is probably going to be stronger than its rival—although not necessarily twice as strong. In addition, at least one recent study (Alcock and Newcombe, 1970: 342) has found that military expenditures alone are the most significant single indicator of perceived national power. This was particularly evident when the states involved had prior war experience. Given that an increase in national power is at least one goal of increased armaments expenditures, this supports the use of this indicator (rather than sums of personnel or weapons) as a measure of an arms race. Richardson's tabulation of the military expenditures of the six European major powers from 1908-1914, adjusted to include or exclude states in the coalitions according to the coding rules, appears in Table 4. These data are then converted into percentage shares of the total military expenditures of all six major powers taken in the aggregate. This depicts more clearly the relative distribution of arms outlays between the opposing coalitions. These "Military Expenditures Shares" (MES) are presented in Table 5. A graphic representation of the MES data, including the ratio of expenditures between the Dual Alliance and the Triple Entente, is presented in Figure 3.

Richardson's data on the pre-1914 arms race support the findings obtained from an analysis of the capabilities data, once one controls for membership in a coalition. That is, although the *absolute* value of the military expenditures of the two coalitions increases markedly over time,

TABLE 4
SUMMARY OF MILITARY EXPENDITURES,
1908-1914

Coalition or State	1908	1909	1910	1911	1912	1913	1914
Triple Entente	156.2	165.0	175.8	187.4	197.8	215.1	239.2
Dual Alliance	89.4	96.2	79.8	86.3	90.1	101.5	123.9
(Italy)	–	–	18.9	21.8	23.8	25.7	27.0
Totals	245.6	261.2	274.5	295.5	311.7	342.3	390.1

NOTE: All figures are in 10^6 £ Sterling. In accordance with our coding rules, Italy is included with Germany and Austria-Hungary for 1908-1909. Effective 1910, it is deleted from the Austro-German coalition, but not added to the "Entente" powers. Although we are comparing coalitions, Italian expenditures for 1910-1914 are presented for comparison with the expenditures of the other major powers in the opposing coalitions.

SOURCE: Richardson (1960a: 87).

TABLE 5
SUMMARY OF MILITARY EXPENDITURES SHARES,
1908-1914

Coalition or State	1908	1909	1910	1911	1912	1913	1914
Triple Entente	63.6	63.2	64.0	63.4	63.5	62.8	61.3
Dual Alliance	36.4	36.8	29.1	29.2	28.9	29.7	31.8
(Italy)	–	–	6.9	7.4	7.6	7.5	6.9
Totals (%)	100.0	100.0	100.0	100.0	100.0	100.0	100.0

NOTE: Expressed as percentages of total military expenditures for all six European major powers. As in Table 4, Italy's MES are included with those of Germany and Austria-Hungary in 1908-1909. For 1910-1914, Italian MES are presented separately.
SOURCE: Adapted from data in Table 4.

their *relative* positions change relatively little. The exclusion of Italy from the Austro-German bloc after 1910 affects this relationship only moderately. As with the distribution of major-power capabilities shares, both Germany and Russia have overtaken England by 1914 (if the coalition data are disaggregated by individual states). Finally, the inferior position of the Dual Alliance vis-a-vis the Triple Entente (even without considering the addition of Italian and Japanese expenditures to the latter) is clearly indicated.[6]

BEHAVIORAL AND PERCEPTUAL DATA:
A CASE STUDY OF 1914

From the preceding discussion we have seen the effects of the changes in the alliance system and the relative distribution of power on the earlier major-power "balance." If one were to look at the interstate system in 1914 and compare it with that in existence in 1900, the relatively deteriorating position of the Central Powers is immediately apparent. This could be reflected in various ways. For example, a number of studies have suggested the importance of perceptions of relative capabilities and of another's behavior in the determination of one's own actions (Glenn et al., 1970; Zinnes, 1962, 1967, 1968; Holsti, 1965, 1972; Holsti, North, and Brody, 1968; Holsti, Brody, and North, 1964). Zinnes has even noted (1966: 474) that "war could be said to originate in the minds

6. Similar findings on the pre-1914 arms race may be compiled from data in Wright (1965b: 670-671).

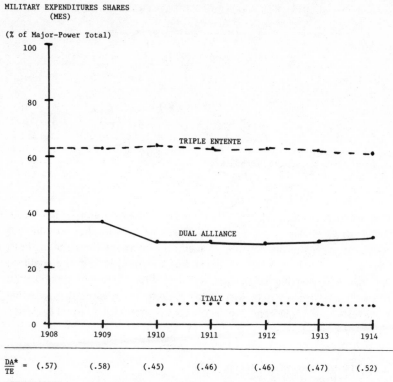

MILITARY EXPENDITURES SHARES
(MES)

(% of Major-Power Total)

$\frac{DA^*}{TE}$ = (.57)   (.58)   (.45)   (.46)   (.46)   (.47)   (.52)

NOTE: Military expenditures for the United States and Japan are not included in this summary. As in the preceding tables, the Entente includes England, France, and Russia. The "Dual Alliance" includes Germany, Austria-Hungary and—until 1910—Italy. From 1910-1914, Italy's MES are displayed separately. Finally, the ratio $\frac{DA^*}{TE}$ is that of the MES of the Alliance coalition to those of the Entente.

SOURCE: Adapted from Richardson (1960a: 87) as presented in Table 5 of this paper.

Figure 3: GENERAL SUMMARY OF MILITARY EXPENDITURES SHARES (MES), 1908-1914

of . . . top-level decision-makers, as a consequence of the way in which they see the world." In fact, under conditions of extreme danger, even perceptions of inferior capability might not deter a decision maker from initiating a conflict (Zinnes et al., 1961; Holsti, North, and Brody, 1968).

Even if this is correct, there should be some trace of that attitude on the part of the decision makers of the weaker coalition which should distinguish them from their counterparts in the stronger coalition. One test, using a two-step mediated stimulus-response model across perceptual and behavioral data for the Sarajevo Crisis (1914), did not, however, immediately support this position. In this instance (Holsti, North, and Brody, 1968), Spearman rank-order correlations were run with "violent (military) behavior" as the dependent variable and five perceptual variables (hostility, friendship, frustration, satisfaction, and desire to change the status quo) as independent variables. These findings appear in Table 6.

In this case, the only statistically significant predictor of violent behavior (and by implication in an international crisis, war) was perceived hostility. That is, if the decision makers of one coalition perceived hostility on the part of their counterparts in the opposing coalition, they were likely to react by ordering military actions to be taken. These findings are supported by similar studies (Zinnes, 1962, 1968; Holsti, 1965; Raser, 1965). As I have been dealing with opposing coalitions rather than a simple aggregation of all major powers, it was decided to carry this analysis somewhat further. That is, even if perceived hostility was the only significant independent variable for all five major powers in the 1914 crisis, that did not mean that it was the only such variable for each of the opposing coalitions. Therefore, separate correlations were run on each coalition. Although this necessitated using a smaller "n" (= 12), some interesting differences appeared. These are presented in Table 7.

These findings further support the argument that perceived hostility is the strongest single predictor of violent behavior. However, significant differences appear between the two coalitions with respect to the other

TABLE 6
RANK-ORDER CORRELATIONS ON PERCEPTUAL
AND BEHAVIORAL VARIABLES
(Dual Alliance and Triple Entente) (n=24)

Perceived:	Violent Behavior (Military Action)	Significance Level (p =)
Hostility	.663	.001
Friendship	.187	n.s.
Frustration	.321	n.s.
Satisfaction	.318	n.s.
Desire to change the status quo	.257	n.s.

NOTE: Findings reflect Spearman rank-order correlations on the major-power subsystem of the Dual Alliance and the Triple Entente during the 1914 Sarajevo Crisis. Data for the five major powers directly involved in that crisis (Germany, Austria-Hungary, England, France, Russia) aggregated by coalitions.
SOURCE: Holsti, North, and Brody (1968: 148).

TABLE 7
DISAGGREGATED RANK-ORDER CORRELATIONS ON
NONAMICABLE PERCEPTUAL AND BEHAVIORAL VARIABLES

(Independent Variable: The coalition indicated in the table reacts violently to its perception that the other coalition is displaying ____ :)	*(Dependent Variable: Violent Behavior)*			
	Coalition			
	Dual Alliance		*Triple Entente*	
Hostility	r=.629	(p=.05)	r=.805	(p=.01)
Frustration	r=.503	(p=.05)	r=.098	(n.s.)
Desire to change the status quo	r=.049	(n.s.)	r=.531	(p=.05)

NOTE: Spearman rank-order correlations on the major-power subsystem of the Dual Alliance and the Triple Entente in the 1914 Sarajevo Crisis. Disaggregated by coalitions.
SOURCE: Adapted from Holsti, North, and Brody (1968: 147-148).

nonamicable perceptual variables. The Austro-German Dual Alliance responded violently to perceptions of "frustration" on the part of the Entente powers. In contrast, those in the Triple Entente reacted in a similar fashion to perceptions of the Austro-German "desire to change the status quo." Moreover, what registered as a strong correlation for one coalition was not statistically significant in the case of the other coalition. That is, what may be statistically weak or without significance across an entire system can be statistically significant for one or more individual members of that system.

SUMMARY AND CONCLUSION

Between 1900 and 1914, the major-power subsystem underwent a transformation which significantly altered the existing European balance of power. That transformation was essentially completed between 1905 and 1910. In the intervening years, what came to be known as the Triple Entente gradually became both numerically larger and markedly stronger than the opposing Austro-German coalition. This is reflected in the changing pattern of major-power alliances, the distribution and shift in distribution of overall capabilities between the contending coalitions, and, in lesser degree, the relative arms expenditures of those coalitions. In 1905, the major-power subsystem was still in a general state of equilibrium. By 1910, that equilibrium had been upset and the balance altered in favor of the Entente coalition. When war finally broke out in the summer of 1914, the Dual Alliance (or Central Powers) as a coalition had not overtaken the Triple Entente as a coalition, either in the arms race or in overall capabilities. In fact, the positions of the two blocs were basically the same as they had been in 1910. And the latter itself reflected a clear deterioration of the balance which had obtained at the beginning of the century.

This situation was mirrored in the perceptions and actions of the decision makers in both coalitions during the 1914 Sarajevo Crisis. The leaders of the weaker coalition, the Dual Alliance, were "revisionists": they wanted to change what had become an unfavorable status quo. However, they had been unable to accomplish this in the precrisis years. Major increases in Austro-German arms outlays had been matched by their opponents, who had also been able to increase both the number and the cohesiveness of their own alliance bonds. For their part, the decision makers of the Triple Entente preferred the existing international order to one in which they might have to play a diminished role. But they were also aware of the Dual Alliance's desire to alter that distribution of power. Precisely how (or even if) that challenge could be deflected was unclear to the Entente's leadership. This conflictful setting was subjected to additional strains during the 1914 crisis, when decision makers in both the "revisionist" and the "status quo" coalitions overperceived the hostility of their rivals. The outcome was a major war.

From our analysis, it appears that the war-proneness of the interstate system may be influenced as much by the composition and the degree of flexibility in the contending coalitions as it is by the existence of a given number of major-power alliances. A flexible set of such alliances, approximating those in a classical balance of power system (Kaplan, 1957: 22-36), may well increase the possibility that crises will arise in the first place. But it may also facilitate the resolution of those crises short of war, or at least serve to restrict the scope of conflicts which do occur. Other circumstances involving a similar number of major-power alliances, however, may have the opposite effect. If there is a prolonged period of alliance aggregation around the same contending power centers (as preceded World War I), or a relative absence of any clear pattern to the alliances (as obtained before World War II), then the system may become both more crisis-prone and more war-prone. And this could apply both to bipolar and to multipolar configurations.[7]

7. The relationship between system polarity and the incidence of war continues to be the subject of considerable debate. For discussions of the major positions, see

Yet "polarity" reflects a concentration of capabilities as well as the number of major powers in the system (Singer, Bremer, and Stuckey, 1972). For example, a bipolar configuration made up of two states (or two coalitions) of comparable power could promote systemic equilibrium. In contrast to this, the same configuration which was characterized by an imbalance of power could have the opposite effect. Moreover, a prolonged sense of inferiority on the part of one such "pole" (be it a single state or a coalition), combined with an inability to change that situation and an unwillingness to accept a permanently inferior status, may adversely affect the stability of the system. In addition, the longer the weaker party finds itself unable to improve its position, the less reluctant it may be to resort to war, whatever its prospects for success. Conversely, either parity or the possibility that a temporarily inferior position can be improved in the near future may reduce the likelihood of war. That is, it may be less the fact (or the fear) of "inferiority" or "encirclement" of one party to a dispute which may increase the war-proneness of the system than the apparent immutability of that condition.[8]

In many instances, of course, crises do involve states of unequal power. In such cases, a major conflict might best be avoided if the stronger party demonstrates a willingness to compromise with the weaker state. This is simply because only it can take such a step without risking a significant deterioration of an already inferior position. The stronger party also has relatively little to gain from pressing an issue to the point of war. It can do no more than reaffirm its existing superiority even if it wins. And that outcome, while probable (Rosen, 1972), is never certain, with "victory" (however that might be defined) often entailing severe losses for both sides.[9] If the attempt to reach a compromise fails, the stronger party's actions may have given additional legitimacy to its position in the dispute.

Deutsch and Singer (1964), Waltz (1967), and Rosecrance (1966). Other analyses are in E. Haas (1953), M. Haas (1970), Singer and Small (1968), and Zinnes (1967). It should be noted that another study (Wallace, 1973) which appeared in print after the completion of this paper also concluded that there might be a curvilinear relationship between alliance polarization and the incidence of war.

8. This could account for the German decision to go to war in 1914 under unfavorable conditions, as has been discussed by Holsti, North, and Brody (1968: 137). One could also infer from the fact that because the Soviet Union was improving its position vis-à-vis the United States during the Cold War, this was one of the factors that helped forestall a general war between the two rival powers.

9. Success in war undoubtedly seems most certain when a major power is opposed to a minor state or nation. And in fact, Singer and Small (1972: 368-369)

In any case, it is irrational to expect the weaker party in a crisis to initiate a compromise, unless it is devoid of support from other states. It can do so only to its continuing disadvantage, whereas resistance may eventually bring assistance from other states.

Essentially, then, states involved in crisis situations would do well to recognize that moderation and prudence are more than proverbial virtues. They are vitally necessary guides for crisis behavior, particularly in the present era. As the outcome of the Sarajevo Crisis demonstrates, an attempt by one side to maximize its gains can end in its incurring maximum losses. Given the destructiveness of contemporary weapons systems, a rational strategy for states would entail the acceptance of smaller gains (or even the minimization of one's anticipated losses), rather than a more ambitious course of action with the attendant risks. It may be that the Cuban Missile Crisis of 1962 was an example of a "nuclear Bosnia." It is clearly in the interests of all of us to work to ensure that a "nuclear Sarajevo" never occurs.

Alan Ned Sabrosky (Ph. D. University of Michigan, 1976) is Assistant Professor of Social Science at the U.S. Military Academy and a Research Associate at the Foreign Policy Research Institute. He is coauthor of The Conventional-Revisionist Controversy and the U.S. Role in World Affairs *(1975), editor and contributor to* Blue-Collar Soldiers? *(1977), and author of* Defense Manpower Policy *(1978).*

---

have found that the major power involved in such a war usually does win. However, there are some rather striking exceptions to this. Great Britain, Austria-Hungary, Germany, the Soviet Union, and the United States each had reason to believe that they would defeat the Boers (1899), Serbia (1914), Poland (1939), Finland (1939), and North Vietnam and the "Viet Cong" (1965), respectively, with the application of massive force. In each instance, the outcome was obviously quite different than what the major power had anticipated. Great Britain and the Soviet Union finally did win, although their losses were far higher than those whom they defeated. Austria-Hungary and Germany were initially successful, yet their actions began world wars which eventually brought about their own defeat and dismemberment. The consequences of the American intervention in Indochina need no elaboration. In other words, when a major power miscalculates its chances for success in a conflict, the results are sufficiently costly to give any state good reason to be reluctant about going to war.

Capability Distribution, Uncertainty, and Major Power War, 1820-1965

J. DAVID SINGER
STUART BREMER
JOHN STUCKEY   *Chapter* **7**

We have synthesized from the literature two distinct and incompatible views of the way in which the distribution and redistribution of capabilities affects the incidence of major power war. One predicts that there will be less war when there is approximate *parity* (and change toward it) among the nations and a relatively *fluid* power hierarchy. The other predicts that there will be less war when there is a *preponderance* (or change toward it) of power concentrated in the hands of a very few nations, and a relatively *stable* rank order among the major powers. While both schools agree that parity and fluidity increase decisional uncertainty, only the first would hold that such uncertainty makes for peace; the preponderance and stability school sees uncertainty as leading to war.

These two viewpoints were consolidated into a single basic model incorporating the three predictor variables (capability concentration, rate and direction of change in concentration, and the movement of capability shares among the powers) and the outcome variable (amount of inter-state war involving major powers). Since the classical theorizers say little regarding the sequence in which the variables should exercise their effects, or the way in which those effects might combine, we articulated and tested four versions: an additive and a multiplicative form with the measurement of concentration *prior* to the measurement of its change and movement, and an additive and multiplicative one with concentration measured *after* change and movement.

For the 19th century, the additive version of the parity-fluidity model produces a close fit to historical reality (R^2 = .73), while the multiplicative preponderance-stability model matches the 20th century, but not nearly as well (R^2 = .46). When capabilities are highly concentrated and there is little movement ir their distribution, then, one finds more war in the 19th century and less in the 20th.

Originally published in B. Russett (ed.) *Peace, War and Numbers,* 1972.

INTRODUCTION

In any systematic effort to identify the immediate or remote sources of international war, one has a variety of more or less equally reasonable options. First of all, one can focus either on the behavior of the relevant governments, or on the background conditions within which such behavior occurs. And if one leans toward ecologically oriented models—as we do—the choice is between the attributes of the nations themselves and the attributes of the system or sub-system within which the nations are located. Further, one may choose to focus on the structural attributes of the nations or the system or on their cultural or physical attributes.

In the Correlates of War project, we have recently begun to examine the behavioral patterns of nations in conflict, in order to ascertain whether there are recurrent patterns which consistently distinguish between those conflicts which eventuate in war and those which do not (Leng and Singer, 1970). But even though we contend that no model is adequate unless it includes such behavioral and interactional phenomena, we also believe that behavior cannot be understood adequately except in its ecological context.

Hence, the first two phases of the project have been restricted to the attributes of the system and those of the nations and pairs of nations that comprise the system. In the process, we have found it necessary to allocate more energy to data generation and acquisition (not to mention data management) than to data analysis, and in addition to making these data sets available via the International Relations Archive of the Inter-University Consortium for Political Research, we have published a fair number of them (Singer and Small, 1966a, 1966b; Russett, Singer, and Small, 1968; Small and Singer, 1969 and 1970; Wallace and Singer, 1970). In due course three handbooks will be published, embracing respectively the fluctuating and cumulative incidence of war (Singer and Small, 1972), the changing structure of the international system since the Congress of Vienna (Singer, Wallace, and Bremer, 1973), and the capabilities of the states which constitute that system (Singer and Small, 1973). We prepare these volumes not only to make our data as widely available as possible, but also in order to explain why and how we construct our most important measures. That is, unlike some other social science sectors, the international politics field finds very little data of a ready-made nature, requiring those of us in that particular vineyard to first convert our concepts into operational indicators, prior to any analysis. And even though we still have some major index construction and data generation tasks before us, we have not been completely inattentive to the possibilities of some modest theoretical analyses (Singer and Small, 1966c and 1968; Singer and Wallace, 1970; Wallace, 1971; Bremer, Singer, and Luterbacher, 1972; Gleditsch and Singer, 1972; and Skjelsbaek,

Authors' Note: Comments on an earlier version of this paper by Karl Deutsch, Melvin Small, Michael Wallace, and James Ray were particularly helpful. We would also like to thank Dorothy LaBarr for her patience and thoroughness in preparing the tables and text, and to acknowledge the support of the National Science Foundation under Grant number 010058.

1971). These partial and tentative analyses are, of course, essentially of a brush-clearing nature, preliminary to the testing of more complex and complete models.

The report at hand falls into that same brush-clearing category, designed to help us sort out some of the dominant regularities in the international system, and to aid in evaluating a number of equally plausible, but logically incompatible, theoretical formulations. To be quite explicit about it, we suspect that anyone who takes a given model of war (or most other international phenomena) very seriously at this stage of the game has just not looked at the referent world very carefully. Just as our colleagues in the physical and biological sciences have found that nature is full of apparent inconsistencies and paradoxes, requiring a constant interplay between theoretical schemes and empirical investigations, we believe that the complexities of war and global politics will require more than mathematical rigor and elegant logical exercises. So much, then, for the epistemological case on which we rest our research strategy. In the Conclusion, we will address ourselves to the equally important normative case, but let us turn now to the investigation at hand.

THE QUERY AND ITS RATIONALE

Our concern here is to ascertain the extent to which the war-proneness of the major powers, from 1820 through 1965, can be attributed to certain structural properties of the sub-system which they constitute. The first of these properties is the distribution of national capabilities within it at given points in time, and the second is the direction and rate of change in that distribution between any two of those points in time.

Before presenting our measures and analyses, however, it is pertinent to ask why one might expect to find any relationship between the distribution of "power" on the one hand, and the incidence of war, on the other. Without either tracing the discussion as it has unfolded in the literature of diplomatic history and international politics, or developing a full articulation of our own line of reasoning, we may nevertheless summarize what looks to us like a fairly plausible set of considerations.

The Major Powers' Preoccupation with Relative Capability

We begin with the assumption that the foreign policy elites of all national states are, at one time or another, concerned with their nation's standing in the power and/or prestige pecking order.[1] For any given nation at any given time,

1. While power and prestige are far from identical, and nations may well have statuses on these two dimensions that are quite inconsistent with each other, there is usually a high correlation between the two. In this paper, we focus only on power, but will deal with prestige (or attributed diplomatic importance) in a later one; for some tentative analyses, see Midlarsky (1969), East (1969), Wallace (1971), and Wallace (1972). For more detail on the composition of the international system and its sub-systems, see Singer and Small (1966a) and Russett, Singer, and Small (1968).

certain ranking scales will be of considerably greater salience than others, as will the relative position of one or another of their neighbors. Normally, we would not expect the decision makers of Burma to worry very much about their nation's military-industrial capability vis-a-vis that of Bolivia, or find the Swedish foreign office attending to the rise in Afghanistan's diplomatic prestige. Nor would it be particularly salient to the Mexican defense ministry that Australia's preparedness level had risen sharply over the previous half-decade. That is, the salience of a given nation's rank position on a given power or prestige dimension will only be high for the foreign policy elites of those other nations that are relatively interdependent with the first, and are "in the same league."

But we are talking here only about major powers, which—almost by definition—are highly interdependent one with the other, and clearly in the same upper strata on most of the recognized power or prestige dimensions. This becomes more evident if we indicate which states comprise the major power sub-system during the different periods of the century and a half which concerns us here. While the data introduced in a later report will indicate how valid the classification is, we emphasize that our criteria—quite intentionally—are less than operational. That is, rather than define the major power sub-system over time in terms of certain objective power and/or prestige indicators, we adhere to the rather intuitive criteria of the diplomatic historians. On the other hand, the consensus among those who have specialized in the various regions and epochs is remarkably high (especially from 1816 through 1945), and it leads to the following.

As the post-Congress period opens, we find Austria-Hungary, Prussia, Russia, France, and Britain constituting this select sub-system. Italy joins the group after unification in 1860, as does Germany as the successor state to Prussia in 1870. The two non-European newcomers are Japan in 1895, following its victory over China, and the United States, after defeating Spain in 1898. These eight continue as the sole major powers until World War I, which sees the dismemberment of the Austro-Hungarian empire, and the temporary loss of position for Germany (from 1918 to 1924) and Russia (from 1917 to 1921). World War II leads to the temporary elimination of France (from 1940 to 1944) and the permanent (i.e. at least through 1965) elimination of the Axis powers of Italy, Germany, and Japan. As the victors in that war, Britain, Russia, and the United States continue as members of the major power category; France regains membership in 1945, and China qualifies as of 1950.

It should not be difficult to argue that these states become major powers by dint of close attention to relative capability, and remain so in the same way. Of course, mere allocation of attention to their power and prestige vis-a-vis others will not suffice. They must begin with a solid territorial and demographic base, build upon that a superior industrial and/or military capability, and utilize those resources with a modicum of political competence.[2] Nor would it be difficult

2. If one accepts the propositions that successful war experience usually leads to increases in national power, and that the more powerful nations usually "win" their wars,

to argue that all of the major powers are sufficiently interdependent, directly or indirectly, to warrant treatment as a discernible sub-system. To a very considerable extent, during the epoch at hand, the policies of each impinge on the fate of the others; and as Campbell (1958) has urged in another context, this condition, plus a similarity of attributes, permits us to think of them as a single social system. We could, of course, go on to construct and apply a number of indices which might reflect the similarities and the interdependence of the major powers, but such an exercise is probably not necessary here.

If, then, we can assume that the states which constitute this oligarchy (Schwarzenberger, 1951) do indeed represent the most powerful members of the international system and that they are in relatively frequent interaction with one another, the next question is the extent to which they all collaborate to preserve the status quo, or conversely, vie with one another for supremacy. Our view is that neither extreme holds very often, and that the cooperative and competitive interactions among them fluctuate markedly over time. Further, as Langer (1931), Gulick (1955), Kissinger (1957), and others have demonstrated, even when they work together to impose a common peace, they keep a sharp eye on their relative capabilities. Each major foreign office is, at a given point in time, deeply concerned with the growth of some of their neighbors' strength and the decline of others'. Moreover, yesterday's allies are often tomorrow's rivals or enemies. Even as domestic political power has passed from the hands of the kings, kaisers, czars, and emperors to party bureaucrats and elected bourgeois rulers, the instability of coalitions has abated but slightly. Despite the inhibitory effects of articulated ideologies, competition for public office, and all the demagoguery which comes in the train of popular diplomacy, major power relationships continue to shift, albeit more slowly.

The Role of Uncertainty

It is, however, one thing to argue that the distribution and redistribution of relative capability will turn out to be a major factor in the behavior of national states, and quite another to predict the strength—and direction—of its relationship with war. As a matter of fact, we contend that a rather strong case can be made for two alternative, but incompatible, models. In each of these models, capability configurations represent the predictor or independent variables, and decision makers' uncertainty serves as the (unmeasured) intervening variable. By uncertainty we mean nothing more than the difficulty which foreign policy elites experience in discerning the stratifications and clusters in the system, and predicting the behavior of the other members of that system.

How does uncertainty link up with capability patterns on the one hand and with war or peace, on the other? Considering the latter connection first, those who believe that it is *un*certainty which usually makes for war will argue that most war is the result of misjudgment, erroneous perception, and poor predictions. The opposing view is that high levels of *certainty* are, on the

the high war involvement and win-lose scores of the major powers offer some evidence that the majors are not only attentive to, but high on relative capabilities (Small and Singer, 1970).

contrary, often at the root of war, and that the major inhibitor to war is a *lack* of clarity, order, and predictability. When relative capabilities are difficult to appraise, and when coalition bonds are ambiguous, outcomes are more in doubt, and it is that very uncertainty which helps governments to draw back from the brink of war (Haas and Whiting, 1956, p. 50).

Shifting from the possible link between uncertainty and war to that between capability distributions and such uncertainty, both schools of thought tend to converge. Here, the assumption is that three different variables will affect uncertainty in the system: the extent to which capabilities are highly concentrated in the hands of a very few nations, whether the distribution is changing toward higher or lower concentration, and the rate at which relative capabilities are moving. The model, as we see it, holds that uncertainty levels will rise when: (a) capabilities are more equally distributed and not concentrated; (b) the direction of change is toward such equal distribution and away from high concentrations; and (c) when there is high fluidity, rather than stability, in capability distributions.

To summarize, we find two contending models of more or less equal plausibility. One, which we might call the "preponderance and stability" model, holds that war will *in*crease as the system moves away from a high and stable concentration of capabilities. The other, which might be called the "parity and fluidity" model, holds that war will *de*crease as the system moves away from such a high and stable concentration and toward a more ambiguous state of approximate parity, coupled with a relatively fluid movement of the nations up and down the power hierarchy.

For the moment, we will leave these models in their pre-operational and verbal form. Then, after describing the measures and the resulting data in some detail, we can return to their formal articulation and to an examination of the extent to which each fits the empirical world of the past century and a half. It should, of course, be emphasized that even if our design were flawless, our measures impeccable, and our analyses beyond reproach, the findings would nevertheless be far from conclusive. First of all, there is Popper's dictum (1965a) regarding the disconfirmability, as opposed to the confirmability of empirical generalizations. Second, we must stress that the generalizations being tested here are very gross and undifferentiated. This, we believe, is as it should be in the early stages of a particular line of theoretical investigation, but we recognize at the same time that a more refined set of tests, with attention to additional variables and tighter analytical controls, is ultimately required.

THE VARIABLES AND THEIR MEASUREMENT

Space limitations and the conventions of scientific reporting usually preclude a fully detailed description of the precise operations by which one's verbalized constructs are converted into machine-readable data. This is especially unfortunate when most of these constructs or variables are not found in ready-made operational form (such as votes) and have not yet achieved even partial acceptance as reliable and valid indices (such as gross national product). But as we noted at the outset, we have been neither bashful nor niggardly in publishing our data, and we can therefore refer to those separate studies in which our rationale, procedures, and results are presented in greater detail. Thus, we will describe and justify our measures in only the briefest fashion here, beginning with the outcome variable (war) and then moving on to our predictor variables: concentration, change in concentration, and movement

The Incidence of War

We begin by distinguishing among inter-state, extra-systemic, and civil wars; the latter two are of no concern here, and we deal only with those of the first type in which at least one major power was an active participant and in which each side sustained at least 1,000 battle-connected fatalities. The particular index used in the analysis at hand is a reflection of the magnitude of war underway, as measured in nation months of such major power inter-state war. And since our time unit is the half-decade, we measure the warlikeness of each such period as the average annual amount of war underway during that period. The war data for each of the 29 periods from 1820 to 1965 are shown in Table 1, at the end of this section.[3]

National Capabilities

To this juncture, we have alluded to power, strength, and capability, but have side-stepped any definitions; that delicate chore can no longer be avoided. As one of us (Singer, 1963) emphasized some years ago, power is to political science what wealth is to economics, but not nearly as measureable. The focus there was on the influence *process*, and the range of strategies appropriate to each basic type of inter-nation influence situation; relative capabilities, or the bases of power, were by and large ignored.

Recently, several serious efforts to convert the intuitive notions of national capability or power base have appeared (German, 1970; Fucks, 1965), but rather than examine them or compare our approach to theirs, we will merely summarize our measures here. In a later volume we plan to discuss the several existing efforts, indicate the theoretical reasoning behind our own measures, and present our data in considerable detail.

We begin with six separate indicators, combine them into three, and then combine those into a single power base or war potential (Knorr, 1956) score for

3. Despite the modest fluctuations in the size of the major power subsystem, we do not normalize the war measure. Full details of our data generation and index construction procedures, and the considerations of validity and reliability upon which the indices rest, along with extensive tabular materials, are found in our forthcoming *Wages of War* (Singer and Small, 1972).

each nation every half decade. The six fall into three groupings of two dimensions each. The *demographic* dimension includes, first, the nation's total population, and second, the number of people living in cities of 20,000 or larger. The *industrial* dimension embraces both energy consumption (from 1885 on) and iron or steel production. The energy may come from many sources, but is converted into coal ton equivalents, and the iron/steel production is based on the former only until 1895, at which time we shift to steel alone. The third pair of measures are *military* expenditures and armed forces size, excluding reserves.

As to the more obvious validity questions, we carefully considered the need for separate indicators of social organization, national unity and motivation, and technical skills, but concluded that each of those was adequately reflected in one or more of the six specific indices. Closely related to the choice of indices and sub-indices is the matter of their relative contributions to a nation's power base. And while we are still experimenting with a number of weighting and interaction effect schemes, our tendency is to treat them as equally important, and additive in their effect. In line with these tentative assumptions, we first compute the total score (in people, tons, dollars, etc.) for the system, and then ascertain each nation's percentage share. This has the virtue of normalizing all of our data, reduces the computational problems associated with fluctuating currency conversion rates, avoids that of changes in purchasing power, and puts the figures into ideal form for the computation of our concentration-distribution scores, to which we will turn in a moment.

In addition, since the validity of the composite six-dimensional score is a long way from being demonstrated, we computed these percentage share scores not only for all six dimensions combined, but for the three two-dimensional indices of demographic, industrial, and military capability, and then for each of the six separately. There are, thus, ten power indices for each nation every half-decade, but only the *composite* scores are utilized in our analyses here.

The Distribution of Capabilities

In our discussion of the impact of certainty and uncertainty on the incidence of major power war, we indicated that capability distributions should exercise a strong effect on these certainty levels. How do we measure CON, or the extent to which these capabilities are concentrated or diffused among the nations which comprise the major power sub-system?

Once more, the measurement problem is sufficiently complex to warrant reference to a fuller statement elsewhere (Singer and Ray, 1972). To summarize here, we have been struck with the empirical inadequacy of several measures of inequality which have been rather widely used, and have thus devised our own.[4] To operationally measure the concentration of capabilities (within the

4. For example, the Gini is often as sensitive to a changing N as to the allocation of shares, when the N is low. And the Schutz index, because it sums the ratios of advantage of those above the equal share point, is sensitive only to their shares *as a group* and is not sensitive to the distributions *within* that group. Thus, the index would be the same (.5) for

grouping of from five to eight major powers) we proceed as follows. First, we compute the standard deviation of the *observed* percentage shares. Second, we divide that figure by the *maximum* standard deviation of the percentage shares that is possible for a given N; that maximum would occur if one nation held 100 percent of the shares, and the others had none at all. The resulting index ranges from zero (reflecting perfect equality in the distribution) to 1.0 (in which case one nation holds 100 percent of that capability), and—if our interpretation of the relevant data is correct—should turn out to be high in face validity. The concentration scores are listed in Table 1, along with the war data and the change and movement measures, to which we now turn.[5]

Movement and Change of Capability Distributions

Having dealt with the measurement of our outcome variable and the key predictor variable, we can now shift to the indices which reflect change across time in the latter. As the scores in Table 1 make clear, the distribution of power in the major power sub-system is by no means a static thing. How do we measure such shifts?

Two rather distinct indices are employed. The first is a straightforward reflection of the extent to which the concentration index has gone up or down during the period (usually five years) between any two observations. We call it simply change in concentration, or ΔCON. The second is a bit more complex, and it reflects the number of percentage shares which have been exchanged between and among the major powers during each period, whether or not that redistribution leads to a change in the rank ordering.

We begin by comparing the percentage of capability shares held by each of the nations at the beginning and the end of the half-decade. If, for example, the top ranked nation held 30 percent of the composite capability shares at the beginning of a half-decade, and the other four held, respectively, 25, 20, 15, and 10 percent, and the distribution at the end of the period were 35, 25, 15, 15, and 10, there would have been a movement of 10 percentage shares. That is, the top nation picked up 5 percentage shares, number three lost 5, and the remaining three scores remained constant. But in order to make the movement

---

each of the following percentage distributions; 70-20-10-0-0; 70-7.5-7.5-7.5-7.5; and 70-15-15-0-0. The same holds if the index is computed on the basis of those below the equal share point. An alternative approach is that of Brams (1968), and a useful discussion is in Alker and Russett (1964).

5. The formula for computing concentration is as follows:

$$CON = \sqrt{\frac{\sum\limits_{i=1}^{n} (Si)^2 - \frac{1}{n}}{1 - \frac{1}{n}}}$$

where n = number of nations in system, and Si = nation i's share (from .00 to 1.00) of the system's capabilities.

index (called MOVE) comparable across all 30 periods in our 150 years, with the size (and composition) of the sub-system changing from time to time, it must be normalized. That normalization is achieved by dividing by the *maximum possible* amount of movement or redistribution. That maximum, in turn, would occur if the lowest ranked nation picked up all the shares between the two observations, and ended up with 100 percent of them. Thus, our denominator is computed by subtracting the lowest nation's score from 100 percent and multiplying that difference by 2, since whatever it gained will have been lost by the others.[6]

It is now time to mention two irregularities that must be dealt with in computing our capability distribution and war measures. First, as already noted, the major power sub-system (as we define it) gains and loses members at several points during the century and a half under study. This not only requires us to normalize for its size when measuring capability distributions, but also to eliminate the distortions that could arise in measuring change or movement between two observations that are based on dissimilar sub-system membership. We do this by counting only the movement of shares between and among nations which were members at *both* observation points, and thus avoid any artifact which could arise merely because the 100 percent is divided among a smaller or larger population at the separate data points.

The second irregularity stems from the fact that we would get rather distorted indices of relative capability if we measured the military, industrial, and demographic strengths during the two world wars. Thus, in place of the 1915, 1940, and 1945 observation years, we use 1913, 1938, and 1946, respectively. But this makes several of our inter-observation intervals longer or shorter than five years. For the war measure, as mentioned earlier, we solve that problem by converting each period's total nation months of inter-state war underway into an *average annual* index. For the change in concentration and the movement measures—which are essentially rate of change measures—we merely divide all the inter-observation scores by the number of years which have elapsed between them; this again produces an average annual index.

Having now summarized, albeit briefly, the ways in which we convert our separate war and capability concepts into operational indices, we can present the resulting figures. In Table 1, then, we list the CON, ΔCON, MOVE, and WAR indices for each of the 29 observation points embraced in the study. Bear in mind that CON is the only one of our indices which is measured at a *single* point

---

6. The formula for computing movement is as follows:

$$MOVE = \frac{\sum_{i=1}^{n} \left| Si_{t-1} - Si_t \right|}{2(1 - Sm_t)}$$

where n = number of nations in system, Si = nation i's share of the system's capabilities, m = nation with lowest share of capabilities, and t, t−1 = observation points.

in time; the change and movement indices reflect the average annual magnitudes during the period immediately following the CON observation, and the amount of war is also that underway during the years immediately following that observation. However, a variety of time lags and leads will be introduced when we turn to our analyses, resulting in re-alignments across the rows as we move the various columns upward and downward.

Table 1. Capability and War Indices

Period Beginning (T0)	CON (T0)	Average Annual ΔCON (T0→T1)	Average Annual MOVE (T0→T1)	Average Annual Nation-Months of WAR Underway (T0→T1)
1820	0.241	−0.15	0.40	(2.92)
1825	0.233	0.17	0.47	6.68
1830	0.242	0.02	0.41	0.00
1835	0.243	−0.22	0.88	0.00
1840	0.232	0.50	0.60	0.00
1845	0.257	0.06	0.28	6.40
1850	0.260	0.34	0.67	9.36
1855	0.276	0.07	0.38	17.24
1860	0.280	−0.49	0.82	16.82
1865	0.255	−0.45	1.23	12.98
1870	0.233	−0.15	0.46	5.44
1875	0.225	0.02	0.34	3.52
1880	0.226	−0.36	0.53	2.64
1885	0.208	−0.10	0.65	2.12
1890	0.203	0.39	0.55	0.00
1895	0.223	−0.41	0.67	0.00
1900	0.202	0.09	0.93	4.32
1905	0.207	0.10	0.37	3.40
1910	0.212	−0.14	0.74	8.47
1913	0.208	2.34	1.69	87.06
1920	0.371	−2.49	1.26	0.00
1925	0.247	−0.13	0.80	0.00
1930	0.241	−0.25	2.57	6.68
1935	0.228	−0.37	2.23	8.73
1938	0.217	2.50	2.82	123.97
1946	0.417	−3.10	1.88	0.00
1950	0.293	0.76	0.99	103.34
1955	0.331	−0.56	1.36	0.52
1960	(0.303)	(0.09)	(1.21)	0.44

Note: For display convenience the values of ΔCON and MOVE have been multiplied by 100. The original values were used in all computations. Figures shown in parentheses ( ) are shown for information only; they are not used in the univariate statistics of Table 2 or in the CON LEADS models.

Examining the Data

Before we get to our analyses and the testing of the contending models, certain characteristics of the several data sets merit a brief discussion. Our motives are two-fold. The careful examination of one's data series, time plots, and scatter plots is, in our judgment, an important prerequisite to the conduct of statistical analyses. In addition, there are the well-known constraints which one's data distributions can impose in the selection and interpretation of the statistical analyses employed. The relevant summary statistics for our four variables are shown in Table 2.[7]

Looking at the measures of central tendency, we note that the differences between the means and medians for our three predictor variables are quite small in all three time spans. This suggests that these variables do not have seriously skewed distributions. The same cannot be said for the war variable, however. The mean nation-months of war figure for the 20th century is 24.78, while the median value is only 3.86, indicating that the distribution is positively skewed. This condition is no doubt due to the extreme values associated with World War I, World War II, and the Korean war.

Examining the measures of dispersion (range and standard deviation), we find that, as one might expect, all of our measures vary less in the 19th century than in the 20th. With one exception these differences are not serious, and that exception is the war variable. Again we find the three large wars in our series exerting a disproportionate influence on the distributional properties of the war variable. The standard deviation of war in the 19th century is 6.08, while the comparable figure for the 20th century is 44.07. Although Chauvenet's criterion (Young, 1962) might cast some doubt on the analyses associated with such outliers, we feel that the brush-clearing nature of this work suggests neither the transformation nor the elimination of these data points. We realize, however, that these values may weaken the predictive power of our models, particularly in the 20th century.

Two additional descriptors will also be important when we turn to our analyses. One of these is the *auto-correlation* coefficient, reflecting the extent to which each successive value of a given variable is independent of, or highly correlated with, the prior value of that same variable. For the entire time span, several of our indices show rather high auto-correlations, with ΔCON at −.58 and MOVE at .63. These turn out, however, to be quite different when we examine the centuries separately, suggesting further that these epochs are divided by more than a change in digits. Now we find that CON shows a .62 auto-correlation in the earlier epoch but only .13 in the present. The two indices of redistribution are negligibly auto-correlated in the 19th, but discernibly so

7. As we move into the examination and analysis of our data, we want to acknowledge our debt to Dan Fox of The University of Michigan Statistical Research Laboratory, for the creation of a set of programs particularly suited to time series data management and analysis in the social sciences.

Table 2. Descriptive Statistics

	CON	ΔCON	MOVE	WAR
Entire Span (N=28)				
Mean	.250	−.0007	.0096	15.36
Median	.237	−.0012	.0071	3.92
Maximum	.417	.0250	.0282	123.97
Minimum	.202	−.0310	.0028	0.0
Standard Deviation	.0504	.0105	.0069	32.33
Range	.215	.0560	.0254	123.97
Auto-correlation	.21	−.58	.63	−.15
Secular trend (beta)	.30	−.09	.66	.32
(b)	.0004	−.00002	.0001	.2501
19th Century (N=14)				
Mean	.244	−.0005	.0058	5.94
Median	.242	−.0004	.0050	4.48
Maximum	.280	.0050	.0123	17.24
Minimum	.208	−.0049	.0028	0.0
Standard Deviation	.0201	.0028	.0026	6.08
Range	.072	.0099	.0095	17.24
Auto-correlation	.62	.18	.01	.72
Secular trend (beta)	−.24	−.37	.17	−.01
(b)	−.0002	−.0005	.00002	−.0042
20th Century (N=14)				
Mean	.257	−.0009	.0315	24.78
Median	.226	−.0014	.0113	3.86
Maximum	.417	.0250	.0282	123.97
Minimum	.202	−.0310	.0037	0.0
Standard Deviation	.0692	.0149	.0078	44.07
Range	.215	.0560	.0245	123.97
Auto-correlation	.13	−.60	.50	−.32
Secular trend (beta)	.61	−.14	.56	.18
(b)	.0020	−.0001	.0002	.3849

Note: The auto-correlation coefficient shown is first-order only. For the separate century series, each variable was divided according to its lag-lead relationship in the ADD/CON LEADS model. Thus, the statistics shown above for the 19th century include the CON observation at 1885, ΔCON and MOVE 1885-1890, and WAR 1890-1894. The 20th century series begins with the following observation on each variable.

(−.60 and .50) in the 20th. As to the amount of war underway in each half decade, there is a high .72 correlation between successive periods in the earlier century, but a low −.32 in this century. We will return to the implications of these in the context of our multivariate analyses, but we should point out here that the important consideration is not so much that of auto-correlation of the indices, but of the auto-correlations of the differences between the predicted and observed values (i.e., residuals) of the outcome variable.

Then there is the closely related problem of secular trends. If one's variables are steadily rising or falling during the period under study, they can produce statistical associations that are largely a consequence of such trends. Hence the widespread use of "first differences" and other techniques for de-trending in the analysis of time series data. How serious is the problem in the study at hand? If we standardize each variable and regress the resulting series on the year of observation, also standardized, we can then estimate the trend of our various series by comparing the resulting slopes (or beta weights, which of course are equal to the product-moment correlation coefficients).

For the entire time span, MOVE shows the steepest slope, with a standardized regression coefficient of .66; CON and WAR are moderately steep with coefficients of .30 and .32 respectively. In the 19th century, ΔCON (−.37) and CON (−.24) show downward slopes, MOVE is slightly positive (.17), and WAR (−.01) shows virtually no trend whatever. CON develops a sharp positive trend (.61) in the 20th century, as does MOVE (.56). The other variables show weak 20th century trends, −.14 for ΔCON and .18 for WAR.

Before turning to our analyses, one additional data problem requires brief attention. Important, from both the substantive and methodological viewpoints, is the extent to which the predictor variables covary with each other, and these coefficients are shown under the correlation matrices in Tables 4, 5, and 6. For the entire span, the product-moment correlation between CON in one period and ΔCON in the next is −.71; that between CON and ΔCON during the preceding half-decade is .47. When CON is correlated with the amount of movement in the subsequent half-decade, we find a coefficient of .21, and it is .50 when correlated with the half decade preceding it. As to the two indices which reflect the durability of capability distribution, any suspicion that they might be tapping the same phenomenon is quickly dispelled; the correlation between ΔCON and MOVE is a negligible .08. When we turn to our multivariate analyses and discuss the problem of multi-collinearity, these correlations as well as those that obtain within the separate centuries will be examined further.

THE BIVARIATE ANALYSES

With our theoretical rationale, index construction, and data summaries behind us, we can return to the query which led to the investigation in the first place: what are the effects of capability distribution and redistribution on the incidence of war involving the members of the major power sub-system? We approach the question in two stages, the first of which is a series of bivariate analyses. These are employed not only because it seems useful to know as much as possible about such relationships prior to the examination of more complex models, but also because the theoretical argument suggests that CON, ΔCON, and MOVE should exercise independent—as well as combined—effects on decision maker uncertainty and on war. From there, we will move on to a number of multivariate analyses, in which we compare the war fluctuation patterns *predicted* by several additive and multiplicative models against the patterns which were actually *observed.*

We begin in a direct fashion and ask whether there is any discernible association between our several measures of capability distribution on the one hand, and fluctuations in the incidence of war, on the other. Bear in mind that: (a) CON is measured as of the first day (more or less) of every fifth year (except for the 1913, 1938, and 1946 substitutions noted earlier); (b) ΔCON and MOVE are measured between two successive readings of CON; and (c) WAR is measured during the period immediately following either the observation of CON or the second of the two observations on which ΔCON and MOVE are based. (A typical set of observations would be: ΔCON and MOVE from 1 January 1840 to 1 January 1845; CON at 1 January 1840; and WAR from 1 January 1845 through 31 December 1849.) The working assumption here is that whatever independent effects each of the predictor variables will have upon the incidence of war will be felt within the subsequent half-decade. In the multivariate analyses, we will experiment with these time lags and leads, and in a follow-up study (when our annual data are in) we will further explore the effects of different, and more precisely measured, time lags and leads.

Turning, then, to the product-moment correlations between these predictor variables and major power inter-state war, we examine the coefficients reported in Table 3. If those who view high concentration, upward change in concentration, and low movement as conducive to decisional certainty (and thus to low levels of war) are correct, we should find negative correlations for the CON-WAR and ΔCON-WAR association and positive ones for the MOVE-WAR association. Conversely, if the world is closer to the model articulated by those who see low concentration, downward change in concentration, and high movement as conducive to uncertainty (and thus to low levels of war), the signs would be just the opposite. What do we find?

Examining the total century and a half first, it looks as if the preponderance and stability school has the better of the predictive models. While correlation

Table 3. Bivariate Correlation Coefficients (r) and Coefficients of Determination Between Capability Indices and WAR in Succeeding Time Period

AVERAGE ANNUAL NATION-MONTHS OF
WAR UNDERWAY$_{t_1 \to t_2}$

	Total Span (N=28)		19th Century (N=14)		20th Century (N=14)	
	r	r^2	r	r^2	r	r^2
CON$_{t_0}$	−.10	.01	.81	.66	−.23	.05
ΔCON$_{t_0 \to t_1}$	−.38	.14	.19	.04	−.41	.17
MOVE$_{t_0 \to t_1}$	.34	.12	−.01	.00	.24	.06

coefficients of −.10, −.38, and .34 are not impressively high, all three are in the direction predicted by that particular model.[8] But as we have already intimated, there seem to be intuitive as well as empirical grounds for treating the centuries separately. Not only have many historians noted the transitional role of the 1890's, but several of our own analyses to date (Singer and Small, 1966c, 1968, and 1969) reinforce that impression.[9] Our suspicions are further reinforced when we compute the correlations for the centuries separately. We now find that those who recommend high concentration and low movement in order to reduce the incidence of war do not do quite so well. In the 20th century, the signs are all in the direction predicted by their model, while for the 19th century (or more precisely, the period ending with the 1890-1895 observations), the signs are reversed.[10]

Before leaving the bivariate analyses, however, a brief digression is in order that we might check for the presence and effect of cross-lag correlations. Here the search is not for the impact of the predictor variable on the outcome at subsequent observations, but for the impact of the "outcome" variable on chronologically subsequent values of the putative "predictor" variable. In the case at hand, we expected to find a number of cross-correlations, and some did indeed turn up. That is, when we correlated the amount of war underway in any period against the concentration measure in the subsequent period, we found a coefficient of .80 for the full 150 years, .52 for the 19th century, and .81 for the 20th. Similarly, for the impact of prior war on ΔCON, the coefficients were −.66, −.51, and −.68; and for its effect on MOVE, they were .30, .46, and .17. Most of these are sufficiently strong to suggest the need for re-examining the extent to which our capability indices predict to subsequent war when the effects of *prior* war have been removed. Hence, we predicted the CON, ΔCON, and MOVE measures from preceding levels of war; the variance in those measures which could *not* be so explained (i.e. residual variance) was then used as a relatively less biased predictor of war in the following half-decade.

For the entire period, the residual correlation between CON and WAR is a negligible .01; the effect on the 19th century coefficient is to reduce it from .81 to .65, and for the 20th, the association drops from −.23 to −.03. As to the

8. Throughout this paper we employ standardized measures of association (correlation coefficients and standardized regression coefficients). Our objective is to evaluate the relative contribution of variables rather than to establish empirical laws, and in this regard we have adopted what Blalock (1961) has called the "quantitative" criterion for evaluating the importance of variables.

9. In this and prior studies we have examined the effects of dividing the 150 years into three or more periods, or of using such salient years as 1871 or 1914 as our cutting point, but the clearest distinctions tend to be found when the 1890-1900 decade is used as our inter-epoch division.

10. The scatter plots, while not reproduced here, reveal the stronger linear relationships quite clearly, and in the case of the 20th century CON-WAR association, suggest a possible curvilinear pattern; the conversion to logarithmic plots does not, however, produce a linear association. On the other hand, a rank order (rho) correlation of −.53 also suggests that the CON-WAR association in the 20th century is far from negligible.

relationship between the residuals of ΔCON and WAR, the coefficients drop from −.29 to −.01, from .18 to −.03, and −.34 to −.06, for the full and the separate epochs respectively. The impact on the predictive power of MOVE, however, is to strengthen rather than reduce it. The full span's coefficient rises from .34 to .45, and those for the 19th century rise from −.01 to −.17, and from .23 to .41, respectively.[11]

Having emphasized the importance of such a cross-lag correlation check, however, we would now back off and argue that residuals should *not* be used in either the bivariate analyses at hand or in the multivariate ones which follow in the next section. That is, our theoretical concern here is exclusively with the effect of the concentration and redistribution of capabilities upon the incidence of war in the following period, regardless of what produced those capability configurations. Thus, while the war-to-capability association must be kept in mind, it is of minor consequence in the analyses at hand. We will, however, return to it in later reports, in which a number of feedback models will be put to the test.

Thus we conclude this section on the associations between capability concentrations and major power inter-state war by noting that the evidence is, for the moment, quite divided. While high concentration and changes toward it do—as the preponderance and stability school suggests—tend to reduce the incidence of war in the current century, such is clearly not the case in the previous century. Those patterns are much closer to what is predicted by the peace-through-parity-and-fluidity model. Let us turn, then, to a more detailed and complex scrutiny of the question.

THE MULTIVARIATE ANALYSES

With the bivariate analyses and some very tentative conclusions behind us, we can now turn to the multivariate models and consider the possible *joint* effects of capability configurations on the incidence of major power war. We do this via the consideration of four different versions of our model, reflecting those of an additive and those of a multiplicative type, and distinguishing between those in which we measure CON before ΔCON or MOVE and those in which CON follows ΔCON and MOVE chronologically. Before examining the several models and the extent to which they match the historical realities, we consider the rationale behind each type.

Looking at the additive-multiplicative distinctions first, let us think of our

11. Given the fact that most of the changes in the size of the major power sub-system occur as the result of high magnitude wars, we also examined the extent to which such changes themselves might be affecting the value of CON. It turns out—not surprisingly—that whatever decrease is found in the predictive power of CON vis-a-vis subsequent war is already accounted for by prior war; thus there is no need to control for the effects of both prior war *and* change in system size.

three predictor variables as if they were merely binary in nature, with 1 reflecting a high value of each and 0 reflecting a low value. Let us assume, further, that war will result if the variables, singly or in combination, reach a threshold of 1 or more. If their effects are additive, it is clear that we will have wars as long as *any one* of them is equal to 1. On the other hand, if their effects are *multiplicative, all* of them must equal 1, since a 0 value on any one of them will give us a product of 0. Another way to look at this distinction is to think of the road to war as having either fixed or flexible exits. In the multiplicative case, there are several exits, since we only need to have a low value (i.e., 0, for *any* one of them to avoid war; hence the flexibility of exits from the road to war. In the additive case, however, the exits are quite fixed; unless *every* one of the predictors is low (i.e. 0), war will result. We might also think of the additive version as a "marginal" one, in that the magnitude of each variable can only exercise a marginal effect on the probability of war, whereas the magnitude of each in the multiplicative case can be determining, at least in the negative sense.[12]

In addition to considering additive and multiplicative versions of the basic model, we need to consider the chronological sequence in which the variables are combined in accounting for the incidence of war. In the bivariate analyses, since the effects of each predictor variable upon war were measured separately, this was no problem. But here, especially since we already know that there is some interdependence among the three predictors, that sequence becomes critical. Unless we want to assume that the capability configurations could exercise their impact later than five years after being observed—which we do not—there are two major options. In one, we measure CON at 1870 (for example), ΔCON and MOVE between 1870 and 1875, and WAR from 1875 through 1879; we call this the CON LEADS version. In the other, we measure CON at 1875, with ΔCON and MOVE observed between 1870 and 1875, and WAR again measured during the 1875-1879 period; this is the CON LAGS version.

Thus, the basic model can be represented in four different forms:

ADD/CON LEADS: $WAR_{t_1 \to 2} = \alpha + \beta_1(CON_{t_0}) + \beta_2 (\Delta CON_{t_0 \to 1}) + \beta_3 (MOVE_{t_0 \to 1}) + \epsilon$

ADD/CON LAGS: $WAR_{t_1 \to 2} = \alpha + \beta_1(\Delta CON_{t_0 \to 1}) + \beta_2(MOVE_{t_0 \to 1}) + \beta_3(CON_{t_1}) + \epsilon$

MULT/CON LEADS: $WAR_{t_1 \to 2} = \alpha \times (CON_{t_0}^{\beta_1}) \times (\Delta CON_{t_0 \to 1}^{\beta_2}) \times (MOVE_{t_0 \to 1}^{\beta_3}) \times \epsilon$

MULT/CON LAGS: $WAR_{t_1 \to 2} = \alpha \times (\Delta CON_{t_0 \to 1}^{\beta_1}) \times (MOVE_{t_0 \to 1}^{\beta_2}) \times (CON_{t_1}^{\beta_3}) \times \epsilon$

where α = estimated constant term, or intercept; β = estimated regression coefficient, and ϵ = error term, or unexplained variance. How well do the several versions predict to the actual historical pattern of major power inter-state war? In Table 4 we show the following for each version of the model: the multiple regression coefficient (R), the multiple coefficient of determination (R^2), and the corrected multiple coefficient of determination ($\bar{R}^2$), as well as the beta

12. For an illuminating discussion of the statistical treatment of multiplicative and other interactive models, see Blalock (1965).

weights, or standardized regression coefficients (*b*), and the squared partial correlation coefficients (r^2) between each of the separate predictor variables and war, controlling for the other two.[13]

Table 4. Predictive Power of Four Versions of the Capability-War Model, ENTIRE SPAN (N=28)

Version	MULTIPLES			CON		ΔCON		MOVE	
	R	R^2	$\bar{R}^2$	b	r^2	b	r^2	b	r^2
ADD/CON LEADS	.56	.31	.23	−.28	.04	−.61	.20	.45	.20
ADD/CON LAGS	.55	.30	.22	−.18	.02	−.33	.11	.46	.18
MULT/CON LEADS	.43	.19	.09	−.27	.04	−.57	.15	.21	.04
MULT/CON LAGS	.43	.18	.08	−.22	.03	−.28	.07	.24	.05

R = Multiple correlation coefficient
R^2 = Coefficient of multiple determination
$\bar{R}^2$ = Corrected coefficient of multiple determination
b = Standardized regression coefficient
r^2 = Squared partial correlation coefficient

Correlations among the predictor variables:

$\Delta CON_{t_0 \to t_1}$	1.00	−.71	.47
$MOVE_{t_0 \to t_1}$	.08	.21	.50
	$\Delta CON_{t_0 \to t_1}$	CON_{t_0}	CON_{t_1}

The overall impression is that all four versions of the preponderance and stability model do moderately well in predicting to the incidence of war. Every one of the signs is in the direction predicted by that model, with high CON and

13. $\bar{R}^2$ is the coefficient of multiple determination, corrected for degrees of freedom in the following way:

$$\bar{R}^2 = 1 - \left[\frac{(1 - R^2)(N - 1)}{N - k - 1} \right]$$

where N = number of observations, and k = number of predictor variables. This index thus conservatively adjusts the goodness-of-fit estimate, penalizing the researcher for a large number of predictor variables and a small number of observations. This rewards parsimony and high N/k ratios; see Ezekiel and Fox (1959, Chap. 17) and Deutsch, Singer, and Smith (1965).

The regression coefficients of the multiplicative models were estimated by means of a $\log_e (X + C)$ transformation on all the variables, where C = 1.0 minus the minimum value of variable X. As Russett et al. explain (1964, pp. 311-313), *addition* of these transformed series is equivalent to the *multiplication* of their original values, and permits the researcher to isolate a unique coefficient for each variable's contribution to the combined multiplicative term. Without this transformation, only a gross coefficient for the interactive effect of the three variables could be estimated.

upward ΔCON preceding low levels of war (i.e. negative correlations with war) and high movement predicting to high levels of war. But the direction of the signs is a relatively crude index; how close is the fit between predicted and observed war levels?

Here we see that the two additive versions of the model, accounting as they do for 31 and 30 percent of the variance, do fairly well, whereas the multiplicative versions do not do as well. But this is only true before we correct for the degrees of freedom lost or gained by the number of observations and the number of predictor variables. When we introduce those corrections, none of the versions turns out to be particularly powerful in accounting for the observed levels of war. We also note that it makes little difference whether we observe CON before or after the two redistribution indices (ΔCON and MOVE). As to the predictive power of the separate indices, the impact of CON in the additive versions is consistently less than that of ΔCON and MOVE; in the multiplicative versions, this pattern is less clear. In sum, however, it is noteworthy that a model could predict as well as this one does, given the already apparent differences between the 19th and 20th century systems. One indication of its overall predictive power is revealed in Figure 1; the observed war values are shown as o's and those predicted by the ADD/CON LEADS version are shown as plus signs. What we see, in the distance between each pair of half-decade points, is that our fit is considerably better for the earlier than for the later epoch. More specifically, while it seems to predict fairly well to the occurrence and non-occurrence of war, it seriously underestimates the war levels generated by the two World Wars and the Korean War, for example.

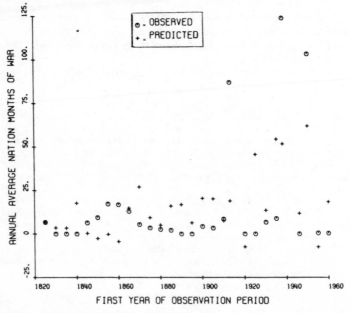

Figure 1. ADD/CON LEADS Model, Full Span

Do the several versions of our model do better when we examine the two centuries separately? As Tables 5 and 6 indicate, their predictive power is impressively high for the 19th century and rather low for the 20th; this disparity would account for the mixed results in the overall time span. In Table 5, reflecting the earlier epoch, we find that the additive versions are once again considerably more powerful than the multiplicative ones. More important, however, are the differences among the corrected coefficients of determination. This very conservative index shows that the additive versions account for at least 65 percent of the variance in our outcome variable (WAR) in the first of our two epochs.

Table 5. Predictive Power of Four Versions of the Capability-War Model, 19TH CENTURY (N=14)

Version	MULTIPLES			CON		ΔCON		MOVE	
	R	R^2	$\bar{R}^2$	b	r^2	b	r^2	b	r^2
ADD/CON LEADS	.85	.73	.65	.85	.72	.29	.19	−.38	.00
ADD/CON LAGS	.85	.73	.65	.96	.71	−.31	.17	−.39	.00
MULT/CON LEADS	.72	.52	.38	.73	.52	.16	.04	−.08	.01
MULT/CON LAGS	.72	.52	.38	.83	.50	−.35	.13	−.08	.01

Correlations among the predictor variables:

$\Delta CON_{t_0 \to t_1}$	1.00	−.14	.49
$MOVE_{t_0 \to t_1}$	−.46	.19	−.12
	$\Delta CON_{t_0 \to t_1}$	CON_{t_0}	CON_{t_1}

Table 6. Predictive Power of Four Versions of the Capability-War Model, 20TH CENTURY (N=14)

Version	MULTIPLES			CON		ΔCON		MOVE	
	R	R^2	$\bar{R}^2$	b	r^2	b	r^2	b	r^2
ADD/CON LEADS	.59	.35	.15	−.50	.12	−.85	.29	.44	.19
ADD/CON LAGS	.56	.31	.10	−.31	.07	−.32	.10	.45	.17
MULT/CON LEADS	.68	.46	.30	−.81	.31	−1.11	.46	.37	.18
MULT/CON LAGS	.64	.41	.23	−.58	.24	−.24	.07	.42	.18

Correlations among the predictor variables:

$\Delta CON_{t_0 \to t_1}$	1.00	−.75	.49
$MOVE_{t_0 \to t_1}$	.14	.16	.51
	$\Delta CON_{t_0 \to t_1}$	CON_{t_0}	CON_{t_1}

R = Multiple correlation coefficient
R^2 = Coefficient of multiple determination
$\bar{R}^2$ = Corrected coefficient of multiple determination
b = Standardized regression coefficient
r^2 = Squared partial correlation coefficient

As to the 20th century, the multiple coefficients of determination (R^2) are far from negligible, but unlike the findings for the entire period and the 19th century, here we find the multiplicative version to be more powerful than the additive one. This is not only quite consistent with our bivariate results, but is understandable in the context of our interpretation of multiplicative models. That is, the $-.23$ correlation between CON and WAR in the 20th century suggests that there is *some* association between the two, and an examination of our scatter plots showed that while most war did occur when CON was low, there were several periods in which CON was low, but *no* war occurred. To put it another way, low CON was *necessary* in order for large wars to occur, but it was far from sufficient. The multiple exit interpretation would suggest, then, that the absence of a downward change in CON (i.e. $-\Delta$CON), a high MOVE, or the effect of some unmeasured intervening variables(s) nevertheless permitted the low CON state of affairs to remain a peaceful one.

Looking at the beta weights, we find that all the signs but one are in the directions predicted by the parity-fluidity school's version of the model in the 19th century, and by the preponderance-stability version in the 20th. That exception occurs in the 19th century ADD and MULT models, when we observe CON after ΔCON and MOVE in the unfolding of events. Whereas a change toward higher concentration makes for more war when CON itself leads, it makes for less war (as the preponderance-stability school would predict) when CON follows behind ΔCON and MOVE. This result is a consequence of the high auto-correlation (.62) in CON in the 19th century.[14]

Returning to the other beta weights, we ask which of the separate indicators

14. The explanation for this phenomenon is somewhat lengthy and several discussions of it may be found in Harris (ed., 1963). To put the matter briefly, suppose that the true CON measures at t_0 and t_1 were equal. ΔCON would then be positively related to the errors in CON at t_1 and negatively related to the errors in CON at t_0, since ΔCON would under these circumstances be equal to the difference between these error terms. If the simple correlation between WAR and ΔCON were positive, as we have found, then the partial relationship between WAR and ΔCON controlling for CON at t_0 would also be positive. This necessarily follows since by controlling for CON at t_0 we are controlling for its error as well; thus the partial association between WAR and ΔCON is the equivalent of the relationship between WAR and the error in CON at t_1, controlling for the error in CON at t_0. As the error in CON at t_1 increases, ΔCON will also increase, and since the relationship between ΔCON and WAR is positive, so also must the relationship between WAR and the error in CON at t_1 be positive.

However, when we control for CON at t_1, rather than at t_0, and investigate the relationship between ΔCON and WAR, we are analyzing the relationship between WAR and the error in CON at t_0, controlling for the error in CON at t_1. As the error in CON at t_0 increases, ΔCON will decrease, and since the relationship between ΔCON and WAR is positive, the relationship between WAR and the error in CON at t_0 must be negative.

Even though our ΔCON measure is not, as assumed above, simply a function of error, the error components are present and apparently responsible for the observed sign reversal. This reversal supports the positive effect of ΔCON on WAR in the 20th century, but it also points up some of the problems which may be encountered when both a variable and its first-difference derivation are used in a regression equation.

exercises the strongest impact. In the 19th century, CON is by far the most potent variable in the regression equation, with all r^2 values greater than .50. This is, of course, fully consonant with the bivariate findings, as is the negligible strength of the movement index. And, as noted above, the effect of ΔCON (when we control for CON and MOVE) is a moderately strong and positive one when CON leads the redistribution measures, and almost as strong but negative when CON follows in the chronological sequence. In the 20th century, on the other hand, we find that all three predictor variables exercise approximately the same impact.[15] And whereas the additive versions give the better fit in the earlier epoch, the multiplicative ones do better in the current century. As a matter of fact, the MULT/CON LEADS version shows fairly strong predictive power, with an R^2 of .46 and partial r^2s of .31 and .46 for CON and ΔCON, respectively. Again the bivariate and multivariate analyses point quite consistently in the same direction.[16]

An examination of Figures 2 and 3 will not only reaffirm, but strengthen, the above statistical results. Plotted on the same scale as Figure 1, these indicate the discrepancy between the levels of war predicted by the **ADD/CON LEADS** model and the amounts that actually occurred in each half-decade. The deviations (i.e. the distances between 0 and + for each half-decade) are remarkably small in the 19th century, but much less consistent in the 20th century plot. The parity-fluidity school is thus strongly vindicated in the earlier

15. Parenthetically, for those who suspect that the definition of war used here may be too broad in that it embraces *all* inter-state war involving major powers, we mention a relevant finding. That is, if we look only at those eight wars in which there is a major power on *each* side, we find that there was a decline in CON during the half decade preceding all but one of those wars. Since these are almost equally divided between the centuries, they lend some support to the peace through preponderance doctrine.

16. We mentioned earlier the problems of multi-collinearity (high correlations among the predictor variables) and auto-correlated error terms. Because our predictor variables are highly correlated in several cases, we omitted one of them at a time and computed the predictions each of our models would have made from each pair of predictor variables, to see the effect of deleting a variable which was highly correlated with another in the equation. The coefficients from those equations were, predictably, similar in sign and strength to the predictions made from our three-variable models, although they naturally produced somewhat poorer overall results. Had we been interested in finding the "perfect" model we would not have included all three variables each time, but for the purposes of this paper, we considered it useful to present the results for each of the variables in all four variations of the multivariate model. As noted earlier, the correlations between the various predictor variables for each time period are shown beneath Tables 4, 5, and 6, respectively.

As to the auto-correlation problem, Table 2 shows that several of our variables do exhibit noticeable first-order auto-correlation r's: $-.13$ for the 150 year WAR series, and .73 and $-.29$ for the separate centuries. The predictions of our four models do a fair job of explaining, where it exists, the auto-correlation in the war variable. The most highly auto-correlated residual terms result from our 19th century predictions; in the case of the ADD/CON LEADS model, the coefficient of that residual series is .47, which, although sizeable, is considerably lower than the amount of auto-correlation in the original series. The coefficients for the residuals of its predictions are .27 for the 150 year span, .47 for the 19th century, and $-.13$ for the 20th.

epoch, while those who look to peace-through-preponderance-and-stability have the better of the argument in the later one.

A close look at Table 7 permits us to see more specifically wherein the amount of war predicted by the models deviates from that which actually occurred. Note, by way of introduction, that even though the same basic model is employed (i.e. ADD/CON LEADS, reflected in the first line in Tables 4, 5, and 6), the difference in the predictions made by the full span model and those for the separate centuries is a result of the difference in signs, as already mentioned. That is, since the best-fitting equation for the entire span has the same signs as that which is nearly the best for the 20th century, it therefore imposes *its* predictions on the 19th century.[17]

Shifting to the columns for the war levels predicted by the parity-fluidity (19th century) and preponderance-stability (20th century) models, a number of specific discrepancies merit explicit comment. Working our way down, we first note that the model underestimates—or more accurately, lags in predicting—the amount of war in the 1820-1840 period. From there on to the end of the 19th century, the fit is fairly good, giving us our estimated standard error of 3.60, which is a function of the actual discrepancy between the predicted and the observed values.

Moving into the later of our two eras, the 20th century model tends to overestimate the levels for 1925-29 and 1935-37, to underestimate the magnitudes of World War I, World War II and the Korean War, and to overestimate the final decade's warlikeness. This latter discrepancy may well be accounted for by the coding rules used for this particular study, excluding as they do the appreciable levels of *extra*-systemic war which marked that period. In general, the 20th century model spreads out the total amount of war more evenly, rather than predicting the radical fluctuations which do in fact occur; the standard error of the prediction is 40.48. For both centuries, of course, the inclusion of additional variables would have given us a better fit, but our objective was not so much to create or discover a best-fitting model as it was to *test* an *a priori* one.

CONCLUSION

Before we summarize the results of these analyses, it is important to make very explicit the tentative nature of our findings. Nor is this a mere genuflection in the direction of scientific custom. The study is preliminary in several fundamental meanings of the word.

First, there are the standard problems associated with any "first cut" investigation. Among these are: (a) the absence of any prior analyses of the same type; (b) the possibility of inaccuracies in our data, and as Morgenstern (1963) reminds us, the soures of error may indeed be considerable; and (c) the lack of

17. We say "nearly," because we actually get the best fit in the 20th century with the multiplicative version.

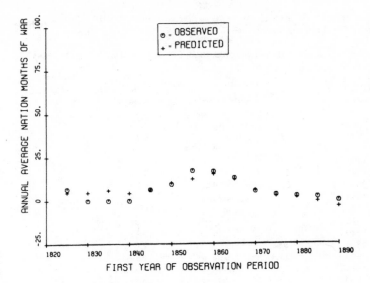

Figure 2. ADD/CON LEADS Model, 19th Century

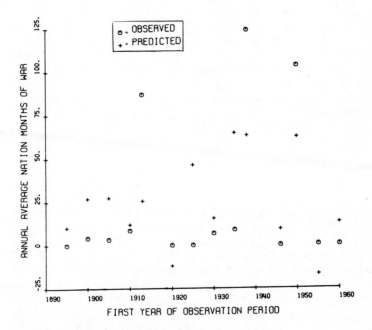

Figure 3. ADD/CON LEADS Model, 20th Century

Table 7. Observed Levels of War and Levels Predicted by ADD/CON LEADS Model: Entire Time Span and Separate Centuries

AVERAGE ANNUAL NUMBER OF NATION-MONTHS UNDERWAY

Period Beginning	Observed	Full-Span Model Predictions	19th Century Model Predictions	20th Century Model Predictions
1825	6.68	6.72	4.80	
1830	0.0	3.51	4.78	
1835	0.0	3.44	6.06	
1840	0.0	17.79	4.39	
1845	6.40	0.36	6.32	
1850	9.36	−2.54	10.23	
1855	17.24	−0.20	12.41	
1860	16.82	−4.35	15.33	
1865	12.98	14.87	12.32	
1870	5.44	27.10	5.92	
1875	3.52	9.31	2.69	
1880	2.64	5.06	1.89	
1885	2.12	16.03	−0.43	
1890	0.0	16.84	−3.51	
1895	0.0	6.35		10.16
1900	4.32	20.44		26.92
1905	3.40	20.15		27.39
1910	8.47	7.47		11.91
1913	87.06	18.96		25.62
1920	0.0	−7.29		−11.95
1925	0.0	45.64		46.28
1930	6.68	13.56		15.36
1935	8.73	54.36		64.54
1938	123.97	51.70		63.13
1946	0.0	11.83		9.12
1950	103.34	61.94		62.24
1955	0.52	−7.36		−16.90
1960	0.44	18.45		13.12

any hard evidence against which the validity of our predictor variables might be measured. In this vein, our use of the composite index of capability may possibly conceal certain important differences that could be revealed by each of the separate (demographic, industrial, and military) indices.

Secondly, the reliance on quinquennial observations might well account for an untoward portion of the results, in both the positive and negative sense of the word. The cutting points between the half-decades can so distribute the capability and war scores that, by accident alone, they may fall into either the "right" or "wrong" time period. Had we used a measure of the amount of war *begun* in a given period, that problem would have been even more accentuated; by measuring war underway, we minimize but do not eliminate the dangers of such an artifact. And any *annual* fluctuation in the predictor variables is concealed. In addition, the fixed interval between observations forecloses the use of briefer or longer spans in experimenting with various lag and lead relationships. In a follow-up study, when our annual capability data are available, we will have much more flexibility in our design, and will be able to ascertain whether the quinquennial time units do indeed represent a source of distortion in the results.

Third, our use of the single nation as our object of analysis may not only be an inaccurate reflection of who the "real" actors are, but produce distorted measures of capability and its distribution. Fourth, as we noted, our decision to defer the analysis of the feedback loops which connect *prior war to concentration* as well as *concentration to subsequent war* leaves our analysis of the problem far from complete. Fifth, it may well be that these findings will continue to hold as we re-examine our model's applicability to the major sub-system, but turn out to be quite inapplicable to the power and war dynamics of other sub-systems or the international system as a whole. Finally, it should be emphasized that this investigation is at the systemic level only and that no inferences can be made as to which particular nations, blocs, or dyads become involved in war resulting from the distribution or redistribution of capabilities.

With these caveats in mind, let us summarize what we have done in the investigation at hand, and what we think has been discovered. To recapitulate the theoretical argument, we have synthesized from the literature two distinct and incompatible models of the way in which the distribution and redistribution of capabilities affects the incidence of major power war. One, which we see as a formal and integrated version of the classical balance of power viewpoint (Haas, 1953) predicts that there will be less war when there is: (a) approximate parity among the major nations; (b) change toward parity rather than away from it; and (c) a relatively fluid power hierarchy. The other, reflecting the hegemony view, predicts that there will be less war when there is: (a) a preponderance of power concentrated in the hands of a very few nations; (b) change, if any, toward greater concentration; and (c) a relatively stable rank order among, and intervals between, the major powers. Even though a variety of intervening variables may be introduced as the link between such capability configurations and the preservation of peace, we suggest that decisional uncertainty is a parsimonious and appropriate one, and is implied in many of the traditional analyses. While both schools agree that parity and fluidity increase that uncertainty, only the first would hold that such uncertainty makes for peace; the preponderance and stability school sees uncertainty as leading to war.

These two sets of predictions have been consolidated into a single basic model incorporating the three predictor variables (capability concentration, rate and direction of change in concentration, and the movement of capability shares among the powers) and the outcome variable (amount of inter-state war involving major powers). But the classical theorizers were less than precise in their formulations, and said little in regard either to the sequence in which the variables should exercise their effects, or the way in which those effects might combine, making it necessary to construct alternative representations. Since an examination of only the most obvious version would be less than a fair test, we articulated and tested four versions: an additive and a multiplicative form with the measurement of concentration prior to the measurement of its change and movement, and an additive and multiplicative one with concentration measured after change and movement.

The first test of all four versions was for the entire century and a half since the Congress of Vienna, and it showed the preponderance and stability school's predictions to be closer to historical reality than those of the parity and fluidity school. But even though the correlations were all in the direction predicted by the preponderance school, their goodness of fit was not very impressive. Then, on the basis of prior findings, as well as a number of visual and statistical examinations of the data, we divided the century and a half into two separate eras of equal length, and re-tested the models.

This time, the predictions of the *parity and fluidity* school turned out to be correct in the direction of their associations and strong in their fit with 19th century reality. Particularly powerful was the additive form of the model with concentration measured prior to its redistribution. And, not surprisingly, given the results of the full 150 year analyses, the *20th* century findings matched the predictions of the *preponderance and stability* school. But whereas the corrected coefficient of determination ($\bar{R}^2$) for the parity model in the earlier era was .65, the best of those for the preponderance model in the contemporary era was .31.

Bearing in mind the opening paragraphs in this section, as well as the relatively clear empirical results, we conclude that the concentration of major power capabilities does indeed exercise an impact on the incidence of war and that its impact has been a radically different one in the past and present centuries. As to possible explanations for these radical differences, space limitations preclude any lengthy consideration. For the moment, though, we might speculate that uncertainty—our unmeasured intervening variable—plays a different role in the two centuries. When diplomacy was still largely in the hands of small elite groups, the uncertainty factor (allegedly resulting from an equal distribution of power, and fluidity in the rank orderings) may have been modest in both its magnitude and its effects. Schooled in the accepted norms of the game, these professionals might be uncertain as to exactly who ranked where, but nevertheless fairly confident as to general behavior patterns. The shared culture made it relatively clear what each would do in given—and familiar—situations of conflict or crisis, and their relative freedom of action made it easier to conform to such regularized expectations.

By the turn of the century, however, industrialization, urbanization, and the democratization of diplomacy may have begun to erode the rules of the game. Conventional definitons of the national interest were no longer widely accepted at home, and political oppositions and interest groups could make certain foreign policy moves difficult and costly to a regime. The increasing need to mobilize popular support as well as material resources meant that the vagaries of domestic politics would intrude more fully into a nation's diplomacy. And a grasp of other nations' domestic politics has never been a strong point in the foreign offices of the world. Hence, the normal uncertainties of the "balance of power" system were aggravated by these additional uncertainties, meaning that the probability of war could only be kept within bounds when power configurations were exceptionally clear and the pecking order was quite unambiguous. This is, of course, only one of several possible interpretations, and a highly speculative one at that.[18] In due course, then, we hope to bring more solid evidence to bear on the power-war relationships which are reported here; in that context, a number of technological, sociological, and political hypotheses will receive due consideration.

Given our findings and the associated caveats, are any policy implications worth noting? On the one hand—as our critics continue to remind us—such macro-level phenomena as the distribution of military-industrial capabilities are not exactly susceptible to short run policy control. In this, as in other of our analyses to date, the independent variables are indeed "independent" as far as immediate human intervention is concerned. They change rather slowly, and worse yet, they seldom seem to change in response to conscious and intelligent planning.

On the other hand, a fuller understanding of these structural conditions is much to be valued. Not only do they appear to exercise a powerful impact on the peacefulness of the international system, but they also constitute some of the major constraints within which men and groups act and interact. Despite the views of Rapoport (1970) and others that "there is no lack of knowledge about 'what men could do' to insure peace," we are struck with the evidence to the contrary.

Closely related is the familiar issue of how similar the world of the 1970's and 1980's is to that of the 1816-1895 or 1900-1965 periods. If the system has changed drastically on one or more occasions in this century, or is likely to do so in the near future, how relevant are the results of historical analyses? Our findings in the Correlates of War project to date suggest rather strongly that: (a) today's world *is* different from that of the 19th century, but (b) the most discernible changes occurred around the turn of the century and not with the first or second World War or with the advent of nuclear weapons and ballistic missiles. For the moment, then, all we can say is that it behooves us to treat all such alleged transformations as empirical questions, and to ascertain the extent

18. It has been alleged (e.g. Bleicher, 1971) that one abuses the scientific method by advancing alternative interpretations without supporting data. Our view is that such a practice not only enhances the quality and cumulativeness of science by suggesting possible follow-up investigations, but helps keep our discipline relevant to the real problems of war and peace in the immediate future.

to which such changes have affected the probability of war. We suspect, as noted above, that the 20th century system *is* a less stable and less easily understood one than the 19th, and that we *are* experiencing different types of war brought on by differing conditions. But it may also have given us the knowledge and skills that make it more tractable to us than the 19th century was for those who sought to understand and control the international politics of that era.

In saying this, however, we have no illusions that social scientific discoveries related to war (or other problems of social justice) will inevitably be utilized to better the lot of humanity (Singer, 1970). Knowledge can not only remain *un*applied; it can also be *mis*applied. But that is no justification for eschewing knowledge. Rather, our job is to ask the most important questions, seek the answers in the most efficient and rigorous fashion, publish our findings and interpretations in an expeditious fashion—and act on them in a forthright manner. As we see it, peace research—especially on the structural conditions that make for war—*is* peace action of a critical sort. Thus, as we continue to press for the policy changes that we *suspect* may improve man's chances for survival and dignity, we nevertheless continue that research which will permit us to replace mere suspicion with relatively hard knowledge.

J. David Singer (Ph.D. New York University, 1956) is Professor of Political Science at the University of Michigan and has also been associated with Vassar College, The Naval War College, and the Universities of Oslo and Geneva. Among his books are Financing International Organization *(1961):* Deterrence, Arms Control, and Disarmament *(1962):* Human Behavior and International Politics *(1965):* Quantitative International Politics *(1968):* The Wages of War, 1816-1965 *(1972): and* The Study of International Politics *(1976).*

Stuart A. Bremer (Ph.D. Michigan State University, 1970) is Research Director at the Wissenschaftszentrum in Berlin and was formerly associated with the University of Michigan. He is the author of Simulated Worlds *(1977) and a number of papers dealing with international conflict, global modeling, and methodology.*

John Stuckey (M.A. Kansas State University, 1968) is a Research Associate at Wissenschaftszentrum in Berlin. He is currently developing computer models of global systems.

The Population Density and War Proneness of European Nations, 1816-1965

STUART BREMER
J. DAVID SINGER
URS LUTERBACHER

Chapter **8**

Research on animal behavior and interpersonal conflict has found some association between "crowding" and aggressiveness. This study, with a temporal domain extending from 1816 to 1965, tests this association at the international level among members of the European state system. Members' population densities and their rates of change in population density are used as measures of objective and subjective crowding. Neither indicator shows any significant association with members' propensities to enter or initiate wars. When another indicator of crowding is used, urbanization, the association between war experience and crowding is still insignificant. There is, however, some association between urbanization and a system member's record of war initiation. Analysis of covariance was used in these experiments to control for the effects of national culture and changes in the level of technology.

There exists today a wide and suggestive literature on the relationship between demographic pressure and war. As far back as Malthus (1798) and as recently as popularizations by Lorenz (1966) and Ardrey (1966), the connection has intrigued students of the human condition. In his history of pre-1900 demographic thought, Hutchinson (1967) reminds us that the "pessimistic doctrine" of population dynamics—linking such pathologies as war, homicide, revolution, and disease with crowding—has been with us a long time. Among the pre- and post-Malthusian writers, we find such names as Thomas Hobbes (1651), and Sir Walter Raleigh (1650) as well as Botero, Bruckner, Gray, Hale, Petty, and Wallace. More recently, the sociological literature has included similar speculation by such scholars as Bouthoul (1953), Ross (1927), Thompson (1953), and Devaldes (1933). This preoccupation takes on renewed salience as the global community has become more concerned over the "ecology" question. Playing a central role in many of the analyses, reports, and sermons that have clogged the

AUTHORS' NOTE: *We are indebted to Albert Somit and Karl Deutsch, as well as our colleagues on the Correlates of War Project for their comments on an earlier draft of this paper. We also acknowedge the support of the National Science Foundation under grant GS-28476X1.*

Originally published in *Comparative Political Studies*, Vol. 6, No. 3, October 1973.

world's communication channels is the demographic factor (Ehrlich, 1969; Meadows et al. 1972). As an independent or intervening variable, crowding has been a key element in the optimistic as well as the pessimistic models, suggesting that the links among population, resources, and pathology remain less than obvious.

In the study of animal societies, while all the evidence is not yet in, the pattern does seem rather clear. The experiments of Calhoun (1962), Christian (1963), and King (1957), for example, seem to point to a crowding-combat syndrome. But in human groups, the pattern is less clear. Examining the association between population density and the incidence of pathology in several New York neighborhoods, for example, Srole et al., (1962) found crowding to be strongly associated with delinquency, suicide, accidents, alcoholism, tuberculosis, and infant mortality. While the causal connection is far from clear, and this sort of field research must cope with a variety of confounding variables, the results by and large coincide with those of several other investigations (Clinard, 1968; Buss, 1966).

On the other hand, there is some evidence that crowding, and the related conditions that are normally associated with urbanization, are not always dysfunctional for the individuals exposed to them. In a recent study of over 5500 respondents in six "developing" nations, Inkeles and Smith (1970) found that the "personal adjustment" of (ex-rural) urban factory workers was significantly better than that of their country cousins. By and large, these men showed consistently lower levels of psychosomatic stress than their village or rural counterparts; whether or not this is merely a consequence of self-selection is, however, an open question.

Shifting from the village and the city to the nation as a whole, is there any indication that nations with high concentrations of people are the ones which also experience a high level of domestic conflict and fighting? If we look at Tables 9 and 29 in the *World Handbook of Political and Social Indicators* (Russett et al., 1964: 267), for example, we see little similarity between the rankings of nations on urbanization and on deaths from domestic group violence in the 1950s. The product-moment correlation, as it turns out, is moderate and negative (−.31) for the 72 nations on which data were available.

Even if it could be demonstrated that there is a strong association between crowding and combat within cities and within nations, this need not point inexorably toward the same pattern at the *inter*national level. That is, despite the frequent speculation that there is a positive correlation between a nation's domestic and foreign conflict levels, it is reasonable to assume that the dynamics are not quite identical.[1]

This distinction raises a delicate definitional problem for the social scientist in general and for the student of cross-national and international politics in particular. On the one hand, all humans belong, by definition, to the same species. But this is essentially a physiological classification, and a rather crude one at that. We certainly know that there are discernible differences in overt physical appearance between races, and that such differences also extend to such less obvious attributes as pelvic structure and skull shape. More important, there seem to be some systematic differences across racial and ethnic lines in behavioral patterns and associated brain functions; perhaps Erikson is correct in referring to them as "pseudo-species."[2] Without venturing into the morass of cross-racial comparisons, individuous or otherwise, or equating such human differences with interspecies animal differences, it is clear that the species homo sapiens embraces a rather diverse range of physiological and behavioral attributes.

For us, the question is whether we can, or should, for the purposes of the analogy at hand, treat separate social groups as if they belonged to the same genera or species. One anthropologist (Livingstone, 1967: 65) puts it as follows: "Ecologically, they do act like different species, which, I think, is another reason for the great prevalence of fighting among populations of the human species. Genetically, of course, man *is* one species." Others might, however, contend that even the above-mentioned racial differences are insignificant, or are overshadowed by the fact that *intra*racial distribution ranges are greater than *inter*racial ones. At the opposite extreme, it could be argued that even so ambiguous a distinction as that between socioeconomic classes justifies the interspecific parallel. If this latter point of view is adopted, it follows that any equation of the inter-nation and the inter-specific (or inter-genus) distinctions would be quite legitimate.

The legitimacy of the metaphor need not, however, rest solely on biological grounds or on the folklore of racial, class, or national difference. That is, we can treat it as an empirical, behavioral question. Thus, if it turns out that the behavioral patterns and biochemical processes associated with inter-nation conflict are more similar to comparable animal phenomena of an inter-specific (or inter-genus) nature (Park, 1954, 1948) than to those of an intra-specific sort, we may be justified in looking upon nations as separate species or subspecies for certain purposes. And, of course, one way to get at those parallels is to examine the relative incidence of intra-nation and inter-nation combat, and compare the behavioral and physiological processes which accompany each. In this study, however, we will restrict ourselves to a much more modest concern: to what extent do national groups engage in combat *against other such groups* under conditions of crowding?

Given the greater complexity of human—as opposed to animal—societies, and the lack of highly consistent and unequivocal associations between crowding and combat in all types of society, it seems reasonable to pay closer attention to certain variables that may intervene between crowding and combat to either enhance or inhibit the allegedly causal process. For the international system, two intervening variables would seem to be of particular importance; and since their inclusion is critical to our research design, we summarize them here. One of these is the cultural variable, and the other is technology.

Turning first to the *cultural* norms which characterize a social system, crowding need not always lead to combat. There may be a variety of culturally accepted (if not sanctioned) responses to this increased density, of which combat and war are merely the most dramatic. And as Bouthoul (1953) has noted, some cultures have well-developed practices by which the crowding problem is headed off before it reaches disastrous proportions. Among those practices are monasticism, exploration and migration, slavery, sexual mutilation, and infanticide. The war-combat response increases in probability as the availability of alternative responses declines. Given the likelihood, then, of differences among national cultures vis-a-vis the high population density syndrome, it is imperative that we control for their effects in examining, for the past century and a half, the crowding-combat association in Europe.

A similar line of reasoning applies to the role of *technology* in the crowding-combat process. Compared to animals, which are remarkably homogeneous within species regardless of locale, humans differ widely both in the cultural norms noted above and in their technology. Some will be much more discommoded that others by the same population density, if they lack the technology which permits the support of a given population by a given resource base. If the production of food, clothing, and shelter, for example, is enhanced by technological innovation, the more innovative society should have a higher density threshold before crossing over into the condition known as crowding. On the other hand, we must not overlook the fact that advanced technology is a two-edged sword. While it certainly can make more effective the society's exploitation of its limited resources, it also generates new uses for and demands upon those same resources (Choucri and North, 1972). Regardless of the extent to which these tendencies might cancel each other out, it is necessary that we control for the effects of technology when we get into our analyses of the crowding and combat data.

THE INTERNATIONAL SETTING: OPERATIONALIZING THE VARIABLES

Whenever a theoretical proposition or model is put to the test for the first time in a given empirical domain, there is the inevitable problem of index construction and measurement. Constructs that convey a good amount of shared information may be perfectly satisfactory for the purpose of preliminary discussions or tentative speculation. But to go beyond that, we need to arrive at reliable and valid measures of those constructs, and this usually requires some difficult choices. Before indicating how we propose to operationalize the crowding and the combat variables, let us specify the spatial-temporal domain within which the analysis will be carried out.

THE SPATIAL-TEMPORAL DOMAIN

As the title indicates, our concern is with the European state system from the close of the Napoleonic Wars to the immediate past; thus the temporal domain extends from January 1, 1816 through December 31, 1965. Since we have only gathered our demographic data for every fifth year, and since a single year is too brief a period for such factors to exercise their impact—if any—on the war proneness of the nations, we aggregate all of our data into thirty periods of five years each. In that form, our data will permit us to investigate the relationship between our predictor (i.e., population density) variable at every fifth year, and the amount of war that began in the half-decade immediately following each such observation.

The political entities which define our spatial domain are the national states of the European continent—including Turkey—which were qualified members of the interstate system for 25 or more years during the 150 years under study. Basically, system membership requires that the nation have most of the traditional earmarks of sovereignty, plus a minimum population of one-half million, plus diplomatic recognition from France and Britain; this latter requirement served for the 1816-1919 period, after which membership in the League of Nations or United Nations is the criterion.

TABLE 1
COMPOSITION OF EUROPEAN STATE SYSTEM

Nation	Tenure	Number of Observations[b]
England	1816-	29
Holland	[a]1816-	29
France	[a]1816-	29
Switzerland	1816-	29
Spain	1816-	29
Portugal	1816-	29
Bavaria	1816-1870	11
Germany (Prussia)	1816-1945	26
Baden	1816-1870	11
Saxony	1816-1867	10
Wuerttemberg	1816-1870	11
Hesse Electoral	1816-1866	10
Hesse Grand Ducal	1816-1867	10
Austria-Hungary	1816-1918	20
Italy (Sardinia)	1816-	29
Papal States	1816-1860	9
Two Sicilies	1816-1861	9
Tuscany	1816-1860	9
Russia	1816-	29
Sweden	1816-	29
Denmark	[a]1816-	29
Turkey	1816-	29
Greece	[a]1828-	26
Belgium	[a]1830-	26
Hanover	1838-1866	5
Yugoslavia (Serbia)	[a]1878-	16
Rumania	1878-	16
Norway	[a]1905-	11
Bulgaria	1908-	10
Albania	[a]1914-	9
Czechoslovakia	[a]1918-	9
Poland	[a]1919-	8
Austria	[a]1919-	6
Hungary	1919-	9
Finland	1919-	8
Luxembourg	[a]1920-	8
Ireland	1922-	7

a. Ignores periods of less than five years during which the nation was militarily occupied.
b. Each nation loses one observation in the time span since a one period time lag is used in the analyses.

The detailed procedures and justifications are spelled out elsewhere (Singer and Small, 1966; and Russett et al., 1968), but the above tells enough about our criteria to permit a listing of the qualifying states and the years of their tenure in the above-defined European state system.

In addition to our interest in the relationship between density and war proneness of the separate individual nations, we must eventually examine that relationship at two other levels of analysis. One of these is the system level, in which we would treat all of Europe as a single unit of analysis and ask whether fluctuations in the amount of war within that regional system can be accounted for by population density and its rate or direction of change. The other level of analysis is the dyad, perhaps focusing on those pairs of nations that share a common border on the continent. Both the systemic and the dyadic analyses will, however, be deferred for the moment and covered in a subsequent paper.

THE DEPENDENT VARIABLE: EUROPEAN WAR EXPERIENCES

Having specified our spatial-temporal domain, and the level of analysis which concerns us here, we can move on to a brief description of the dependent, or outcome, variable. What do we mean by international war, and how do we measure it? Since the procedures and problems of measurement, as well as the resulting data, are covered in great detail in Singer and Small (1972), we need only summarize them here.

We begin by differentiating between two types of international war: intra-European and extra-European. In the first, we include all sustained military combat between the regular armed forces of European members of the interstate system, in which each side suffered at least 1,000 battle-connected fatalities among military personnel. Our data show 24 intra-European wars (i.e., those in which at least one protagonist on each side was European), resulting in 22,032,480 European battle deaths during the 150 years under investigation here. The second type of war (extra-European) is one in which a European member of the system fought only against a national entity—sovereign or not—located *outside* the continent. The period under study saw 49 such wars, resulting in 732,400 European battle deaths. Inasmuch as it was nearly impossible to ascertain battle death figures for those nonsovereign polities (e.g., Zulus, Mamelukes, or the Achinese) who fought in some of these wars, we used the 1,000 fatalities threshold only for the European belligerents in deciding whether it was sufficiently severe to include in our compilation. Whatever the ethnocentric implications of such a procedure, it at least seems to pose no serious threat to the validity of our nominal measure of war-no war, since the nonsovereign nations generally sustained many more casualties than the better-armed Western troops, against whom they fought in these colonial and imperial wars.

Once the qualifying wars have been identified, we can go on to derive or compute a number of other indicators of our dependent or outcome variables: the "war proneness" of each European nation during each of the half-decades (up to the maximum of 29) in which it was a system member. Thus for each such nation-period, we ascertain: a) the number of months of war it entered into; and b) the number of battle deaths it suffered from all wars (intra- plus extra-European) and from European wars (intra-European only). Note that even if a war extended in time beyond a given five-year period, our measure is concerned with the amount of war experience which began for each nation in each period.

Before leaving the war-proneness measure, one important refinement needs to be made. That is, even though we are interested in the extent to which population density predicts a nation's war proneness, that inquiry could turn out to be quite misleading. The theoretical literature on the subject, while recognizing that high (or rapidly rising) density might make a nation more likely to *be attacked* by another, is primarily concerned with the opposite relationship. In a latter section we will examine the proposition that high density nations *initiate* war with considerable regularity. We need, therefore, to distinguish between those which merely participate in a given war and those which actually initiate hostilities. We must emphasize, however, that the differentiation used here is extremely crude. While we are now generating the conflict behavior data which will eventually permit us to speak with some confidence as to which side was the "aggressor" in each of these 24 intra-European wars, we are restricted for the nonce to a mere specification of the initiator. By that term, we mean only the nation whose military personnel either first crossed an international boundary in force, or fired the first major fusillade. In other words, there will almost certainly be some cases in which the initiator was *not* the nation most responsible for escalating conflict into a shooting war, but here we merely identify the one(s) which committed the final catalytic act.

Were space available, in order to make visible any possible sources of disagreement, we would list each of the 73 qualifying wars, their initiators and other active participants, and the duration and severity of the war for all the participants collectively and separately. Those data may, however, be readily found in Singer and Small (1972: Tables 4.2, 4.4, 14.7).

THE PREDICTOR VARIABLES: POPULATION DENSITY

So much, then, for the referent world in which our historical experiment will be carried out, and the ways in which we measure our outcome, or dependent variable. Let us shift now to population density and some of the problems associated with its measurement. In order to measure or estimate the density of our European nations, two sets of data are essential: population and area. In a forthcoming handbook on national capabilities, these—as well as many other indicators of national size and capability—will be presented for each interstate system member, year by year. Thus, it will suffice to say that our half-decade estimates of each nation's total population and its area in square kilometers are based on a wide range of sources; for the most part, we relied on such standard annuaires as *Almanac de Gotha* and *Statesman's Yearbook,* supplemented by the more specialized demographic and geographic monographs.

While these quinquennial observations of each nation's total population and area provide the ingredients for the conventional ratio measure of population density, it should be noted that it is quite primitive and may well not be the most valid index of "crowding." That is, one nation's population distribution may have perhaps 60% of its citizens in cities of 20,000 or more, and another might have only 20% of its population so urbanized, while they both have the same overall average density. Despite that problem, and while examining alternative indices, in the present analysis we use the conventional measure.

We do, however, go slightly beyond that static ratio in an effort to capture what might be an important distinction. Crowding may be thought of in both objective and subjective terms, and a valid measure of the latter aspect is even more elusive than that of the former. In addition to the cultural and technological factors we noted earlier, differing responses to, and perceptions of, a given density might flow from such additional factors as acclimatization, or the extent to which a given population takes its density levels for granted. One obvious way of tapping this dimension is to ascertain how rapidly each society's density ratio is changing (usually upward) each half-decade. That is, when density rises very slowly, it may be nearly imperceptible to the inhabitants or their political elites, and they will find it easier to adapt to the rise when it is of so gradual a nature. But if the rate of increase is high, its objective and subjective consequences will be felt more rapidly and with greater force. Hence our use of both the quinquennial density ratio for each nation and the amount by which it changed since the prior half-decade observation.

THE ANALYSES

With the specification of our empirical domain and the variables whose association concerns us, we may readily move on to the procedures by which those associations, if any, might be ascertained.

ANALYSIS OF COVARIANCE:
CONTROLLING FOR THE MEDIATING VARIABLE

As we urged earlier in the paper, there are some sound reasons for not expecting the association between crowding and combat to be uniform across all nations or across so extended a period as the 150 years which concern us here. Rather, we suggested the importance of ascertaining the crowding-combat connection while explicitly controlling for the effects of: (a) national cultures, and (b) changes in the technology available to the separate nations. That is, we would—under ideal conditions—introduce indicators of these potentially intervening variables directly into our model, in order to control for their effects. But in the absence of the data reflecting cross-national and cross-temporal differences in culture or technology, we fall back on an approximation of the ideal design.

To do so, we need to make certain assumptions which, while plausible, are far from self-evident. As to the cultural variable, we assume that most of the variation within the European system over our century and a half will be found between and among the separate *nations,* and not between and among separate time *periods.* That is, not only are the nations more culturally similar within than between at a given point in time, but each is more similar to itself at two different times than it is to any other nation at the same or different points in time. To put it still another way, we can think of the European cultural mix and then ask whether more of the variation in that mix is accounted for by cross-national differences than by cross-temporal ones.

Just as we assume that culture is spatially heterogeneous and temporally homogenous, we assume—in turning to the technological variable—quite the opposite. Here, we assume that the European nations are, by and large, at roughly the same stage of technological development at any given time, but that there is a great deal of change across time. That change (increase) in technological development, we assume, is fairly radical over the 150 years which concern us, while most of the several nations are advancing at approximately the same rate and from approximately the same base line in 1816. Put more specifically, we assume that although the technological differences between France and Britain or between Italy and

Russia in 1816 or 1900 or 1965 are quite discernible, these are considerably less than the differences between the technology of France (or Britain, or Italy, or Russia) in 1816 and in 1965.

With these assumptions made explicit, we then proceed to our analyses, in which we measure the association between a nation's population density and its war proneness, controlling for the effects of the mediating variables. Using the analysis of covariance technique (Blalock, 1960; Alker, 1968), we can estimate the extent to which the relationship between density and war is similar across all nations and across all time periods. It estimates the linear relationship between these two interval scale variables for each of the possible categories of the nominal scale (culture or technology), and then tests (using the F statistic) for any interaction effects.

If the linear relationships between density and war are sufficiently homogeneous across the several categories of the nominal scale phenomena, there is no serious interaction, and we are then justified in computing a *single* estimate of the relationship between density and war. That is, a low or nonexistent interaction tells us that the relationship between our predictor and outcome variable is essentially the same for all categories of the intervening nominal variable. The *presence* of any significant interaction, on the other hand, tells us that we have two or more distinct linear patterns in the density-war relationship. Under those conditions, it would *not* be legitimate to assume that a single estimate of the regression slope would be equally applicable to all the sets of observations. Any remaining ambiguities as to our analysis of covariance should disappear as we now move to its application in the empirical context.

DENSITY AND WAR MEDIATED BY NATIONAL CULTURE

With our variables defined and the rationale behind our data analysis procedures spelled out, we turn to the analyses one at a time. Here, we ask: (a) how strong is the association between the density of the European nations and the amount of war they experienced in the half-decade following each density observation; and (b) how different are those associations from one nation to the next. A fact worth recalling is that we use two separate indices of crowding (density and $\triangle$ density) and four indices of national war (war months experienced and battle deaths sustained in all wars into which the nation entered during the five years following the density or density change observation, and the same for wars against other European system members only).

TABLE 2
ASSOCIATIONS BETWEEN CROWDING AND COMBAT INDICES,
CONTROLLING FOR NATION-SPECIFIC DIFFERENCES

Crowding Measure	Combat Measure	b	SE	r^2	F
Density	All months	.0022	.0021	.002	0.51
Density	All deaths	.069	.052	.003	1.33
Density	Eur. months	.0027	.0014	.007	0.95
Density	Eur. deaths	.070	.052	.003	1.32
△ Density	All months	.0012	.0010	.000	0.39
△ Density	All deaths	.107	.255	.000	0.21
△ Density	Eur. months	.0006	.0068	.000	0.68
△ Density	Eur. deaths	.112	.255	.000	0.20

Turning, then, to Table 2, the first concern is with the general associations between our several crowding and combat indices.

The b values indicate the magnitude of the change in war, given an increase in density. The standard errors (SE), on the other hand, give us an idea as to the error margins of these predictions. For example, the first b in Table 2 tells that, for each increase of one person per square kilometer, we can expect the average nation's war involvement to increase by .002 months. The standard error, on the other hand, reminds us that this change could easily be .002 months more or less than this predicted value. In other words, the change in war may reasonably be expected to vary from 0.0 to .004 months. Given this error range, it would be unwise to infer a strong relationship!

Generally, then, the b coefficients and their standard errors give us an idea as to the magnitude and quality of the relationship. The percent of variance-explained values (r^2) provides us with a compatible but slightly different basis for evaluation. A survey of these coefficients in Table 2 indicates that there is virtually no association for the pairs of predictor and outcome variables. Nation-years characterized by high density or rapid increases in density are followed by periods which are neither particularly high nor particularly low in the nations' war involvement.

The second question, however, is whether this lack of relationship between crowding and combat is consistent across all nations, or whether different groups of nations show distinctive patterns which are then canceled out by other groups with equally distinctive but opposite patterns. If this were the case, we would find F values of greater magnitude, reflecting significant differences between and among the various types of nations. The fact is that none of the F values is significant at even the .05 level, indicating that there are no important cross-national differences in the crowding-combat association. As suggested earlier, this permits us to not only conclude that cultural differences between and among the nations do not mask some strong associations, but also that no nation-specific differences are doing so. On the other hand, the analysis of covariance does not permit us to say that cultural differences have no effect at all on the associations; it merely permits us to say that whatever those effects may be in raising or lowering the intercept of the regression line, they do not affect its slope (b).

DENSITY AND WAR MEDIATED BY TECHNOLOGICAL INNOVATION

Having found little relationship between density and war when *nation*-specific differences, such as national culture, are partialled out, we now turn to the analysis of this relationship controlling for the effects of *time*-specific differences, such as technological innovation. We will again be looking at two measures of density and four measures of war participation, and our primary concerns will be: (a) the nature of the relationship, and (b) how well the relationship characterizes all 29 time periods in our century and a half.

Turning to Table 3 our first concern is with the general association between our several crowding and combat indices. Looking at the b values, their standard errors, and the associated r^2 values, we find little evidence for inferring an association between the predictor and outcome variables. On the average, nations characterized by high density or increasing density are neither more nor less war prone than those nations which are not.

TABLE 3
ASSOCIATIONS BETWEEN CROWDING AND COMBAT INDICES, CONTROLLING FOR TIME-SPECIFIC DIFFERENCES

Crowding Measure	Combat Measure	b	SE	r^2	F
Density	All months	.0004	.0010	.000	0.97
Density	All deaths	−.026	.026	.000	0.55
Density	Eur. months	.0001	.0006	.000	1.41
Density	Eur. deaths	−.020	.026	.001	0.95
△ Density	All months	.0035	.0096	.000	0.62
△ Density	All deaths	.075	.238	.000	0.05
△ Density	Eur. months	.0032	.0056	.001	0.77
△ Density	Eur. deaths	.081	.238	.000	0.05

The F values given in Table 3 reveal that this lack of relationship between density and war is generally consistent across all the time periods under study. The absence of interaction, as indicated by the failure of any of the F values to achieve significance at the .05 level, suggests that as technology has advanced from 1816 to the present, the cross-national relationship between population density and war proneness has become neither more nor less pronounced.

DENSITY AND THE INITIATION OF WAR

To this juncture, our data permit the conclusion that population density by itself tells us little about a nation's war proneness. Even when we control for cross-national cultural differences or cross-temporal technological differences, there is no evidence that the high-density nations of Europe are any more likely to end up in war than those of medium or low density. But as we suggested earlier in describing the distinction between mere *participation* in war and the actual *intiation* of combat, there may well be some association between this latter propensity and a nation's population density. That is, if high-density nations generally attack others of low density, the previous analyses, using only war participation, would not reveal this association. Under these circumstances, both more and less densely populated nations could have high war participation scores. Since there are good theoretical reasons for supposing that more densely populated nations may intiate war against less densely populated nations, we should attempt to determine whether initiators of war have higher population densities than those they attack.

We know the magnitudes of both population density and change therein for both initiators and defenders in most of the 24 intra-European wars in the 150 years under study. Comparing the two groups on these variables measured immediately before the outbreak of each war, we find that initiators are neither more nor less dense than defenders.

Table 4 presents the results of t-tests between the two groups. They do not appear to be significantly different with respect to either the level of density or the change in density since neither of the t-values is significant at the .05 level. We are somewhat assured, then, that our previous analyses have not masked important relationships of the sort outlined above.

URBANIZATION AND THE INITIATION OF WAR

An argument can be made that our basic measure of crowding— population per square kilometer—is an inadequate one. This conventional

TABLE 4

DENSITY OF INITIATORS AND DEFENDERS IN EUROPEAN WAR

Variable:	Density		△ Density	
Group:	Initiators	Defenders	Initiators	Defenders
N	23	23	21	21
Maximum	143.0	110.0	6.0	43.0
Minimum	3.0	3.0	−7.0	−22.0
Mean	54.2	47.0	2.00	1.81
Standard deviation	34.3	33.7	2.89	11.03
t-value	0.715		0.076	

measure may be conservative since it measures how spatially diffused a nation's population may be, rather than how crowded it is.

A measure which would be more accurate in this regard would require data on what proportion of a nation's population occupies what proportion of the available space. Given this information, we could construct an index of population concentration along the lines of a Gini coefficient. Lacking data for this type of index at this time, we can nevertheless take a partial step in this direction using the data gathered by Banks (1971). The two variables of interest here are the percent of a nation's population in cities of over 50,000 and over 100,000. We have been able to determine these percent figures for most of the initiators and defenders prior to the outbreak of the previously mentioned 24 wars. When possible, we also determined the change in percent in these two variables over the five year period which preceded the war.

Table 5 presents the results of the comparisons of the degree of urbanization variables for the initiators and defenders. Looking just at the

TABLE 5

LEVEL OF URBANIZATION FOR INITIATORS AND DEFENDERS IN EUROPEAN WAR

Variable:	% in Cities > 50,000		% in Cities > 100,000	
Group:	Initiators	Defenders	Initiators	Defenders
N	15	15	16	16
Maximum	36.9	26.3	32.1	20.7
Minimum	3.1	3.1	0.0	0.0
Mean	12.3	10.4	9.1	7.4
Standard deviation	10.2	6.6	8.9	5.5
t-value	0.60		0.62	

results concerning the percent of people in cities over 50,000, we find that a t-test reveals little difference between initiators and defenders. Similarly, the t-value associated with percent in cities over 100,000 is also not significant at the .05 level. In both of these cases the mean percent figures for initiators and defenders are quite close, as can be seen from Table 5.

Turning to the change of percent scores, we find some evidence to indicate that those who initiate war tend to be urbanizing faster than those whom they attack. As Table 6 indicates, the mean percent change (usually increase) in cities over 100,000 is significantly different for initiators and defenders at the .05 level of significance. For cities over 50,000 it is significant at the .12 level.

Upon inspection of the data concerning percent change in cities over 100,000 we find that, of the fourteen wars, nine are characterized by initiators who are urbanizing faster than the nations they attack and three cases exhibit the reverse pattern. The remaining two show equal amounts of change for the initiators and defenders.

The difficulty of interpreting these results in terms of our theoretical focus should be readily apparent. The link between urbanization and economic development is well established, and these findings may support the equally plausible industrialization-war relationship, rather than the crowding and combat hypothesis (Haas, 1965). We need not, of course, interpret this as an either-or proposition, since one of the causal factors underlying an industrialization-war relationship may be the crowding associated with urbanization. Perhaps the best that can be said is that there is a need for a more refined analysis focusing upon the urbanization process and its bearing on the war-proneness of nations.

TABLE 6
CHANGE IN URBANIZATION FOR INITIATORS AND DEFENDERS IN EUROPEAN WAR

Variable:	$\triangle$% in Cities > 50,000		$\triangle$% in Cities > 100,000	
Group:	Initiators	Defenders	Initiators	Defenders
N	13	13	14	14
Maximum	5.2	1.2	4.3	1.0
Minimum	−0.9	−0.1	0.0	−0.7
Mean	1.3	0.6	1.2	0.4
Standard deviation	1.7	0.4	1.3	0.5
t-value	1.62		2.21[a]	

a. Significant at the .05 level.

CONCLUSION

The findings which emerge from the above analyses may be summarized quite simply. There does not seem to be much support for the crowding and combat hypothesis at the international level. Using both an objective measure of crowding (population density) and a subjective measure of crowding (change in population density), we found little relationship over time between how crowded a nation was and several measures of its war participation, controlling for nation-specific differences such as culture. There seem to be no major exceptions to this pattern among the members of the European state system.

We found also that the proposed relationship did not emerge when cross-time differences such as technological development were controlled for. We found, rather, that the cross-national relationship between density and war is negligible and generally constant over the 150 year period. The additional finding that initiators of war were neither more nor less densely populated than those who were attacked gives added credence to our main conclusion.

Shifting to a different measure of crowding—urbanization—we found that initiators of war were generally urbanizing faster than those whom they attacked. However, our feeling is that this latter result, for a variety of reasons, may be more reflective of a link between industrialization and war proneness than between crowding and combat.

There are several factors which should be considered here in regard to our findings. The first is that we have not tested for a *non*-linear relationship between crowding and combat. This may be a critical shortcoming of the present study since much of the biological evidence points to the existence of a "crowding threshold," at which combatative behavior is activated. It may be, for example, that all the European state system members are below this threshold, but are approaching it. Under these conditions, it would be unwise for us to conclude that the crowding and combat syndrome, having not been present in the past, will not be present in the future.

Another limitation of the present study concerns the degree to which we can generalize our findings to non-European nations. There are two reasons for being cautious in this regard. First, it should be noted that many of the most densely populated nations, such as Japan, are not European, and these nations may be much closer to, or even beyond, the "crowding threshold" alluded to above. Secondly, we should note that in spite of our efforts to control for cultural and technological variables, it must be recognized that, comparatively speaking, the European state system is by no means typical of the global system with respect to these variables. Taking into account the far greater variety in culture and technology in the global system may reveal that the link between crowding and combat is evident in some of its subsystems, but not in others.

Going beyond this, we acknowledge that good reasons exist for postulating that cultural and technological factors may interactively mediate the density-war relationship. It may be, for example, that cultural norms which prohibit relieving the pressures of crowding by nonwar means and a low stage of technological development are each necessary, but not by themselves sufficient, for the crowding and combat process to take effect. It may require the presence of both conditions before combat will result from crowding in human societies.

A final point is one which appeared in our opening discussion on the relationship between crowding and combat in animal societies: the role of social disorganization as the critical intervening variable. In the Calhoun experiments and others, it turned out that mere crowding did not always suffice to produce high levels of combat. It usually had to be accompanied by a shattering of the established social patterns and hierarchies, such that the distribution of goods (space, food, mates, and so on) was no longer easily arranged. To anthropomorphize somewhat, customary allocations became subject to dispute, traditionally effective rules of dominance and submission had to be constantly renegotiated, and modest threats were converted into outright combat.

The parallel to the international system is not beyond recognition. As the number of people and nations grows and outstrips natural and man-made resources, objective and subjective levels of relative deprivation are likely to rise sharply. As people begin to feel that the norms of distributive justice are not being satisfied, they will increasingly challenge the global pecking order and the institutions which perpetuate it. Thus, as the animal experimenter could so rearrange access to, and the distribution of, valued objects as to permit the groups to adapt to larger populations, so must those who control resources in the global system. If our follow-up studies confirm these suspicions, we may well find that population pressure does indeed lead to war when, by virtue of the ways in which the continents and the entire world are organized, key resources are inaccessible to some. In that case, it behooves us to accelerate our efforts to redesign the global system and reallocate the goods which all people increasingly believe to be rightfully theirs. Unless we do, the entire globe may soon become what the ethologists refer to as one vast "behavioral sink."

NOTES

1. Several studies covering many nations in the 1950s have, as a matter of fact, shown almost no association between levels of domestic and foreign conflict; see Rummel (1963) and Tanter (1966). For a longer time span but fewer nations, see Sorokin (1937), and for a reanalysis of the Rummel and Tanter studies, suggesting that there is an association when we control for type of governmental regime, see Wilkenfeld (1968).

2. His point is that awareness of cultural and ethnic differences is often accompanied by a tendency to believe that only one's own group is "man" and that others are "non-man." Once that differentiation (or "pseudo-speciation") occurs, we have eliminated a major inhibition against killing people in other groups.

Stuart A. Bremer (Ph.D. Michigan State University, 1970) is Research Director at the Wissenschaftszentrum in Berlin and was formerly associated with the University of Michigan. He is the author of Simulated Worlds *(1977) and a number of papers dealing with international conflict, global modeling, and methodology.*

J. David Singer (Ph.D. New York University, 1956) is Professor of Political Science at the University of Michigan and has also been associated with Vassar College, The Naval War College, and the Universities of Oslo and Geneva. Among his books are Financing International Organization *(1961):* Deterrence, Arms Control, and Disarmament *(1962):* Human Behavior and International Politics *(1965):* Quantitative International Politics *(1968):* The Wages of War, 1816-1965 *(1972): and* The Study of International Politics *(1976).*

Urs Luterbacher (Ph.D. University of Geneva, 1972) is Associate Professor at the Graduate Institute of International Studies, Geneva, and has been associated with the University of Michigan on several occasions since 1970. Among his publications are Dimensions Historiques de Modeles Dynamique de Conflit *(1974) and numerous articles on international conflict and arms races.*

Behavioral Indicators of
War Proneness in Bilateral Conflicts

RUSSELL J. LENG with
ROBERT A. GOODSELL   *Chapter* **9**

An attempt is made to identify behavioral patterns characterizing international conflicts that are most likely to end in war. Five dyadic conflicts (the Schleswig-Holstein War, the Moroccan Conflict, World War I, the Suez Crisis, and the Cuban Missile Crisis) are chosen as representative of war or no-war outcomes in different historical periods. Internation acts are compiled from various secondary sources. Negative and positive acts are differentiated by their immediate objective impact on the target, adjusted according to the tempo. Thus, if Nation A states that it intends to refrain from a clash, the impact is positive. The first hypothesis holds that action taken by each side during a conflict will be symmetrical in type as well as magnitude. This is supported in three of the cases, but not in the Suez or Cuban Missile Crisis. Suez is the only case that subsided as a result of outside pressures; the exception of the Cuban Missile Crisis is consistent with the belief that the Russians "backed-down." The other hypotheses posit that as the military threat threshold is crossed, conflict behavior will increase and cooperative behavior will decrease until either side initiates escape behavior or war occurs. These hypotheses are supported.

Lord Palmerston once said that only three men ever understood the implications of the Schleswig-Holstein question and that, unfortunately, one (the Prince Consort) was dead, one (a former Foreign Office clerk) had gone mad, and he himself, the third, had forgotten them.

—Gordon Craig
Europe Since 1815

AUTHOR'S NOTE: Grateful acknowledgement is due to the National Science Foundation for support of this work under Grant Number 33120, and to Robert A. Goodsell for exceptional advice and assistance.

Originally published in C. W. McGowan, Jr. (ed.) Sage International Yearbook, II, 1974.

THE PROBLEM

The problem is the outbreak of war. This paper is a beginning step in an attempt to identify the behavioral patterns which characterize international conflicts which are most likely to end in war. Recognizing that the conflict behavior of rival nations is often only the last link in a causal chain that must include the attributes of the international system and its member actors,[1] we, nevertheless, assume that the overt actions of the rivals will have a profound influence over the outcome of conflicts.

Two basic ingredients are necessary for this undertaking. One is a base of theoretical work on the dynamics of inter-nation conflict behavior. The other is some means of extracting valid traces of that behavior from the available sources. Assuming that both requirements have been met, the search for indicators of prewar behavior patterns is analogous to studying electro-cardiograms for traces of symptoms signaling the onset of organic abnormalities. To a large degree, indices of the pathology are determined inductively, by continuing comparisons between "normal" and "abnormal" behavior traces. On the other hand, whether the search is for symptoms of an intra-human or international pathology, one must begin with some theoretical prognosis. As more data is generated and interpreted, the behavioral model becomes increasingly well defined, allowing for more reliable mappings of the course of the pathology. Ideally, the process would move by increments to the explanation necessary for the control of the disease, as well as the identification of its symptoms.[2]

This paper represents the first step in our investigation: the construction of a crude descriptive model of potential prewar conflict patterns. The model is based on five propositions drawn from the literature on conflict behavior, as well as our own speculation. But, before turning to these propositions, a brief statement of our assumptions regarding the nature of the social pathology—the prewar conflict—is in order.

We assume that relations among nations involve elements of both competition and cooperation. The scarcity of the values nations seek, national expectations of assertiveness as the norm in external behavior, and a decentralized international system based on the concept of self-help, all encourage competition in inter-nation relations. The interdependence of nations and the need for reciprocity demand some inter-nation cooperation. Within this framework, international actors attempt to influence the behavior of each other through a wide range of acts. Competing interests and mutual distrust may raise the competitive element in the mix to the point where the pattern of behavior between or among certain nations is significantly more competitive than cooperative. When the nations involved are aware of the increasingly competitive situations, but continue the same or a more competitive mix of behavior, the relationship may result in a conflict. Many such conflicts are likely to be exacerbated by the effects of positive (self-aggravating) feedback and "lock-in" effects (Deutsch, 1963; Rapoport and Chammah, 1965).

Thus, while we do not discount calculated aggression as an important source of war, we assume that conflicts in which rival nations become so enmeshed that they cannot extricate themselves, despite their desires to avoid a violent confrontation, are a major source of war in the modern international system. This perspective leads us to concentrate on the behavioral patterns which may make war more difficult to avoid, as well as the systemic and national attributes which influence the outbreak of war. We consider the following five propositions compatible with these assumptions.

PROPOSITIONS

The first proposition is that as a conflict develops over time, a tit-for-tat pattern may be observed as the opposing forces attempt to balance each other with reciprocal behavior. Triska and Finley (1970), who attribute the proposition to Eugéne Dupréel of the University of Brussels (1948), have found indicators of this pattern of behavior in the Cold War. These authors state (1970: 135) that in an extended conflict, "any stimulus inserted into the process by one of the opponents may be expected to bring about a *proportionate response* in *kind* from the other." North (1967) has observed a symmetrical pattern in the *intensity* of hostility in pre-World War I conflict escalation; Azar (1972) has observed a similar pattern in the escalatory phase of the 1956 Suez conflict; North, Brody and Holsti (1964) have found a high correlation in the level of violence exchanged between the United States and the Soviet Union in the Cuban Missile Crisis of 1962.

A balancing pattern of a less determined sort would be plausible in inter-nation relations, where the decentralized political system makes conflicting nations dependent on each other. Whether the dependence leads to resolution of the conflict in the form of a negotiated settlement or recourse to the use of military force, the nature of a system of self-help and reciprocity suggests balancing behavior. The remaining propositions suggest how this process can end on the path to war.

The "fight" process serves as the basis for the second and third propositions. This pattern, which was observed by Lewis Richardson (1960) in his model of a prewar arms race, has been elaborated to apply to a wider range of international conflict behavior by Pruitt (1965). Rapoport (1960) sees the model as applicable to conflicts occurring at all levels. Whether it is Tom Sawyer and Alfred Temple meeting on the street in Hannibal, one of Konrad Lorenz's coral fish invading the territory of another (1967), or the Great Powers on the eve of World War I, the scenario is the same. Rapoport (1960: 2) describes the confrontation between Tom Sawyer and Alfred Temple:

The two enemies stand poised for combat. What follows is a series of maneuvers, verbal jabs, and feints, in which invitation to join the combat is mixed with caution (the enemy's strength is being gauged). Each jab, however, calls for a counterjab, and so must be followed by another, *somewhat bolder* one. . . . The thrusts follow one another to the inevitable outburst of physical violence. The physical combat, too, must run its course. It is terminated only when the proper stimulus for its termination occurs: when the defeated boy "hollers 'nuff." [emphasis added]

Each adversary responds to a conflictive act from the other with a "somewhat bolder one." We no longer have an eye for eye, but the well-known process of escalation in the form of self-aggravating feedback. The conflict model proposed by Dupréel may or may not escalate; the fight process must. A pattern of escalation resembling the fight model has been observed in the rising casualty rates of the Vietnam War by Alcock and Lowe (1969). Studies by North (1967) and North, Brody, and Holsti (1964) of perception and action in the pre-World War I crisis, have indicated a pattern of increasingly threatening and injurious actions; this also is consistent with the assumptions of the fight model.

The third proposition is implied by the fight model, but stated more explicitly in one of Rapoport's more recent works (Rapoport and Chammah, 1965). It is the notion of a "lock-in" effect. He has found that in repeated experimental plays of the Prisoner's Dilemma game, the players are likely to become locked into either conflictive or cooperative strategies for extended periods. Applied to real world conflicts, this means that once the conflict escalation process is begun, it is likely to continue until one side surrenders to the will of the other. Stated absolutely, this means that, if the fight process obtains, then war must occur. On the other hand, if the proposition is applied in more relative terms, we may conceive of a conflict approximating the fight model to some degree. It would exhibit more or less of a lock-in pattern and require more or less of a surrender—that is, some sacrifice—to be terminated.

The lock-in proposition, as stated here, has not found explicit support in previous studies of inter-nation conflict interaction. A study by McClelland and Hoggard (1969) of world interaction patterns for 1966 indicated that, at least at the systemic level, in times of international crisis, the frequency of *all* types of behavior—cooperative as well as conflictive—increased. Corson (1970) has reported rather mixed observations in his East-West interaction study. Cooperation declined with the escalation of conflict during the Berlin blockade in 1949, the start of the Korean War in 1950, and the peak of the Vietnam War in 1964-1965; but cooperation remained high during the

Taiwan straits crisis of 1958, the Laotian and Cuban crisis periods of 1962, and the Berlin crisis of 1961.[3]

The fight scenario depicts a nonrational process. Actions lead automatically to reactions, as opposed to a *game* where each action is calculated to achieve particular values.

> In short, the essential difference, as we see it, is that a fight can be idealized as devoid of the rationality of the opponents, while a game, on the contrary, is idealized as a struggle in which complete 'rationality' of the opponents is assumed. [Rapoport, 1960: 10]

We propose that elements of both the fight and the game appear in most conflicts, and those conflicts which result in wars—wars which do not appear to have been desired by either adversary—are likely to be characterized by a pattern of behavior more strongly approximating the fight process. The all too familiar cycle of threat and counterthreat, commitments of national honor and pride which become mutually exclusive, not to mention the passions which may blind statesmen to cooperative solutions or bind them to winning at all cost, turn the game into a fight.

As the game becomes more of a fight, the means eat up the ends. Behavior predicts more strongly to behavior, with less relationship to "rational" objectives. If we accept this notion, two important questions remain. When is the nonrational process most likely to begin? What actions are necessary to make it stop short of a war? Some hypothetical answers to these questions are proposed by our fourth and fifth propositions.

The fourth proposition states that conflicts are more likely to escalate into the fight pattern when one adversary attempts to persuade or dissuade the other through the threat of military violence.[4] The notion that the use of threatening or coercive behavior is a turning point in the development of a conflict, of course, is not new.[5] In a system of self-help, the "threat" ups the ante for both sides. In our examination of potential prewar conflicts, we will consider military threats only; that is, those attempts to influence the behavior of the other side by the threat of the use of military violence will be distinguished from threats of political or economic sanctions. We do not suggest that the latter are not valid indicators of the development of an ongoing conflict, or that they are unrelated to the onset of war. Rather we propose that the fight threshold is most likely to occur when one or both sides threaten the use of military violence. This event was chosen on intuitive grounds based on the author's reading of diplomatic history; however, other scholars (K. Holsti, 1966; Young, 1968) have suggested it as a salient indicator of the probability of violent conflict.

Not all conflicts in which the above pattern of behavior is observed are condemned to terminate in war. But it is unlikely that, at this point, the conflict will be terminated short of war without some sacrifice on the part of at least one of the adversaries. Our fifth proposition is that, once the military threat threshold has been exceeded, it becomes necessary for at least one of the adversaries to undertake positive action, which we will call "escape behavior," rather than merely avoid certain conflictive actions ("avoidance behavior") to stop the escalation of the conflict. The proposition does not state that the escape behavior is defined conceptually as positive action directed at the adversary, which includes some sacrifice of values or "cost" to the actor. This type of act could be conceived of as akin to hollering "nuff"–as a *partial surrender* by one side, or a compromise by both. The assumption is that once the conflict has escalated to a certain magnitude, commitments to certain conflictive strategies and objectives have become so mutually exclusive that either one side must give in or both must engineer a costly compromise if war is to be avoided. Of course, the same factors which make for mutually exclusive commitments make a sacrifice less likely. At this stage, it would seem that only the fear of war itself could serve as a sufficient incentive to surrender or compromise. Again, we would expect to observe this phenomenon with even greater strength when the military violence threshold is crossed.

Summarizing the above, Propositions One, Two, and Three identify three behavior patterns likely to occur in an inter-nation conflict: symmetry, escalation, and lock-in. Proposition Four suggests that the escalation and lock-in patterns are more likely to occur after the threat of military violence. Proposition Five says that, once these thresholds are crossed, greater sacrifices by either one, or both sides, will be necessary to reverse the pattern of escalation of war.

HYPOTHESIS

The proposition outlined above can be stated as three basic hypotheses. The first allows for operational tests of the two behavioral assumptions in Proposition One, Dupréel's Theorem.

Hypothesis 1. During a conflict, the actions of each adversary are likely to be matched by actions by the other which are similar in (a) type and (b) magnitude.

Hypotheses 2 and 3 combine the notion of conflict escalation suggested by Rapoport's fight process (Proposition Two) with the upward and downward turning points suggested in Propositions Four and Five.

Hypothesis 2. If the military threat threshold is exceeded, then the magnitude of conflictive behavior will increase until one side initiates escape behavior or war occurs.

The third hypothesis states that, once the fight process begins, the lock-in effect described in Propostion Three should obtain. This suggests that as the fight progresses, not only should both sides become locked-in to an increasing amount of negative action, as indicated by Hypothesis 2, but that the magnitude of cooperative action should decrease.

Hypothesis 3. If the military threat threshold is exceeded, then the magnitude of cooperative acts will decrease until one side initiates escape behavior or war occurs.

THE EMPIRICAL DOMAIN

The time interval chosen for our complete sample of cases will be from 1816 to 1965, to correspond with other research undertaken as part of the Correlates of War project. The period begins with the Congress of Vienna and extends into the nuclear age, encompassing the wide range of changes occurring in the modern international system. Eventually, we plan to generate behavioral data from 20 prewar conflicts occurring during that period for comparison with 20 conflicts from the same period that did not result in war. In this paper we consider just five of those conflicts. The five conflicts were not chosen by random selection, but as representative of war or non-war outcomes in different historical eras. Three are from the pre-World War I era: the Schleswig-Holstein Conflict of 1864-1866, the Moroccan Conflict of 1904-1906, and the Austro-Serbian Conflict preceding the Great War. The other two are from the post-World War II era: the Suez Conflict of 1956-1957 and the Cuban Missile Crisis of 1962. Three (Schleswig-Holstein, Suez, and Austro-Serbia) ended in war; the other two did not.

There are other important differences, too. Historians agree that, in the Schleswig-Holstein conflict, Bismarck's Prussia was consciously seeking a war from the start. We now know that Britain, France, and Israel planned the use of military force against Egypt in Suez, well after Nassar's nationalization of the Suez Canal but well before the actual outbreak of fighting. On the other hand, it was hoped up until the final days that war between Austria and Serbia could be avoided. The differences between the two non-war conflicts are no less striking. The Moroccan Crisis of 1904-1906 was a typical nineteenth century style Great Power rivalry for influence in the affairs of a North African kingdom. It was an extended tempest-in-a-teapot compared to the sudden superpower confrontation over Cuba. We will not use these cases to attempt statistical inference to the full population of conflicts occurring during the 1816-1965 time interval; nevertheless, the variety of behavior occurring within the five should provide a good initial look at our propositions.

Having identified our cases, the next step is to delineate the boundaries of the conflicts—their participants, beginnings, and endings. The problem of determining who is a participant, and when, can be as sticky as a Democratic Party credentials dispute. None of our cases is a purely bilateral affair. Each has its own number of large and small actors, entering and exiting from the conflict at different time intervals.[6] Not all the parties to the same conflict are equally involved or even concerned with the same issues.[7] To simplify the matter, we have chosen a single dyadic dispute from each of the five conflicts: Germany versus Denmark in Schleswig-Holstein, France versus Germany in Morocco, Austria versus Serbia on the eve of World War I, Britain versus Egypt over Suez, and the United States versus the Soviet Union over Cuba. Thus, our analysis will be at the level of the bilateral conflict. We have avoided taking more than one dispute within a single conflict to preserve an assumption of independence among the cases.

When does a conflict begin? Assuming that a certain amount of competition and even conflict is normal in relations among rival nations, we must look for a certain magnitude of conflictive action, rather than the mere appearance of conflictive action. But when does the amount of conflictive activity exceed "normal" limits? When does it become a symptom of a potential prewar conflict?

The establishment of specific parameters which could be applied generally would have to be determined inductively, after considering a large sample of cases. Identifying the beginning of a particular conflict, however, is a bit simpler. By beginning our data generation well before the time when the conflict was assumed to have begun, we were reasonably certain to obtain patterns of "normal" activity prior to the conflict. First, we identified the seven-day interval, in the heart of the conflict, at which the highest frequency of conflictive acts was observed. Then we worked back in time until the frequency of conflictive acts receded to a relatively low and constant level, for a period of at least a month prior to the starting data assumed by our data sources. This was not difficult to determine in our five cases because the beginning of each conflict was identified with a salient act by which one adversary was assumed to have threatened the interests of the other.[8] We then reversed our direction and moved forward until we came to the first increase in the frequency of conflictive action. This was assumed to be the beginning of the conflict for our immediate research purposes.

Our conflicts should be terminated either by the outbreak of war or when the conflictive behavior subsides to the pre-conflict level or to some new equilibrium. Although three of our conflicts crossed the Singer-Small (1970) war threshold of at least 1,000 battle deaths, we decided to carry the Schleswig-Holstein and Suez conflicts to their post-war conclusions, as the actual military combat was over relatively quickly. The end points in these, as well as the two non-war conflicts, were determined by reversing our procedure for identifying the beginning of the conflicts. We moved ahead in time, instead of back, from the peak interval of conflictive action. The end of the Austro-Serbian conflict was identified as the outbreak of the military combat signaling the start of the war.

DATA GENERATION PROCEDURES

Before proceeding to operational definitions of the concepts appearing in the three hypotheses, it is necessary to summarize the data generation procedures.

Data Sources

By far the most widely used source for what is generally referred to as "events data," has been the press, most often the *New York Times* or the *New York Times Index*. Our intention is to supplement the media with the accounts of diplomatic historians, official documents, and memoirs. To minimize ideological biases, we will, wherever possible, use an account of the sequence of events as seen by at least one historian or participant from each nation involved in each conflict.[9] We make the assumption that most distortions in historical treatments occur through the neglect of certain actions, rather than the artificial creation of inter-nation acts which never occurred. The addition of historical materials adds an account of those secret consultations and confrontations which would have been unavailable to the contemporary press. The multiple sources also help eliminate some of the bias and distortion one might expect in the media.[10]

For the immediate purposes of this paper, we have generated data from the *New York Times* (daily edition) for each case in order to provide one common data source for all conflicts, along with the following historical narratives and chronologies.

(1) *Schleswig-Holstein:* Lawrence Steefel, *The Schleswig-Holstein Question;* W. E. Mosse, *The European Powers and the German Question, 1848-71.*

(2) *Moroccan Crisis:* Eugene Anderson, *The First Moroccan Crisis, 1904-1906.*

(3) *World War I:* Howard Koch et al., *Documentary Chronology of Events Preceding the Outbreak of the First World War.* [11]

(4) *Suez:* Kenneth Love, *Suez: The Twice Fought War;* Hugh Thomas, *Suez;* and *Middle East Journal* (the chronology).

(5) *Cuban Crisis:* David Larson, *The "Cuban Crisis" of 1962: Chronology and Documents;* Robert Kennedy, *Thirteen Days;* Roger Hilsman, *To Move a Nation.*

A verbal chronology was constructed from each of the above sources. Then the chronologies for each case were merged into a single master chronology, to be converted into machine readable data according to our action typology and coding rules.

The Action Typology

The foundation of any effort to generate and analyze behavioral data must be the constructed typology of behavior. Ours is designed for the identification and description of observable external acts undertaken by the agents of nations or other international actors. We have followed the procedure of Charles McClelland in concerning ourselves only with those acts which we consider politically significant, as opposed to the myriad of day-to-day transactions among nations.[12]

The typology has been constructed with our long-range research objectives in mind, rather than solely for the specific needs of this chapter. It reflects our assumptions regarding the dynamics of international behavior; nevertheless, it has been designed to allow for maximum flexibility in testing a wide variety of plausible hypotheses. Given the need for flexibility inherent in our long-range research goals and our epistemological preference for a valid and reliable description of phenomena prior to attempting analysis, the typology requires a minimum of inference regarding motives or perceptions of actions. Commonly used descriptions of acts, such as "threat" or "accusation," which do include inferences regarding motives, are avoided as much as possible at the data generation stage in favor of more direct and observable descriptions of the concrete acts. We do infer such meanings in our analysis of the data, but as far as is possible we avoid relying on either the data source or the coder to make these inferences.

The actual construction of the typology has been described in detail elsewhere (Leng and Singer, 1970); here we will mention only features of particular relevance to the investigation at hand. First, it is in the form of a hierarchical "choice tree." After describing the date, actor, target, location, and "tempo" (see below), each act is described according to the medium or resource which the actor utilizes to communicate to the target: Information, People, Places, or Things. This is typed more specifically as Military, Diplomatic, Economic-Technical, or Unofficial. Finally, at the last branch in the choice-tree the act is described according to one of 105 possible specific activity types. The choice-tree diagrams appear in the Appendix. This allows us to collapse the data file upward, thus providing the flexibility for a test of the reciprocity pattern, stated in Hypothesis 1, at several levels of specificity. This construction also allows us to collapse data files *across* categories to whatever extent desired; thus permitting the isolation of the types of behavior derived from the concepts appearing in Hypotheses 2 and 3. We have cast a fine-screened net in order to provide the most detailed description of international acts, but it is a simple matter to aggregate or isolate data according to the research problem at hand.

A sensitive mapping of the patterns of behavior over time is facilitated by describing acts according to the *tempo* of action; that is, whether they are *discrete* acts, beginning and ending on the same day, or *continuing* acts which are *starting, increasing, decreasing,* or *stopping.* This, of course, is necessary in the measurement of the magnitude of conflictive and cooperative behavior required by our hypotheses. Finally, each verbal act is "double-coded"; that is, the act of issuing information is described fully, then it is followed by a description of the act commented upon, requested, or stated as intended. As we shall see below, this capability is essential in determining whether or not specific verbal acts meet our definitions of the military threat threshold or escape behavior.

Coding Procedures

Data files were coded from the verbal chronologies according to instructions in *Coder's Manual for Identifying and Describing International Actions* (Leng, 1972a), which the author pretested and revised over a two-year period.[13]

Operational Definitions

Using this action typology, we have composed the following operational definitions of the variables appearing in our three hypotheses.

(1) *Cooperative and Conflictive Behavior.* Operationally, we distinguish between cooperative and conflictive acts according to whether the *immediate*

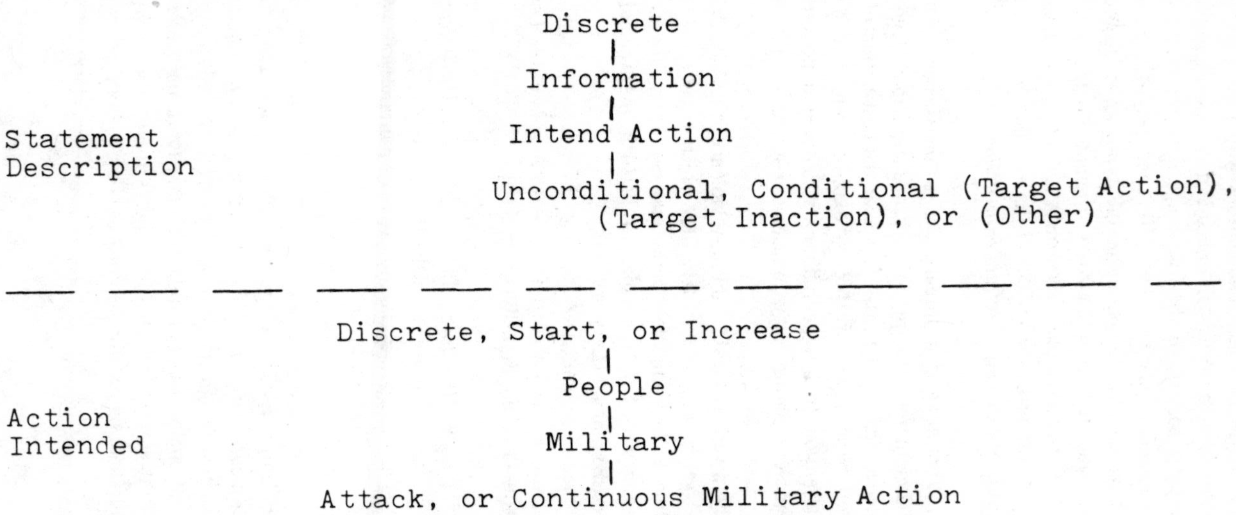

Statement
Description

Discrete
|
Information
|
Intend Action
|
Unconditional, Conditional (Target Action),
(Target Inaction), or (Other)

Action
Intended

Discrete, Start, or Increase
|
People
|
Military
|
Attack, or Continuous Military Action

Figure 1: VERBAL THREATS OF MILITARY VIOLENCE

objective impact on the target would be described as positive or negative. Thus, a military "Clash" between two nations would be coded as having a negative impact on each, even though one side may have desired such a clash for certain political reasons, or the long-range outcome of the event may prove to be beneficial to one or both of the nations.[14] The positive or negative impact on each act appearing in the typology is labeled in "pure form" and then readjusted according to the "tempo" of the action once the act has been coded. For example, if Nation A states that it intends to *refrain from* a *Clash* with Nation B, the impact of the act upon Nation B is adjusted to *positive,* because of the *tempo—refrain from acting.*

(2) *Coercion Threshold.* Conceptually, we say that a coercion threshold is exceeded when one nation attempts to influence another through the threat of military violence; that is, the loss of lives or the destruction of property. We include two basic types of threats, explicit verbal communications indicating an intention to initiate military violence and nonverbal deeds, which, by their very nature, may indicate an intent to initiate military violence.[15]

Operationally, a verbal threat of military violence is defined as any of the "double-coded" verbal acts in our data files which include the descriptors appearing in Figure 1. Complete operational definitions for each of the descriptive categories used in this paper are listed in the Appendix as they appear in the *Coder's Manual* (Leng, 1972a).

Nonverbal threats of military violence include any acts coded as People-Military, where the last descriptor is Change-in-Force Level, Alert, Mobilization, Show-of-Strength, or Blockade.[16]

(3) *Military Violence Threshold.* Military violence is defined conceptually as any military action which results in the loss of lives or the destruction of property. Acts serving as operational indicators of military violence are those within the People-Military category, whose most specific descriptors are Attack, Clash, or Continuous Military Conflict.

(4) *Escape Behavior.* Escape behavior includes any positive act toward the adversary which incurs some sacrifice of values or "cost" to the actor. In this category, we also include agreements whereby each of the adversaries gives up something. Operationally, we define escape behavior as occurring whenever one, or both, of the adversaries either undertakes or unconditionally states its intention to undertake one of the descriptive combinations appearing in the matrix in Table 1.

TABLE 1
ACTS QUALIFYING AS ESCAPE BEHAVIOR*

	Military	*Diplomatic*	*Economic*
People	Domestic Military Act (Negative)	Domestic Political Act (Negative)	Domestic Economic Act (Negative)
	Military Surrender	Political Concession	
Things	Domestic Military Act (Negative)		Domestic Economic Act (Negative)
	Grant		Grant
	Return		Loan
	Remove		Return
	Remove Strategic Weapons		Remove
			Pay Reparations
			Pay Ransom
Places	Domestic Military Act (Negative)	Grant Independence	
	Permit Foreign Military Passage		
	(Allow) Overseas Base		

*With verbal acts, the descriptive sequence would be: *Information-Intend Action-Unconditional-Action Specified*, followed by one of the descriptions appearing above.

(5) *Avoidance Behavior.* Cooperative acts which do not require a significant sacrifice of values are classified as "avoidance behavior." The American-Soviet consultation during the Cuban Missile Crisis, for example, is cooperative behavior, which would be classified as avoidance behavior.

TESTING THE HYPOTHESES

Hypothesis 1 was divided into two parts for testing purposes. First, we tested for "matches" in the *types* of acts taken by the two adversaries. Operationally, we defined 14 types of acts, which were taken from the next to lowest level of specification in the action typology. (See Appendix for the choice-tree "Action–General Differentiation Scheme.") Some subjective judgment was required in choosing the time intervals in which to observe matches of inter-adversary actions. Duprèel's Theorem does not state either that there is an explicit action-response sequence,[17] or that the adversaries would take the same types of acts simultaneously. On the other hand, the idea of nations acting to balance each other suggests that we should expect to find similar acts occurring in more or less the same time intervals. Certainly we would not want to argue that acts occurring at the end of a two- or three-year conflict reciprocated acts occurring at the start of the conflict. We decided to break the conflicts into seven-day intervals and search for matching acts within each.

We found that the most practical measure of symmetry in types of behavior was obtained by using the same formula we had employed to test inter-coder reliability (see note 13). Now the two adversary nations became the "coders," with matches in the coded types of actions providing a "reliability" score for symmetry. The scores for each of the five conflicts are presented in Table 2.

The total percentage scores for each conflict lend support to the hypothesis. Interestingly, the highest scores often appear in the seven-day intervals which include the greatest amount of inter-adversary activity. The more interaction, the greater the similarity in behavior. By the same token, with the exception of the pre-World War I case, the greatest amount of symmetry was observed in the Schleswig-Holstein and Moroccan conflicts, the two longest conflicts. Both of these observations are consistent with Dupréel's assumption that the balancing behavior occurs as "the character of the aggressor and defender inter-mingle and merge."

The second part of Hypothesis 1 states that the adversaries will take action that is similar in *magnitude,* as well as type. Magnitude was defined operationally as the frequency of acts occurring within a specified interval.[18] For this test, we divided the actions into two general types—positive (cooperative) and negative (conflictive). This time it was possible to use a product moment correlation to test for symmetry in the magnitude of acts. A serial correlation in the data required us to abandon a test using magnitude scores within the same seven-day intervals in favor of first differences.[19] The correlation coefficients appear in Table 3.

With a few exceptions, the results in Table 3 lend further credence to the notion of symmetry in conflict behavior. The correlation coefficients also provide a standard measure which is a bit more suggestive than the ICR score. The extent to which the adversaries' negative acts move together is particularly impressive. All cases are significant at the .05 level.[20] The only correlation coefficient below .50 is that for the Schleswig-Holstein conflict, which we previously singled out for its distinctive one-sidedness (see the section entitled "Data Sources").

Two of the correlation coefficients for association in the magnitude of *positive* acts do fall below the .05 significance level. These are the two most recent conflicts, the Cuban and Suez conflicts. A closer look at the pattern of action by the two adversaries in the Cuban conflict indicates a large number

TABLE 2
INTER-ADVERSARY MATCHES OF ACTS BY TYPES, OBSERVED AT SEVEN-DAY INTERVALS

Schleswig-Holstein 10/1/63 — 8/4/64 (pi = 78.06)

N =	23	24	22	21	21	27	43	40	37	9	7	7	8	7	7	16	28	28	30	4	3	0
Score =	100	96	100	100	100	89	81	88	97	100	100	100	87	100	100	100	100	100	97	100	0	0

N =	0	0	0	0	0	0	0	1	0	0	0	0	0	0	0	1	7	12	21	22	24	21	22
Score =	0	0	0	0	0	0	0	100	0	0	0	0	0	0	0	100	75	66	64	63	100	100	95

Moroccan 3/31/04 — 9/29/05 — 12/8/05 — 3/31/06 (pi = 63.70)

N =	1	0	1	0	0	0	0	0	0	3	3	2	0	1	0	1	0	0	1	0	1	1	3
Score =	100	0	100	0	0	0	0	0	100	33	100	0	100	0	100	0	100	0	100	0	100	0	66

N =	8	7	7	8	0	1	0	7	16	17	23	28	28	30	29	22	23	22	21	21	23	11
Score =	100	100	100	100	0	0	0	86	75	100	96	100	100	100	97	95	96	95	100	100	100	100

Pre-WWI 6/15/14 — 7/27/14 (pi = 65.00)

N =	0	1	2	1	2	14	34
Score =	0	100	50	0	50	93	97

Suez 7/12/56 — 12/27/56 (pi = 59.25)

N =	0	0	21	18	26	22	22	31	34	52	50	49	54	63	52	55	75	57	58	59	63	72	71	36	7
Score =	0	0	43	61	54	64	64	55	74	54	58	57	60	59	56	60	67	63	66	59	56	61	75	100	

Cuba 8/22/62 — 1/2/63 (pi = 41.05)

N =	0	2	0	2	2	0	4	16	29	20	27	24	16	8	8	7	7	7
Score =	0	0	0	50	50	100	100	94	93	100	48	100	38	13	12	0	0	0

N = the number of possible matches. Score = the proportion of matches to possible matches. *Pi* = Scott's *pi* for inter-coder reliability. Beginning and ending dates appear over each column of seven-day intervals.

TABLE 3

ASSOCIATION OF INTER-ADVERSARY ACTS BY MAGNITUDE
FIRST DIFFERENCES AT SEVEN-DAY INTERVALS

Conflict	Acts	Product Moment Correlation
Schleswig-Holstein	Total	.52*
	Negative	.30*
	Positive	.60*
Morocco	Total	.82*
	Negative	.52*
	Positive	.90*
Serbia-Austria	Total	.96*
	Negative	.97*
	Positive	(.92)**
Suez	Total	.56*
	Negative	.55*
	Positive	.06
Cuba	Total	.67*
	Negative	.75*
	Positive	.27

*Significant at the .05 level.
**Durbin-Watson score of 3.36, judged outside acceptable limits.

of positive Soviet acts occurring toward the end of the dispute that are not reciprocated by the United States. This is consistent with the popular belief that the Russians "backed-down." (Critics of this view, on the other hand, might question the validity of frequency counts as an adequate indice of cooperation magnitude, not to mention the limited sources available for this case.)

The lowest score for reciprocity in positive acts appears for the Suez conflict. This is partly a reflection of the dearth of positive acts for either adversary, as the nearly identical scores, for negative acts and positive and negative acts combined, indicate. There are sporadic verbal gestures, usually coming from Britain, which are rarely reciprocated. It also is interesting that the Suez conflict is unique among our cases in having subsided as a result of outside pressures, rather than through negotiation on the part of the principal adversaries. A comparison of these two cases with the score for the French-German dispute over Morocco, which involved extensive negotiations and an eventual agreement, is especially striking.

Hypothesis 2 states that, if the *military threat threshold* is exceeded, then the magnitude of conflictive behavior will increase until one side initiates escape behavior or war occurs. In testing this hypothesis, we sought evidence

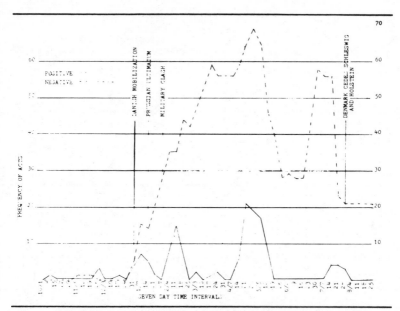

Figure 2: FREQUENCY DISTRIBUTION OF POSITIVE AND NEGATIVE ACTS DURING THE SCHLESWIG-HOLSTEIN CONFLICT 1863-64

of the answers to two questions. First, does the military threat threshold serve as a true turning point in the conflict? Is there a relatively significant increase in the magnitude of negative activity immediately after the threshold is crossed? Second, is the threshold event followed by the long-term escalation stated in the hypothesis?

The graphs appearing in Figures 2 through 6 allow a visual inspection of the frequency distributions of negative acts over time taken at seven-day intervals. The graphs indicate an increase in the magnitude of negative activity immediately following the threshold event in the Schleswig-Holstein, Suez, and Cuban conflicts. There appears to be a brief lull prior to a dramatic escalation in the Austro-Serbian conflict. The Moroccan case, however, indicates that there is a decline in the magnitude of negative action following the threshold event.

A "single-Mood" test was employed to obtain a more explicit measure of the difference in the magnitude of negative behavior before and immediately after the threshold (see Table 4). This is a test of significance for interrupted time-series data to determine the effect the interruption (military threat threshold) has on the variable of interest (magnitude of negative acts) in the

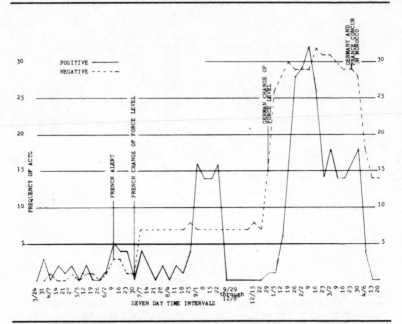

Figure 3: FREQUENCY DISTRIBUTION OF POSITIVE AND NEGATIVE ACTS DURING THE MOROCCAN CONFLICT 1905-06

time interval immediately following the interruption. The slope of the line obtained by least squares regression for the pre-interruption series is used to predict the first Y value following the interruption. In our cases, this is the first seven-day period following the military threat threshold. This estimate of Y is compared to the "real" first value of Y appearing in the data. A significance score, based on the difference between the "real" and estimated Y values, is obtained via a t-test. The t-test is based on an assumption that errors are independent; however, Sween and Campbell (1965a, 1965b) have found that autocorrelated error has very little effect in the single-Mood test. A fuller explanation of the single-Mood test appears in Sween and Campbell (1965a), as well as Caporaso and Pelowski (1971) who provide an example of its application.[21]

The Schleswig-Holstein, Suez, and Cuban conflicts all provide evidence to support the selection of the military threat threshold as a turning point in the pattern of conflict escalation. The low score for the Moroccan case is not surprising. There is little in this conflict to resemble the modern day concept of a "crisis." The threshold event, a French alert, appears to be part of a brief

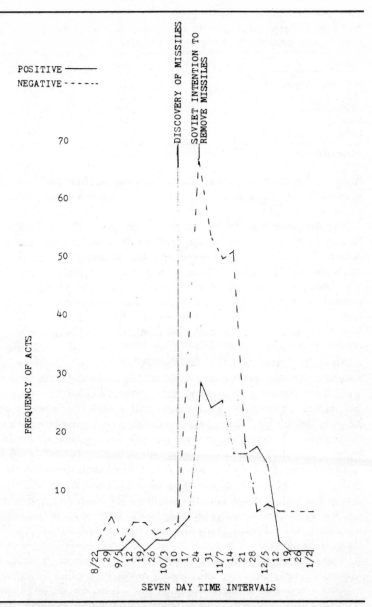

Figure 6: FREQUENCY DISTRIBUTION OF POSITIVE AND NEGATIVE ACTS DURING THE CUBAN CONFLICT 1962

TABLE 4

SINGLE-MOOD TEST OF DIFFERENCE IN MAGNITUDE OF NEGATIVE ACTION
BEFORE AND IMMEDIATELY AFTER THRESHOLD

Conflict	Pre-N*	F-value	Significance Level
Schleswig-Holstein	10	9.23	.01
Moroccan	10	1.32	–
Austro-Serbian	10	.69	–
Suez	10	5.98	.01
Cuba	10	8.17	.01

*Seven-day intervals prior to military threat threshold.

flurry of "sword rattling," which is not reciprocated. Germany's immediate reaction to the French antagonism resembles avoidance behavior, rather than the onset of a "fight."

The Austro-Serbian case is an interesting exception. The threshold event, Serbian mobilization of its forces, produces no immediate reaction, which accounts for the low t-test score, but this is soon followed by rapid escalation. Just 11 days later, Austria delivers its famous ultimatum of July 23rd and the conflict dramatically escalates to war. If we apply the single-Mood test with the Austrian ultimatum as the threshold event, the resultant t-value is 16.66, which is significant at the .01 level.

We can find a somewhat analogous situation in the Cuban Missile Crisis. We chose the American discovery of the Soviet offensive missile emplacements as the threshold event in this conflict. The United States immediately responds with intelligence activities and military preparations which do mark a significant turning point in the escalation of that conflict; however, it does not respond explicitly to the U.S.S.R. until a week later when President Kennedy delivers his famous speech on October 22nd, establishing the naval "quarantine." Testing this later event as a possible threshold, we obtained a higher t-value of .12.55.

In each case, the Austro-Serbian and the Cuban Missile Crisis, there is a lag that extends slightly beyond our one-week interval and that proceeds a very dramatic escalation in the amount of conflict. The historical explanation for the delayed reaction is straightforward enough. Once aware of the danger of war, what Bruce Russett (1962) has termed the "point of surprise," the national decision-making systems of Austria and the United States took time to make important political decisions. This explanation, however, has important implications for the "fight" model of conflict escalation. It suggests a degree of serious deliberation and a consideration of alternative possibilities which do not fit the mechanical reactions of the "fight" model.

On the other hand, once those nations acted on these decisions, the escalation is immediate and dramatic.

Turning now to the long-term post-threshold pattern of negative action, Figures 2 through 6 indicate an extended pattern of growth in the magnitude of conflict exhibited between the military threat threshold and the military violence threshold, or the initiation of escape behavior. This is supported by a comparison of the mean magnitude of negative action observed in this interval, with the period extending from the beginning of each conflict to the military threat threshold. The results of this comparison are presented in Table 5.

The scores in Table 5 indicate that the growth in conflictive behavior, after the threat threshold is exceeded, is substantial in all of the cases. Just *how* substantial is more difficult to say. To gain some idea of its salience relative to succeeding tests, we grouped the cases together, normalized the data for conflict size,[22] and conducted a two-tailed t-test for differences of means for matched pairs. With a normalized average of .297, the results were significant at the .01 level (p = .006).

In each case the conflict continues to grow in magnitude after the threat threshold is exceeded—is this evidence of a *fight* pattern? One could argue that the fight scenario suggests that the conflict not only should continue to grow during this period, but that the conflictive acts should come more quickly, almost as reflex actions, once the fight begins. If this pattern obtains, then the rate of escalation should be greater in the post-military threat period than in the pre-threat period. To obtain a comparison of the rates of escalation before and after the threshold, we employed a Walker-Lev test for significance of the difference between slopes of regression lines for the two series. The test requires an adjustment of the critical F-value for autocorrelated error.[23] Sween and Campbell (1965a, 1965b) have calculated adjusted values which were used in obtaining the adjusted significance levels

TABLE 5

MEAN MAGNITUDE OF NEGATIVE ACTS, OBSERVED IN EXTENDED INTERVALS BEFORE AND AFTER MILITARY THREAT THRESHOLD

Conflict	Pre-Threat	Post-Threat
Schleswig-Holstein	.03	2.52 (mv)*
Morocco	.09	1.90 (eb)
Austro-Serbia	.55	3.00 (mv)
Suez	2.00	13.99 (mv)
Cuba	.62	5.64 (eb)

*Indicates whether interval ends at military violence threshold or escape behavior.

reported in Table 6. It was necessary to make the observations at one-day intervals for this test in order to obtain enough values to calculate the slopes of the regression estimates for the post-threshold to escape behavior or war time series for each of the cases.

With one exception, the Suez conflict, the results fit the impression gained from the single-Mood test. Just two of the cases, Schleswig-Holstein and the Cuban Missile Crisis, are significant at the .01 level after adjusting for autocorrelated error; however, the F-value for the Austro-Serbian conflict is certainly impressive, even though the high level of autocorrelated error makes an adjustment for significance infeasible. The low score for the Moroccan conflict matches our earlier results and it is consistent with our intuitive impression of the events. The acts qualifying as threats of military violence which preceded the negotiations at Algeciras—a French alert, the naval shows-of-strength by the participating powers—appear to be gestures which were more ritualistic than threatening.

The score for the Suez case is a bit puzzling, particularly in light of the high t-value for the single-Mood test and the seven-fold post-threshold increase in the mean magnitude of negative acts in Table 5. A closer look at Figure 5, however, indicates that this should not be so surprising. First, it is apparent that the escalation of the conflict begins in earnest before the military threat threshold is crossed; that is, immediately after Nassar's July 26th announcement of his decision to nationalize the Suez Canal. There is a jump in the level of conflict immediately following the threshold event—the Egyptian alert on the 29th which partially acounts for the high single-Mood

TABLE 6

SIGNIFICANCE TEST FOR DIFFERENCE IN SLOPES BEFORE AND AFTER THRESHOLD

Conflict	Pre-N*	Post-N	Slope Change	F-Value	Signifi-cance Level	Adj. Signifi-cance Level	Auto-correlated Error at Lag 1**
Schleswig-Holstein	21	28	+	21.25	.01	.01	.25
Moroccan	21	298	+	.007	–	–	.90
Austro-Serbian	21	16	+	38.90	.01	–	.74
Suez	21	93	+	.04	–	–	.82
Cuban	21	12	+	52.73	.01	.01	–.01

*Observations at one day intervals.

**Autocorrelation of differences from the separate regression lines for pre-N and post-N.

test score—but this is followed by a lull until the conflict escalates again, four weeks later. Second, the period between the military threat threshold and the outbreak of war is considerably longer than in any of the other cases. This is an extended period of British planning and consultation with her allies. It appears to resemble more closely an incubation stage than a fight process.

In sum, three of the cases, the Schleswig-Hostein, Austro-Serbian, and Cuban Missile conflicts, meet, or come close to meeting, all of our measures of a "fight" pattern of conflict escalation. Some of the elements of this pattern are exhibited in the Suez conflict, but the dramatic escalation characteristic of the fight is missing. One of the cases, the Moroccan Crisis, clearly does not fit the pattern.

The selection of the military threat threshold as a significant turning point in the escalation of a conflict is supported by three of the cases; however, in two of the cases, the conflicts escalated more significantly after a later interval, when the target of the first threshold event issued a more explicit threat of military force. In all of the cases the mean magnitude of negative acts increased in the post-threshold period. Taken in aggregate, the difference was significant at the .01 level. The rate of escalation also grew in this period for all of the conflicts. The difference was significant at the .01 level in two cases and impressive in a third.

Half of the lock-in effect stated in Hypothesis 3 has been supported by our last two tests. The substantial increase in the frequency of negative action occurring after the military threat threshold is crossed is quite consistent with the hypothesis. On the other hand, a glance at the distribution of *positive* acts in Figures 2 through 6 is enough to indicate that the other half of the hypothesis, which states that positive (cooperative) acts should *decrease*, does not hold for our five cases. Applying the same techniques as those we used to measure the mean increase for negative actions, we find that the scores are in the *same* direction. Rather than decrease after the threat threshold is crossed, the positive acts increase in magnitude (see Table 7).

TABLE 7

MAGNITUDE AND INCREASE IN MAGNITUDE, POSITIVE ACTS, OBSERVED IN EXTENDED INTERVALS BEFORE AND AFTER MILITARY THREAT THRESHOLD

Conflict	*Magnitude*	
	Pre-Threat	*Post-Threat*
Schleswig-Holstein	.07	.55
Morocco	.21	1.01
Austro-Serbia	.05	.82
Suez	.18	.43
Cuba	.37	.82

These scores suggest that the lock-in process may work only half way. A plausible explanation would be that nation-states, unlike Tom Sawyers, do not become so single-mindedly locked-in to the heat of the conflict that they lose all sight of the need for some reciprocity to obtain their objectives. Intuitively, it makes sense to conceive to inter-nation conflicts as something of a game-fight hybrid. The national decision makers are neither as coolly rational as the pure game model suggests; nor as locked-in to the escalation of conflict as the fight model indicates in its purest form.

CONCLUSION

We have made a crude start on an important question. Although we find the expected variation in the five conflicts, the behavior traces do indicate patterns which obtain in all five cases. This helps put the lie to the old notion that each international situation is so unique that any generalization is impossible. There is evidence that conflicts escalate when one side begins to threaten the other side with military violence. Whether the escalation that appears in the behavior traces describes a fight process remains unclear. We can say only that there are some indications of such a pattern. We also find a strong degree of reciprocity in conflict behavior for all five cases. Interestingly, the one point on which the fight and reciprocity models diverge shows the strongest variance among the five conflicts considered. The lock-in effect of the fight did not obtain with regard to the expected decrease in cooperative behavior. Unfortunately, reciprocity in cooperative behavior was not demonstrated either, in the two most contemporary cases.

An interesting finding from this first look at conflict behavior patterns is that, with one exception, there appears to be no major difference between the pre-1914 and post-World War II conflicts. The exception is the mean magnitude of negative acts; here the Cuban and Suez conflicts rank first and second. Perhaps this is attributable either to the extensive public exposure which seems to require more aggressive "posturing" and assertiveness than in the era of secret diplomacy or to better reporting in an era of mass communications. But on our tests of symmetry and escalation, the historical eras do not provide significant differences. The Cuban Crisis of 1962, the Schleswig-Holstein conflict of 1864-1866, and the Austro-Serbian conflict of 1914 achieve the highest scores in both the symmetry and escalation of conflictive action. The high scores for the Schleswig-Holstein conflict are especially interesting because this is not only the earliest of the conflicts which we considered, but also because it probably would be regarded by most historians as the most one-sided. The one thing that all three of these conflicts have in common is a very explicit indication of the willingness of one side to go to war, which comes shortly after the military threat threshold is crossed. In each case, there is an ultimatum delivered within a fortnight.

Obviously, in order to go further more data and finer measurements are required. It will be necessary to observe more cases with more data sources for each. As the frequency distributions demonstrate, a conflict model must be devised which takes into account the lulls in activity, as well as the tendency of conflictive behavior to taper off at a certain level, rather than demonstrate a smooth pattern of escalation. Some transformations of the data, such as scaling or weighting acts, may be necessary to provide more accurate mappings. In short, we have completed only the first step in the incremental process mentioned in the Introduction.

Behind all of this is the normative policy question of ends and means symbolized by the game and fight models of conflict behavior. Are international conflicts rational games, where each side calculates its advantages and acts to influence the other in its interest? Or do the means overwhelm the ends, turning the games into fights, where the only objective is to harm, and the conflict is condemned to escalate to either violence or surrender? The answer is bound to be a relative one, with the ratio of the mix of the two types all important. The first step in the quest for an answer must be the construction of models of conflict behavior which will enable us to observe patterns in the behavior traces which identify symptoms of a growing danger of war. Then it might be possible to make probablistic estimates of the costs and risks attendant to the influence techniques used in inter-nation conflicts. The next step is to establish the links between prewar behavioral patterns and the ecological setting; that is, the attributes of the adversaries and the conditions of the international system. But, even at that point, we must make a great *ceteris paribus* assumption with regard to the effects of domestic politics, bureaucratic and organizational variables, and the influences of third parties. Only then would we be able to establish a probablistic model of the basic problem, war.

APPENDIX

HIERARCHICAL DIFFERENTIATION DIAGRAMS
OF THE ACTION TYPOLOGY

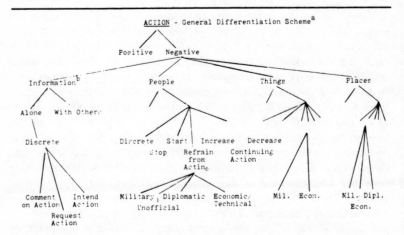

a. We have presented the subcategorization for only one branching in each category, and have labeled for only one category to save space. Each possible branching in each category would be fully differentiated the same way.

b. Down to this level of differentiation all subcategories are the same for each of the four major categories. Below this level each employs a distinctive scheme.

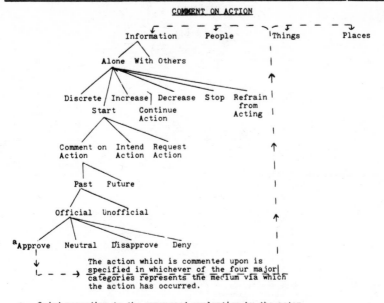

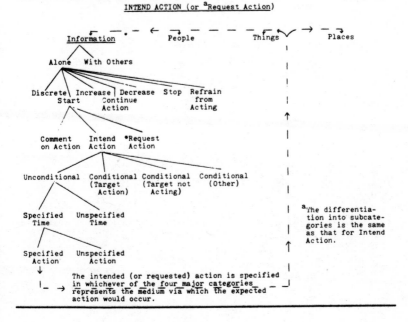

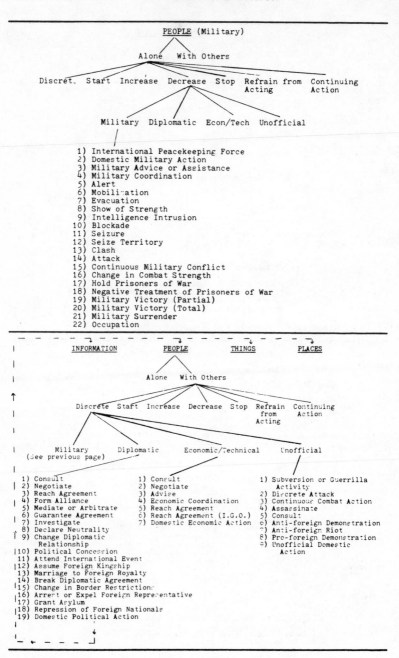

PEOPLE (Military)

Alone   With Others

Discret. Start Increase Decrease Stop Refrain from Continuing
                                         Acting   Action

Military Diplomatic Econ/Tech Unofficial

1) International Peacekeeping Force
2) Domestic Military Action
3) Military Advice or Assistance
4) Military Coordination
5) Alert
6) Mobilization
7) Evacuation
8) Show of Strength
9) Intelligence Intrusion
10) Blockade
11) Seizure
12) Seize Territory
13) Clash
14) Attack
15) Continuous Military Conflict
16) Change in Combat Strength
17) Hold Prisoners of War
18) Negative Treatment of Prisoners of War
19) Military Victory (Partial)
20) Military Victory (Total)
21) Military Surrender
22) Occupation

INFORMATION   PEOPLE   THINGS   PLACES

Alone   With Others

Discrete Start Increase Decrease Stop Refrain Continuing
                                       from   Action
                                       Acting

Military   Diplomatic   Economic/Technical   Unofficial
(See previous page)

1) Consult   1) Consult   1) Subversion or Guerrilla
2) Negotiate   2) Negotiate   Activity
3) Reach Agreement   3) Advise   2) Discrete Attack
4) Form Alliance   4) Economic Coordination 3) Continuous Combat Action
5) Mediate or Arbitrate   5) Reach Agreement   4) Assassinate
6) Guarantee Agreement   6) Reach Agreement (I.G.O.) 5) Consult
7) Investigate   7) Domestic Economic Action 6) Anti-foreign Demonstration
8) Declare Neutrality   7) Anti-foreign Riot
9) Change Diplomatic   8) Pro-foreign Demonstration
   Relationship   9) Unofficial Domestic
10) Political Concession   Action
11) Attend International Event
12) Assume Foreign Kingship
13) Marriage to Foreign Royalty
14) Break Diplomatic Agreement
15) Change in Border Restrictions
16) Arrest or Expel Foreign Representative
17) Grant Asylum
18) Repression of Foreign Nationals
19) Domestic Political Action

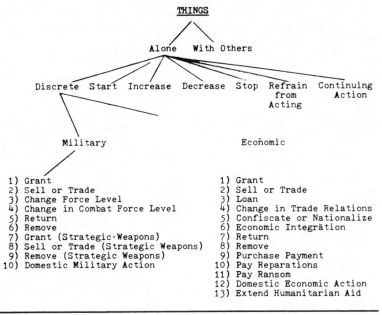

THINGS

Alone   With Others

Discrete Start Increase Decrease Stop Refrain from Acting Continuing Action

Military   Economic

1) Grant
2) Sell or Trade
3) Change Force Level
4) Change in Combat Force Level
5) Return
6) Remove
7) Grant (Strategic·Weapons)
8) Sell or Trade (Strategic Weapons)
9) Remove (Strategic Weapons)
10) Domestic Military Action

1) Grant
2) Sell or Trade
3) Loan
4) Change in Trade Relations
5) Confiscate or Nationalize
6) Economic Integration
7) Return
8) Remove
9) Purchase Payment
10) Pay Reparations
11) Pay Ransom
12) Domestic Economic Action
13) Extend Humanitarian Aid

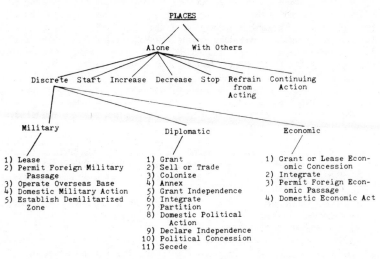

PLACES

Alone   With Others

Discrete Start Increase Decrease Stop Refrain from Acting Continuing Action

Military   Diplomatic   Economic

1) Lease
2) Permit Foreign Military Passage
3) Operate Overseas Base
4) Domestic Military Action
5) Establish Demilitarized Zone

1) Grant
2) Sell or Trade
3) Colonize
4) Annex
5) Grant Independence
6) Integrate
7) Partition
8) Domestic Political Action
9) Declare Independence
10) Political Concession
11) Secede

1) Grant or Lease Economic Concession
2) Integrate
3) Permit Foreign Economic Passage
4) Domestic Economic Act

NOTES

1. Our research on the "Behavioral Correlates of War" is a subset of the larger "Correlates of War Project," under the direction of J. David Singer at the University of Michigan. The overall project is outlined in Singer (1972).

2. This research strategy is chosen over that of developing a comprehensive model or system for which data would be generated and put to the test. We believe that there are so many contending propositions and preoperational models extant in the literature on conflict behavior that investment in a single comprehensive model at this stage would not be practical.

3. Smoker (1969) found evidence of a "lock-in" effect of a different sort in the correspondence of decisionmaking elites of China and India between 1956 and 1964. A lock-in pattern was defined by Smoker as occurring when low "freedom of decision" was exhibited by a high correlation between communication patterns from one week to the next.

4. Our conception of the threat as an attempt to persuade or dissuade parallels that of Singer (1963). We are in the process of generating data for a test of some of the hypotheses stated in Singer's "Inter-Nation Influence" model.

5. Our two thresholds, in fact, mirror those of Oren Young (1968), except that we restrict the coercion to threats of military violence.

6. An interesting discussion of the effect of new actors on the boundaries of conflicts and other situations appears in William Riker (1957). Riker suggests that the addition or subtraction of a member defines a new situation.

7. John Burton's (1969) experiments in "controlled communication" have provided some interesting evidence of the diversity of issues that bring different parties into conflicts. See pp. 14-19.

8. (1) Schleswig-Holstein: March 30, 1863—the proclamation of King Frederick VI of Denmark announcing the annexation of Schleswig. (2) Moroccan Crisis: March 31, 1904—the visit of the German emperor to Tangier. (3) Pre-World War I: June 28, 1914—the assassination of Archduke Francis Ferdinand at Sarajero. (4) Suez Conflict: July 26, 1956—Nassar announces nationalization of the Suez Canal. (5) Cuban Crisis: October 15, 1962—the United States discovers Russian missile emplacements.

9. The data sources used in this paper do not meet our criterion of including an account by at least one historian or participant from each side. These sources will be added as the *Coder's Manual* is translated into the appropriate languages. The hypotheses in this paper do not draw comparison between the adversaries; therefore, this is less of a weakness than it might be otherwise.

10. The source validity question is considered at greater length in an earlier paper (Leng, 1972b). Recently a number of scholars have raised interesting questions regarding the validity of the world press as a data source. See Azar (1970b), Burrows et al. (1971), Hoggard (1969, 1970), Sigler (1970), and Solnick (1972). For a different approach to the problem, see Phillips (1972).

11. The Stanford chronology was constructed from an extensive base of archival material and historical treatments.

12. See McClelland (1968).

13. Inter-Coder reliability scores for the three undergraduate students who generated the data used in this paper averaged .88 (Scott's pi). The basic inter-coder reliability score is computed by dividing matching descriptions times N by the total number of items coded by N coders. Scott's pi subtracts expected agreement for a more conservative score. See Holsti (1969: 140-141).

14. When two nations are involved in a reciprocal act, each qualifies as an actor with the other as target; consequently, two acts are identified.

15. The distinction between the explicit verbal threat and the tacitly threatening deed is discussed extensively by Schelling (1960).

16. The reader may wonder if our operational definition distorts the usual meaning of an act such as a Blockade, which may be conceived of as an act of military force. We assume that unless there is actual conflict resulting from a breach of the blockade, the act remains a threat of physical violence.

17. "Balancing" behavior by one adversary implies a response to behavior by the other, but just what behavior is problematic. We conducted a test of symmetry comparing the actions of Nation A in a one-day time interval ti, with those of Nation B in interval

$$\frac{\Sigma \, (ti \; t_{i+1} \cdots t_{i+6})}{7}$$

The results were slightly weaker than those in tests reported below.

18. We have not attempted any scaling or weighting of the data at this stage of the investigation in order to keep the data in as "pure" a form as possible in the early stages of analysis.

19. A Durbin-Watson Test (Durbin and Watson, 1950) indicated a strong secular trend for *all* variables, an early hint that Hypothesis 3 might be disproven. The first differences provided Durbin-Watson scores within acceptable limits for all cases, except *positive* acts in the Austro-Serbian conflict.

20. The significance scores used here, and in reporting the results of subsequent tests, are presented for comparative purposes. At this stage, our analysis is intended to be descriptive and suggestive, not inferential. We are aware of the argument that significance scores should be used *only* for inference from samples to populations; nevertheless, we believe the test scores provide a useful benchmark for the comparison of a variety of measures. See Winch and Campbell (1969) for a similar argument.

21. A prepared computer program for single-Mood test, Walker-Lev tests, and the double extrapolation technique (Double Mood) appears in Sween and Campbell (1965a). This has been converted to Fortran IV time-sharing use by Alan Pelowski (1969) and for Basic time-sharing use by Helen Haerle at Middlebury College, Middlebury, Vermont.

22. The "size" was normalized relative to the frequency of acts occurring within each conflict.

23. Sween and Campbell (1965a) recommend that in the instance of a true difference between the slopes and/or intercepts of the pre- and post-threshold groups, the autocorrelation of the differences for the separate regression lines be used to obtain the estimate of serial dependency between points.

Russell J. Leng (Ph. D. American University, 1966) is Dean of Sciences at Middlebury College and has been a visiting professor at the University of Michigan. He has written several articles on qualitative research in international relations and is currently investigating the interaction of nations in serious disputes.

Robert A. Goodsell (J.D. University of Michigan, June 1978) is currently a law clerk for a New Jersey State Supreme Court Justice, and plans to continue his law career in public interest service. He was Executive Editor of the Michigan Law Review and served as a research assistant for the Inter-university Consortium for Political and Social Research.

Arms Races and Escalation

SOME NEW EVIDENCE

MICHAEL D. WALLACE   *Chapter 10*

Although major power arms races have been the subject of a great amount of mathematical modelling, there has been little data-based research concerning their impact on international war. This study attempts to determine whether or not these arms races affect the probability that a serious dispute between major powers will escalate to all-out war. To do this, an arms race index is constructed in the following manner: a curve-fitting technique is employed to calculate changes in arms expenditures for each major power as a function of time. The smoothed rates of increase for each of the parties to a dispute are multiplied together, yielding an index whose values will be high only if the two powers have engaged in rapid and simultaneous military expansion prior to the dispute. It was found that disputes preceded by such an arms race escalated to war 23 out of 28 times, while disputes *not* preceded by an arms race resulted in war only 3 out of 71 times. It was concluded that at the very least, arms races are an important early warning indicator of escalation potential, and may well play a central role in the escalation process. The implications of this finding for the current debate over SALT II were noted.

INTRODUCTION

More than 30 years have passed since Lewis Fry Richardson began his pioneering treatise on the dynamics of arms races (Richardson, 1960), and nearly two decades have gone by since David Singer (1958) and Samuel Huntington (1958) staked out their positions on

AUTHOR'S NOTE: Revised version of a paper presented to the Annual Meetings of the Social Science History Association, Ann Arbor, Michigan, October 1977. The research reported here could not have been undertaken without the efforts and assistance of my colleagues and associates on the Correlates of War Project, especially Michael Champion, Charles Gochman, Thomas Kselman, David Singer, and Richard Stoll. I would also like to thank Richard Rosecrance, Bruce Russett, Harold von Riekhoff, and Dina Zinnes for their comments on an earlier draft. Financial assistance for this project was provided by a grant from the Social Sciences and Humanities Research Council of Canada.

Originally published in the *Journal of Conflict Resolution,* Vol. 23, No. 1, March 1979.

opposite sides of the "armaments-tensions" debate. In the inter-vening years, a great deal has been written concerning the onset and dynamic evolution of arms races,[1] and on the relationship between national capabilities and likelihood of violent conflict.[2] Yet, oddly enough, virtually nothing written to date has shed much light on the central question these pioneering works address: does the exist-ence of an arms race between two states significantly increase their probability of going to war?

It is only necessary to peruse the current debate over the partu-rient SALT II negotiations to realize that the outlines of the controversy have remained essentially unchanged since classical times. On the one side, Vegetius's doctrine "si vis pacem, para bellum" finds its contemporary expression amongst the partisans of military expansion in both the Pentagon and the Kremlin. They argue that only a strong military posture can deter an opponent's military adventurism, which, unchecked, would lead to armed con-flict. In other words, it is not arms races that lead to war, but rather a nation's failure to maintain its military capabilities vis-à-vis its potential rivals and adversaries.

On the other side of this debate are those who believe that military expansion per se contributes to the danger of war. It is argued, to begin with, that military expansion is self-defeating, in that it is likely to provoke a similar countervailing expansion by the other side. Moreover, the mutual threat posed by such competitive mili-tary growth intensifies other conflicts and contentions among nations, leading to additional uncertainty and insecurity, further pressures for military expansion, and so on in a vicious, escalating circle. In short, the partisans of the "arms race" school do not see the competi-tive acquisition of military capability as a neutral instrument of policy, still less as a means to *prevent* war, but rather as a major link in the complex chain of events leading to armed conflict.

Given the central role this debate has played in current policy discussions, and considering the magnitude of the stakes involved in the nuclear age, it is long past time that some direct scientific

1. Useful summaries and critiques of this extensive literature are to be found in Rapaport (1958), Busch (1970), Chaterjee (1974), Zinnes (1976), Gillespie et al. (1977), and Hollist (1978).

2. See, for example, Singer, Bremer, and Stuckey (1972); Wallace (1974); and Choucri and North (1974).

evidence were brought to bear on the matter. That is what I shall attempt here.

In order to address the question in a systematic manner, two preliminary conceptual matters must be dealth with. First, we must decide what is to be meant by an "arms race," and second, we must specify the *process* by which arms races may be thought of as influencing the probability of war.

THE DEFINITION OF AN ARMS RACE

Turning first to the definition of an arms race, the literature presents numerous alternatives.[3] While many of these differ in some respects, there are two elements common to all. First, arms races involve simultaneous abnormal rates of growth in the military outlays of two or more nations. Second, in an arms race these result from the competitive pressure of the military rivalry itself, and not from domestic forces exogenous to this rivalry.

Beginning with the second of these two components of a definition, it is clear that, at a minimum, we can only speak of an "arms race" between nations whose foreign and defense policies are heavily interdependent; the behavior and capabilities of each nation must be highly salient to the other nations. Thus, it is meaningless to speak of an "arms race" between nations with little contact with or interest in each other. But more than this is required. The capabilities of the putative military rivals must not only be mutually salient, but also roughly comparable. However great their mutual antagonism, and however rapidly their armed forces grow, it would make little sense to speak of an "arms race" between, say, the United States and Cuba, or the Soviet Union and Iran. In short, arms races can exist only amongst the great powers, or amongst local powers of comparable military standing within the same region.

The next question is, what are we to understand as the "abnormal growth" which constitutes an arms race? Clearly, not *all* competitive or simultaneous increases qualify. Throughout most of the nineteenth and twentieth centuries, a majority of nations, and virtually all of the great powers, have made continual qualitative and quantitative addi-

3. See Huntington (1958); Richardson (1960); Milstein and Mitchell (1968); and Busch (1970).

tions to their armed forces. More often than not, these have been undertaken in a spirit of rivalry—country X wishing to possess bigger battleships than Y or more armoured divisions than Z. Yet these competitive acquisitions are not "arm races"; the average annual rate of growth has not usually exceeded 4 or 5% in real terms, and an examination of historical accounts indicates that contemporary elites have worried very little about them.

At frequent intervals, however, this pattern of normal arms *competition* is transformed into a runaway arms *race* through some combination of domestic, diplomatic, and strategic pressures.[4] The competition now becomes a matter of great, perhaps paramount salience for both sides. The annual rate of growth in military capability occasionally climbs to a figure in excess of 10%, even as much as 20 or 25%. In short, the onset of an arms race is characterized by a sharp acceleration (significant increase in the rate of increase) in military capability. It is these "runaway accelerations" that we shall term "arms races" for purposes of this paper.

FROM ARMS RACE TO WAR

In specifying the impact which rapid military growth has upon the probability of war, two problems arise. First, how do we distinguish empirically between genuine competitive arms races as described above, and mere coincidental military "accelerations"? For example, between 1937 and 1939, both Britain and the United States increased the size and quality of their armed forces many times over, yet it would be absurd to speak of them as engaging in an arms race.

The second problem arises from the fact that military acquisitions by *themselves* are extremely unlikely to provoke military hostilities. Even in the era of "counterforce" and "flexible response," few responsible observers suggest that any nation would initiate violent hostilities with a power of comparable size *solely* to protect or enhance its military-strategic position. Some other factor or factors must lead nations into a dispute or confrontation of sufficient severity that the military dangers created by the arms race are transformed from chronic irritants into acute threats to national survival.

Both of these problems are easily solved by turning the central question on its head. Instead of asking whether or not bilateral or

4. See Luterbacher (1975), and Wallace (1976; 1978).

multilateral runaway arms growth enhances the likelihood of war, we can pose the problem this way: "do serious disputes between nations engaged in an arms race have a significantly greater probability of resulting in all-out war than those between nations exhibiting more normal patterns of military competition?" Presumably, if two nations are on opposite sides of a serious dispute, any military acquisition they might make will be directed towards each other at least in part. At the same time, such a dispute provides the theoretical preconditions for the transition from war preparation to war initiation.

THE DOMAIN

As is customary with studies using Correlates of War Project data, the test period for our hypotheses will extend from 1816 to 1965. In this paper we shall consider only *great power* disputes and wars occurring during this period, that is, those in which there was at least one great power on each side. There are two reasons for this. First, we noted that rough equivalence of capability was a crucial prerequisite for an arms race, ruling out consideration of "major vs. minor" wars and disputes. Although rough equivalence of capability often obtains among hostile lesser powers, these are often dependent upon great powers for weapons and political support to the extent that their decisional autonomy is open to question. A second difficulty is that data concerning the military capability of, and disputes concerning, lesser powers is far less reliable than the corresponding information for the majors.

In sum, it was felt that any major extension of the test population at this stage would muddy the waters, and possibly confuse the results. There is one important exception, however. In those cases where there occurs a dispute between a great power and a minor power bound in a military alliance to another great power, we consider this to be a great power dispute.

The population of "great powers" is that used by Singer and Small (1966), and comprises Britain from 1815 to 1965; France from 1816 to 1940, and 1945 to 1965; the United States from 1898 to 1965; Germany from 1816 to 1918, and 1923 to 1945; Austria-Hungary from 1816 to 1917; Russia from 1816 to 1917, and from 1920 to 1965; Japan from 1904 to 1945; and China from 1950 to 1965.

SERIOUS DISPUTES

As the data collected by the Correlates of War Project on serious international disputes have not yet appeared in print, a brief summary of the coding rules is in order here. Briefly, for our purposes a *dispute* is a military confrontation between two or more nations not deadly enough to qualify as a war defined by Singer and Small. However, it must be "serious enough for one of the parties involved to threaten to commit, or actually commit, significant military resources to resolve the dispute" (Levy, 1977). We consider this a commitment to have a specific series of acts initiated by the official representatives of a power and clearly a commitment directed towards another great power. This series of acts comprises the following: the act of blockade, declaration of war, seizure or occupation of territory, the use of military forces, the mobilization of armed forces, and the seizure of foreign personnel or materiel. In all, a total of 99 disputes between major powers met our criteria; a complete list will be found in Table 1.

THE WARS

Of these 99 serious dispute dyads, only 23 resulted in the outbreak of full-scale war as defined by Singer and Small (1972). Included are all military clashes in which at least one great power participated on each side, and which resulted in at least 1,000 battle-related fatalities. Only one departure is made from the Singer-Small codifications. In the case of those wars which involved more than two powers, each dyad is coded separately. Thus, for example, World War II is coded as an initiation of Franco-German and Anglo-German hostilities in 1939, an Anglo-Italian and Franco-Italian outbreak in 1940, and a Russo-German and Japanese-American conflict initiated in 1941. This was done to avoid the practical and conceptual difficulties of aggregating military capabilities of nations entering the conflict at different times.

THE MEASUREMENT OF MILITARY CAPABILITY

The next step in the operational test of our hypotheses is the development of an index of military capabilities. For present purposes, we

TABLE 1
Serious Disputes Between Major Powers, 1816-1965

Year	Nations Involved		Escalation to War	Arms Race Index
1833	UK	Russia	No	2.73
1833	France	Russia	No	0.17
1836	Russia	UK	No	1.00
1840	France	Russia	No	12.90
1840	France	Germany	No	0.66
1849	UK	Russia	No	1.02
1849	France	Russia	No	36.27
1850	Germany	Austria	No	9.54
1853	UK	Russia	Yes	0.06
1853	France	Russia	Yes	31.74
1854	Austria	Russia	No	53.80
1859	France	Austria	Yes	120.91
1861	UK	Russia	No	0.16
1866	Germany	Austria	Yes	148.61
1866	Italy	Austria	Yes	575.14
1867	France	Italy	No	55.00
1870	France	Germany	Yes	8.91
1875	France	Germany	No	1.19
1877	UK	Russia	No	3.22
1878	UK	Russia	No	0.88
1878	Austria	Italy	No	0.48
1885	UK	Russia	No	4.93
1887	Germany	France	No	1.07
1888	Italy	France	No	7.17
1888	Austria	France	No	8.35
1888	England	France	No	1.63
1893	Austria	Russia	No	0.23
1895	Russia	Japan	No	61.53
1897	UK	Russia	No	0.17
1898	UK	France	No	0.35
1899	UK	Germany	No	0.39
1900	Japan	Russia	No	53.17
1902	US	Germany	No	0.15
1902	US	UK	No	0.01
1903	US	UK	No	0.07
1904	UK	Russia	No	0.07
1904	Russia	Japan	Yes	221.00
1905	Germany	France	No	0.04
1911	Germany	France	No	2.48
1911	Germany	UK	No	28.07

TABLE 1 (Continued)

Year	Nations Involved		Escalation to War	Arms Race Index
1912	Russia	Austria	No	0.02
1912	Austria	Italy	No	0.37
1913	Italy	France	No	43.39
1914	Germany	UK	Yes	133.20
1914	Germany	France	Yes	231.25
1914	Germany	Russia	Yes	205.35
1914	Austria	UK	Yes	90.00
1914	Austria	France	Yes	156.25
1914	Austria	Russia	Yes	138.75
1915	Italy	Germany	Yes	811.30
1915	Italy	Austria	Yes	912.38
1917	US	Germany	Yes	349.68
1923	UK	Russia	No	0.04
1931	US	Japan	No	0.53
1932	UK	Japan	No	0.85
1932	US	Japan	No	1.05
1934	Italy	Germany	No	14.58
1934	Russia	Japan	No	0.13
1935	Japan	Russia	No	106.13
1935	UK	Italy	No	38.21
1936	UK	Germany	No	112.68
1936	France	Germany	No	5.56
1937	Russia	Japan	No	51.47
1937	Japan	US	No	28.28
1938	Russia	Japan	No	14.96
1938	UK	Germany	No	90.06
1938	France	Germany	No	25.97
1939	Japan	France	No	11.49
1939	UK	Japan	Yes	261.23
1939	France	Germany	Yes	495.51
1939	UK	Germany	Yes	420.08
1940	Italy	UK	Yes	559.65
1940	Italy	France	Yes	643.70
1940	Japan	UK	No	39.98
1940	Japan	France	No	11.49
1941	Germany	Russia	Yes	221.61
1941	US	Germany	Yes	536.89
1941	US	Italy	Yes	543.07
1941	US	Japan	Yes	314.58
1945	Japan	Russia	Yes	102.93
1946	US	Russia	No	0.03
1948	Russia	US	No	0.32
1948	Russia	UK	No	0.25

TABLE 1 (Continued)

Year	Nations Involved		Escalation to War	Arms Race Index
1948	Russia	France	No	10.01
1953	Russia	US	No	68.72
1953	Russia	UK	No	41.80
1954	China	UK	No	22.89
1956	China	US	No	25.03
1956	Russia	France	No	61.89
1956	Russia	UK	No	53.05
1958	China	US	No	65.02
1958	UK	Russia	No	0.19
1960	US	Russia	No	6.34
1961	US	Russia	No	14.14
1962	US	China	No	103.73
1962	US	Russia	No	122.10
1964	US	Russia	No	30.70
1965	China	UK	No	81.43
1965	China	US	No	47.97

shall use annual *aggregate military expenditures*. Included in this total are both regular and extraordinary expenditures for all regular armed forces, as well as proceeds from borrowings in aid of the military. Both metropolitan and colonial expenditures are included. However, we *exclude* unexpended appropriations, military pensions, and expenditures on police, frontier guards, and reserves.

At this point, a few words of justification are in order. Obviously, many will argue that expenditures for armed forces do not always reflect true military capabilities; to use expenditures as an index would be to assume that military "cost-effectiveness" remains constant through time and space. Obviously, this is not the case, and represents a major potential source of bias in the index. But, in mitigation, two points may be made.

First, while military efficiency varies widely, it tends to change fairly slowly. As we shall see, our measurement of the severity of an arms race is made with reference to a time-span of ten years. Within this time period, changing cost-effectiveness is unlikely to be a problem.

Moreover, we shall be concerned here not with the absolute level of military expenditures, but rather with their *rates of change* (deltas) from year to year. Thus, the problem of comparing absolute levels across nations does not arise.

We have now specified operational criteria for wars, disputes, and military capabilities. It remains to distinguish operationally between those instances of military growth which are to be characterized as "arms races," and those which are not. This is not quite as easy as it might seem at first blush, and to make a valid and useful distinction, we shall have to enlist the aid of some recent developments in applied mathematics that are unlikely to be familiar to most social scientists.

AN ARMS RACE INDEX

It is easier to set down the conditions which an operational definition of an arms race must satisfy than it is to meet them. First and foremost, the measure should distinguish clearly between the "normal" incrementation of arms levels and abnormal "runaway" growth. Second, it should be sensitive only to *competitive* growth, where both sides are increasing rapidly and simultaneously. Third, given the occasional problems of data accuracy which persist despite our best efforts, the measure should be founded on as solid a data base as possible. Finally, it should be relatively more sensitive to the situation immediately prior to the dispute or war, and relatively *less* sensitive to the rates of arms growth further away in time.

The application of these criteria rules out several initially plausible index construction procedures. Measures based upon mean rates of increase do not satisfy the first and fourth criteria, as they are likely to average together observations made before and after the onset of the arms race. Moving averages go a long way towards satisfying the fourth criterion, but are still likely to "average out" periods of fast and slow growth. Indices based upon growth immediately prior to the dispute are likely to involve only two or at most three data points, leaving themselves extremely vulnerable to error. Finally, indices based upon the direct measurement of the *acceleration* of the arms race also run into problems with criterion three, since more data points are required for an unbiased estimate of the rate of acceleration than for the simple rate of change.

In this paper, a completely different approach will be employed. Instead of detecting the existence of an arms race by measuring the rate of increase or acceleration in arms spending directly, the issue shall be determined by extrapolating from a polynomial function fitted to the arms expenditure data for ten years prior to the onset of the dispute or war.[5] This polynomial function shall be used to estimate the time rate of change (delta) for each nation for the year prior to the dispute. The existence of an arms race prior to the dispute or war shall be determined by obtaining the *product* of the national rates of change for each side, with higher values representing "arms-race" dyads. By calculating national rates of growth on the basis of a ten-year data series, and by constructing the final index in a multiplicative fashion, we ensure that only long-term, intense, bilateral growth in arms expenditures will score high on our arms race scale. The calculated arms race index values for each dyad are displayed in Table 1.

5. The mathematically trained reader may be interested in the procedure used to derive the polynomial functions from which the time rates of change of national arms levels are calculated. Given a set of $(m + 1)$ data observations, $y_0, y_1 \ldots y_m$ corresponding to evenly spaced points in time, let us express the value of y at time u as $Y(u) \approx \beta_0(u)y_0 + \beta_1(u)y_1 + \ldots \beta_m(u)y_m$, where $\beta_0(u), \beta_1(u), \ldots \beta_m(u)$ represent

$$\beta_i(u) = \sum_{\lambda=i}^{p-2} a_i |u|^\lambda + \sum_{\epsilon=0}^{m} b_{i\epsilon} |u-\epsilon|^p$$

and p represents the specified degree of the plynomial function. Now it can be shown (Sard and Weintraub, 1971) that if p is a real, positive integer, there exist matrices A, B

$$A = \begin{vmatrix} a_{0i} & a_{0m} \\ a_{i1} & a_{im} \end{vmatrix} \qquad B = \begin{vmatrix} b_{01} & b_{0m} \\ b_{i1} & b_{im} \end{vmatrix}$$

whose elements (the so-called "cardinal splines"), are unique, and define a unique approximation function $Y \approx F'(t)$, which is continuous with respect to the $p-1^{th}$ derivative. Sard and Weintraub have calculated the elements of A and B for p = 3, 4, 5, 6, and 10, and m = p, p + 1, ... 20. Since our hypotheses are concerned only with the first and second derivatives (the rate of change and acceleration of arms expenditures), we take p = 3, and since we estimate the function on the basis of ten annual observations, m = 9. Using Sard and Weintraub's values, we can calculate that, for the year prior to a dispute,

$$\Delta y \approx \frac{k - y_9}{k + y_9}$$

where $k = -.000025y_0 + .00014y_1 - .00059y_2 + 00317y_3 - .01929y_3 + .0307y_5 - .1148y_6 + .43097y_7 - 1.60773y_8 + 2.26581y_9$ and $y_0 \ldots y_9$ are the arms expenditure values for the ten years prior to the dispute.

THE RESULTS

Given these values, how does our hypothesis fare? Even by inspection, it is clear that the mean arms race score for nation-dyads entering into full-scale warfare is much greater than the corresponding score for "no war" dyads—292.2 compared with only 23.0. The probability that this difference would occur by chance is less than one in 10,000.

In other words, pairs of nations which end up going to war are characterized by much more rapid military growth in the period immediately prior to the conflict than those which do not resolve their conflicts by other means. The predictive power of this relationship can be seen more clearly if we dichotomize the independent variable to produce a 2x2 table. In Table 2, we see that a high arms race score for a pair of nations correctly predicts the outbreak of war 23 out of 28 times, and conversely, a low score correctly predicts the *non*escalation of a dispute 68 out of 71 times, for an overall 'batting average" of 91 cases out of 99. For those addicted to correlational statistics, the overall strength of the relationship as measured by Yule's Q is .96; using the more conservative ϕ coefficient, it is .75.

As interesting as the strength of the relationship are the identities of some of the "incorrect predictions." Included among the five conflicts preceded by an arms race which did *not* result in war are the remilitarization of the Rhineland, the Munich Crisis, and the Cuban Missile Crisis. In each of these cases, the consensus of historians has it that war was averted only by the narrowest of margins.

INTERPRETING THE FINDINGS

The relationship between arms races and conflict escalation uncovered in this study is unusually strong. For this very reason, great caution must be exercised in interpreting its meaning. First, it is worth emphasizing that these findings do *not* imply that an arms race between the powers necessarily results in war. To prove this, it would be necessary to show not only that arms races lead to the escalation of conflicts, but also that they play an important role in the *initiation* of such conflicts. No such evidence has been adduced here.

Moreover, the findings do not provide incontrovertible proof of a *causal* link between arms races and conflict escalation; they establish

TABLE 2

	Arms Race	No Arms Race
War	23	3
No War	5	68

only that rapid competitive military growth is strongly *associated* with the escalation of military confrontations into war. It is conceivable that this result is a spurious effect of the level of ongoing hostility and tension between powers. It is possible that, when they are very great, such tensions simultaneously stimulate military competition and induce a greater propensity to war. If such is the case (and this itself would have to be demonstrated by further research), then arms races, while remaining a valuable "early warning indicator" of war, could not be considered a causal factor in war onset.

But despite these caveats, it will not do to interpret the findings too conservatively. When two great powers engage in acts of military force or violence against one another, we cannot but assume that their relationship is characterized by a considerable degree of hostility and tension. Yet, in only 3 of 71 cases did such acts lead to war when not preceded by an arms race. Conversely, when an arms race *did* precede a significant threat or act of violence, war was avoided only 5 out of 28 times. It is difficult to argue, therefore, that arms races play *no* role in the process of leading to the onset of war.

The policy implications of this are obvious and immediate. The findings support with hard evidence the intuitive fears of those who argue that an intensification of the superpower arms competition could lead to a "hair-trigger" situation in which a major confrontation would be far more likely to result in all-out war. Thus, they underline the urgency of present efforts to curb the looming quantitative and qualitative expansion of superpower strategic arsenals.

Michael D. Wallace (Ph.D. University of Michigan, 1970) is Associate Professor of Political Science at the University of British Columbia, and has held several visiting appointments at the University of Michigan. He is the author of War and Rank Among Nations *(1973), and coeditor of* To Augur Well *(1979), and has written many articles on arms races and the causes of war.*

Clusters of Nations in the Global System, 1865-1964

SOME PRELIMINARY EVIDENCE

MICHAEL D. WALLACE   *Chapter 11*

This is an effort to identify clusters of nations according to the distance between and among them in terms of common membership in intergovernmental organizations. In addition to reliability and convenience, shared IGO memberships tap a number of dimensions of effective distance. Using hierarchical cluster analysis, the structure of the international system is mapped every five years for the period 1865-1964. We can identify four approximately equal subperiods. The first, 1865-1894, can be characterized by a single, European-centered cluster. The second period, 1895-1919, although showing no evidence of the European cluster diminishing in either "stature or cohesion," sees the development of a closely bound Latin American cluster. In the third period, 1920-1944, one can identify three clusters: (1) a European cluster, now extending to include Asia and Africa; (2) a more tightly bound Latin American cluster, including the United States; and (3) a British Commonwealth cluster. The fourth period, 1945-1964, although showing considerably less homogeneity as a result of the increased system membership, does reveal a number of regularities. The analysis supports the view that the global system can best be described as a single, continuously evolving entity, rather than a sequence of distinct systems.

A major focus in recent international relations literature has been the problem of measuring the "effective distance" (Deutsch and Isard, 1961) between and among nation-states. Hard, quantitative data have been generated on a variety of indices which are designed to measure the volume and intensity of interaction or the closeness of the relationship between pairs of nations: among others, diplomats exchanged (Russett and Lamb, 1969), airline traffic (Gleditsch, 1967, 1969), diplomatic notes and official visits (Galtung, 1966), trading patterns (Russett, 1967; Alker and Puchala, 1968; Savage and Deutsch, 1960), and common membership in international organizations

AUTHOR'S NOTE: An earlier version of this paper was presented to the Western Region meetings of the International Studies Association, in San Francisco, March 26-27, 1971. The author would like to thank J. David Singer for his helpful comments on the manuscript.

Originally published in *International Studies Quarterly,* Vol. 19, No. 1, March 1975.

as well as simple geographic distance (Russett, 1967) have been used. Stimulated by speculative inquiries which suggested the existence of regional subsystems, some scholars have attempted to use these data to delineate regions or clusters of nations characterized by relatively close relationships among their membership and relatively loose bonds between member nations and other state actors (Russett, 1967; Gleditsch, 1967; Alker and Puchala, 1968). Unfortunately, these studies have thus far been confined to a rather narrow time span. In some cases, they examine no more than a decade of the postwar era, and even those which do reach back before World War II begin only during the interwar years. This restricted temporal domain imposes three important limitations on their utility.

To begin with, a major *raison d'etre* of such studies is that they permit the researcher to test his hypothesis on a systematically selected subpopulation of nations where a test comprising all nations in the system would be inappropriate (Russett, 1967: 8-12). For example, many propositions about international integration (Deutsch, 1954), the effect of national status on international behavior (Wallace, 1971, 1972, 1973) and the outcome of internation interactions (Holsti, 1968), are all predicated on the selection of a spatial domain comprising nations with close mutual relationships. Since there is an increasing tendency for scholars to employ long time spans in testing hypotheses to avoid possible short-run idiosyncracies in their data, the narrow temporal domain of existing studies of international clusters leaves them little option but to rely on unsupported intuitive ju dgment in selecting test populations (Wallace 1973: ch. 3), with unpredictable consequences for their findings.

Second, a narrow time span makes it difficult to delimit the temporal as well as the spatial boundaries of one's observational universe. Many hypotheses about international phenomena are explicitly valid only for those periods in which international groupings of the appropriate number, membership, and tightness exist; familiar examples are the numerous propositions about national behavior restricted to "multipolar" or "bipolar" situations (Kaplan, 1957; Hoffman, 1961; Rosecrance, 1963). Even those scholars concerned with hypotheses of a more general nature must contend with the problem of nonadditivity (Alker, 1966); it is more than likely in many cases that the statistical relationship between two variables will vary with changes in these international groupings, requiring that the hypothesis in question be tested over a series of shorter time periods to obtain the best fit. Since intuitive assessments of changes in these configurations over time have a notoriously low intersubjective reliability (Singer, 1969), the lack of hard evidence is felt keenly when it is time to decide on appropriate temporal segmentations.

Finally, confining the empirical delineation of clusters of nations to a relatively limited and recent time period makes it impossible to employ their configurations as variables in their own right, even though such variables play a central role in many well-known models and hypotheses. For example, it is often asserted that a configuration of clusters characterized by many close relationships within each grouping, and only distant relationships between the nations of the separate clusters, is more likely to be associated with international conflict than a configuration manifesting many cross-cutting links between and among clusters (Kaplan, 1957; Deutsch and Singer, 1964). Since reliable, data-based tests[1] of such an hypothesis require a large and heterogenous universe of observations on both independent and dependent variables, and since the basic characteristics of these international clusters (in common with most structural attributes of the global system) change relatively slowly, it follows that such tests must comprise a good number of "readings" over a considerable time span and hence cannot be undertaken on the basis of existing clustering studies.

This paper represents a first step toward filling the need to delineate clusters or groups of nations over a lengthly historical period according to hard, operational criteria measuring the effective distance between and among the state members of the global system. In this preliminary analysis, we shall confine ourselves to a century of time (1865-1964) and to a single index of effective distance (common membership in intergovern-

1. An examination of this hypothesis based on formal alliance bonds was made by Singer and Small (1968). This study illustrates very clearly the need for a large temporal domain when measuring variations in structural attributes of the global system.

mental organizations). In the larger study of which this is a part, many more data sets will be employed, and additional analyses run over a still longer period.[2] Nevertheless, even these partial findings may be of use to scholars for some theoretical purposes. Moreover, the techniques employed in obtaining them may serve a heuristic function for those interested in the systematic description of the structure of the international systems.

The Index of Distance—IGO Common Memberships

The first step in the empirical delineation of international clusters is the measurement of the effective distance between each pair of nations. Ideally, multiple indicators should be used to do this. Nations may enter into relationships with one another in so many different ways, and interact by such a wide variety of means at so many different levels, that no single measure, however comprehensive, can claim to be completely adequate. Not only is there no reason in principle why the numerous possible indices should yield the same results, but in practice it has been discovered that the internation "distances" they measure often diverge quite markedly (Russett, 1967: 168).

However, against the greater validity of the multidimensional approach must be weighed considerations of reliability and sensitivity which rule out many possible indices for purposes of this study. On the one hand, there are those measures for which it has thus far proved impossible to obtain complete and reliable data for all nations over a long period of time: examples are trade, mail flows, and numbers of diplomatic personnel exchanged. On the other hand, there are those indices of effective

2. The author is one of a group of scholars headed by J. David Singer at the University of Michigan who are presently collaborating in an attempt to produce a structural history of the global system from 1816 to 1970 comprising not only the clustering or grouping of nations according to various measures of effective distance, but also the measurement of such diverse structural attributes of the system as the distribution of material capability among its members, relationships of status and hierarchy among nations, and rates of horizontal and vertical mobility within the system.

distance for which complete data are available but which are not sufficiently sensitive measures as they stand: for example, the existence or nonexistence of an alliance bond or formal diplomatic ties between nations yields only a binary measure of distance. Even if several categories of alliance and recognition are established (Singer and Small, 1966a, 1966b), one is left at best with a three- or four-point scale, insufficient to establish even an ordinal ranking among internation distances.[3]

Given these difficulties, I decided to use a single index of effective distance, devised by Russett (1967), which meets the requisite criteria of reliability and sensitivity: the number of intergovernmental organizations to which a given pair of nations both belong. Not only are complete data available on the membership of all IGOs for the century under study (Wallace and Singer, 1970), but this number of common memberships can take on any integer value and thus assure us of at least an ordinal scale of effective distance.

Reliability and convenience are not the only advantages of this index, however. Equally attractive is its apparent ability to tap a number of dimensions of effective distance. Since the activities of IGOs touch upon so many different mutual interests, shared problems, and common foci of attention in the affairs of nations, pairs of states possessing large numbers of institutional affiliations are likely to be those exhibiting a variety of close relationships and high rates of interaction on many levels. Conversely, nations with relatively few such associations are likely to be closely related in only a very limited number of ways, with looser, more distant ties the rule. Of course, it must be stressed that the extent to which institutional links are associated with low internation effective distances on any given dimension or profile of dimensions remains an empirical—and open—question (Russett, 1967: 94-99; Singer, 1969: 27). Nevertheless, in this preliminary study

3. Of course, there exist analytic techniques to detect clusters in such data, but these all involve making (explicitly or implicitly) many complex assumptions about one's data and theoretical model. I shall argue that this is unwise at this stage of knowledge about the international system.

it is not unreasonable to consider the number of common IGO memberships possessed by two nations as indicating, to a first approximation at least, the overall effective distance between them.

Having decided what index to use, I then specified the operational procedures to be used in its construction. Which of the many international institutions are to be considered IGOs and what form of association with them constitutes membership? The criteria used here are spelled out in detail elsewhere (Wallace and Singer, 1970), but a brief resume is in order.

The Data-Making Procedures

There are five criteria which govern the decision to include or to exclude an organization from the compendium of IGOs used here. First, the organization must consist of two or more qualified state members of the international system (Singer and Small, 1966a). Second, it must hold plenary meetings at intervals not greater than every ten years. If an organization ceases to meet this requirement, it is deemed to have passed out of existence; conversely, an organization is added to the list from the date of its first plenum. Third, an IGO must possess a permanent secretariat distinct from that of other organizations. Fourth, it must be established by an instrument of agreement between governments. Fifth, its membership must not be selected by another IGO.

Having selected the population of IGOs to be used in constructing this index, I set out the criteria for national membership in them. These are three in number. First, the nation in question must be a qualified state member of the system, as above. Second, it must send working delegations with voting rights to the plenary meetings; if a nation fails to do so for two plenary sessions, it is deemed to have lost membership. Third, where a colony, province, or dependent territory participates in an organization on behalf of the metropole, the latter is counted as a member.

Employing these coding rules, I obtain national membership data for each five-year period in the century beginning with 1865-1869 and ending with 1960-1964.[4] The number of common memberships for each pair of nations are then determined for each period. These are arranged, according to analytic convention, into a square, symmetric matrix in which cell (i,j) represents the number of IGO memberships held in common by a row nation i and column nation j. Since the larger this number, the closer the nations i and j, I refer to these entries as proximities. Let us now turn to a discussion of the various procedures whereby these twenty proximity matrices may be analyzed to delineate international clusters.

Normalizing and Transforming the Matrix

Before beginning the analysis proper it is necessary to perform two operations on the matrices: normalization to a zero-one scale and transformation of the matrix values from proximities to distances.

Beside analytic convention, there are two reasons for normalizing. The first is to facilitate the transformation of the matrix to one whose entries are *distances,* as outlined below. A second and more substantive consideration is that of comparability. Since the absolute number of IGOs in the system increases roughly exponentially with time (Wallace and Singer, 1970) it would be impossible to make meaningful comparisons between widely separated time points using the raw data, and this would negate a major justification for the entire enterprise.

Russett (1967: 99) performs this normalization on similar matrices by dividing by the largest cell in each matrix, that is, by the largest number of common IGO memberships possessed by any single pair of nations. This procedure was not followed

---

4. Because it proved difficult to determine the precise membership of some IGOs on an annual basis, a five-year measurement period was employed. If a nation was a member of an IGO at any time during the five-year period, it is counted as a member for that entire period; the births and deaths of IGOs themselves are treated in the same way.

here for two reasons. For one thing, it detracts from the general "robustness" of the resulting values; all entries are made dependent on that of a single cell, increasing the vulnerability of the results to measurement error. Second, it only partially solves the problem of comparability over time; in cases where the largest cell changed markedly between two periods while the entries in the rest of the matrix remained relatively constant, the two normalized matrices would look substantially (and misleadingly) different.

The alternative procedure followed here was to normalize each matrix by the total number of IGOs extant in the system for each period. This not only increases reliability, but is also more satisfactory from a theoretical point of view. Each cell (i,j) can now be interpreted as the fraction of all possible IGO relationship opportunities utilized by nations i and j.

Once the matrices have been normalized, the next step is to transform their values to distances. As noted above, as they stand the matrices contain proximities; since we wish to measure effective distance we must turn things around so that the larger the cell entry, the greater the distance between the corresponding nations. To do this, simply subtract each of the normalized proximity values from one; thus, a proximity of .35 becomes a distance of .65. With the 20 matrices thus normalized and transformed, we may now consider the various means of analyzing them to detect clusters or groupings of nations.

FACTOR ANALYSIS–THE PROBLEMS

The most common analytical technique employed on matrices of this type is of course factor analysis. Although originally intended to detect patterns among a large number of variables, it has often been applied to the analysis of both similarities and distances among actors in various types of social systems (Cattell, 1965b: 414-417). However, despite its widespread use there are two important reasons why it is inappropriate for the present task of detecting clusters of nations over a long period of time.

First, it requires that the measure of effective distance used be in the form of ratio scale, so that we can say, for example, that a distance of .50 is precisely twice as large as one of .25. This poses three problems. Even when (as in the present case) the data are in ratio scale form, one may not wish to presume on this too much. Given that we have not used any procedure to weight the common memberships by the importance of the organizations in which they occur, it is surely unwise to insist, for example, that 20 common memberships constitute precisely half the effective distance represented by 10. (The reasons why such a weighting has not been attempted are discussed in detail in Wallace and Singer, 1970: 270.) It would be preferable to make only the less ambitious claim that the 10 memberships constitute the greater distance. A second point is that this requirement puts a heavy burden on the method used to normalize the matrix, since in the case of a ratio scale the *absolute* as well as the relative magnitude of the coefficients is assumed to be meaningful. Thus, if the analysis were re-run after normalizing by a figure twice as large, the clusters identified would be quite different, Finally, even if one could use the technique with the present data, the ratio scale requirement precludes its use on other indices of internation distance for which the construction of even ordinal scales may pose problems. Since, as mentioned above, eventually it will be necessary to compare these results with those obtained using different distance measures, it behooves one not to select so restrictive a technique.

However, the strong assumptions required by the factor analytic model are not limited to the metric which generates the input data, and herein lies its second major weakness. At several stages in the complex sequence of operations intervening between input matrix and delineated factors or clusters, choices must be made to how the algorithm shall proceed. While often masquerading as technical decisions, they have crucial theoretical implications (Russett, 1967: 100-101). In deciding whether or not to normalize the factor matrix prior to rotation one in effect decides whether or not a nation's membership in several clusters shall be deemed to attenuate its affiliation with each (Russett, 1967: 101-102); in choosing the number of factors to be extracted and rotated, one chooses at what point the number of common IGO memberships is small enough to be considered "trivial" or "noise" (Cattell, 1965a: 204); in settling on a criterion for factor rotation, one decides whether to emphasize each nation's strongest affiliation with a particular cluster or its membership in several (Cattell, 1965a: 211). The need to make such crucial theoretical decisions at the very outset makes factor analytic procedures considerably less inductive than they appear at first sight; given the still underdeveloped state of knowledge, this constitutes a powerful argument against its use at the present juncture, particularly in a "first-pass" analysis such as this one.

Any clustering algorithm will make some assumptions about the data. The problem is to find one which produces clearly delineated clusters without forcing one to place excessive confidence in measurement procedures or to make unpalatable theoretical decisions. Perhaps the simplest of the available alternatives is heirarchical cluster analysis, and it is this technique that shall be employed here.

HIERARCHICAL CLUSTER ANALYSIS

Unlike factor analysis, which employs a variety of complex mathematical procedures to arrive at a "solution," hierarchical cluster analysis uses a relatively simple algorithm. It constructs clusters by the successive merger of nations, beginning with the most proximate and gradually extending outward to include nations at ever greater distances. In doing so, the algorithm attempts to include the maximum number of nations in the minimum number of clusters while at the same time minimizing the intracluster diameter, that is, the distance between the two nations in the cluster that are the farthest apart. Since the procedures for doing this are very simple and are crucial to an understanding of the results, they are worth reproducing here in brief. (A complete description is found in Johnson, 1967: 247-249.)

There are three steps to the clustering process. First, the program searches the input matrix of normalized distances to find the smallest cell entry, i.e., the pair or pairs of objects "closest" to one another, and to merge these objects into a new object or cluster. The second step is to measure the distance between this new object and each of the other objects in the system. Where d(i,j) is the distance between objects i and j, x and y are the objects to be merged, and z is another object in the matrix,

$$d\,[(x,y),z] = \max\,[d(x,z),d(y,z)]$$

In other words, the distance between the new cluster and any other object in the matrix is defined as the greater of the distances between each of the merged objects and the outside object. The third step is to repeat the first two steps on the reduced matrix (consisting now of both clusters and nations) until all objects have been merged into a single cluster whose diameter is the distance between the two most distant nations in the matrix.

The output thus consists of a hierarchy of ever-expanding clusters which identifies (a) which nations group with which others, (b) how loosely or tightly bound each nation is in its cluster, and (c) the distances between the clusters themselves. The result is a kind of contour map of the international system. We begin our examination of the international terrain from the top, viewing first the very highest peaks (most tightly clustered nations). Then, as the vantage point moves downward, the peaks grow broader and more numerous, merging into ranges and then broad plateaus separated only by the deepest of valleys (the most distant clusters and nations).

Cluster Analysis—A Caveat

A brief digression regarding the assumptions implicit in this procedure is in order. As noted above, while the clustering algorithm demands less of the data and models than factor analysis, it is by no means "theory-free"; it makes assumptions both about the nature of the input data and the attributes of the output clusters which are of crucial importance.

With regard to the former, the algorithm assumes that the entries in the matrix can be arranged in the form of a true ordinal ranking. This means not only that a larger number must represent a greater distance, but also that all the entries are unique numbers with no ties (Johnson, 1967: 249). Since the present data are in fact only weakly ordered with a number of ties in most of the matrices, a certain amount of care is necessary in interpreting the results. This is particularly true in the case of clusters with large diameters containing small numbers of nations.

Turning to the theoretical assumptions of the analysis, the one we need take note of here concerns a crucial decision which must be made with regard to any clustering algorithm, namely, what property of the resulting clusters interests us most and is therefore to be emphasized in their generation. Here, I have chosen compactness; clusters are selected to minimize the distance between all pairs of nations in the cluster. However, I could have chosen instead to stress the connectedness of the clusters, in other words, to minimize the length of all direct and indirect links between and among all nations in each cluster. To do this, one could change the procedure for measuring the distance between a newly formed cluster (x, y) and an outside object z so that

$$d\ [(x,y),z] = min\ [d(x,z),d(y,z)]$$

That is, connectedness is measured if at each iteration the distance between an object and a cluster is defined as the minimum rather than the maximum distance between the object and each component nation in the cluster (Johnson, 1967: 249-250).

With the present data this "minimum method" was not used, since it is difficult to assign much intuitive importance to the concept of *indirect* distance between nations when the measure of distance is the number of IGO memberships held in common. To build clusters on such a principle would imply, for example, that an increase in common IGO memberships between Mexico and the United States would bind Mexico more closely to Central America via the latter's close institutional links with the United States; in fact, such an increase could just as easily be interpreted as implying the opposite. However, with different measures of internation distance—alliance bonds may represent one example—the connectedness rather than the compactness of the clusters may be of greater theoretical interest, and in such cases the minimum rather than the maximum method may be the more appropriate. With this caveat in mind, let us turn to the results of the cluster analysis. These are presented in graphic form in the appendix. Their main features will be summarized in two ways: first, a look at the basic structural patterns revealed by the analysis: what are the major clusters and how do they change over time? Second, we will examine the results from the point of view of individual nations: which states tend to cluster tightly, which ones loosely, and what is their degree of mobility, both between periphery and center of a single cluster and among different clusters?

The Results

THE BASIC STRUCTURE

The most striking feature of the results is the continuity of the basic structure over time. In some cases the clusters change scarcely at all over a five-year period; moreover, changes that do occur take place gradually over longer periods. This steady pace of change and the degree of continuity throughout makes it difficult and somewhat misleading to speak of the results in terms of distinct epochs, but for the sake of descriptive convenience I may divide the century into four approximately equal subperiods: 1865-1894, 1895-1919, 1920-1944, and 1945-1964.

The first period, 1865 to 1894, is characterized by a monocentric clustering pattern. Having its nucleus and tightest bonds among the major powers of Europe, a single cluster expands outward to comprise the smaller European states, the larger states of North and South America, and finally encompasses the smaller and weaker states of Asia, Latin America, and the Near East at its periphery. This clustering pattern, of course, accords well with the intuitive understanding of this period; marking the apex of European colonization and predating the rise of extra-European great powers, it is dominated by a Europe whose member nations, regardless of political divisions, were knit together by a host of relationships—economic, cultural, and dynastic—which had no parallel anywhere in the globe.

The second period, 1895-1919, sees the development of a second cluster in Latin America. Although the most important American states (the United States and Brazil) still are bound most closely to the European great power grouping, the system is no longer totally Europe-centered. The smaller nations of Latin America are now closer to one another than they are to the European core, forming an independent grouping. But the European cluster itself is diminished neither in stature nor cohesion. Outside Latin America, nations are still less distant from the European great powers than from any other group of nations.

The third period, 1920-1944, shows clearly the changes wrought in the system by World War I. The largest cluster, as before, centers around the European powers, with concentric circles radiating outward to embrace the Asian and African periphery. As might be expected, this grouping is no longer as tightly bound as before the war. In particular, the losers and successor states move toward the periphery. Moreover, there are now two additional clusters which group together some distance from the European core: (a) a new and more tightly bound Latin American cluster strengthened by the addition of the United States, and (b) a cluster composed of the British Commonwealth states which, surprisingly, do not join the mother country in the European cluster, but group together on their own.

The post-World-War-II period (1945-1964) shows considerably less homogeneity than the previous three, largely because of the rapidly expanding membership of the system during these two decades. Nevertheless, several important regularities are visible in the clustering patterns of this period.

First, the gradual loosening of ties within the European grouping has culminated in its complete fission. While a nucleus of Western European states centering around the "Six" of the EEC is bound together as firmly as ever, the Soviet bloc states of Eastern Europe form a completely independent cluster a considerable distance away. Moreover, the Scandinavian and neutral states of Europe develop during the course of this period into a distinct group, although this cluster does not move far from the Western European core.

This split in the European core is paralleled by a falling away at the periphery. The Afro-Asian nations which once clustered loosely around the European inner circle (albeit at a distance) now either emulate Latin America and the Commonwealth in forming separate groupings of their own or simply join these older independent clusters. The major new groupings comprise two clusters of Arab states (one "traditional" and one "modern"), one containing former British East Africa along with several West Indian states, one made up of former French Africa, and one including that group of socialist states headed by China which were not accorded diplomatic recognition by most Western states. In addition, a number of South and Southeast Asian states join the former Commonwealth cluster, along with the former British colonies in West Africa when they achieved independence; and, toward the end of this period, those Southeast Asian nations with close military ties to the United States group themselves with the American cluster. In short, the postwar changes in the clustering patterns clearly reflect the eclipse of Europe as the center of the global system, the rise of the Cold War as a major dimension of cleavage both in Europe and Asia, and the entry into the system of a multitude of new states attempting to establish ties with other nations apart from those with their former metropoles and the Cold War conflict system.

NATIONAL CLUSTERING PATTERNS

Having outlined the major configurations of clusters in the global system as determined by the analysis, I now focus on the tightness with which nations are bound in clusters and the extent of their mobility between clusters.

As might have been anticipated from the examination of the cluster groupings themselves, the picture is one of almost complete continuity throughout the century under examination. With regard to the tightness of the cluster bonds, no matter which of the twenty periods we look at, we can distinguish three major types of nations. The most tightly bound are the European and North Atlantic nations, excepting only the socialist states. All of these enter into clusters at distances of less than .50, and indeed in some periods form clusters with diameters less than .10. In other words, these nations consistently possess common memberships with others in over half of the IGOs extant at the time. A second recognizable type of nation lies in the middle range, not as tightly bound as the "Atlantic core" but by no means on the periphery of the cluster structure. Entering into clusters at distances between .50 and .80, these nations include most of the Latin American nations, such "peripheral" great powers as the Soviet Union and Japan, the larger Third World states, and the old Commonwealth. The third type of nation is the true peripheral, clustering at distances greater than .80. The smaller and more remote Third World states, and, latterly, those socialist states long considered "pariahs" in the West, fall into this category.[5]

5. Note the great degree of similarity between these findings and the earlier classificatory scheme used by Singer and Small (1966a) which distinguished between a "central" and "peripheral" system of nations. Not only is this monocentric portrait of the pre-World-War-I international system largely borne out by the present findings, but the two studies largely correspond with regard to the nations classed as "central" and "peripheral." No nation classed by Singer and Small as peripheral clusters at a distance of less than .5, and most enter at .8 or greater. Conversely, no Singer and Small "central" nation is found clustering at a distance of more than .8.

Furthermore, while the clusters have tended to divide and become more complex from period to period, once a cluster has become established there is remarkably little mobility of nations in or out of it or even much change in the tightness of its bond with that cluster. With the exception of the changes already noted in the periods immediately following the two world wars, intercluster mobility is almost exclusively confined to peripheral states. Equally rare are major movements toward or away from the center of clusters. The only exceptions involve the casting out of the losers and revolutionary pariahs in the aftermath of major conflict.

A NOTE OF CAUTION

Now that the main features of the results have been outlined, it remains to examine their implications for knowledge about the system. Before I do so, however, let me digress a moment to stress the limitations of the present study and the restraints which they put on the inferences that may legitimately be made from the findings.

This study has tested no models and examined no hypotheses: it is solely an exercise in systematic description, and it is entirely illegitimate to interpret its findings as evidence for causal statements. Thus, for example, while some intuitive inferences have been made in the previous section regarding the factors which may be responsible for changes in the clustering patterns, in the absence of hard data on the independent variables, these must be tendered as hypotheses rather than as conclusions.

Second, this preliminary study employed only one index of effective distance to obtain these results, and as a consequence the picture presented here may be biased. It could be argued, for example, that as IGOs are often the least salient of nation's foreign policy concerns—membership in them cannot be taken as indicative of a nation's important relationships with others. In the case of more vital relationships such as trade flows and alliance bonds, a totally different set of factors may come into play. Moreover, given the relative longevity of IGOs (Singer, 1969: 28), the continuity of the results may be misleading; different indices might easily show more short-run variation. These are, of course, empirical questions, but until they are answered by further analysis it cannot be claimed that the findings produced here are in any way a definitive portrayal of the clusters in the global system.

Third, this study represents a preliminary effort as well in terms of the analytic technique used. While there are good reasons for selecting hierarchical clustering (as will be noted), there are disadvantages to such a choice as well. One is that in general (as will be seen), hierarchical clustering produces somewhat different results from other techniques such as factor analysis, making comparisons with other findings problematic. Another and more important problem is that knowledge of the complex relationships between data, results, and technique is not sufficiently rigorous to assume that results here represent precisely what was asked for and are free from distorting effects caused by the interaction of the algorithm with some unperceived feature of the data matrix. Once again, only replication can shed light on this question, and, in the interim, caution should be exercised in interpretation, especially with regard to the smaller and weaker clusters.

Having made it clear what these results do not mean, let us now turn to what they do show. We may discern in them three important implications.

Implications of the Findings

The results of these analyses provide strong empirical support for the view that the global system is most profitably described as a single, continuously evolving entity rather than a sequence of distinct "systems" separated by sharp temporal boundaries (Singer, 1969: 31). Almost without exception, major changes in the way nations clustered together proved to be gradual rather than abrupt, and as we saw, most of the major clustering patterns persisted over a long period of time. Of course, as noted, other relationships between and among nations may change much more abruptly. But the existence of such continuity in so important an area of interstate relations should lead one to examine much more critically many of the explicit and implicit assumptions of temporal *discontinuity* which occur so often in our models and hypotheses. In particular, one should avoid the common practice of using such dubious assumptions to set a priori (and often very narrow) limits on the temporal domain chosen for analysis.

Second, the results seem to call into question the common assumption that geographic regions delineate distinct groupings or subsystems which can usefully be examined separately from the global system as a whole. While geography obviously plays a role in determining cluster membership, it is really central in only two cases, Western Europe and Latin America. In virtually all other cases, physical proximity is strongly attenuated by a variety of other linkages. For example, the evidence suggests that many of the states of "South Asia" (Brecher, 1968), the "Middle East" (Binder, 1958), and "West Africa" (Hodgkin, 1961) are more closely bound to groupings outside their respective areas than they are to most of the other nations in the vicinity. Of course different indices would show a different result, but as Russett (1967) shows, this is an empirical question, and one, moreover, which is not always answered in favor of geography. Furthermore, lest it be argued that the lack of common IGO bonds within some areas is only the result of a lag between the development of common ties and their institutionalization, a quick glance at the changes in cluster patterns shows that, with the exception of Latin America, the cohesion of most geographic regions has either not increased or has actually decreased over time. Indeed, looking over the changes in the clustering patterns for the one hundred years as a whole, one is tempted to draw the opposite conclusion from that heard so often in the literature on regional subsystems and regional integration: that geographical proximity has decreased and not increased in importance as a factor in determining cluster patterns.

Third, in addition to these theoretical implications the findings demonstrate the crucial methodological point stressed throughout: that the substantive findings produced by such analyses are dependent on—in fact, inseparable from—the theoretical assumptions underlying the analytic technique used. This is readily apparent if we compare the clusterings for 1950-1954 and 1960-1964 with Russett's factor analyses of IGO memberships for 1951 and 1962 (Russett, 1967: chs. 6-7). We see at once that while the largest and most tightly clustered groups are the same, many of the more peripheral groups identified by Russett are divided into subgroups by this analysis. Examples are his "Asia" and "Arab" factors (1967: 103-104). To some degree, these differences at the periphery may be due to minor idiosyncracies in data-generation procedures, but they are no doubt also the result of substantive differences in the theoretical orientation of the two techniques. Whereas the hierarchical clustering algorithm is designed to produce clusters of maximum compactness, factor analysis as used by Russett is oriented toward discovering "simple structure" (Cattell, 1965a: 207), that is, toward minimizing the number of clusters. We can argue endlessly about the best mix of parsimony and detail in descriptive studies of this sort, but the point is that the choice is the researcher's, and no mathematical tricks can make it for him.

In summary, what is offered here is a first step toward the systematic description of an important structural attribute in the global system. The findings are in no sense final or complete, and nothing would please the author more than to see substantial efforts made to hasten their obsolescence. In the meantime, it is hoped that other scholars who require such systematic descriptions in their own work will be able to put them to good use.

Michael D. Wallace (Ph.D. University of Michigan, 1970) is Associate Professor of Political Science at the University of British Columbia, and has held several visiting appointments at the University of Michigan. He is the author of War and Rank Among Nations *(1973), and coeditor of* To Augur Well *(1979), and has written many articles on arms races and the causes of war.*

Measuring the Concentration of Power in the International System

JAMES LEE RAY
J. DAVID SINGER

Chapter 12

The purpose of this paper is to examine some earlier efforts to measure the inequality of distribution within several different substantive contexts and to see how appropriate these different measures might be if they were applied to the distribution of "power potential" in the international system or any of its subsystems. We discuss several measures which we find would not be appropriate. We then present a measure which we find better suited for the purpose and go on to compare it to earlier measures of inequality. Several of these turn out to be very similar to the one we present, even though they were originally devised for quite different purposes, such as measuring the degree of economic differentiation in a society. We conclude with a demonstration of the essential similarities among most of the measures discussed.

While notions of equality and distributive justice are dear to the hearts of most social scientists, the hard fact of life is that almost nothing is equally distributed. Whether the valued object is something as tangible as income, land, or votes, or so

AUTHORS' NOTE: We would like to acknowledge the helpful comments of our colleague Stuart Bremer, those of two anonymous readers for this journal, and the financial support of the National Science Foundation, under grant GS-28476X1.

Originally published in *Sociological Methods and Research,* Vol. 1, No. 4, 1973.

elusive a thing as status or influence, some individuals usually have more than others. The same holds for groups, be they social classes, labor unions, political parties or nations; in any social system, the chances are slim that each will possess the same fraction or share of valued objects. Nor is the problem restricted to the distribution of "goods." Such neutral distributions as age or hair color may be of concern, as might the distribution of such "bads" as the tax burden or the incidence of crime. This ubiquitous phenomenon is, furthermore, not merely a matter of idle curiosity or a simple question of social description. To the contrary, many theoretical arguments rest heavily on the predictive or explanatory power of a given set of distributions. From the primary group up through the international system, theoretical enlightenment often flows from an understanding of the pattern in which certain values or attributes are distributed among the component units.

Measuring such inequality in these varying contexts may seem, at first blush, to be a simple and straightforward matter. In a system having two component units, for example, we need merely measure the arithmetic difference or the ratio of their percentage shares in order to get an intuitively reasonable measure of the equality of a given distribution. A more difficult problem arises, however, when we try to quantify the inequality among *more than* two units. Even if the system at hand contains only three units, there are no longer such obvious ways to measure the inequality of a given distribution. Among three groups, for example, which of the following distribution patterns is most unequal: 70%, 20%, 10%; 70%, 30%, 0%; 70%, 15%, 15%? The answer is far from clear.

The purpose of this paper is to examine some earlier efforts to measure the inequality of distribution within several different substantive contexts, and to see how appropriate these different measures might be if they were applied to the distribution of "power potential" in the international system or any of its subsystems. In the course of our discussion, we will describe the fascinating, if sometimes laborious journey we have taken through a maze of indices reflecting an impressive variety of related—but not identical—concepts. Our hope will be to share with the reader some of that fascination, while saving him most of the labor involved in tracking these various indices back to their disparate origins. We shall conclude by describing an index we have found to be especially helpful if one is dealing with a system containing a relatively small, but variable number of units or categories.

There have been several illuminating discussions of measures of inequality in the last decade, among which the one by Alker and Russett (1964) is perhaps most familiar to political scientists. Others of importance are Alker (1965), Hall and Tideman (1967), Nutter (1968), Horvath (1970), Silberman (1967), and Singer (1968). But rather than summarize all of them here, we will introduce them in context as they become relevant to the issues at hand. We begin by delineating briefly some of the more important characteristics we expect to find in a useful measure of inequality or concentration.

We should admit, and indeed will even emphasize, that the criteria for selection of an index will vary as research purposes change. Generally speaking, however, we suggest that an index should have a range of zero to one; while not an essential requirement, such a range is readily accomplished in most cases, and it makes the measure easier to interpret, and index scores easier to compare. Second, its magnitude should *in*crease if there is an upward redistribution of shares from any lower-ranked unit to any higher-ranked unit, and vice versa. Third, it should reflect the shares of *all* the units in the system and not be largely or entirely determined by the shares of only a few of the component members. Finally, it is critical that the measure react to changes in system size in a manner which is appropriate to one's theoretical concerns. Such "appropriateness" is a major preoccupation in this paper, and we focus first on that particular problem.

SENSITIVITY TO SYSTEM SIZE

Most of the indices we will discuss here satisfy the first three criteria mentioned above. However, several of them are inadequate (for our purposes) in their response to changes in system size, especially when N (referring to the number of component units, groups, or categories, regardless of how many subgroups or individuals are in each) is small. Some existing indices tend to *in*crease in value when N increases, others *de*crease, and some are relatively insensitive to the size of the system, or, alternatively, to the number of categories used. Which of these relationships between an index of inequality and system size or category number is desirable? It turns out that there is no single answer to that question; rather, it depends very much on one's substantive concern. Consider the following examples.

If nation A possesses 90% of the military aircraft within a three-nation subsystem, and the rest of the aircraft are distributed evenly between the other two, the inequality in the subsystem is certainly high. But if two or more nations entered the subsystem, and nation A managed to increase production or imports enough to maintain its share at 90%, one might say the inequality within the subsystem is higher. That is, 90% of the hardware was originally "concentrated" in the hands of 33-1/3% of the actors (i.e., nation A), while, later on, that 90% is concentrated in the hands of a mere 20% of the units. The percentage controlled by A has remained the same, as has the percentage controlled by the rest of the subsystem members. Despite this basic similarity, from one point of view it seems obvious that an increase in N has led to a greater inequality or concentration within the subsystem. If one accepts this point of view, then one would want an index of inequality that *in*creases with N.

However, if one were interested in inequality of a different kind—e.g., industrial concentration—there are good reasons for wanting a different kind of index, even if one is dealing with exactly the same distributions. If an industry was formerly concentrated entirely in the hands of three firms, and two firms are added, the concentration of this industry has decreased, even if the largest firm manages to maintain its 90% share of the market, because the entire economic pie is now divided among five rather than three firms. This situation would suggest the need for an index that *de*creases when N increases.

Finally, there may be times when any kind of sensitivity to N will be inappropriate. Lieberson (1969), discussing a concept which is admittedly different from, but still related to, inequality—i.e., "religious diversity"—suggests such a case. Suppose we are comparing the diversity between two campus fraternities. Both fraternities have ten Jews and twenty Catholics, but the second fraternity also has one Protestant. Lieberson points out that a measure which increased with N (which in this case equals the number of categories) would give a significantly higher score to the second fraternity. This "radical difference" would be misleading, as would any significant difference that resulted from an index' sensitivity to the number of categories, Lieberson maintains, because the groups have nearly identical religious composition.

These examples make it clear that, depending on one's theoretical concerns and the particular concept at hand, one may want an inequality index which rises with N, falls when N rises, or which is not sensitive to changes in system size or category number. In a recent paper of ours (Singer et al., 1972), one of the predictor variables in the model was the changing distribution of power potential among the major powers during the 1816-1965 period.[1] During that epoch, the size of the major power subset ranged between 5 and 8. In such a longitudinal analysis, where one of the goals was to ascertain the effect of changing concentration of power upon variations in the incidence of major power war, the concentration measure has to be *comparable* from one observation to the next, despite fluctuations in size. That led us into a literature search in pursuit of such a measure, and that pursuit—plus the difficulty we had in finding such a measure—led to the paper at hand.

EVALUATING SOME PREVIOUS MEASURES

While the idea of concentration or unequal distribution seems unambiguous, attempts to make it operational, verbally or mathematically, reflect a remarkably wide range of interpretations. On the other hand, the diversity is not nearly as great as the number of alternative indices might lead one to suspect. Many of the indices of inequality (as well as indices of a variety of related concepts) turn out, despite surface differences, to be functionally equivalent. One set of measures is based on the sum of squares, or ΣP_i^2 approach, and the other is based on deviations from a line of perfect equality. And in the conclusion we will show that even these two types of indices are translatable into equivalent terms.

Sum of Squares Indices

The first category contains measures known variously as indices of concentration, fractionalization, diversity, or heterogeneity. Perhaps the best known of these is the Herfindahl-Hirschman index of industrial concentration, which simply equals the sum of the squares of each unit's percentage share, or ΣP_i^2 (Herfindahl, 1950). While this measure uses information about all the units in the system, its magnitude is heavily influenced by the scores of those with the largest shares of the market. That is, the squares of small percentages are very small indeed, and thus have a disproportionately modest impact on the final index score.

To illustrate, if the shares of the market (or other valued objects) are equally distributed in a five-unit system, HH = $(20\%)^2 + (20\%)^2 + (20\%)^2 + (20\%)^2 + (20\%)^2 = .20$. If ten new units are added to the system, and each controls .1%, leaving the original five with 19.8% each, that makes virtually no impression on HH, reducing it slightly to .196. This decrease in the index score occurs despite the fact that the addition of ten almost totally deprived units to the system—and the resulting predominant position of the original five units—has, at least from one point of view, substantially *increased* the inequality in the system.

However, we should remember that HH is a measure of a special kind of inequality (i.e., industrial concentration) and one can certainly argue, as we already have, that the addition of ten new firms is "deconcentrating" even if those firms only capture a very small share of the market. This kind of reasoning leads Hall and Tideman (1967) to argue that "a measure of concentration should be a decreasing function of N." The ten new firms in this example are "underprivileged" to a marked degree, but they still have succeeded in breaking into a market formerly dominated completely by five firms. The inequality added by the ten new firms exerts an upward pressure on HH, but that is more than offset by the increase in N—i.e., an increase in the number of firms which have managed to capture a share, no matter how small, of the market.

Such sensitivity to N may be appropriate when measuring industrial concentration, but its appropriateness is at least questionable when measuring the concentration of power potential in an international system. Consider these two simple systems:

I			II	
States	% shares		States	% shares
A	90		A	85
B	5		B	5
C	5		C	2.5
			D	2.5
			E	1
			F	1
			G	1
			H	1
			I	0.5
			J	0.5
HH = .82			HH = .73	

The HH index suggests that there is more inequality in system I than in system II. In some contexts, that judgment would be acceptable, but it should be noted that, in the first system, 90% of the power potential is in the hands of the upper third of the states, whereas in the second, 90% of the power potential is controlled by an even smaller minority—i.e., the upper fifth of the states.

The results in both examples are, of course, affected by the fact that HH does not have a range of zero to one. The lower limit of HH is $1/N$, which means that HH can approach zero only as N approaches infinity. When N is as small as three, or even ten, the lower limits of HH are .33 and .10, respectively. In the example immediately above, HH "starts out" from a higher level in system I than in II, and the final index score is higher in that case, even though (to repeat) 90% of the power potential in II is concentrated in a smaller proportion of its component units.

A perusal of the literature reveals that there are several measures which are similar, or algebraically identical, to HH, even though some of them are not designed to measure industrial concentration, or even inequality per se. The discussion which follows should make obvious the similarity of such concepts as inequality, concentration, fractionalization, ethnicity, diversity, and heterogeneity. Greenberg (1956), for example, presents a measure of linguistic diversity, which is basically the sum of the probabilities that two individuals randomly chosen from a population will belong to the same linguistic group.[2] If one group makes up 50% of the society, then the probability that any two individuals chosen from the total population will be chosen from *that* particular group is .50 x .50, or .25. If .25 is added to the probability of randomly choosing two individuals from each of the remaining groups (whose number and size are of consequence only when *their* probability value is being computed), the result is Greenberg's index.

But this index turns out to be identical to ΣP_i^2, where P_i in this case is the percentage share of the total population held by the ith group, rather than the percentage share of the market controlled by the ith firm. The linguistic diversity index is functionally and arithmetically equal to the Herfindahl-Hirschman index of industrial concentration.

Similar to both these measures is the Rae and Taylor (1970) index of fragmentation. Their formula is

$$1 - \frac{1}{N(N-1)} \, \Sigma f_i(f_i - 1),$$

where f_i equals the number in the ith subgroup and N equals the number in the total group. A slight rearrangement of terms[3] reveals that this formula is equivalent to

$$1 - \sum \frac{(f_i)}{(N)} \frac{(f_i - 1)}{(N - 1)}.$$

It then becomes obvious that f_i/N is a term representing the proportion of the whole made up by the ith subgroup, and that $(f_i - 1)/(N - 1)$ is only a very slight modification of that term. In short, this measure is equivalent to—or, more precisely, the complement of—ΣP_i^2.

However, we should point out that, if one is measuring fragmentation of a comparatively *small* body, such as a committee or legislature, the second term in Rae and Taylor's equation will not be identical to the first term, and the index will deviate perceptibly from the simple ΣP_i^2. To illustrate, if there were 100 representatives in a legislative body, the contribution of a group of 25 to the fragmentation index score would be 25/100 x 24/99, or .0606, whereas if ΣP_i^2 were the index, that group's contribution to the score would be .0625. Such differences, when summed over several groups, can lead to a noticeable difference between the Rae and Taylor index and ΣP_i^2.

Furthermore, the small difference will make conceptual sense. If we reason that the measure should reflect the sum of probabilities that two individuals randomly chosen from the legislative body will belong to the same party, then the smallness of the body makes it strictly incorrect to calculate those probabilities by simply squaring f_i/N. Replacement of individuals drawn from a population, and/or an infinitely large population should not be assumed; therefore f_i/N should be multiplied by $(f_i - 1)/(N - 1)$ in order to obtain those probabilities.

Yet another index which is based on the ΣP_i^2 is the Michaely (1962) concentration index, which does not measure industrial concentration, but "tendencies toward geographic concentration in transactions" (Puchala, 1970). It shows the extent to which an actor's transactions are widely distributed throughout the system (low score), focused on a small cluster of partners (high score), or shared with a single partner only (highest score). The index formula is $100 \sqrt{\Sigma(X_{sj}/X_{.j})^2}$, where X_{sj} equals j's transactions with s, and $X_{.j}$ equals the total transactions for j; $X_{sj}/X_{.j}$ is a proportion, of course, and since it is squared, the similarity of this measure to ΣP_i^2 is obvious. Taking the square root of the summed squares changes the range within which the index is most sensitive. We used this same technique in constructing the measure to be described below.

This list of measures based on ΣP_i^2 can be continued almost indefinitely. Another important one is Lieberson's (1969) index of population diversity, as are several which he discusses: the Bachi (1956) and Simpson (1949) indices of diversity, the Bell (1954) index of ecological segregation, and the Gibbs and Martin (1962) measure of diversification in an industry.

Finally we would like to mention a measure of industrial concentration which "owes its intellectual parentage to the Herfindahl Summary Index" (Horvath, 1970), but which is sufficiently different to be worth considering if the ΣP_i^2 is not deemed satisfactory. Horvath's measure,

$$CCI = x_i + \sum_{j=2}^{n} (x_j)^2 (1 + [1 - x_j]),$$

where $I = 1$, $j = 2, 3, 4, \ldots$, n, and n = the number of firms in the industry, and x = the decimal fraction of assets (or sales, employment, or profit) belonging to each individual firm. A detailed discussion of this measure would be out of place here, since for our purposes this measure shares the disadvantages of its intellectual parent, ΣP_i^2. Suffice it to say that this measure focuses upon—and therefore reflects—both *absolute* concentration (having to do with the smallness of the number of firms in the industry) and *relative* concentration (having to do with comparisons of the sizes of the firms in the industry, regardless of the number of firms which exist).[4]

Deviation from Equality Indices

Our second category contains perhaps the best known measures of inequality in economics and political science—the Gini index[5] and the Schutz coefficient. Both are based upon the deviation of a Lorenz curve from the "line of perfect equality." The rationale behind these measures is indeed intuitively appealing. If one constructs a graph (see Figure 1a) indicating what percentage of a good is held by each percentage of a population, and if each 1% of the population possesses 1% of the good, the Lorenz curve will fall completely on the line of perfect equality, whose slope equals one. However, if the goods are not distributed evenly, the Lorenz curve will deviate from the line of perfect equality, as in examples in Figure 1b and 1c.

The Gini index and the Schutz coefficient measure these deviations in slightly different ways. According to Alker (1965), "the Gini index sums for each individual in the population, the difference between where he is on the Lorenz curve and where he would be expected to be in the case of democratic equality." The Schutz coefficient, on the other hand, sums "ratios of advantage" for each population percentile above *or* below the equal share point. It is based on the *slope* of the Lorenz curve, and in effect reflects how close the slope of the line below the equal share point is to zero, *or* how close the slope of the line *above* the equal share point is to infinity.

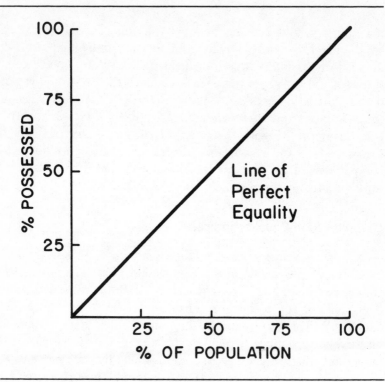

Figure 1a: LORENZ CURVE INDICATING PERFECT EQUALITY OF
          DISTRIBUTION

The Gini index appears to meet most of the basic requirements of a good measure of inequality. It utilizes the
information available about all units, increases in response to
exchanges of shares from lower- to higher-ranked units, and vice
versa. However, if one is measuring the concentration of power
potential in a rather small international subsystem, the Gini
index has some properties which might *not* be desirable. Some
of these are related to the fact that it has an upper limit of $1 -
1/N$, because it was originally designed for continuous, rather
than discrete, distributions. Figure 2—in which A holds all and
B holds none—illustrates this problem. Even though the
inequality of this situation is complete, only *half* of the "area of

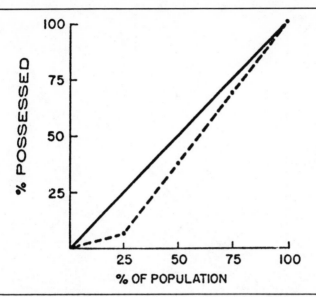

Figure 1b: LORENZ CURVE INDICATING 'SOME' INEQUALITY IN THE DISTRIBUTION

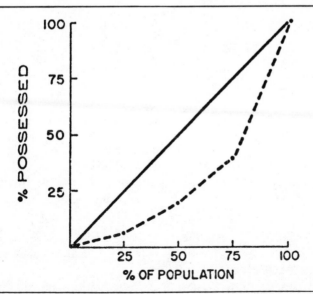

Figure 1c: LORENZ CURVE INDICATING 'GREATER' INEQUALITY IN THE DISTRIBUTION

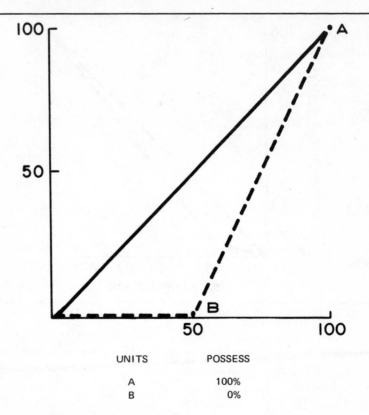

UNITS	POSSESS
A	100%
B	0%

Gini index = $2\Sigma(X_i - Y_i)\Delta X_i$

$= 2[(.50 - 0).50 + (1.00 - 1.00).50 = .50$

Figure 2: LORENZ CURVE WITH ONE UNIT POSSESSING ALL, AND THE OTHER UNIT NONE

inequality" (the triangle below and to the right of the line of perfect equality) lies between the line of perfect equality and the Lorenz curve. Therefore, the Gini index—reflecting the percentage of the total area of inequality falling between the Lorenz curve and the line of perfect equality—equals .50, the upper limit in the two-unit case. In the three-unit case, of course, the upper limit would be .67.

This fluctuation in the upper limit of the Gini index, much like that of the lower limit of HH, can have an undesirable effect on index scores. Consider, for example, an attempt to measure the concentration of power potential at two points in time in a small international subsystem.

t_0			t_1	
States	% share	States		% share
A	90	A		70
B	6	B		15
C	4	C		10
		D		3
		E		2

| Gini = .57 | | Gini = .59 | |

If the Gini index—calculated according to Alker's (1965) formula for approximations in case of discrete distributions—is used as one's measure of concentration of power potential, the subsystem appears to be marked by greater concentration at the second point in time.

In fact, however, the Gini index is slightly higher in the second case, *not* because the subsystem more nearly approaches the condition of perfect concentration (with one state so "unequal" as to control 100% of the power potential) in the latter case, but because the upper limit of the index has been increased by the addition of two states to the subsystem at that point in time. Although Gini has probably not been used in exactly this way, it would not be obviously unreasonable to make such a use of it. Our point here is that if it is used for this (or similar) purposes, it will be very sensitive to differences in system size when N is small, and the user should be sure that this sensitivity is appropriate for his purposes.

Gini Versus HH

As we have seen above, Gini has an upper limit of $1 - 1/N$, while HH (and the various similar measures) has a lower limit of $1/N$. There is at least one other striking difference which should be mentioned here. Hall and Tideman claim that if "a [system]

A has k times the number f units as [system] B, with $k > 1$, and the P_i's [percentage shares] in A are distributed such that corresponding to each P_i in B there are k units of size P_i/k, then the measure of concentration for A should be $1/k$ times the measure for B." The explanation is that "if each [unit] in a given [system] is divided into two [units] of equal size, the effect on a measure of concentration should be to reduce it by $1/2$."

Although we agree that such a property may be desirable if industrial concentration is being measured, we are less certain that it is appropriate when measuring concentration of power potential, or other kinds of inequality. In any case, HH and the Gini index react very differently to situations such as that described above by Hall and Tideman. For example, consider the following two subsystems.

I		II	
States	% shares	States	% shares
A	40	A	20
B	30	B	20
C	20	C	15
D	10	D	15
		E	10
		F	10
		G	5
		H	5
HH = .30		HH = .15	
Gini = .25		Gini = .25	

It is readily seen that HH for system II equals $1/2$ the HH score for system I, which, according to Hall and Tideman, is expected and desirable. But the Gini index remains unchanged, since in both system I and system II the upper 25% of the units control 40% of the goods, the next 25% control 30% of the goods, and so on. The "blindness" of the Gini index to the differences in these two cases is again attributable to the fact that it was not designed for discrete distributions. This difference between these indices cannot be resolved by "controlling for" N. If N is controlled for, HH = .20 in both cases, while Gini = .33 in the first case, and .29 in the second.

Another Gini "Blind Spot"

Kravis (1962) has pointed out that the Gini index assumes that "equal importance may be attached to equal absolute differences in income . . . even though one of the differences is taken between two low [value positions] and the other between two high ones." This means that very different distributions can and will generate Lorenz curves which deviate to the same extent from the line of perfect equality. The following very disparate distribution patterns, for example, both have a Gini value of .50.

I	II
70%	45%
7.5%	35%
7.5%	20%
7.5%	0%
7.5%	0%

If one is particularly interested in an inequality which tends toward monopoly (one unit controls 100%), then one would probably want system I to receive a higher score. On the other hand, if one's interest is in the extent to which the smaller units in a system are deprived, system II should receive a higher score. (Of course, no single measure can satisfy all theoretical needs, since one which would rank both of these cases "higher" is obviously not feasible.)[6]

The Schutz Coefficient

Shifting now to the Schutz coefficient, we find that it is similar to the Gini index in that its upper limit is also $1 - 1/N$. However, the reason for this may not be so intuitively clear.

The Schutz coefficient sums "ratios of advantage," and these ratios are comparisons of the holdings of the advantaged (or the disadvantaged) to the *average* percentage of holdings of all the units in the system. (Formally, the Schutz coefficient is

$$\sum_{v_i \geq \bar{v}} \left(\frac{v_i}{\bar{v}} - 1 \right) \Delta X_i,$$

or

$$\sum_{v_i \leq \bar{v}} \left(1 - \frac{v_i}{\bar{v}} \right) \Delta X_i,$$

where $\bar{v}$ = the average share of the units in the system; v_i = the share of the ith unit; and $\Delta X_i = X_{i+1} - X_i$, when $X_i = i/N$.) These average holdings become smaller with every increase in N. Again, in the extreme case, if the system has only two units, the *average* holding is 50% no matter how unequally the holdings may be distributed, and when N increases to 4, 5, or 10, the average holding decreases to 25%, 20%, and 10%, respectively. The larger N is, the larger is the ratio of advantage of the one unit which controls 100% of the goods, and the larger is the upper limit of the Schutz coefficient.

Perhaps the most unattractive characteristic of this measure is that it does not make use of all available information. Alker (1965) points out that Schutz can be calculated either by summing the ratios of advantage for those above the mean or by summing the ratios of *dis*advantage for those below the mean. Of course, this means that the coefficient cannot be sensitive to variations within that part of the distribution which is *not* included in the calculations. Furthermore, because the coefficient *sums* the ratios of advantage, and since different combinations of ratios can give the same sum, the coefficient can also be insensitive to variations in the distribution in the group which *is* included in the calculations. For example, the Schutz coefficient equals .50 in all three of the cases below.

I	II	III
70%	70%	70%
20%	7.5%	15%
10%	7.5%	15%
0%	7.5%	0%
0%	7.5%	0%

Before turning to our own proposed index, we should mention briefly several other measures of inequality, some of which may be excellent for certain purposes. One widely used measure of industrial concentration, CR, equals the fraction of the market held by the L largest firms, where L usually equals 4, 8, or 20. Another measure of industrial concentration, introduced by Hall and Tideman, is TH, defined as $1/(2\Sigma iP_i) - 1$, where i equals the rank of the ith largest unit, and P_i equals the percentage share of that unit. Several other measures are discussed by Alker and Russett (1964), including the ratio of the percentage controlled by the largest unit to the percentage controlled by the smallest unit, the Pareto coefficient, and the skewness of a distribution. Though it is possible that one of the measures might be ideal for some specialized purpose, we agree with Alker and Russett that in most cases they are not as generally applicable as the other measures discussed above.

THE PROPOSED INDEX OF CONCENTRATION

Before describing the index which we decided to use for our own purposes, let us restate briefly the criteria we hope to satisfy. First, we want our measure to have a range of zero to one, even at the lower end of the size spectrum, because we seek to measure concentration in both the full international system, with an N as large as 135, and in its smaller regional and functional subsystems—with Ns as low as 5. Also its magnitude should increase if there is an upward redistribution of shares from any lower-ranked to any higher-ranked unit, and vice versa. Furthermore, it should reflect the shares of *every* unit in the system, and not merely of those which fall, for example, above or below the mean. Finally, it is critical that the measure react to changes in system size in a manner which is appropriate to our theoretical concern.

With the few exceptions that we have mentioned explicitly above, most measures satisfy the first three criteria, but meeting the fourth criterion proves to be more problematical. As we have implied in the discussion above, because the measures we looked at had different *ranges* for different Ns, they appeared to us to be overly sensitive to changes in N. This led us to prefer a *standardized* measure which has the same range regardless of system size. The basic formula for our index of concentration (or CON) is: standard deviation of the percentage shares ÷ maximum possible standard deviation in a system of size N. Fortunately, this simplifies to

$$\text{CON} = \sqrt{\frac{\Sigma P_i^2 - 1/N}{1 - 1/N}}$$

The maximum possible standard deviation of the percentage shares occurs when one unit controls 100% of the goods, while the rest of the units control none at all. And the minimum (zero) occurs when all the units control equal shares. Thus CON is equal to 1 whenever a single unit controls 100% of the goods, regardless of system size. It also has the virtue of taking into account information regarding all units, and it increases in value if there is a shift in shares from a lower-ranked to a higher-ranked unit, and vice versa.[7]

Now the fact that we opted for a standardized measure does not mean that we wanted or have a measure that is *totally* insensitive to system size. While the *range* of this measure is constant, and therefore insensitive, the *scores* on the index will rise and fall with system size, even when nothing else changes. For example, consider this subsystem at two points in time:

	t_0			t_1
States	% share		States	% share
A	90		A	90
B	6		B	6
C	4		C	4
			D	0
			E	0
	CON = .85			CON = .88

The only difference is that two units have been added at t_1; no shares have been shifted from some units to others. Yet CON is higher (because of the change in the standardizing denominator), as we believe it should be, since more power potential is concentrated in the hands of a smaller percentage of the subsystem's members. Had we wanted a measure that was insensitive to N (when nothing else changes), we could have used an *un*standardized measure such as HH. In the case at hand, HH would equal .82 on both occasions; the *range* of HH is sensitive to changes in N in such cases, but the *scores* are not. The advantage, we believe, of a standardized measure such as CON is that scores are comparable, in the sense that a score of .33, for example, indicates that the system shows one-third as much concentration as is possible, no matter what the size of the system. Unstandardized measures such as HH or Gini will reflect changes in N only because their ranges will change (and therefore may appear to be too sensitive to such changes) but not necessarily because the degree of concentration has changed. And in examples like the one above, the *scores* may not change when N changes, but those scores will not be comparable.

Now the price of this comparability as we have defined it is an insensitivity to changes in N at the extremes of the index. For example, if there are 5 units in a system and 1 unit controls 100%, CON = 1. If 7 units are added to the system, but 1 unit still controls 100%, CON still equals 1. This is so even though all the goods are concentrated in the hands of 20% of the units in the first case, but in the hands of an even smaller minority of

12.5% of the units in the second case. Such changes in N (when nothing else changes) will be reflected in CON as long as no one unit controls 100%. If one is dealing with that rare empirical domain in which such extreme cases occur, and one wants an index that will be sensitive to changes in N, then CON should not be used. In our case, these extreme distributions are not possible, and it seemed worthwhile to forego sensitivity to N in such cases for the sake of comparability across the much more common cases where there is some, but not absolute, inequality.

Perhaps the best way to illustrate the characteristics of the CON measure is to show how it varies vis-à-vis several alternative indices in a few simple examples. Assume that we are measuring the concentration of power potential among states in two different international subsystems containing three and five states, respectively.

I			II	
States	% shares		States	% shares
A	90		A	70
B	6		B	15
C	4		C	10
			D	3
			E	2
.57		Gini		.59
.82		HH		.52
.85		CON		.64

While HH and CON produce the intuitively reasonable higher index score for case I, the Gini scores are just the opposite, albeit not by much. This latter result is largely a function of N, since the upper limit of the Gini index is only .67 in case I, but .80 in case II. If we correct Gini for N (by dividing it by $1 - 1/N$), it rises to .85 in I and only to .74 in II, making it more consonant with the HH and CON results. However, when Gini is corrected in this fashion, it has less discriminating power in this example (i.e., the sensitivity of the index as reflected in the *difference* between the scores in the two cases is diminished), a characteristic which also showed up when we used this modified Gini on our own historical data. One can enhance the discriminating power of some indices by taking the square root of the raw scores. But when we used that technique on our data with the Gini index, its discriminating power *decreased,* as it does in this example above (that is, the square root values of the Gini corrected for N are .92 and .86).

As we noted, the HH and CON scores seem to be in the "correct" order, but the HH pattern is largely a function of its lower limits, which are .33 and .20, respectively. And while such sensitivity to N happens to produce the appropriate scores in the cases at hand, it often will not. Consider the following pair of subsystems.

I			II	
States	% shares		States	% shares
A	33 1/3		A	32
B	33 1/3		B	32
C	33 1/3		C	32
			D	2
			E	2
.33 1/3		HH		.31
.00		CON		.37

HH indicates that the concentration of power potential in I is slightly higher, even though its equality of distribution is perfect. CON, on the other hand, reacts more appropriately in this empirical and theoretical context, since its upper and lower limits do not vary with the size of the system.

Let us consider one more example.

	I			II	
States	% shares		States	% shares	
A	40		A	20	
B	30		B	20	
C	20		C	15	
D	10		D	15	
			E	10	
			F	10	
			G	5	
			H	5	

.25	Gini	.25
.30	HH	.15
.26	CON	.17

While the HH results are appropriate according to the Hall and Tideman criterion, with its value in case I twice that produced for case II, the Gini index scores are identical. For our purposes, the face validity of both of these results leaves something to be desired. Conversely, the CON scores of .26 and .17 seem to us to reflect most appropriately the differences in the inequality of the distribution of power potential in the two systems. In any case, these illustrations demonstrate that—at least when one is measuring concentration or inequality among a rather small, but changing number of units—there are differences among such measures as HH, the Gini index, the Schutz coefficient, and CON which should be taken into account by any potential user.

SIMILARITY TO OTHER MEASURES

Over 15 years ago, in the conclusion of an article analyzing indices of segregation, Duncan and Duncan (1955) lamented that

one lesson to be learned from the relatively unproductive experience with segregation indexes to date is that similar problems are often dealt with under different headings. Most of the issues which have come up in the literature on segregation indexes. . . . had already been encountered in the methodological work on measures of inequality, spatial distribution, and localization in geography and economics.

We have learned a similar lesson from our experience with indexes of inequality. The major problem we have discussed here—i.e., comparability in the face of a small but changing N—has been dealt with under different headings and solved in essentially the same manner. For example, Amemiya (1963) has developed an index of economic differentiation (IED) which equals

$$\sum_{i=1}^{n} \frac{n}{n-1} \left(\frac{P_i - 1}{n} \right)^2 ,$$

where n = the number of classifications of industry, and P_i is defined as the proportion of workers in the ith industry. If we say that n = N = the number of units in the system, and that P_i is the percentage controlled by the ith unit, we can see that IED is essentially the same as CON. That is,

$$IED = \sum_{i=1}^{N} N/N - 1(P_i - 1/N)^2 = N/N - 1\Sigma(P_i - 1/N)^2$$

$$= N/N - 1\Sigma(P_i^2 - 2P_i/N + 1/N^2) = N/N - 1\Sigma P_i^2$$

$$- 2/N\Sigma P_i + N[1/N]^2 = N/N - 1\Sigma P_i^2 - 2/N[1] + 1/N$$

$$= N/N - 1\Sigma P_i^2 - 1/N = \frac{\Sigma P_i^2 - 1/N}{N - 1/N} = \frac{\Sigma P_i^2 - 1/N}{1 - 1/N}$$

Thus, CON is equivalent to the square root of IED.

Similarly, Labovitz and Gibbs (1964) present a measure of the degree of division of labor (D) which equals

$$1 - \frac{(\Sigma X^2 / [\Sigma X]^2)}{1 - 1/N},$$

where N equals the number of occupations, and X is the number of individuals in each occupational category. This is also essentially equal to CON. The term $\Sigma X^2 / [\Sigma X]^2 = \Sigma P_i^2$, which means that $D = 1 - \Sigma P_i^2 / 1 - 1N$. Therefore,

$$\sqrt{1 - \frac{1 - \Sigma P_i^2}{1 - 1/N}} = \text{CON}.$$

In short, $\sqrt{1 - D} = \text{CON}$. It can further be shown that the index of qualitative variation (IQV), presented by Mueller et al. (1970), which equals

$$\frac{\Sigma n_i n_j}{\frac{k(k-1)}{2} (n/k)^2}$$

(where n_i = the number in the ith category, $i \neq j$, and k = the number of categories) is related to CON in the same way. That is, $\sqrt{1 - \text{IQV}} = \text{CON}$.

Aside from the fact that we use the index as a measure of concentration, rather than of economic differentiation, division of labor, qualitative diversity, and so on, the only substantial difference between CON and these other measures is that we use the square root of the same basic formula. We do this for several reasons. First, this procedure increases the discrimination of CON within the range of inequality in the small N systems that are of concern to us here. Second, we find the conceptual definition of CON as the standard deviation of the percentage shares divided by the maximum possible standard deviation in a system of size N an intuitively appealing one; this means that by definition, we should use the square root. Finally, one critic has already pointed out that, despite the fact that we criticize HH on the grounds that the squares of small percentages are very small, and that therefore they have a disproportionately small impact on the final index score, we turn around and use the squares of small percentages in our own index. But, by using the square root of the difference between these small squared percentages and $1/N$, and even more importantly, by standardizing the measure the way we do, CON avoids this insensitivity to small percentages that HH displays, even though the squares of small percentages are used in both indices.

CONVERGENCE OF MEASURES

In examining the important differences among the available measures of concentration, we noted that they nevertheless fall into two basic classes. While retaining the distinction (sum of squares versus deviation from equality) for the sake of clarity, we now follow up the earlier suggestion that even this distinction is far from fundamental.

The mathematical convergence among these diverse measures begins to become evident when we note that all of them can be expressed in the same basic terms: P_i, i, and N, where P_i equals the percentage share of the ith unit, i equals the rank of the ith largest unit, and N equals the number of units in the system. This equivalence is further reflected by the fact that—with the exception of the Schutz coefficient—all the major measures are a function of either: (a) the sum of squared percentage shares, or (b) the sum of rank share products.

The most obvious similarity, already discussed above, is that between CON and HH, both of which are originally expressed in terms of P_i and N. If

$$CON = \sqrt{\frac{\Sigma P_i^2 - 1/N}{1 - 1/N}} \; ,$$

and HH = ΣP_i^2, we can also express CON as

$$\sqrt{\frac{HH - 1/N}{1 - 1/N}} \; .$$

Hence, it is clear that CON^2—and therefore CON itself—is a perfectly predictable function of HH, as long as we know the value of N. What is true of the relationship between CON and HH is also true, of course, of the relationship between CON and all those other measures discussed which are based on the sum of squared percentage shares, or some slight mutation thereof.

The Gini index can also be expressed in terms of P_i, i, and N, as may be seen by referring to Figure 3. What the Gini formula does, in effect, is to sum the area of the rectangles in the figure, and subtract that sum from one, the total "area of inequality" that lies above and below the line of perfect equality. The resulting difference is the proportion of the *total* area that lies between the Lorenz curve and the line of perfect equality; that proportion *is* the Gini index score. By referring to Figure 3, one can see that there are 2i − 1 rectangles associated with each group. For example, group A, which is the *fourth* largest group, has (2 x 4) − 1, or 7 rectangles associated with it. The area of each of the rectangles in the figure equals the product of 1/N (i.e., the proportion of the whole which each group constitutes, which is represented by the *length* of each rectangle as measured along the *horizontal* axis), and P_i (the proportion of the whole which each group controls, which is represented by the *width* of each rectangle as measured along the vertical axis), or P_i/N. Therefore, the area of the rectangles associated with group A is .25 x .10, or .10/4, which equals .025. There are 7 such rectangles, so group A's contribution is 7 x .025, or .1750. The contribution of all the other groups can be calculated in the same way. The Gini index is thus equal to $1 - \Sigma(2i - 1 [P_i/N])$. But this can be simplified to

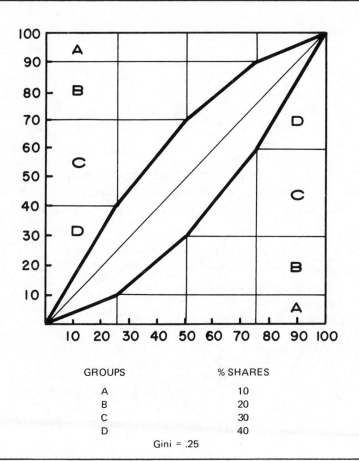

GROUPS	% SHARES
A	10
B	20
C	30
D	40

Gini = .25

Figure 3: LORENZ CURVES ENCOMPASSING PROPORTION OF TOTAL AREA EQUAL TO THE GINI INDEX

$$1 - \frac{\Sigma(2i - 1)(P_i)}{N} = 1 - 1/N\Sigma(2i - 1)(P_i)$$

$$= 1 - 1/N\Sigma(2iP_i - P_i) = 1 - 1/N\Sigma 2iP_i - 1/N\Sigma P_i.$$

Since $\Sigma P_i = 1$, and the constant 2 can be brought outside the summation sign, this further simplifies to $1 - (2/N\Sigma iP_i) - 1/N$. Thus, it can be seen that the Gini index is a function of the rank share products, or $\Sigma i P_i$, as is TH, which, as we recall, equals $1/(2\Sigma i P_i) - 1$.

Turning to the Schutz coefficient, we find that it, too, can be expressed in terms of P_i and N. Recall that the original formula is

$$\sum_{v_i \geqq \bar{v}} (v_i/\bar{v} - 1)\Delta X_i.$$

However, v_i is equivalent to P_i, and both v and $\Delta X_i = 1/N$. (As long as each unit represents an equal percentage of the total number of units.) Thus for formula can be rewritten as:

$$\sum_{P_i \geqq 1/N} \frac{P_i}{1/N - 1} \frac{1}{N},$$

and this in turn simplifies to

$$\sum_{P_i \geqq 1/N} (P_i - 1/N).$$

Similarly, the alternative formula for the Schutz coefficient simplifies to

$$\sum_{P_i \leqq 1/N} (1/N - P_i).$$

SUMMARY

The measurement of inequality and related concepts is a pervasive problem in several social sciences. We have discussed various attempts to solve this problem and have found that the measures often differ in their reaction to changes in system size. In that discussion, we pointed out that some measures might not be appropriate if one were measuring the concentration of power potential in the international system or its subsystems. We have presented a measure that seems appropriate for such a purpose, and then examined its similarity to other measures which have been used for quite different purposes. Finally, we concluded, by focusing on the essential similarity of most of the measures we discussed, that they are all a function of P_i, N, and/or i, where P_i equals the percentage share of the ith unit, N equals the number of units in the system, and i equals the rank of the ith largest unit.

In closing, it might be appropriate to suggest that the establishment of a journal such as this was long overdue. In the literature of 5 disciplines, at least 25 scholars have utilized over 15 different journals to present their efforts to get at a central problem in the social sciences. Our fairly thorough search in the more likely sectors, as well as conversations with other political scientists, however, turned up only about half these efforts; until our first draft was circulated to specialists in sociology, the remaining sources remained beyond our ken. Even now, we suspect that economists and psychologists, for example, might lead us to additional papers on the same class of problem. Had this journal been available as a prominent solution, these independent "discoveries" and the attendant costly digressions might have been avoided.

Be that as it may, we trust that this effort represents a modest accretion to our methodological armamentarium. In addition to offering a small improvement on some existing indicators of concentration, it should help to put the problem into fuller context, offering as it does a synthesis and a codification of those which have gone before. At the least, its circulation among political scientists should serve as a reminder that crossing disciplinary boundaries may often be a salutary, sobering experience.

NOTES

1. The power—or more accurately, power potential—index reflects three sets of dimensions, each of which taps two phenomena; military (personnel and expenditures); industrial (energy consumption and iron/steel production); and demographic (total population and urban population). The 1816-1965 data base, plus the derived measures and their rationale, will appear in Singer and Small (forthcoming).

2. Greenberg also presents a more complex measure which is modified to reflect the dissimilarity of the languages involved.

3. Charles Taylor (1970) uses this formula to measure party concentration in legislatures.

4. A good discussion of the measure can be found in Horvath's article. For those who want to compare "within subset" concentration to "between subset" concentration, see Hexter and Snow (1970). And for a discussion of the special problem of inferring the concentration of an industry from the observation of a few firms, see Silberman (1967), and Hart and Prais (1956).

5. Several indices similar to the Gini index have been used to measure "segregation." For example, see the "nonwhite section index" and the "nonwhite ghetto index" (Jahn et al., 1947), the Cowgills' (1951) index of segregation, and the "reproducibility index" (Jahn, 1950). For a discussion of all these measures and their similarity to the Gini index and to each other, see Duncan and Duncan (1955), and Hornseth (1947).

6. It should be noted also that this example does not involve a change in the number of units (since we could have given the lowest two units in the second case a percentage only slightly larger than zero to meet the objection that system II "really" only contains three units); this is another case in which Gini cannot be made more "reasonable" simply by correcting it with a denominator of $1 - 1/N$.

7. It was interesting to discover while preparing this paper that Janda (1971) has come up with exactly the same formula to cope with the problem of measuring "party articulation."

James Lee Ray (Ph.D. University of Michigan, 1974) is Assistant Professor of Political Science at the University of New Mexico. He has written the textbook Global Politics *(1979) as well as numerous articles on international conflict, political economy, and methodology.*

J. David Singer (Ph.D. New York University, 1956) is Professor of Political Science at the University of Michigan and has also been associated with Vassar College, The Naval War College, and the Universities of Oslo and Geneva. Among his books are Financing International Organization *(1961):* Deterrence, Arms Control, and Disarmament *(1962):* Human Behavior and International Politics *(1965):* Quantitative International Politics *(1968):* The Wages of War, 1816-1965 *(1972): and* The Study of International Politics *(1976).*

REFERENCES

ABEL, T. (1941) "The element of decision in the pattern of war." Amer. Soc. Rev. 6: 853-859.

ADAMS, J. S. (1965) "Inequity in social exchange," in L. Berkowitz (ed.) Advances in Experimental Social Psychology, Vol. II. New York: Academic Press.

ADELMAN, M. A. (1959) "Differential rates and changes in concentration." Rev. of Economics and Statistics 41 (February): 68-69.

AITCHISON, J. and J. A. BROWN (1954) "On criteria for descriptions of income distribution." Metroeconomica 6 (December): 88-107.

ALBERTINI, L. (1967) The Origins of the War of 1914 (I. Massey, trans. and ed.). London: Oxford Univ. Press.

ALCOCK, N. and K. LOWE (1969) "The Vietnam war as a Richardson process." J. of Peace Research 2: 105-112.

ALCOCK, N. and A. NEWCOMBE (1970) "The perception of national power." J. of Conflict Resolution 14, 3 (September): 335-343.

ALDRICH, J. and C. F. CNUDDE (1975) "Probing the bounds of conventional wisdom: a comparison of regression, probit, and discriminant analysis." Amer. J. of Pol. Sci. 19: 571-606.

ALKER, H. (1968) "The structure of social action in an arms pact." Delivered at the Sixth North American Peace Research Conference. Peace Research Society (International), Cambridge.

——— (1968) "The long road to international relations theory: problems of statistical non-additivity," in M. Kaplan (ed.) New Approaches in International Relations. New York: St. Martin's.

——— (1965) Mathematics and Politics. New York: Macmillan.

——— and R. T. BRUNNER (1969) "Simulating international conflict: a comparison of three approaches." International Studies Q. 13 (March): 70-110.

ALKER, H. and D. PUCHALA (1968) "Trends in partnership: the North Atlantic area, 1928-1963," in J. D. Singer (ed.) Quantitative International Politics. New York: Free Press.

ALKER, H. and B. RUSSETT (1964) "On measuring inequality." Behavioral Sci. 9, 3 (July): 207-218.

ALLISON, G. T. (1971) Essence of Decision: Explaining the Cuban Missile Crisis. Boston: Little, Brown.

ALMOND, G. A. (1960) The American People and Foreign Policy. New York: Praeger.

AMEMIYA, E. C. (1963) "Measurement of economic differentiation." J. of Regional Sci. 5 (Summer): 84-87.

ANDERSSON, I. (1956) A History of Sweden. London: Widenfeld & Nicholson.

ANDO, A., F. FISHER, and H. A. SIMON (1963) Essays on the Structure of Social Sciences. Cambridge: MIT Press.

ARDREY, R. (1966) Territorial Imperative. New York: Atheneum.

ARON, R. (1967) Peace and War. New York: Praeger.

——— (1954) The Century of Total War. Garden City: Doubleday.

ASCH, S. E. (1952) Social Psychology. Englewood Cliffs: Prentice-Hall.

AZAR, E. (1972) "Conflict escalation and conflict reduction in an international crisis: Suez, 1956." J. of Conflict Resolution 26: 183-202.

——— (1970a) Analysis of international events. Peace Research Reviews 4 (November).

——— (1970b) "The dimensionality of violent conflict: a quantitative analysis." Peace Research Papers 15: 122-167.

BACHI, R. (1956) "A statistical analysis of the revival of Hebrew in Israel," pp. 179-247 in R. Bachi (ed.) Scripta Hierosolymitana. Jerusalem: Magnus.

BANKS, A. S. (1971) Cross-Polity Time-Series Data. Cambridge: MIT Press.

——— and P. M. GREGG (1965) "Grouping political systems: Q-factor analysis of A Cross-Polity Survey." Amer. Behavioral Scientist 9 (November): 3-6.

——— and R. B. TEXTOR (1963) A Cross Polity Survey. Cambridge: MIT Press.

BEER, S. (1966) "An operational approach to the nature of conflict." Pol. Studies 14: 119-132.

BELL, W. (1954) "A probability model for the measurement of ecological segregation." Social Forces 32 (May): 357-364.

BENTLEY, A. F. (1954) "Inquiry into inquiries: essays in social theory," in S. Rutner (ed.) Boston: Beacon Press.

BERELSON, B. and G. A. STEINER (1964) Human Behavior: An Inventory of Scientific Findings. New York: Harcourt Brace Jovanovich.

BERKOWITZ, L. (1962) Aggression: A Social Psychological Approach. New York: McGraw-Hill.

BERNARD, L. S. (1944) War and Its Causes. New York: Holt, Rinehart & Winston.

BERRY, B.J.L. (1966) Essays on Commodity Flows and the Spatial Structure of the Indian Economy. Chicago: Univ. of Chicago Press.

BINDER, L. (1958) "The Middle East as a subordinate international system." World Politics 10, 3: 408-429.

BLAINEY, G. (1973) The Causes of War. New York: Free Press.

BLAIR, J. M. (1956) "Statistical measures of concentration in business." Bull. of Oxford Univ. Institute of Statistics 18 (November): 355-356.

BLALOCK, H. M. (1969) Theory Construction. Englewood Cliffs: Prentice-Hall.

——— (1967) "Causal inferences, closed populations, and measures of association." Amer. Pol. Sci. Rev. 61, 1 (March): 130-136.

——— (1966) "The identification problem and theory-building: the case of status inconsistency." Amer. Soc. Rev. 31 (February): 52-61.

——— (1965) "Theory building and the statistical concept of interaction." Amer. Soc. Rev. 30, 3 (June): 374-380.

——— (1964) Causal Inferences in Nonexperimental Research. Chapel Hill: Univ. of North Carolina Press.

——— (1961) "Evaluating the relative importance of variables." Amer. Soc. Rev. 26, 1 (December): 866-874.

——— (1960) Social Statistics. New York: McGraw-Hill.

BLEICHER, S. (1971) "Intergovernmental organization and the preservation of peace: a comment on the abuse of methodology." International Organization 25, 2 (Spring): 298-305.

BLOCH, J. de (1903) The Future of War. Boston: Ginn.

BLOOMFIELD, L and A. LEISS (1969) Controlling Small Wars. New York: Knopf.

BOBROW, D. and N. E. CUTLER (1967) "Time-oriented explanations of national security beliefs: cohort, life stage, and situation." Peace Research Society (International) Papers 8: 31-57.

BOBROW, D. and J. SCHWARTZ [eds.] (1968) Computers and the Policy Making Community: Applications to International Relations. Englewood Cliffs: Prentice-Hall.

BODART, G. (1916) Losses of Life in Modern Wars. Oxford: Clarendon.

BOEKE, J. H. (1946) "The evolution of the Netherlands Indies economy." New York: Netherlands and Netherlands Indies Council, Institute of Pacific Relations Research Series.

BOGARDUS, E. S. (1933) "A social distance scale." Sociology and Social Research 17: 265-271.

——— (1925) "Measuring social distance." J. of Applied Sociology 9: 299-308.

BOUDON, R. (1968) "A new look at correlation analysis," pp. 199-235 in H. M. Blalock and A. B. Blalock (eds.) Methodology in Social Research. New York: McGraw-Hill.

BOULDING, K. E. (1962) Conflict and Defense. New York: Harper & Row.

——— (1959) "National images and international systems." J. of Conflict Resolution 3, 2: 120-131.

BOUTHOUL, G. (1953) War. New York: Walker.

——— (1951) Les Guerres: Elements de Polemologie. Paris: Payot.

——— and R. CARRERE (1976a) Le defi de la Guerre. Paris: PUF.

——— (1976b) "La Violence Mondiale en 1975." Etudes Polemologiques 20-21: 49-74.

BRAMS, S. (1968) "Measuring the concentration of power in political systems." Amer. Pol. Sci. Rev. 62, 2 (June): 461-475.

BRECHER, M. (1963) "International relations and Asian studies: the subordinate state system of Southern Asia." World Politics 15, 2: 212-235.

BREMER, S. (1979) "The powerful and the war-prone: relative national capabilities and war experience, 1820-1965," in J. D. Singer (ed.) The Correlates of War, Vol. 2. New York: Free Press.

——— (1970) "National and international systems: a computer simulation." Michigan State University, Ph.D. dissertation.

——— J. D. SINGER, and U. LUTERBACHER (1972) "Crowding and combat in animal and human societies: the European nations, 1816-1965," in A. Somit et al. (eds.) Biology and Politics. Chicago: Aldine.

BRODY, R. (1963) "Some systemic effects of the spread of nuclear weapons technology: a study through simulation of a multi-nuclear future." J. of Conflict Resolution 7, 4 (December): 663-753.

BUCHANAN, W. and H. CANTRIL (1953) How Nations See Each Other. Urbana: Univ. of Illinois Press.

BUENO de MESQUITA, B. (1975a) "Measuring systemic polarity." J. of Conflict Resolution 19: 187-216.

——— (1975b) Strategy, Risk, and Personality in Coalition Politics. New York: Cambridge Univ. Press.

BURROWES, R. (1969) "Conflict and cooperation within and between nations: Israel, the United Arab Republic and the major Arab states of South West Asia, 1949-1969." New York: Amer. Pol. Sci. Assoc.

—— D. MUZZIO, and B. SPECTOR (1971) "Mirror, mirror, on the wall . . .: a source comparison study of inter-nation event data." Presented at the Annual Meeting of the International Studies Association, San Juan, Puerto Rico, March.

BURTON, J. W. (1969) Conflict and Communication: The Use of Controlled Communications in International Relations. New York: Free Press.

—— (1962) Peace Theory. New York: Knopf.

BUSCH, P. C. (1970) "Mathematical models of arms races," in B. M. Russett, What Price Vigilance? New Haven: Yale Univ. Press.

BUSS, A. H. (1966) Psychopathology. New York: John Wiley.

BUTTERFIELD, H. (1959) The Origins of Modern Science. New York: Macmillan.

CALHOUN, J. B. (1962) "Population density and social pathology." Scientific Amer. 206 (February): 139-146.

CAMPBELL, D. T. (1958) "Common fate, similarity, and other indices of the status of aggregates of persons as social entities." Behavioral Sci. 3, 1 (January): 14-25.

CAPORASO, J. and A. PELOWSKI (1971) "Economic and political integration in Europe: a quasi-experimental analysis." Amer. Pol. Sci. Rev. 65: 418-433.

CASPARY, W. R. [ed.] (forthcoming) Reaction Process Models of International Conflict. New York: Free Press.

—— (1970a) "Dimensions of attitudes on international conflict, internationalism and military offensive action." Peace Research Society (International) Papers 13: 1-10.

—— (1970b) "The 'Mood Theory': a study of public opinion and foreign policy." Amer. Pol. Sci. Rev. 64, 2 (June): 536-547.

CATTELL, R. (1965a) "Factor analysis: an introduction to essentials (I)." Biometrics 21, 1 (March): 190-215.

—— (1965b) "Factor analysis: an introduction to essentials (II)." Biometrics 21, 2 (June): 405-435.

—— and R. GORSUCH (1965) "The definition and measurement of national morale and morality." J. of Social Psychology 67, 1: 77-96.

CATTON, W. R., Jr. (1965) "The concept of 'mass' in the sociological version of gravitation." in F. Massarik and P. Ratoosh (eds.) Mathematical Explorations in Behavioral Science. Homewood, IL: Richard Irwin.

CHAMBERS, F. P., C. P. HARRIS, and C. C. BAYLEY (1950) This Age of Conflict. New York: Harcourt Brace Jovanovich.

CHATERJEE, P. (1975) Arms, Alliances, and Stability. Delhi: Macmillan.

CHESTER, L., G. HODGSON, and B. PAGE (1969) An American Melodrama: The Presidential Campaign of 1968. New York: Viking.

CHOUCRI, N. (1974) Population Dynamics and International Violence: Propositions, Insights, and Evidence. Lexington, D. C. Heath.

—— (1970) "Applications of experimental econometrics to forecasting in political analysis." Paper for the Conference on Forecasting International Relations.

—— and R. C. NORTH (1975) Nations in Conflict: National Growth and International Violence. San Francisco: W. H. Freeman.

—— (1972) "Dynamics of international conflict," in R. Tanter and R. H. Ullman (eds.) Theory and Policy in International Relations. Princeton: Princeton Univ. Press.

—— (1969) "The determinants of international violence." Peace Research Society Papers 12: 33-63.

CHRIST, C. F. (1965) Econometric Models and Methods. New York: John Wiley.

CHRISTIAN, J. J. (1963) "The pathology of overpopulation." Military Medicine 128, 7 (July): 571-603.

CLAUDE, I. L., Jr. (1962) Power and International Relations. New York: Random House.

CLINARD, M. (1968) The Sociology of Deviant Behavior. New York: Holt, Rinehart & Winston.

COFER, C. N. and M. H. APPLEY (1964) Motivation: Theory and Research. New York: John Wiley.

COLEMAN, J. (1957) Community Conflict. New York: Free Press.

CONNERY, D. S. (1966) The Scandinavians. New York: Simon & Schuster.

COPLIN, W. D. [ed.] (1968) Simulation in the Study of Politics. Chicago: Markham.

CORSON, W. H. (1970) "Measuring conflict and cooperation intensity in East-West relations: a manual and codebook." Ann Arbor: Institute for Social Research, University of Michigan.

——— (1970) "Conflict and cooperation intensity in East-West relations." Harvard University, Ph.D. dissertation.

——— (1970) "Conflict and cooperation in East-West relations: measurement and explanation." Presented at the Annual Meeting of the American Political Science Association, Los Angeles.

COSER, L. (1963) "Peaceful settlements and the dysfunctions of secrecy." J. of Conflict Resolution 7, 3 (September); 246-253.

——— (1961) "The termination of social conflict." J. of Conflict Resolution 5, 4 (December): 347-353.

——— (1956) The Functions of Social Conflict. New York: Free Press.

COWGILL, D. O. and M. S. COWGILL (1951) "An index of segregation based on block statistics." Amer. Soc. Rev. 16 (December): 825-831.

CUTRIGHT, P. (1967) "Inequality: a cross-national analysis." Amer. Soc. Rev. 32 (August): 562-578.

DEHIO, L. (1965) The Precarious Balance: Four Centuries of the European Power Struggle (C. Fullman, trans.). New York: W. W. Norton.

DENTON, F. H. (1966) "Some regularities in international conflict, 1820-1949." Background 9, 4: 283-296.

DE RIVERA, J. (1968) The Psychological Dimensions of Foreign Policy. Columbus, OH: Charles E. Merrill.

DEUTSCH, K. W. (1968) The Analysis of International Relations. Englewood Cliffs: Prentice-Hall.

——— (1966) "Power and communication in international society," in A.V.S. de Reuck and J. Knight (eds.) Conflict in Society. London: J. & A. Churchill.

——— (1963) Nerves of Government. New York: Free Press.

——— (1957) Political Community and the North Atlantic Area: International Organization in the Light of Historical Experience. Princeton: Princeton Univ. Press.

——— (1954) Political Community at the International Level. Garden City: Doubleday.

——— et al. (1957) Political Community and the North Atlantic Area. Princeton: Princeton Univ. Press.

DEUTSCH, K. W. and W. ISARD (1961) "A note on a generalized concept of effective distance." Behavioral Sci. 6, 4 (October): 308-311.

DEUTSCH, K. W. and R. L. MERRITT (1965) "Effects of events on national and international images," in H. Kelman (ed.) International Behavior: Social-Psychological Analysis. New York: Holt, Rinehart & Winston.

DUETSCH, K. W. and D. SENGHAAS (1969) "Toward a theory of war and peace: propositions, simulations and realities." New York: Amer. Pol. Sci. Assoc.

DEUTSCH, K. W. and J. D. SINGER (1964) "Multipolar power systems and international stability." World Politics 16 (April): 390-406.

—— and K. SMITH (1965) "The organizing efficiency theories: the N/V ratio as a crude rank order measure." Amer. Behavioral Scientist 9, 2 (October): 30-33.

DEUTSCH, M. (1965) "Conflict and its resolution." Presented to the Annual Meeting of the American Psychological Association, Chicago, September.

DEVALDES (1933) Croitre et Multiplier, C'est la Guerre. Paris.

DINERSTEIN, H. S. (1965) "The transformation of alliance systems." Amer. Pol. Sci. Rev. 54, 3 (September): 589-601.

DODD, S. C. (1947) Dimensions of Society. New York: Macmillan.

DOLLARD, J. et al. (1939) Frustration and Aggression. New Haven: Yale Univ. Press.

DUMAS, S. and K. VEDEL-PETERSON (1923) Losses of Life Caused by War. Oxford: Clarendon.

DUNCAN, O. D. and B. DUNCAN (1955) "A methodological analysis of segregation indexes." Amer. Soc. Rev. 20 (April): 210-217.

DUPREEL, E. (1948) Sociologie Générale. Paris: Presses Universities de France.

DURBIN, J. and G. S. WATSON (1950) "Testing for serial correlation in least squares regression." Biometrika 37: 409-417.

DUSCHA, J. (1965) Arms, Money, and Politics. New York: Ives Washburn.

DUVALL, R. (1976) "An appraisal of the methodological and statistical procedures of the Correlates of War project," in F. W. Hoole and D. A.Zinnes (eds.) Quantitative International Politics: An Appraisal. New York: Praeger.

EAST, M. A. (1971) "Stratification in the international system: an empirical analysis," in V. Davis et al., The Analysis of International Politics. New York: Free Press.

—— (1969) "Stratification and international politics." Princeton University, Ph.D. dissertation.

EASTON, D. (1953) The Political System: An Inquiry into the State of Political Science. New York: Knopf.

EDELMAN, M. (1964) The Symbolic Uses of Politics. Urbana: Univ. of Illinois Press.

EHRLICH, P. (1969) Population Bomb. New York: Sierra Club.

—— and A. M. ERLICH (1970) Population, Resources, Environment. San Francisco: W. H. Freeman.

EISENSTADT, S. N. (1963) The Political Systems of Empires. New York: Free Press.

ELLIOT, J. [ed.] (1891) The Debates in the Several State Conventions on Adoption of the Federal Constitution. Philadelphia.

ETZIONI, A. (1965) Political Unification: A Comparative Study of Leaders and Forces. New York: Holt, Rinehart & Winston.

EZEKIEL, M. and K. A. FOX (1959) Methods of Correlation and Regression Analysis. New York: John Wiley.

FALLS, C. (1962) A Hundred Years of War, 1850-1950. New York: Collier.

FARRELL, R. B. (1966a) "Foreign politics of open and closed political societies," in R. B. Farrell (ed.) Approaches to Comparative and International Politics. Evanston: Northwestern Univ. Press.

—— [ed.] (1966b) Approaches to Comparative and International Politics. Evanston: Northwestern Univ. Press.

FAY, S. (1928) The Origins of the World War. New York: Macmillan.

FERRIS, W. H. (1973) The Power Capabilities of Nation-States: International Conflict and War. Lexington: D. C. Heath.

FESTINGER, L. (1964) Conflict, Decision, and Dissonance. Stanford: Stanford Univ. Press.

——— (1957) A Theory of Cognitive Dissonance. Stanford: Stanford Univ. Press.

FINKELSTEIN, M. and R. M. FRIEDBERG (1967) "The application of an entropy theory of concentration to the Clayton Act." Yale Law J. (March): 671-717.

FIORINIA, M. (1975) "Axiomatic models of risk and decision: an expository treatment." Presented at the 1975 meeting of the International Studies Association.

FISHER, F. M. (1966) The Identification Problem in Econometrics. New York: McGraw-Hill.

——— (1963) "On the cost of approximate specification in simultaneous equation estimation," in A. Ando, F. M. Fisher, and H. A. Simon, Essays on the Structure of Social Sciences. Cambridge: MIT Press.

FISHER, R. (1969) International Conflict for Beginners. New York: Harper & Row.

FORBES, H. D. and E. R. TUFTE (1968) "A note of caution in causal modeling." Amer. Pol. Sci. Rev. 62, 4 (December): 1258-1264.

FORRESTER, J. W. (1969) Urban Dynamics. Cambridge: MIT Press.

FOSSUM, E. (1967) "Factors influencing the occurrence of military coups d'etat in Latin America." J. of Peace Research 3: 225-251.

FRANKEL, J. (1964) International Relations. New York: Oxford Univ. Press.

FRIEDHEIM, R. L. and J. B. KADANE (1970) "Quantitative content analysis of the United Nations seabed debates: methodology in a continental shelf case study." International Organization.

FRISCH, R. (1947) Elements of the Theory of Business Cycles. Oslo, Norway: Aschehoug.

FUCKS, W. (1965) Formeln zur Macht. Stuttgart: Duetsch Verlagsanfalt.

GALTUNG, W. (1969) "Violence, peace and peace research." J. of Peace Research 3: 167-191.

——— (1967) "Public opinion on the economic effects of disarmament," in E. Benoit (ed.) Disarmament and World Economic Interdependence. Oslo: Universitetsforlaget.

——— (1966) "East-West interaction patterns." J. of Peace Research 3: 146-177.

——— (1966) "Rank and social integration: a multidimensional approach," in J. Berger et al., Sociological Theories in Progress, Vol. I. Boston: Houghton Mifflin.

——— (1964a) "Summit meetings and international relations." J. of Peace Research 1: 36-54.

——— (1964b) "A structural theory of aggression." J. of Peace Research 2: 95-119.

——— M. MORA y ARAUJO and S. SCHWARTZMANN (1966) "The Latin American system of nations: a structural analysis." J. of Social Research.

GAMSON, W. A. (1961) "A theory of coalition formation." Amer. Soc. Rev. 26, 3 (June): 373-382.

GARNHAM, D. (1976) "Power parity and lethal international violence, 1969-1973." J. of Conflict Resolution 20, 3 (September): 379-394.

GERMAN, F. C. (1960) "A tentative evaluation of world power." J. of Conflict Resolution 4, 1 (March): 138-144.

GIBBS, J. P. and H. L. BROWNING (1966) "The division of labor technology, and the organization of production in twelve countries." Amer. Soc. Rev. 31 (February): 81-92.

GIBBS, J. P. and W. T. MARTIN (1962) "Urbanization, technology, and division of labor: international patterns." Amer. Soc. Rev. 27 (October): 667-677.

GILLESPIE, J. V., D. A. ZINNES, P. A. SCHRODT, G. S. TAHIM, and R. M. RUBINSON (1977) "An optimal control model of arms races." Amer. Pol. Sci. Rev. 81, 1 (March): 226-244.

GINI, C. (1912) Variabilita e Mutabilita. Bologna.

GLEDITSCH, N. P. (1969) "Rank and interaction: a general theory with some application to the international system." Presented at the Third Conference of the International Peace Research Association. Karlovy Vary, Czechoslovakia.

——— (1969) "The international airline network: a test of the Zipf and Stouffer hypotheses." Peace Research Society Papers 11: 123-153.

——— (1967) "Trends in world airline patterns." J. of Peace Research 4: 366-408.

——— and J. D. SINGER (1972) "Spatial predictors of national war-proneness, 1816-1965." Oslo: Peace Research Institute.

GLENN, E., R. JOHNSON, P. KIMMEL, and B. WEDGE (1970) "A cognitive interaction model to analyze culture conflict in international relations." J. of Conflict Resolution 14: 35-55.

GLENN, N. (1970) "Problems of comparability in trend studies with opinion poll data." Public Opinion Q. 21, 1 (Spring): 82-91.

GOCHMAN, C. S. (1975) "Status, conflict, and war: the major powers, 1820-1970." University of Michigan, Ph.D. dissertation.

GOLDBERGER, A. S. (1964) Economic Theory. New York: John Wiley.

GONZALES CASANOVA, P. (1966b) "Internal and external politics of underdeveloped countries," in R. B. Farrell (ed.) Approaches to Comparative and International Politics. Evanston: Northwestern Univ. Press.

GOOCH, G. (1938) Before the War: Studies in Diplomacy. London: Longmans, Green.

GORT, M. (n.d.) "Analysis of stability and change in market shares." J. of Pol. Economy 71: 51-63.

GREENBERG, J. (1956) "The measurement of linguistic diversity." Language 32: 109-115.

GUETZKOW, H. et al. (1963) Simulation in International Relations. Englewood Cliffs: Prentice-Hall.

CULICK, E. V. (1955) Europe's Classical Balance of Power. New York: W. W. Norton.

GURR, T. (1970) Why Men Rebel. Princeton: Princeton Univ. Press.

GUTTMANN, L. (1968) "A general nonmetric technique for finding the smallest coordinate space for a configuration of points." Psychometrika 33: 469-506.

HAAR, J. E. (1970) "The issue of competence in the Department of State." International Studies Q. 14 (March): 95-101.

——— (1969) The Professional Diplomat. Princeton: Princeton Univ. Press.

HAAS, E. B. (1970) "The study of regional integration: reflections on the joy and anguish of pretheorizing." International Organization 24, 4.

——— (1964) Beyond the Nation-State. Stanford: Stanford Univ. Press.

——— (1953) "The balance of power: prescription, concept, or propaganda." World Politics 5, 3 (April): 442-477.

——— and A. WHITING (1956) Dynamics of International Relations. New York: McGraw-Hill.

HAAS, M. (1970) "International systems: stability and polarity." Amer. Pol. Sci. Rev. 64, 1 (March): 98-123.

—— (1968) "Social change and national aggressiveness, 1900-1960," in J. D. Singer (ed.) Quantitative International Politics. New York: Free Press.

—— (1965) "Societal approaches to the study of war." J. of Peace Research 4: 307-323.

HALL, E. T. (1969) The Hidden Dimension. Garden City: Doubleday-Anchor.

—— (1959) The Silent Language. Garden City: Doubleday.

HALL, M. and N. TIDEMAN (1967) "Measures of concentration." J. of Amer. Statistical Assn. 62 (March): 162-168.

HARBOTTLE, T. (1904) Dictionary of Battles from the Earliest Date to the Present Time. London: Sonneschein.

HARMAN, H. (1967) Modern Factor Analysis. Chicago: Univ. of Chicago Press.

HARRIS, C. [ed.] (1963) Problems in Measuring Change. Madison: Univ. of Wisconsin Press.

HART, H. (1946) "Depression, war and logistic trends." Amer. J. of Sociology 52: 112-122.

HART, P. E. (1957) "On measuring concentration." Bull. of Oxford Univ. Institute of Statistics 19 (August): 225.

—— and S. J. PRAIS (1956) "The analysis of business concentration: a statistical approach." J. of Royal Statistical Society 119: 150-181.

HAYDON, B. (1962) The Great Statistics of War Hoax. Santa Monica, CA: Rand.

HAYS, W. L. (1963) Statistics for Psychologists. New York: Holt, Rinehart & Winston.

HEINTZ, P. (1969) Ein Soziologisches Paradigma de Entwicklung mit Besonderer Berucksichtigung Lateinamerikas. Stuttgart: Ferdinand Enke Verlag.

HELMER, O. (1973) The Systematic Use of Expert Judgement in Operations Research. Santa Monica, CA: Rand.

HERFINDAHL, O. C. (1950) "Concentration in the steel industry." Columbia University, Ph.D. dissertation.

HERMANN, C. [ed.] (1972) International Crisis. New York: Free Press.

—— and M. HERMANN (1967) "An attempt to simulate the outbreak of World War I." Amer. Pol. Sci. Rev. 61: 400-416.

HEXTER, J. L. and J. W. SNOW (1970) "Entropy measure of relative aggregate concentration." Southern Economic J. 36 (January): 239-243.

HITCH, C. J. and D. McKEAN (1960) The Economics of Defense in the Nuclear Age. Cambridge: Harvard Univ. Press.

HOBBES, T. (1651) Leviathan. New York: Oxford Univ. Press (1909 ed.).

HODGKIN, T. (1961) "The new West African state system." Univ. of Toronto Q. 31: 74-82.

HOFFMANN, S. [ed.] (1961) Contemporary Theory in International Relations. Englewood Cliffs: Prentice-Hall.

HOGGARD, G. D. (1970) "Differential source coverage and the analysis of international interaction data." Los Angeles: Univ. of Southern California.

—— (1969) "Comparison of reporting for the *New York Times Index, Asian Recorder,* and *Deadline Data*—Chinese interaction, January through October, 1962." Los Angeles: Univ. of Southern California.

HOLLIST, W. L. [ed.] (1978) Exploring Competitive Arms Processes. New York: Marcel-Dekker.

HOLSTI, K. J. (1970) "National role conceptions in the study of foreign policy." International Studies Q. 14: 233-309.

—————— (1966) "Resolving international conflicts: a taxonomy of behavior and some figures on procedures." J. of Conflict Resolution 10, 3: 272-296.

HOLSTI, O. (1972) Crisis, Escalation, War. Montreal: McGill-Queens Univ. Press.

—————— (1970) "Individual differences in 'definition of the situation'." J. of Conflict Resolution 14: 303-310.

—————— (1969) Content Analysis of the Social Sciences and Humanities. Reading, MA: Addison-Wesley.

—————— (1965) "Measuring affect and action in international reaction models: empirical materials from the 1962 Cuban crisis." Peace Research Society Papers 2: 170-190.

—————— (1965) "Perceptions of time, perceptions of alternatives, and patterns of communication as factors in crisis decision-making." Peace Research Society (International) Papers 3: 79-120.

—————— (1965) "The 1914 case." Amer. Pol. Sci. Rev. 59: 365-378.

—————— R. NORTH, and R. BRODY (1968) "Perception and action in the 1914 crisis," pp. 123-158 in J. D. Singer (ed.) Quantitative International Politics. New York: Free Press.

HOLSTI, O., R. BRODY, and R. NORTH (1964) "Affect and action in international reaction models. J. of Peace Research 1: 170-190.

HOLSTI, O. and J. D. SULLIVAN (1969) "National-international linkages: France and China as nonconforming alliance members," pp. 147-195 in J. N. Rosenau (ed.) Linkage Politics. New York: Free Press.

HOMANS, G. C. (1961) Social Behavior: Its Elementary Forms. New York: Harcourt Brace Jovanovich.

HOPMANN, T. P. and C. E. WALCOTT (forthcoming) Bargaining in International Arms Control Negotiations.

HORNSETH, R. A. (1947) "A note on 'the measurement of ecological segregation' by Julius Jahn, Calvin F. Schmid, and Clarence Schrag." Amer. Soc. Rev. 12 (October): 603-604.

HORVATH, J. (1970) "Suggestion for a comprehensive measure of concentration." Southern Economic J. 36 (April): 446-452.

HOWARD, A. and R. A. SCOTT (1965) "A proposed framework for the analysis of stress in the human organism." Behavioral Sci. 10, 2 (April): 141-160.

HUDDLESTON, S. (1954) Popular Diplomacy and War. Rindge, NH: Richard R. Smith.

HULA, E. (1959) "Comment." Social Research 26 (Summer): 154-161.

HULL, C. L. (1943) Principles of Behavior. New York: Appleton-Century-Crofts.

HUNTINGTON, S. P. (1958) "Arms races: prerequisites and results," in C. J. Friedrich and S. E. Harris (eds.) Public Policy. Cambridge: Harvard Univ. Press.

HUTCHINSON, E. P. (1967) The Population Debate. Boston: Houghton Mifflin.

IJRI, Y. and H. A. SIMON (1964) "Business firm growth and size." Amer. Economic Rev. 54 (March): 77-89.

IKLE, F. C. (1964) How Nations Negotiate. New York: Praeger.

INKELES, A. and D. SMITH (1970) "The fate of personal adjustment in the process of modernization." International J. of Sociology (June).

Institut Francais de Polemologie (1968) "Periodicité et intensité des actions de guerre, 1200-1945," Guerres et Paix 2: 20-32.

JACOB, P. E. and H. TEUNE (1964) "The integrative process: guidelines for analysis of the bases of political community," in P. E. Jacob and J. V. Toscano (eds.) The Integration of Political Communities. Philadelphia: Lippincott.

JAHN, J. A. (1950) "The measurement of ecological segregation: derivation of an index based on the criterion of reproducibility." Amer. Soc. Rev. 15 (February): 100-104.

―――― C. F. SCHMID, and C. SCHRAG (1947) "The measurement of ecological segregation." Amer. Soc. Rev. 12 (June): 293-303.

JANDA, K. (1971) "Conceptual equivalence and multiple indicators in the cross-national analysis of political parties." Prepared for the ISS/UNESCO/ECPR Workshop on Indicators of National Development, August.

JENSEN, L. (1968) "Approach-Avoidance Bargaining in the Test Ban Negotiations." International Studies Q. 12: 152-160.

JOHANSSON, O. (1967) "The gross domestic product of Sweden and its composition, 1861-1955." Stockholm Economic Studies 18. Stockholm: Almquist & Wikfell.

JOHNSON, S. C. (1967) "Hierarchical clustering schemes." Psychometrika 32, 3 (September): 241-254.

JOHNSTON, J. (1963) Econometric Methods. New York: McGraw-Hill.

de JOUVENAL, B. (1967) The Art of Conjecture. New York: Basic Books.

KAHN, H. (1960) On Thermonuclear War. Princeton: Princeton Univ. Press.

―――― and WIENER, A. (1967) The Year 2000. New York: Macmillan.

KAPLAN, A. (1964) The Conduct of Inquiry. San Francisco: Chandler.

KAPLAN, M. (1957) System and Process in International Politics. New York: John Wiley.

KATZ, D. (1967) "Group processes and social integration: a system analysis of two movements of social protest." J. of Social Issues 23: 3-22.

KENDE, I. (1977) "Dynamics of war, arms trade, and of military expenditure." Helsinki: Armament, Tension, and War Symposium, September.

―――― (1971) "Twenty-five years of local wars." J. of Peace Research 8, 1.

KENNAN, G. (1957) U.S. Senate Subcommittee on Control and Reduction of Armaments. Hearings, Part 11, p. 1075. Washington, DC: Government Printing Office.

KIMBERLEY, J. C. (1966) "A theory of status equilibration," in J. Berger et al., Sociological Theories in Progress, Vol. 1. Boston: Houghton Mifflin.

KING, J. A. (1957) "Intra- and interspecific conflict of Mus and Peromyscus." Ecology 38: 355-357.

KISSINGER, H. (1957) A World Restored: Metternich, Castlereagh, and the Problems of Peace, 1812-22. Boston: Houghton Mifflin.

KLINGBERG, F. L. (1966) "Predicting the termination of war." J. of Conflict Resolution 10, 2 (June): 147-148.

―――― (1952) "The historical alternation of moods in American foreign policy." World Politics 4, 2: 239-273.

KNORR, K. (1970) Military Power and Potential. Lexington, MA: D. C. Heath.

―――― (1956) The War Potential of Nations. Princeton: Princeton Univ. Press.

KRASLOW, D. and S. H. LOORY (1968) The Secret Search for Peace in Vietnam. New York: Vintage.

KRAVIS, I. B. (1962) The Structure of Income. Philadelphia: Univ. of Pennsylvania Press.

LABOVITZ, S. and J. P. GIBBS (1964) "Urbanization, technology and the division of labor: further evidence." Pacific Soc. Rev. 7 (Spring): 3-9.

LAFORE, L. (1971) The Long Fuse: An Interpretation of the Origins of World War I. Philadelphia: Lippincott.

LAGERSTROM, R. P. and R. C. NORTH (1969) "An anticipated gap, mathematical model of international dynamics." Stanford: Stanford University.

LAGOS, G. (1963) International Stratification and Underdeveloped Countries. Chapel Hill: Univ. of North Carolina Press.

LANDIS, J. R., D. DATWYLER, and D. S. DORN (1966) "Race and social class as determinants of social distance." Sociology and Social Research 51, 1: 78-86.

LANGER, W. (1931) European Alliances and Alignments, 1871-1890. New York: Knopf.

LANKFORD, P. (1974) "Comparative analysis of clique identification methods." Sociometry 37: 287-305.

LARSEN, K. (1948) History of Norway. Princeton: Princeton Univ. Press.

LASSWELL, H. D. (1954) "Key signs, symbols, and icons," in L. Bryson et al., Symbols and Values: An Initial Study. New York: Harper & Row.

——— and A. KAPLAN (1950) Power and Society: A Framework for Political Inquiry. New Haven: Yale Univ. Press.

LASSWELL, H. D., N. LEITES, and Associates (1949) Language of Politics: Studies in Quantitative Semantics. Cambridge: MIT Press.

LAUMANN, E. O. (1965) "Subjective social distance and urban occupational stratification." Amer. J. of Sociology 71 (July): 26-36.

LAURING, P. (1960) A History of the Kingdom of Denmark. Copenhagen: Hoss & Son.

LEISERSON, M. (1966) "Coalitions in politics: a theoretical and empirical study." Yale University, Ph.D. dissertation.

LEISS, A. C., L. P. BLOOMFIELD et al. (1967) The Control of Local Conflict: A Design on Arms Control of Limited War in the Developing Areas. Cambridge: Center for International Studies, MIT.

LENG, R. J. (1972a) "Coder's manual for identifying and describing international actions." Middlebury, VT: Middlebury College. (mimeo)

——— (1972b) "Problems in events data availability and analysis." Presented at the Annual Meeting of the New England Political Science Association, Kingston, Rhode Island; April 21-22.

——— and J. D. SINGER (1970) "Toward a multi-theoretical typology of international behavior." Ann Arbor: University of Michigan, Mental Health Research Institute. (mimeo)

LENSKI, G. (1966) Power and Privilege: A Theory of Social Stratification. New York: McGraw-Hill.

LEPAWSKY, A., E. BUEHRIG, and H. LASSWELL [eds.] (1971) The Search for World Order. New York: Appleton-Century-Crofts.

LERCHE, C. O. (1956) Principles of International Politics. New York: Oxford Univ. Press.

LEVI, W. (1970) "Ideology, interests, and foreign policy." International Studies Q. 14 (March): 1-31.

LEVY, A. (1977) "Coder's manual for identifying serious inter-nation disputes, 1816-1965." Correlates of War Project, Ann Arbor, Michigan. (internal memo)

LEWIN, K. (1964) Field Theory in Social Science in D. Cartwright (ed.) New York: Harper Torchbooks.

LIEBERSON, S. (1969) "Measuring population diversity." Amer. Soc. Rev. 34 (December): 850-862.

——— (1964) "An extension of Greenberg's linguistic diversity measure." Language 40 (November): 526-531.

LINGOES, J. C. (1966) "Recent computational advances in nonmetric methodology for the behavioral sciences." Presented at the International Symposium on Mathematical and Quantitative Methods in Social Sciences, Rome, July 4-6.

——— (1965) "An IBM—7090 program for Guttmann-Lingoes' smallest space analysis —I." Behavioral Sci. 10: 183-184.

LIPPMANN, W. (1955) The Public Philosophy. Boston: Little, Brown.

LIPSET, S. M. (1960) Political Man. Garden City: Doubleday.

LISKA, G. (1962) Nations in Alliance. Baltimore: Johns Hopkins Univ. Press.

——— (1956) International Equilibrium. Cambridge: Harvard Univ. Press.

LIU, T. C. (1955) "A simple forecasting model for the U.S. economy." International Monetary Fund, Staff Papers: 434-466.

LIVINGSTONE, F. (1967) The effects of warfare on the biology of the human species." Natural History (December): 61-65.

LORENZ, K. (1966) On Aggression. New York: Harcourt Brace Jovanovich.

LORENZ, M. O. (1905) "Methods of measuring the concentration of wealth." Amer. Statistical Assn. J. 9 (June): 209-219.

LUTERBACHER, U. (1977) Dimensions historiques de modes dynamiques de conflict. Leiden: A. W. Sythoff.

McCLELLAND, C. A. (1968) "International interaction analysis: basic research and some practical applications." World Event/Interaction Survey, Technical Report No. 2. Los Angeles: Univ. of Southern California.

——— (1968) "Access to Berlin: the quantity and variety of events," in J. D. Singer (ed.) Quantitative International Politics. New York: Free Press.

——— and G. HOGGARD (1969) "Conflict patterns in interactions among nations," in J. N. Rosenau (ed.) International Politics and Foreign Policy. New York: Free Press.

McKELVEY, R. and W. ZAVOINA (1971) "An IBM FORTRAN IV program to perform N chotomous multivariate probit analysis." Behavioral Sci. 16: 186-187.

McNEIL, E. B. [ed.] (1965) The Nature of Human Conflict. Englewood Cliffs: Prentice-Hall.

MALTHUS, T. R. (1798) Essay on the Principle of Population as It Affects the Future Improvement of Society.

MARGENAU, H. (1950) The Nature of Physical Reality. New York: McGraw-Hill.

MARSH, R. M. (1967) Comparative Sociology. New York: Harcourt Brace Jovanovich.

MAY, E. R. (1973) Lessons of the Past: Uses and Misuses of History in American Foreign Policy. New York: Oxford Univ. Press.

MEADOWS, D. et al. (1972) The Limits to Growth. Washington, DC: Potomac Associates.

MERTON, R. K. (1957) Social Theory and Social Structure. New York: Free Press.

MICHAELY, M. (1962) Concentration in International Trade. Amsterdam: North Holland.

MIDLARSKY, M. (1975) On War: Political Violence in the International System. New York: Free Press.

——— (1969) "Status inconsistency and the onset of international warfare." Northwestern University, Ph.D. dissertation.

MILLER, G. A., E. GALANTER, and K. H. PRIBRAM (1960) Plans and the Structure of Behavior. New York: Holt, Rinehart & Winston.

MORGENTHAU, H. J. (1948, 1960, 1967) Politics Among Nations: The Struggle for Power and Peace. New York: Knopf.

MORSE, E. L. (1970) "The transformation of foreign policies: modernization, interdependence, and externalization." World Politics 22, 3 (April): 371-392.

MOSES, L. E., R. A. BRODY, O. R. HOLSTI, J. B. KADANE, and J. S. MILSTEIN (1967) "Scaling data on inter-nation action." Sci. 156 (May 26): 1054-1059.

MUELLER, J. (1970) "Presidential popularity from Truman to Johnson." Amer. Pol. Sci. Rev. 64, 1 (March): 18-34.

—— K. F. SCHUESSLER, and H. L. COSTNER (1970) Statistical Reasoning in Sociology. Boston: Houghton Mifflin.

MULHALL, M. G. (1880) The Progress of the World. London: Edward Stanford.

MYDANS, C. and S. MYDANS (1968) The Violent Peace. New York: Atheneum.

NAROLL, R., V. L. BULLOUGH, and F. NAROLL (1974) Military Deterrence in History: A Pilot Cross-Historical Survey. Albany: State Univ. of New York Press.

NELSON, R. L. (1963) Concentration in the Manufacturing Industries of the United States. New Haven: Yale Univ. Press.

NEWCOMBE, H., W. ECKHARDT, and C. YOUNG (n.d.) "Voting blocs in the U.N. General Assembly, 1946-1970: A typal analysis." (mimeo)

NICOLSON, H. (1961) The Congress of Vienna: A Study of Allied Unity. New York: Viking.

NORTH, R. (1971) In collaboration with Nazli Choucri. "Population and the future international system." International Organization.

—— (1969) "The determinants of international violence." Peace Research Society Papers 12: 33-63.

—— (1967) "Perception and action in the 1914 crisis." J. of International Affairs 27: 16-39.

—— (1967) "Steps toward developing a theory." Stanford: Studies in International Conflict and Integration.

—— R. BRODY, and O. HOLSTI (1964) "Some empirical data on the conflict spiral." Peace Research Society (International) Papers: 1-14.

NORTH, R. and N. CHOUCRI (1968) "Background conditions to the outbreak of the First World War." Peace Research Society (International) Papers 9: 125-137.

NORTH, R. C. and R. LAGERSTROM (1971) War and Domination: A Theory of Lateral Pressure. New York: General Learning Press.

NORTH R., O. HOLSTI, G. ZANINOVICH, and D. ZINNES (1963) Content Analysis: A Handbook with Applications for the Study of International Crises. Evanston: Northwestern Univ. Press.

Norway (1968) Historical Statistics. Oslo: Statistisk Sentralbyra.

NUTTER, G. W. (1968) "Industrial concentration," pp. 218-222 in D. Sills (ed.) International Encyclopedia of the Social Sciences. New York: Free Press.

NYE, J. S. (1970) Comparing common markets: a revised neo-functional model." International Organization 24, 4: 796-835.

OAKLEY, S. (1966) A Short History of Sweden. New York: Praeger.

OGBURN, C., Jr., H. F. HAVILAND, Jr., and Associates (1960) The Formulation and Administration of United States Foreign Policy. Report for the Committee on Foreign Relations of the United States Senate. Washington, DC: Brookings Institution.

OLSSON, G. (1965) Distance and Human Interaction: A Review and Bibliography. Philadelphia: Regional Science Research Institute.

ORCUTT, G. H. et al. (1961) Microanalysis of Socioeconomic Systems: A Simulation Study. New York: Harper & Row.

ORGANSKI, A.F.K. (1968) World Politics. New York: Knopf.

PAIGE, G. (1972) Political Leadership. New York: Free Press.

PARK, T. W. (1969) "Asian conflict in systemic perspective: application of field theory (1955 and 1963)." University of Hawaii, Ph.D. dissertation, and Dimensionality of Nations Project Research Report No. 35.

PARK, T. (1954) "Experimental studies of interspecies competition II." Physiol. Zoology 27: 177-238.

——— (1948) "Experimental studies of interspecies competition I." Ecological Monographs 18: 265-308.

PARKMAN, M. A. and J. SAWYER (1967) "Dimensions of ethnic intermarriage in Hawaii." Amer. Soc. Rev. 32 (August): 593-607.

PATEL, J. J. (1964) "The economic distance between nations: its origin, measurement and outlook." Economic J. 74 (March): 119-131.

PELOWSKI, A. (1969) "*Pintr:* a version of timex for on-line use." Evanston: Northwestern University. (mimeo)

PHILLIPS, W. P. (1969) "Dynamic patterns of international conflict." University of Hawaii, Ph.D. dissertation, and Dimensionality of Nations Project Research Report No. 33

PHILLIPS, W. R. (1972) "Two views of foreign policy interaction: substantially the same or different?" Presented at the Midwest Regional Meeting of the International Studies Association and the Peace Research Society (International), Toronto, May 11-13.

PLATIG, E. R. (1967) International Relations Research. Santa Barbara: ABC Clio.

PLATT, J. R. (1964) "Strong inference." Sci. 146 (October): 347-353.

POINCARE, H. (1952) Science and Hypothesis. New York: Dover Publications.

POLLATSEK, A. and A. TVERSKY (1970) "A theory of risk." J. of Mathematical Psychology 7: 540-553.

POOL, I. de S. (1951) Symbols of Internationalism. Stanford: Stanford Univ. Press.

POPPER, K. (1961) The Logic of Scientific Discovery. New York: Science Editions.

——— (1959) The Logic of Scientific Discovery. London: Hutchinson.

PRESTON, L. E. and N. R. COLLINS (1961) "The size structure of the largest industrial firms." Amer. Economic Rev. 51 (December): 986-1011.

PRUITT, D. (1965) "Definition of the situation as a determinant of international action," pp. 393-432 in H. Kelman (ed.) International Behavior. New York: Holt, Rinehart & Winston.

——— and R. C. SNYDER [eds.] (1969) Theory and Research on the Causes of War. Englewood Cliffs: Prentice-Hall.

PUCHALA, D. (1970) "International transactions and regional integration." International Organization 24 (Autumn): 732-763.

Public Papers of the Presidents of the United States, containing the public messages, speeches, statements of the President: Lyndon B. Johnson (1964-1968). Washington: Government Printing Office.

QUANDT, R. E. (1966a) "Old and new methods of estimation and the Pareto distribution." Metrika 10: 55-82.

——— (1966b) "On the size distribution of firms." Amer. Economic Rev. 56 (June): 416-432.

RAE, D. W. and M. TAYLOR (1970) The Analysis of Political Cleavages. New Haven: Yale Univ. Press.

RALEIGH, W. (1650) Discourse on War in General.

RAPAPORT, A. (1970) "Is peace research applicable?" J. of Conflict Resolution 14, 2 (June): 277-286.

—— (1960) Fights, Games, and Debates. Ann Arbor: Univ. of Michigan Press.

—— (1957) "Lewis F. Richardson's mathematical theory of war." J. of Conflict Resolution 5, 1 (September): 249-299.

—— and A. CHAMMAH (1965) Prisoner's Dilemma. Ann Arbor: Univ. of Michigan Press.

RASER, J. (1965) "Learning and affect in international relations." J. of Peace Research 2: 216-227.

REMAK, J. (1967) The Origins of World War I. New York: Holt, Rinehart & Winston.

RENOUVIN, P. and J. B. DUROSELLE (1967) Introduction to the History of International Relations. New York: Praeger.

REVENTLOW, E. (1916) Deutschlands auswärtige Politik. Berlin: Mittler.

RICHARDSON, J. D. [ed.] (1904) A Compilation of the Messages and Papers of the Presidents, 1789-1902. Washington, DC.

RICHARDSON, L. F. (1960a) "Statistics of deadly quarrels," in Q. Wright and C. Lienau (eds.) Chicago: Quadrangle.

—— (1966b) "Arms and insecurity," in N. Rashevsky and E. Trucco (eds.) Chicago: Quadrangle.

RIKER, W. (1957) "Events and situations." J. of Philosophy 54, 3 (January).

—— and P. ORDESHOOK (1972) An Introduction to Positive Political Theory. Englewood Cliffs: Prentice-Hall.

ROBINSON, J. P., J. RUSK, and K. HEAD (1968) Measures of Political Attitudes. Ann Arbor: University of Michigan, Institute of Social Research.

ROSECRANCE, R. (1973) International Relations: Peace or War? New York: McGraw-Hill.

—— (1966) "Bipolarity, multipolarity, and the future." J. of Conflict Resolution 10: 314-327.

—— (1963) Action and Reaction in World Politics: International Systems in Perspective. Boston: Little, Brown.

—— A. ALEXANDROFF, B. HEALY, and A. STEIN (1974) Power, Balance of Power, and Status in Nineteenth Century International Relations. Beverly Hills: Sage.

ROSEN, S. (1972) "War power and the willingness to suffer," pp. 167-183 in B. Russett (ed.) Peace, War, and Numbers. Beverly Hills: Sage.

—— (1971) "Cost-tolerance in human lives for foreign policy goals." Peace Research Society (International) Papers 15.

—— (1970) "A rational actor model of war and alliance," in J. Friedman, C. Bladen, and S. Rosen (eds.) Alliance in International Politics. Boston: Allyn & Bacon.

ROSENAU, J. [ed.] (1969) Linkage Politics: Essays on the Convergence of National and International Systems. New York: Free Press.

—— (1967a) "Foreign policy as an issue area," in J. Rosenau, Domestic Sources of Foreign Policy. New York: Free Press.

—— (1967b) "Of boundaries and bridges: a report on a conference on the interdependencies of national and international political systems." Center of International Studies Research Monograph No. 27. Princeton University.

—————— (1966) "Pre-theories and theories of foreign policy," in R. B. Farrell (ed.) Approaches to Comparative and International Politics. Evanston: Northwestern Univ. Press.

ROSENBERG, M. J. (1967) "Attitude change and foreign policy in the Cold War era," in J. N. Rosenau (ed.) Domestic Sources of Foreign Policy. New York: Free Press.

ROSENBLUTH, G. (1955) "Measures of concentration," in National Bureau of Economic Research (ed.) Business Concentration and Price Policy. Princeton: Princeton Univ. Press.

ROSS, E. A. (1927) Standing Room Only? New York: Appleton-Century-Crofts.

RUMMEL, R. (1972) Dimensions of Nations. Beverly Hills: Sage.

—————— (1970a) Applied Factor Analysis. Evanston: Northwestern Univ. Press.

—————— (1970b) "New developments in field theory: the 1963 behavior space of nations." Presented at the Seventh European Peace Research Society (International) Conference, Rome, August 30-31.

—————— (1970c) "Social time and international relations." Published for the Eighth World Congress, International Political Science Association, Munich, September 1-7.

—————— (1969a) "Field and attribute theories of nation behavior: some mathematical interrelationships." Presented at the First Far East Peace Research Conference. Tokyo, August.

—————— (1969b) "Field theory and indicators of international behavior." Presented at the American Political Science Association Convention, New York, September.

—————— (1969c) "Indicators of cross-national and international patterns." Amer. Pol. Sci. Rev. 68, 1 (March): 127-147.

—————— (1969) "Some empirical findings on nations and their behavior." World Politics 21: 226-241.

—————— (1968) "The relationship between national attributes and foreign conflict behavior," in J. D. Singer (ed.) Quantitative International Politics. New York: Free Press.

—————— (1966a) "A foreign conflict behavior code sheet." World Politics 18, 2 (January): 283-296.

—————— (1966b) "Some dimensions in the foreign behavior of nations." J. of Peace Research 3: 201-224.

—————— (1965) "A field theory of social action with application to conflict within nations." Yearbook of the Society of General Systems 10.

—————— (1963a) "Dimensions of conflict behavior within and between nations." General Systems Yearbook 8: 1-50.

—————— (1963b) "Testing some possible predictors of conflict behavior within and between nations." Peace Research Society Papers 79-111.

—————— (1961) "Technology and war: a correlational analysis." University of Hawaii, Master's thesis.

RUSSETT, B. [ed.] (1972) Peace, War, and Numbers. Beverly Hills: Sage.

—————— (1971) "An empirical typology of international military alliances." Midwest J. of Pol. Sci.

—————— (1970) What Price Vigilance? New Haven: Yale Univ. Press.

—————— (1968a) "Components of an operational theory of alliance formulation." J. of Conflict Resolution 12, 3 (September): 285-301.

—————— (1968b) "'Regional' trading patterns, 1938-1963." International Studies Q. 12, 4 (December): 360-379.

—————— (1967a) International Regions and the International System. Chicago: Rand McNally.

—————— (1967b) "Pearl Harbor: deterrence theory and decision theory." J. of Peace Research 2: 89-105.

—————— (1965) Trends in World Politics. New York: Macmillan.

—————— (1963a) Community and Contention: Britain and America in the Twentieth Century. Cambridge: MIT Press.

—————— (1963b) "The calculus of deterrence." J. of Conflict Resolution 7, 2 (June): 97-109.

—————— (1962) "Cause, surprise, and no escape." J. of Politics 24: 3-22.

—————— et al. (1964) World Handbook of Political and Social Indicators. New Haven: Yale Univ. Press.

RUSSETT, B. and W. C. LAMB (1969) "Global patterns of diplomatic exchange, 1963-64." J. of Peace Research 1: 37-55.

RUSSETT, B., J. D. SINGER, and M. SMALL (1968) "National political units in the twentieth century: a standardized list." Amer. Pol. Sci. Rev. 62, 3 (September): 932-951.

SABROSKY, A. (1970) "The Bosnian crisis of 1908-1909: a diplomatic perspective." Ann Arbor: University of Michigan. (mimeo)

SARD, A. and S. WEINTRAUB (1971) A Book of Splines. New York: John Wiley.

SAVAGE, R. I. and K. W. DEUTSCH (1960) "A statistical model of the gross analysis of transaction flows." Econometrica 28, 3: 551-572.

SCHELLING, T. C. (1960) Strategy of Conflict. Cambridge: Harvard Univ. Press.

SCHILLING, W. (1965) "Surprise attack, death, and war." J. of Conflict Resolution 9, 3 (September): 385-390.

SCHMITT, B. (1916) The Annexation of Bosnia, 1908-1909. London: Cambridge Univ. Press.

SCHUMPETER, J. (1939) Business Cycles. New York: McGraw-Hill.

SCHWARTZMAN, S. (1966) "International development and international feudalism: the Latin American case." Proceedings of the IPRA Inaugural Conference. Assen, the Netherlands: Van Gorcum.

—————— and M. M. Y ARAUJO (1966) "The images of international stratification in Latin America." Peace Research J. 3: 225-243.

SCHWARZENBERGER, G. (1951) Power Politics. New York: Praeger.

SCOTT, A. M. (1970) "Environmental change and organizational adaptation: the problem of the State Department." International Studies Q. 14 (March): 85-94.

—————— (1969) "The Department of State: formal organization and informal culture." International Studies Q. 13 (March): 1-18.

SCOTT, F. D. (1950) The United States and Scandinavia. Cambridge: Harvard Univ. Press.

SCOTT, W. (1958) "Rationality and non-rationality of international attitudes." J. of Conflict Resolution 2: 8-16.

SEALLY, K. (1957) The Geography of Air Transport. London: Hutchinson.

SEARS, R. R. (1951) "Social behavior and personality development," in T. Parsons and E. A. Shils (eds.) Toward a General Theory of Action. New York: Harper & Row.

SECEROV, S. (1919) Economic Phenomena Before and After War. London.

SEGAL, D. R. (1969) "Status inconsistency, cross pressures, and American political behavior." Amer. Soc. Rev. 34 (June): 352-359.

SHIMBOR, M. et al. (1963) "Measuring a nation's prestige." Amer. J. of Sociology 64: 63-68.

SHIRER, W. L. (1955) The Challenge of Scandinavia: Norway, Sweden, Denmark and Finland in Our Time. Boston: Little, Brown.

SIGLER, J. H. (1970) "Reliability problems in the measurement of international events in the elite press." Presented at the Michigan State University International Events Data Conference, East Lansing, April.

SILBERMAN, I. H. (1967) "On log normality as a summary measure of concentration." Amer. Economics Rev. 57: 807-831.

SIMMEL, G. (1904) "The sociology of conflict." Amer. J. of Sociology 9 (January): 490-525.

SIMON, H. A. (1953) "Causal ordering and identifiability," in W. C. Hood and T. C. Koopmans (eds.) Studies in Econometric Method. New York: John Wiley.

—— and C. P. BONINI (1958) "The size distribution of business firms." Amer. Economic Rev. 48 (September): 607-617.

SIMPSON, E. H. (1949) "Measurement and diversity." Nature 163 (April): 688.

SINGER, E. M. (1968) Antitrust Economics. Englewood Cliffs: Prentice-Hall.

SINGER, J. D. (1973) "The peace researcher and foreign policy prediction." Peace Sci. Society (International) Papers 21: 1-14.

—— (1972) "The 'Correlates of War' project: interim report and rationale." World Politics 24, 2 (January): 243-270.

—— (1970) "The outcome of arms races: a policy problem and a research approach." Proceedings of the International Peace Research Association, Third General Conference 2: 137-146.

—— (1970) "Knowledge, practice and the social sciences in international politics," pp. 137-149 in N. Palmer (ed.) A Design for International Relations Research. Philadelphia: American Academy of Political and Social Science.

—— (1969) "National alliance commitments and war involvement, 1818-1945," pp. 513-542 in J. Rosenau (ed.) International Politics and Foreign Policy. New York: Free Press.

—— (1969) "The global system and its subsystems: a developmental view," in J. N. Rosenau (ed.) Linkage Politics. New York: Free Press.

—— [ed.] (1968a) Quantitative International Politics: Insights and Evidence. New York: Free Press.

—— (1968b) "Man and world politics: the psycho-cultural interface." J. of Social Issues 24, 3 (July): 127-156.

—— (1965) "Data-making in international relations." Behavioral Sci. 10: 68-80.

—— (1963) "The return to multilateral diplomacy." Yale Rev. 54: 36-48..

—— (1962) Deterrence, Arms Control, and Disarmament. Columbus: Ohio State Univ. Press.

—— (1961) "The level-of-analysis problem in international relations." World Politics 14, 1 (October): 77-92.

—— (1958) "Threat-perception and the armament-tension dilemma." J. of Conflict Resolution 2, 1 (March): 90-105.

—— and S. JONES (1971) Beyond Conjecture: Data-Based Findings in International Politics. Chicago: Peacock.

SINGER, J. D. and M. SMALL (1972) The Wages of War, 1816-1965: A Statistical Handbook. New York: John Wiley.

—— (1969) "Formal alliances, 1816-1965: an extension of the basic data." J. of Peace Research 3: 257-282.

—— (1968) "Alliance aggregation and the onset of war, 1815-1945," pp. 247-286 in J. D. Singer (ed.) Quantitative International Politics. New York: Free Press.

—— (1967) "National alliance commitments and war involvement, 1815-1945." Peace Research Society Papers 5: 109-140.

—— (1966a) "The composition and status ordering of the international system: 1815-1940." World Politics 18 (January 2): 236-282.

—— (1966b) "Formal alliances, commitments and war involvement, 1815-1939: a quantitative description." J. of Peace Research 1: 1-32.

SINGER, J. D. and J. L. RAY (1972) "Measuring distributions in macro-social systems." Ann Arbor: University of Michigan Mental Health Research Institute.

SINGER, J. D. and M. D. WALLACE (1970) "Inter-governmental organization and the preservation of peace, 1816-1965: some bivariate relationships." International Organization 24, 3 (Summer): 520-547.

SINGER, J. D. and P. WINSTON (1969) "Individual values, national interests and political development in the international system." Presented to the Annual Meeting of the American Political Science Association, Washington, DC.

SINGER, J. D., S. BREMER, and J. STUCKEY (1972) "Capability distribution, uncertainty, and major power war, 1820-1965," pp. 19-48 in B. Russett (ed.) Peace, War, and Numbers. Beverly Hills: Sage.

SIVARD, R. L. (1977) World Military and Social Expenditures, 1977. Leesburg, VA: WMSE Publications.

SKJELSBAEK, K. (1971) "Shared memberships in intergovernmental organizations and dyadic war, 1865-1964," in E. H. Fedder (ed.) The United Nations: Problems and Prospects. St. Louis: Center for International Studies.

SMALL, M. and J. D. SINGER (1969) "Formal alliances, 1816-1965: an extension of the basic data." J. of Peace Research 3: 257-282.

—— (1970) "Patterns in international warfare, 1816-1965." Annals of American Academy of Political and Social Science (September): 145-155.

—— (1973) "The diplomatic importance of states, 1816-1970: an extension and refinement of the indicator." World Politics 25 (July): 577-599.

SMOKER, P. (1969) "A time series analysis of Sino-Indian relations." J. of Conflict Resolution 13: 172-191.

—— (1968) "Analyses of conflict behaviors in an international processes simulation and an international system, 1955-1960." (mimeo)

—— (1967) "Nation state escalation and international integration." J. of Peace Research 4: 61-75.

—— (1963) "A mathematical study of the present arms race." General Systems Yearbook 8: 51-59.

SOLNICK, J. M. (1972) "Observations about selected aspects of the use of conflict event data in empirical cross-national studies of conflict." Presented at the Annual Meeting of the International Studies Association, Dallas, March 14-18.

SONTAG, R. (1933) European Diplomatic History, 1871-1932. New York: Appleton-Century-Crofts.

SOROKIN, P. (1943) Sociocultural Causality, Space, Time. Durham: Duke Univ. Press.

—— (1937) Social and Cultural Dynamics, Vol. 3. New York: American.

—— (1938) "A neglected factor of war." Amer. Soc. Rev. 3, 4 (August): 475-486.

SPROUT, H. and M. SPROUT (1965) The Ecological Perspective on Human Affairs with Special Reference to International Politics. Princeton: Princeton Univ. Press.
———— (1962) Foundations of International Politics. New York: Van Nostrand.
SROLE, L. et al. (1962) Mental Health in the Metropolis. New York: McGraw-Hill.
STARR, H. (1972) War Coalitions: The Distribution of Payoffs and Losses. Lexington, MA: D. C. Heath.
STILLMAN, E. O. (1970) "Civilian sanctuary and target avoidance policy in thermo-nuclear war." Annals of the American Academy of Political and Social Science 392 (November): 119.
STRAUSZ-HUPE, R. and S. T. POSSONY (1954) International Relations in the Age of the Conflict Between Democracy and Dictatorship. New York: McGraw-Hill.
SULLIVAN, J. D. (forthcoming) "Cooperation in international politics: quantitative perspectives on formal alliances," in M. Haas (ed.) Behavioral International Relations. San Francisco: Chandler.
———— (1970) "The location of social science research for the foreign policy decision-maker." Prepared for the Conference on Social Science Research and Foreign Affairs. Arlie House, VA.
———— (1969) "National and international sources of alliance maintenance." Stanford University, Ph.D. dissertation.
SULLIVAN, M. P. (1970) "Commitment and the escalation of conflicts." Tucson: University of Arizona.
———— (1969) "International conflict systems: two models." Tucson: University of Arizona.
SWEEN, J. and D. CAMPBELL (1965a) "The interrupted time series as quasi-experiment: three tests of significance." Evanston: Northwestern University. (mimeo)
———— (1965b) "A study of the effects of proximally autocorrelated error on tests of significance for the interrupted time series quasi-experimental design." Evanston: Northwestern University. (mimeo)
TANTER, R. (1966) "Dimensions of conflict behavior within and between nations, 1958-1960." J. of Conflict Resolution 10, 1 (March): 41-64.
TAYLOR, A.J.P. (1954) The Struggle for Mastery in Europe, 1848-1918. London: Oxford Univ. Press.
TAYLOR, C. (1970) "Turmoil, economic development, and organized political opposition as predictors of irregular government change." Presented at the Sixty-Sixth Annual Meeting of the American Political Science Association, Los Angeles, September 8-12.
TEUNE, H. and S. SYNNESTREDT (1965) "Measuring international alignment." Orbis 9, 1 (Spring).
THEIL, H. (1970) "On the estimation of relationships involving qualitative variables." Amer. J. of Sociology 76 (July): 103-154.
———— (1967) Economics and Information Theory. Chicago: Rand McNally.
THOMPSON, W. S. (1953) Population Problems. New York: McGraw-Hill.
THURSTONE, L. (1935) The Vectors of Mind. Chicago: Univ. of Chicago Press.
TOLMAN, E. C. (1951) "A psychological model," in T. Parsons and E. A. Shils (eds.) Toward a General Theory of Action. New York: Harper & Row.
TRISKA, J. F. and D. D. FINLEY (1969) "Soviet-American relations: a multiple symmetry model," in D. V. Edwards (ed.) International Political Analysis: Readings. New York: Holt, Rinehart & Winston.

TURNER, M. E. and C. D. STEVENS (1959) "Regression analysis of causal paths." Biometrics 15, 2: 236-258.

URLANIS, B. T. (1960) Wars and the Population of Europe. Moscow: Government Publishing. (Russian and Czech)

VANDENBOSCH, A. (1955) Dutch Foreign Policy Since 1815: A Study in Small Power Politics. The Hague: Mantinus Nijhoff.

VON den BERGHE, P. L. (1960) "Distance mechanisms of stratification." Sociology and Social Research 44 (January-February): 155-164.

VOTH, A. (1967) "Vietnam: studying a major controversy." J. of Conflict Resolution 9, 3 (December): 438.

WALL, C. and R. J. RUMMEL (1969) "Estimating missing data." Dimensionality of Nations Project Research Report No. 20, University of Hawaii.

WALLACE, M. D. (1976) "Arms races and the balance of power: a preliminary model." Applied Mathematical Modelling 1, 2 (September): 83-92.

——— (1973) "Alliance polarization, cross-cutting, and international war, 1815-1964: a measurement process and some preliminary evidence." J. of Conflict Resolution 17: 575-604.

——— (1973) War and Rank Among Nations. Lexington, MA: D. C. Heath.

——— (1972a) "The radical critique of peace research: an exposition and interpretation." Peace Research Reviews 4, 4 (February): 24-51.

——— (1972b) "Status, formal organization, and arms levels as factors leading to the onset of war, 1820-1964," pp. 49-69 in B. M. Russett (ed.) Peace, War, and Numbers. Beverly Hills: Sage.

——— (1971) "Power, status and international war." J. of Peace Research 1: 23-35.

——— (1970) "Arms races and the balance of power: a preliminary model." Applied Mathematical Modelling 1, 2 (September): 83-92.

——— (1970) "Status inconsistency, vertical mobility, and international war, 1825-64." University of Michigan, Ph.D. dissertation.

——— and J. D. SINGER (1970) "Inter-governmental organization in the global system, 1816-1964: a quantitative description." International Organization 24, 2 (Spring): 239-287.

WALLACE, M. D. and J. M. WILSON (1978) "Non-linear arms race models: a test of some alternatives." J. of Peace Research 15, 2: 175-192.

WALLENSTEEN, P. (1973) Structure and War: On International Relations, 1920-1968. Stockholm: Raben & Sjogren.

WALTZ, K. (1967) "International structure, national force, and the balance of world power." J. of International Affairs 21: 215-231.

——— (1964) "The stability of a bipolar world." Daedalus 93: 881-909.

——— (1959) Man, the State, and War. New York: Columbia Univ. Press.

WARNER, L. G. and M. L. DeFLEUR (1969) "Attitude as an interactional concept: social constraint and social distance as intervening variables between attitudes and action." Amer. Soc. Rev. 34 (April).

WATANABE, S. (1969) Knowing and Guessing. New York: John Wiley.

WEINSTEIN, F. (1969) "The concept of a commitment in international relations." J. of Conflict Resolution 13: 39-56.

WEISS, H. (1963) "Stochastic models for the duration and magnitude of a deadly quarrel." Operations Research 11: 101-121.

WEISS, L. W. (1963) "Factors in changing concentration." Rev. of Economics and Statistics 44 (February): 70-77.

WESOLOWSKI, W. (1966) "Some notes on the functional theory of stratification," in R. Bendix and S. M. Lipset, Class, Status and Power. New York: Free Press.

WHITE, R. K. (1968) Nobody Wanted War: Misperception in Vietnam and Other Wars. Garden City: Doubleday.

WICKER, T. (1968) JFK and LBJ: The Influence of Personality on Politics. New York: William Morrow.

WIENER, N. (1948) Cybernetics; or Controlled Communication in the Animal and the Machine. Cambridge: MIT Press.

WILKENFELD, J. (1969) "Some further findings regarding the domestic and foreign conflict behavior of nations." J. of Peace Research 2: 147-156.

——— (1968) "Domestic and foreign conflict behavior of nations." J. of Peace Research 1: 56-69.

WILKINSON, D. (1969) Comparative Foreign Relations: Framework and Method. Encino, CA: Dickenson.

WILLIAMS, E. (1963) Holland Growing Greater. Amsterdam: Bezige Bij.

WILLIAMS, R. M., Jr. (1947) The Reduction of Intergroup Tensions. New York: Social Science Research Council.

WILSON, J. H. (1977) "Foreign policy trends since 1920." Society for Historians of American Foreign Relations Newsletter 8, 3: 1-17.

WINCH, R. and D. T. CAMPBELL (1969) "Proof? No. Evidence? Yes. The significance tests of significance." Amer. Sociologist 4, 2 (May): 140-143.

WOHLSTETTER, A. (1968a) "Illusions of distance." Foreign Affairs 46 (January).

——— (1968b) "Theory and opposed-systems design." J. of Conflict Resolution 12, 2 (September): 302-331.

WOLD, H.O.A. (1960) "A generalization of causal chain models." Econometrica 28, 2 (April): 443-463.

——— in association with L. JUREE (1953) Demand Analysis. Baltimore: Johns Hopkins Univ. Press.

WOOD, D. (1968) Conflict in the Twentieth Century. Adelphi Papers, No. 48. London: Institute for Strategic Studies.

WOODS, F. A. and A. BALTZLY (1915) Is War Diminishing? Boston: Houghton Mifflin.

WRIGHT, Q. (1965) "The escalation of international conflicts." J. of Conflict Resolution 9, 4 (December): 434-449.

——— (1957) "Design for a research proposal of international conflict . . . " Western Pol. Q. 10: 263-275.

——— (1955) The Study of International Relations. New York: Appleton-Century-Crofts.

——— (1942) The Study of War. Chicago: Univ. of Chicago Press.

——— (1935) The Causes of War and the Conditions of Peace. London: Longmans, Green.

WRIGHT, S. (1960) "The treatment of reciprocal interaction, with or without lag, in path analysis." Biometrica 15, 3 (September): 423-445.

——— (1934) "The method of path coefficients." Annals of Mathematical Statistics 5: 161-215.

WUORINEN, J. H. (1965) Scandinavia. Englewood Cliffs: Prentice-Hall.

YAKOBSON, S. and H. D. LASSWELL (1949) "Trend: May Day slogans in Soviet Russia, 1918-1943," in H. Lasswell, N. Leites et al. Language of Politics. Studies in Quantitative Semantics. Cambridge: MIT Press.

YNTEMA, D. (1933) "Measures of inequality in personal distribution of wealth or income." Amer. Statistical Assn. J. 28 (December): 423-433.

YOUNG, H. D. (1962) Statistical Treatment of Experimental Data. New York: McGraw-Hill.

YOUNG, O. R. (1968) The Politics of Force, Bargaining in International Crises. Princeton: Princeton Univ. Press.

ZECHMAN, M. (1974) "A comparison of the small sample properties of probit and OLS estimators with a limited dependent variable." University of Rochester. (mimeo)

ZINNES, D. A. (1976) Contemporary Research in International Relations. New York: Free Press.

―――― (1968) "The expression and perception of hostility in prewar crisis: 1914," pp. 85-119 in J. D. Singer (ed.) Quantitative International Politics. New York: Free Press.

―――― (1967) "An analytical study of the balance of power theories." J. of Peace Research 4: 270-288.

―――― (1966) "A comparison of hostile behavior of decision makers in simulate and historical data." World Politics 18: 474-502.

―――― (1962) "Hostility in international decision-making." J. of Conflict Resolution 6: 236-243.

―――― and J. WILKENFELD (1971) "An analysis of foreign conflict behavior of nations," in W. F. Hanrieder (ed.) Comparative Foreign Policy Theoretical Essays. New York: David McKay.

ZINNES, D. A., R. NORTH, and H. KOCK, Jr. (1961) "Capability, threat, and the outbreak of war," pp. 469-482 in J. Rosenau (ed.) International Politics and Foreign Policy New York: Free Press.

ZINNES, D. A., J. L. ZINNES, and R. D. McCLURE (1972) "Markovian analyses of hostile communications in the 1914 crises," in C. F. Hermann (ed.) Crisis in Foreign Policy Decision-Making. New York: Free Press.